# New Visions of Graduate Management Education

*a volume in*
Research in Management Education and Development
*Series Editors:* Charles Wankel and Robert DeFillippi

# Research in Management Education and Development

Charles Wankel and Robert DeFillippi, Series Editors

# New Visions of Graduate Management Education

*edited by*

**Charles Wankel**
*St. Johns University*

*and*

**Robert DeFillippi**
*Suffolk University*

INFORMATION AGE
PUBLISHING

Greenwich, Connecticut • www.infoagepub.com

**Library of Congress Cataloging-in-Publication Data**

New visions of graduate management education/edited by Charles Wankel and Robert DeFillippi
   p. cm. -- (Research in management education and development)
  Includes bibliographical references.
  ISBN-13: 978-1-59311-553-1 (pbk.)
  ISBN-13: 978-1-59311-554-8 (hardcover)
  1. Management--Study and teaching. 2. Business education. I.
Wankel, Charles. II. DeFillippi, Robert.
  HD30.4.N468 2006
  658.0071'1--dc22

                                        2006021686


ISBN 13: 978-1-59311-553-1 (pbk.)
         978-1-59311-554-8 (hardcover)
ISBN 10: 1-59311-553-9 (pbk.)
         1-59311-554-7 (hardcover)

Printed in the United States of America

# EDITORIAL REVIEW BOARD

# LIST OF CONTRIBUTORS

| | |
|---|---|
| *Howard Armitage* | University of Waterloo, Waterloo Canada |
| *Jos A. R. Arts* | Technical University Eindhoven, Eindhoven, the Netherlands |
| *Stephen R. Ball* | Lourdes College, Sylvania, OH |
| *Robert J. Bies* | Georgetown University, Washington, DC |
| *Henny P. A. Boshuizen* | Open University Netherlands, Heerlen, the Netherlands |
| *John C. Byrne* | Pace University, New York, NY |
| *Arnaldo Camuffo* | University of Padua, Padua, Italy |
| *Francesca Chiara* | Ca' Foscari University of Venice, Venice, Italy |
| *Denis Collins* | Edgewood College, Madison, WI |
| *Gary Coombs* | Ohio University, Athens, OH |
| *Deborah Crown Core* | Ohio University, Athens, OH |
| *Robert DeFillippi* | Suffolk University, Boston, MA |
| *Peter G. Dominick* | Stevens Institute of Technology, Hoboken, NJ |
| *Mark Fenton-O'Creevy* | Open University, United Kingdom |
| *Fabrizio Gerli* | Ca' Foscari University of Venice, Venice, Italy |
| *Wim H. Gijselaers* | University of Maastricht, Maastricht, the Netherlands |
| *Owen P. Hall, Jr.* | Pepperdine University, Malibu, CA |
| *Anne Herbert* | Helsinki School of Economics, Helsinki, Finland |
| *Brooks C. Holtom* | Georgetown University, Washington, DC |

| | |
|---|---|
| *Edward J. Inderrieden* | Marquette University, Milwaukee, WI |
| *Peter Knight* | Open University, United Kingdom |
| *Kari Lilja* | Helsinki School of Economics, Finland |
| *Judith Margolis* | Open University, United Kingdom |
| *Rod B. McNaughton* | University of Waterloo, Waterloo, Canada |
| *Tunç Medeni* | Japan Advanced Institute of Science and Technology, Ishikawa, Japan |
| *Yongsun Paik* | Loyola Marymount University, Los Angeles, CA |
| *M.S.R. Segers* | University of Leiden, Leiden, the Netherlands |
| *Hugh D. Sherman* | Ohio University, Athens, OH |
| *Charles M. Vance* | Loyola Marymount University, Los Angeles, CA |
| *Charles Wankel* | St. Johns University, New York, NY |

# CONTENTS

# INTRODUCTION TO NEW VISIONS OF GRADUATE MANAGEMENT EDUCATION

**Charles Wankel and Robert DeFillippi**

Graduate management education, especially MBA education, has become a lighting rod for criticism by management scholars (Bennis & O'Toole, 2005; DeAngelo, DeAngelo, & Zimmerman 2005; Gartner, 2005; Mintzberg, 2004). Collectively, these scholars have criticized the overly analytic emphasis of MBA instruction, the stifling of creativity, innovation, and integration within functional teaching and research silos, the disconnect between theory and practice, between knowing and doing, and between rigor and relevance. Moreover, Pfeffer and Fong (2004) infer from their review of the literature that there is little economic benefit for students enrolled in the vast majority of MBA programs.

These sirens of graduate management education criticism are not in harmony regarding either the sources of alleged MBA program dysfunction or how best to remedy their shortcomings. For example, DeAngelo, DeAngelo, and Zimmerman (2005) argue that U.S. business schools are locked in a dysfunctional competition for media rankings that diverts resources from long-term knowledge creation into short-term strategies

*New Visions for Graduate Management Education,* xi–xxi
Copyright © 2006 by Information Age Publishing
All rights of reproduction in any form reserved.

aimed at improving their rankings. MBA curricula are thus distorted by "quick fix, look good" packaging changes designed to influence rankings criteria, at the expense of giving students a rigorous, conceptual framework that will serve them well over their entire careers. These authors do not agree with such critics as Bennis and O'Toole (2005), who suggest a major problem in MBA programs is their faculty member's disconnection from the world of practice and who recommend that recruitment, promotion, tenure, and other rewards be radically restructured to discourage "scientific" research and to promote research with immediate practical payoffs as evaluated by corporate appraisers.

By contrast, DeAngelo, DeAngelo. and Zimmerman (2005) counter-argue that replacing rigorous academic training in functional business disciplines with greater emphasis on practical training short-changes the student. The authors contend that what students lack from their practical experience are the more generalizable analytical skills necessary to recognize and address future business challenges that are not simple extensions of past practical experiences.

With respect to the authors' contention that U.S. business schools are suffering from short-term rankings pressures, it should be noted that the United Kingdom and continental Europe are also coming under the sway of rankings competition (whether based on *U.S. News and World Reports* or the *Financial Times* or other academic business school sources of annual ratings). Hence there is some evidence to suggest that ranking pressures may be influencing MBA curriculum and branding decisions across the United States of America, United Kingdom and continental Europe, and anywhere that business school deans and their university presidents wish to achieve some reputation-based position in any of the available ratings services.

On their face, these critiques demand our attention. Indeed, the issues raised in these critiques are worthy of closer empirical examination. However, we also perceive that some of the criticisms seem directed at a highly stylized vision of American (U.S.) MBA education and these critiques may be ignoring innovations in MBA and graduate management education occurring in the United States and in other countries.

This fifth volume in our book series on Research in Management Education and Development (Information Age Publishing) is thus devoted toward an empirical and conceptual examination of some of these criticisms of graduate management education. This volume also showcases a wide variety of innovative experiments in new visions of master's level graduate management education. We draw upon a rich array of U.S. and non-U.S. scholars and empirical sources in this volume and we are most grateful to our volume's distinguished academic contributors for sustaining our book series' aspiration to both reflect upon and shape innovative thinking and practice on important issues of management education and development.

## Research Evidence on Management Education Outcomes

Our opening section offers three chapters summarizing substantial empirical studies on the impact of MBA and undergraduate business education on students' earnings, career success, and competency development. Our initial chapter by Edward J. Inderrieden (Marquette University), Brooks C. Holtom, and Robert J. Bies (both of Georgetown University) reports on a national panel survey of 3,769 Graduate Management Admission Test (GMAT) takers in 1990-1991 and their subsequent economic and career success in 1998. Their research is among the first national panel studies to empirically examine some of the claims made of Pfeffer and Fong (2002) that MBAs provide economic or career benefit only to graduates of elite MBA programs. In their carefully designed study, Inderrieden, Holtom, and Bies empirically demonstrate that MBA programs of all levels of program quality produce economic and career benefits to their MBA graduates. Indeed, the most intriguing finding of their research is that MBA program quality (defined by whether or not a student's MBA program is ranked in the top 25 business schools listed in the *U.S. News and World Reports* manual survey) does not seem to have much impact on economic and career success. A second significant finding is that cognitive ability, measured by GMAT scores, is a good predictor of career success.

The role of MBA education in fostering cognitive development is the focus of the chapter by Arnaldo Camuffo (University of Padua), Fabrizio Gerli, and Francesca Chiara (both at University of Venice). They analyzed five cohorts of Italian MBA students/graduates (from 2000 to 2004) to assess competency development at the start and at the end of their MBA at the Fondazione Centro Universitario Di Organizzazione Aziendale (CUOA) of Vicenza, one of the top business schools in Italy. In the late 1990s, the CUOA master's program was completely redesigned according to competency-based principles based on the ground breaking work by Boyatzis, Cowen, Kolb, and Associates (1995) at Case Western University's Weatherhead School of Management. The chapter authors assess the impact of a competency-based MBA curriculum on the self-evaluations, peer evaluations, and third party (research team) evaluations of students' managerial and functional competencies. Their findings suggest that an MBA curriculum that is carefully and comprehensively designed according to competency-based principles can indeed foster the development of functional and managerial competencies within its student body.

This section concludes with a chapter by Wim H. Gijselaers (University of Maastricht), Jos A. R. Arts (Technical University Eindhoven), Henny P. A. Boshuizen (Open University Netherlands), and M. S. R. Segers (University of Leiden) reporting on a series of empirical studies of managerial expertise development that compares recent graduates' problem solving performances with those of managerial experts. Although their research is primarily grounded in comparisons of first degree business graduates and experienced managerial experts, their findings support the general criticism cited for MBA programs that business education is too theoretical. They recommend that educational research should form the basis for improving current management educational efforts but they also warn that business schools have a weak tradition in questioning their own assumptions about their own production processes in comparison to medical or science education. The authors also advocate a more practice-based approach to management education, one of the several suggestions detailed in the next section of our volume.

## DESIGNS FOR GRADUATE MANAGEMENT EDUCATION

Our next section features four thoughtful reviews of approaches to designing graduate management curricula. Each of these chapters addresses directly the challenges posed by current critique of contemporary graduate management education and each chapter suggests specific approaches for creatively responding to the education challenges posed by these critiques.

Stephen R. Ball (Lourdes College) opens this chapter by reviewing the sources and substance of calls for the reform of business education over the past 100 years. Ball criticizes business faculty for limiting their curriculum reform efforts to *content* (what will we teach?), *pedagogy* (how will we teach?), and sometimes *sequencing* (in what order will the content be taught?) In place of such piecemeal curriculum design criteria, Ball recommends Stark and Lattuca's (1997) more comprehensive curriculum design framework consisting of curricular purpose, content, the learners, instructional resources, sequence of presentation, instructional processes, and evaluation of outcomes. Ball's chapter indeed helps bridge the gap between higher education researchers, who extensively study curricula and programs, and MBA faculty who are largely unaware of this body of research.

Mark Fenton-O'Creevy, Peter Knight and Judith Margolis (all at Open University) argue that a practice-based approach to designing learning environments and experiences should replace the current emphasis on organizing curriculum "content." They propose an approach that sets up effective dialogues between theory and practice, between different disciplinary perspectives, and between the different experiences of program participants. They illustrate these dialogues in learning episodes extracted from their collective experience as educators of adult learners participating in the online learning programs of the professional diploma in management, which is a 1-year part-time program that forms the first stage of the Open University MBA. A common element in all these dialogues is reflective practice, which encourages the integration of formal, tacit and self-regulative forms of expert knowledge.

The final two chapters of this section draw upon curriculum design principles articulated by Henry Mintzberg and associates for developing managers. Mintzberg suggest that experienced managers require a curriculum and educational framework that fosters experienced reflection to make sense of their life and work experience and that also fosters the development of five distinctive mindsets (Mintzberg & Gosling, 2002). The reflective mindset is concerned with managing the self, the analytic mindset with managing organizations, the worldly mindset with managing context, the collaborative mindset with managing relationships and the action mindset with managing change. Each of these mindsets may be accomplished through a wide range of activities supporting a consistent pedagogy of experienced reflection.

Tunç D. Medeni (Japan Advanced Institute of Science and Technology) provides a conceptually ambitious analysis of key components of the International Masters Program in Practicing Management (IMPM) designed by Mintzberg and his associates according to their principles of the five mindsets. Medeni focuses his attention on two modules and associated mindsets: the reflective mindset module conducted at Lancaster University and the collaborative mindset that guides IMPM activities at JAIST. Medini extends the IMPM concept of reflection (seeing reality as it is) to suggest a complementary focus on refraction (reconceiving reality and changing reality). Medini provides a rich conceptual map for employing the mindsets of the IMPM program to foster a knowledge management mindset that supports both knowledge transfer and knowledge creation managerial competencies.

Our concluding chapter on design principles for graduate management education focuses on the work by Peter Dominick (Stevens Institute of Technology) and John Byrne (Pace University) to develop appropriate "leadership mindsets" in MBA students. This final contribution to design illustrates how each of Mintzberg's five mindsets may be applied to leadership development education and training through specific learning activities. The authors persuasively demonstrate how a "leadership mindset" design for graduate management education helps instill the broader skill sets of reflection and analysis that foster engagement in action (real life applications) in order to make learning possible. Although this chapter is focused upon a particular course pedagogy (leadership development), the leadership mindset has implications far beyond their specialized course offerings.

## Non-U.S.A Centric Models of Graduate Management Education

This section focuses upon two chapters reflecting country-specific responses to creating graduate management educational offerings appropriate to their national contexts. These chapters take a decidedly non-U.S.A centric approach toward graduate management education and their choices also reflect responses to perceived deficiencies of U.S.A MBA models that have taken root in their local contexts. These chapters provide a nuanced view of how specific condition of the national context can spur innovative graduate management education.

Howard Armitage and Rod B. McNaughton (both of University of Waterloo) document Canada's disappointing record in managing entrepreneurial and technological opportunities and a growing concern with the lack of a culture of innovation in Canadian enterprises. Moreover, they suggest that the high number of generalist MBA programs in Canada foster too little innovation. To remedy this gap, the authors describe the programs and offerings of the 12-month long Master of Business, Entrepreneurship and Technology (MBET) program at the University of Waterloo (UW). MBET is a response to the perceived problems with MBA curricula and programs, especially as catalysts of successful innovation and entrepreneurship. The authors document the efforts at MBET to develop a "knowing-doing" curriculum that simulates the commercialization process and provides students with a supportive environment for testing test out new ideas, developing entrepreneurial networks, and developing the self-confidence required for embarking on their entrepreneurial journeys.

Anne Herbert and Kari Lilja (both at Helsinki School of Economics) describe how Helsinki School of Economics (HSE), the leading economics and business focused university in Finland, redesigned its MBA program to better accommodate a changing international context for MBA education within the economic, political and cultural context of Scandinavian society. HSE had developed its country's first MBA program in the 1970s and modeled its curriculum on the then dominant U.S.A models of MBA design. However, the increasing globalization of business and the local context of Scandinavian business require a series of reverse innovations in MBA curriculum and pedagogy that are now underway. These innovations are grounded in HSE's programmatic research on national business systems (NBS) and how different NBS vary in economic, political, and cultural details.

## Partnerships in MBA Innovation

This section features two chapters detailing how university partnerships can assist business schools in creating innovative MBA program offerings. Hugh D. Sherman, Debora Crown Core, and Gary Coombs (all at Ohio University) describe how Ohio University's Business School has benefited from its long standing partnership with Ohio University's Voinovich Center for Leadership and Public Affairs (The Center), a nonprofit organization that is the University's largest service provider to the 29 county Appalachian Ohio region. Through this organization Ohio University' MBA program leaders and faculty have established relationships with regional economic development officials, bankers, and a for-profit venture capital firm. One benefit of this partnership is The Center's ability to provide access to application opportunities for MBA students to engage in action learning and internship projects. Additional benefits include faculty access to Center professional staff and their external business partners.

Charles M. Vance and Yongsun Paik (both at Loyola Marymount University) report on a survey done in support of a proposed partnership by their business school with American Chambers of Commerce (AmChams) to pilot a new delivery model for MBA international internships. Their model integrates distance coursework with direct field learning assignments during the course of the students' internships. Based on field interviews at Chambers of Commerce in Australia and New Zealand and e-mailed survey of 18 American Chambers of Commerce (AmChams) in Europe, South America, and Asia, the authors propose an internship partnership model that can capitalize on the ubiquity of Chambers of Commerce in diverse international settings and the ability of MBA students to engage in meaningful projects in a cost-effective manner.

## Potpourri of Innovative Contributions to Graduate Management Education

Our final section includes a heterogeneous collection of three chapters, each of which attends to specific examples of innovative approaches to graduate management education. Each chapter is focused on how to integrate a particular form of innovative management education into the business curriculum. Our section opens with a chapter by Owen P. Hall (Pepperdine University) on how to design and implement a "hybrid net" learning system that combines the best of both Web-based learning and classroom practices for delivering cost-effective executive management education. Hall documents the significant role that nontraditional teaching methods, such as online teaching, are now playing in top tier executive MBA programs world wide. He details the emergence of online executive education in a growing segment of EMBA programs and compares their delivery systems. The bulk of his chapter details the learning activities, tools and practices that constitute the "hybrid net" learning system to integrate both face-to-face and online learning.

Denis Collins (Edgewood College) demonstrates how educators can integrate the teaching of ethics into the business curriculum by applying innovative teaching methods that engage students in higher level learning and through a host of other activities. The business ethics course described in this chapter is designed according to Kohlberg's stages of moral development (Kohlberg, 1981). Additionally, Collins describes an array of business school activities that can help integrate ethics within the business school. These include service learning projects, brown bag faculty workshops on teaching ethics, and university centers for business ethics to sponsor faculty development, research, and curriculum development in ethics that can be applied across the business school curriculum. Collins provides the reader a wide range of university examples of such ethics-supportive practices that can be applied to a wide range of MBA (and undergraduate) educational settings.

Loykie Loïc Lominé (University of Westminster) concludes our volume with her chapter on how educators can integrate cultural diversity into graduate management education. She reports that graduate management education tends to remain monocultural due to the pressing time priorities of functional business course content. Her chapter reviews a wide range of diversity phenomena (race/ethnicity, religion, sex/gender, sexual orientation, age, and disability). She also details a series of steps business schools can take to integrate diversity: staff development, curriculum audit, adapting current practice, adding a course component on diversity, and embedding cultural diversity in the course's overall pedagogy. Her chapter concludes with a call to business schools to provide their MBA (and undergraduate) students with the capacity to make culturally-informed and culturally-sensitive business decisions in their professional careers.

## FINAL REFLECTIONS ON NEW VISIONS OF GRADUATE
## MANAGEMENT EDUCATION

The preceding chapters offer considerable food for thought on the issues posed by recent critiques of graduate management education. Our opening section "Research Evidence on Management Education Outcomes" suggests that MBA degrees continue to have a positive impact on the incomes and career mobility of GMAT test takers who subsequently complete their MBA studies. Moreover, these income and career benefits (however modest) arise across all levels of MBA program quality. Hence, it would appear that Pfeffer and Fong's (2002, 2004) concerns with the declining value of the MBA degree from nonelite programs may be somewhat over stated. Nonetheless, the relatively modest income and career gains reported by Inderriedem, Holtom, and Bies in chapter 1 does suggest that the MBA may ultimately face a crisis of value if the costs of MBA education continue to escalate, as they have in the United States and Europe.

The next two chapters of our opening section by Camuffo, Gerli, and Chiara, and by Gijselaers, Arts, Boshuizen, and Segers both suggest that graduate management education can play a positive role in promoting the development of managerial competencies of MBA students. However, both chapters suggest that these competencies can only be fully realized if the knowledge and techniques taught in the MBA classroom are integrated with the more dynamic learning that occurs through engagement in real world business practice.

The four chapters on "Designs for Graduate Management Education" suggest some convergent themes. These include the need for graduate management education to pay more attention to practice (what managers do) and to provide learning laboratories for engaging in practice. These calls for work practice engagement in learning outside the classroom were detailed in our fourth volume's focus on *Educating Managers through Real World Projects* (Wankel & DeFillippi, 2005). Also emphasized in the four chapters of this section is the continuing value of the MBA and other forms of graduate management education in providing venues (space and time) for reflection on the links between what one learns in the classroom and their relationship to one's work and life experiences. Hence reflective practice seems to be a common theme in many innovative designs for graduate management education.

Our two chapters on "Non-U.S.A Centric Models of Graduate Management Education" remind us that national and regional culture and context still matter in the design of graduate management education. These national (e.g., Canada) and regional (e.g., Scandinavian) contexts may pose both unique challenges and unique opportunities for graduate management innovations to flourish and for the resulting degree programs to distinguish themselves in comparison to the many look-alike MBA programs that have proliferated in recent years. Also, in contradistinction to the prevailing call for more practice-driven learning, the chapter by Herbert and Lija does propose utilizing the research and knowledge on national business systems that faculty have amassed at Helsinki School of Economics. This point reminds us that the choice in curriculum design is not between academic rigor or practical relevance but rather the more daunting challenge of linking academic scholarship and knowledge to practical know-how and competence.

Our two chapters on "Partnerships in MBA innovation" illustrate how business schools and their graduate management programs can benefit from partnering with both internal university partners (Sherman, Core, and Coomb's chapter on the partnership between Ohio University School of Business and the Voinovich Center for Leadership and Public Affairs) and with external partners (Vance & Paik's chapter on the proposed partnership in global internships with the American Chambers of Commerce). What both these chapters amply illustrate is that no MBA program or graduate management education program is an island. Innovative graduate management programs and business schools devise partnership relationships to extend their internal capabilities (van Baalen & Moratis, 2004).

Our concluding section on "Potpourri of Innovative Contributions to Graduate Management Education" features three seemingly unrelated chapters on Web-based learning systems (Hall) business ethics (Collins) and multiculturalism (Lominé). Despite their substantive differences, each chapter makes significant contributions to visions for both undergraduate and postgraduate (MBA, MA, MSc.) management curriculum development. The overarching theme in each chapter is the need for each innovation to be integrated within the larger body of curriculum, program structures and pedagogic practices of the innovative Business School and its overall management education curriculum. Piecemeal and stand-alone versions of each innovation are seen more as pilots for early stage demonstration of the value of the innovation. Each chapter argues for a more holistic approach to embedding each innovation within the fabric of the entire business school and graduate management education enterprise. This call for holistic, integrative approaches to graduate management education is amply demonstrated in many chapters of this volume and we sincerely hope that you will find some inspiration in the forthcoming pages for furthering your own educational vision.

## ACKNOWLEDGMENTS

We would like to acknowledge the invaluable contributions of our Editorial Associates Matthew Marovich and Brendan Cyrus of Rutgers University. Their high professionalism and articulate analytical acumen have made this volume significantly better.

## REFERENCES

Bennis, W. G., & O'Toole, J. (2005, May). How business schools lost their way. *Harvard Business Review*, 1-9.

Boyatzis, R. E., Cowen, S. S., Kolb, D. A., & Associates. (1995). *Innovation in professional education*. San Francisco: Jossey-Bass.

DeAngelo, H., DeAngelo, L., & Zimmerman, J. L. (2005). *What's really wrong with U.S. business schools?* Retrieved May 20, 2006, from http://ssrn.com/abstract=766404

Gartner, J. (2005, June 19). Are business schools failing the world? Interview with Jeffrey Gartner, Dean, Yale School of Management, *New York Times*, p. BU13.

Kohlberg, L. (1981). *The philosophy of moral development*. New York: Harper Collins.

Mintzberg, H. (2004). *Managers not MBA's: A hard look at the soft practice of managing and management development*. San Francisco: Berrett and Koehler.

Mintzberg, H., & Gosling, J. (2002). Educating beyond borders. *Academy of Management Learning and Education, 1*(10), 64-76.

Pfeffer, J., & Fong, C. T. (2002). The end of business schools? Less success than meets the eye. *Academy of Management Learning and Education, 1*, 78-95.

Pfeffer, J., & Fong, C. T. (2004). The business school "business": Some Lessons from the U.S. Experience. *Journal of Management Studies, 41*(8), 1501-1520.

Stark, J. S., & Lattuca, L. R. (1997). *Shaping the college curriculum: Academic plans in action*. Needham Heights, MA: Allyn & Bacon.

Van Baalen, P., & Moratis, L. (2004). From going alone to going along? European business schools as loosely coupled networks. In C. Wankel & R. DeFillippi (Eds.), *The cutting edge of international management education* (pp. 3-36). Greenwich, CT: Information Age.

Wankel, C., & DeFillippi, R. (Eds.). (2005). *Educating managers through real world projects*. Greenwich, CT: Information Age.

# Part I

## RESEARCH EVIDENCE ON MANAGEMENT EDUCATION OUTCOMES

# CHAPTER 1

# DO MBA PROGRAMS DELIVER?

## Edward J. Inderrieden, Brooks C. Holtom, and Robert J. Bies

A recent broad scale article by Pfeffer and Fong (2002), along with work by Mintzberg (2004), raises a variety of important questions concerning the contribution of business schools. These cast efforts doubt on the relevance of business school education and its impact on the careers of graduates. The current research study investigates one aspect of Pfeffer and Fong's (2002) paper, the impact of an MBA on career success. Pfeffer and Fong (2002) contend that there is little or no economic gain from obtaining an MBA degree unless one attends an elite program. The present study extends existing research in the following ways: direct comparisons are made between individuals who obtained MBA degrees and those who did not; career success is measured in both absolute and relative terms. The sample is representative of MBA programs throughout the United States, allowing for comparisons of schools at all levels of national rankings, along with evaluating the effect of full-time and part-time MBA programs, and assessing the value of attending a public or private institution. Among the findings from the study, results indicate that earning an MBA has a modest impact on income. In addition, graduates report receiving more promotions than nongraduates.

*New Visions for Graduate Management Education*, 3–22
Copyright © 2006 by Information Age Publishing
All rights of reproduction in any form reserved.

## INTRODUCTION

*Business Week* (Hondo, 2002) reported that it takes approximately 5.2 years to recoup the cost, tuition payments, and foregone salary, of attending a full-time MBA program. Is an MBA worth it? Not withstanding the ubiquitous comments that MBA's have an inflated impression of themselves and unrealistic expectations regarding salary and advancement opportunities, does obtaining an MBA make sense? Judging from the number of people taking the Graduate Management Admissions Test (GMAT) each year, many people seem to think so. In 2002, 249,632 GMAT tests were taken, the highest number in history (Bruce, Edgington, & Olkin, 2003). Despite these huge numbers, controversy regarding the merits of an MBA rages on.

Once again, the value of obtaining an MBA has been drawn into question. This seems to happen with regularity and often occurs when the U.S. economy is in a slump: starting salaries for MBAs level off and graduates, even from the most prestigious programs, find they have greater difficulty obtaining that dream job. Most recently, leading academics at renowned universities have joined the fray, directly questioning whether or not MBA programs provide value. The purpose of this proposed work is to investigate whether or not getting an MBA provides value to the student.

The expressed intent of MBA programs has never been to create instant managers, but rather to provide a solid base of business essentials to help prepare individuals for their careers. Unfortunately, instant gratification has become the goal of many. Graduates expect to get the perfect job and employers want to see someone who can immediately step into a leadership role. Are these realistic goals? We think not. In a 2004 book, Mintzberg pilloried MBA programs, indicating that MBA programs do not teach managers or management, but are focusing on analyzing the functional aspects of business rather than on synthesis, which according to Mintzberg is the essence of management. Mintzberg states,

> It is time to recognize conventional MBA programs for what they are—or else to close them down. They are specialized training in the functions of business, not general educating in the practice of managing. Using the classroom to help develop people already practicing management is a fine idea, but pretending to create managers out of people who have never managed is a sham. It is time that our business schools gave proper attention to management. (2004, p. 5)

We agree with Mintzberg that our MBA programs are focusing on the functional aspects of business, however the sole purpose of MBA programs has never been to "train managers." An important question to answer is whether or not MBA programs deliver value. Pfeffer and Fong (2002) would answer this question with a resounding "no," arguing that while business schools have been a commercial success the MBA degree has been of little value to individuals, corporations, and society. If this is true, one has to question the future of MBA programs.

Students enter programs expecting that receiving an MBA degree will increase their career options and enhance their earning power (Bruce et al., 2003). MBA programs must deliver value. Specific to this issue, Pfeffer and Fong (2002) review relevant research and indicate that there is little economic gain for an individual in getting an MBA unless one attends a top-ranked program. Despite the strong argument presented by Pfeffer and Fong (2002), much of the cited research was anecdotal in nature (Livingston, 1971), appeared in the popular press (Leonhardt, 2000), conducted without research controls (Dugan, Grady, Payne, & Johnson, 1999) and focused on narrow samples from three or fewer schools (Dreher, Dougherty, & Whitely, 1985; Pfeffer, 1977).

Most studies investigating the impact of obtaining an MBA degree focus on salary. While income is obviously an extremely important outcome, Baruch, Bell, and Gray (2005) indicate the importance of looking at the "added value" of an MBA degree from a broader perspective. In addition to considering "current salary, we propose that a measure of percentage change in salary may better reflect the specific impact of obtaining an MBA degree. If an individual can enhance his or her relative worth, attending an MBA program may be of value. Career success has also been identified as an important reason for pursuing an MBA (Hawksley, 1996). Existing research has focused primarily on MBA graduates only, assessing the existent to which their careers improved (see Baruch, et al., 2005). This study will compare the careers of MBA and non-MBA graduates on three measures of career success: number of promotions received, satisfaction with pay, and satisfaction with the opportunity for career advancement. Examination of these five outcome measures should shed some light on the value and impact of obtaining an MBA.

MBA programs should be carefully scrutinized to ensure that value is being delivered. However, reactions based on incomplete information are as dangerous as doing nothing. Before we wave the white flag and hastily close down programs, it is important to conduct broad-based research which examines possible shortcomings in MBA programs. The purpose of the current work is to extend our knowledge of the relationship between obtaining an MBA and early career success. We will help to build existing research in the following ways. First, direct comparisons are made between individuals who obtained MBA degrees and those who did not. Second, the sample is representative of MBA programs throughout the United States, allowing for comparisons of schools at all levels of national rankings, along with comparing the effect of full-time and part-time MBA programs. Third, outcomes will be measured from a variety of perspectives including wages, promotions, and general satisfaction. Fourth, this investigation will be guided by previous research efforts investigating the primary determinants of wages. Fifth, we will look at students from both part-time and full-time programs, and examine these samples both together and separately. Part-time and full-time students generally differ both in terms of age, income, and full-time work experience. Thus the impact of receiving an MBA should be examined separately for these groups.

### It's All in the Name!

There is little doubt that attending a top-ranked MBA program provides students with opportunities not always available at less prestigious programs: top-notch placement services, access to corporate recruiters, and networking with executives and successful graduates. Pfeffer and Fong (2002) indicate that high quality students and the opportunities available at top programs are the primary factors influencing the high salaries received by graduates at top-ranked MBA programs. Pfeffer and Fong (2002) cite studies from *The Economist* ("The MBA cost-benefit," 1994) by Dugan et al. (1999) to support this contention.

We expect that individuals from top-ranked schools will receive higher salaries, in general, upon graduation. However, the real question is not just how well off one is, but rather is one better off than before? Studies by Dugan et al. (1999) and *The Economist* ("The MBA cost-benefit," 1994) focus on current salary rather looking at the percentage change in salary during the time studied. In order to establish whether an MBA degree adds value, there is a need to control for salary earned before entering an MBA program, along with the number of years of work experience. Percentage change in salary during that period appears to be a more pertinent measure of the impact of an MBA than current salary. Thus, we expect that quality or ranking of an MBA program will be strongly related to current salary, but there will be a weaker effect for quality of the MBA program on percentage change in salary.

### Literature Review

A large portion of the research on estimating compensation levels has focused on determining the factors than underlie the gender wage gap. In other words, why do women earn less than men? Much of what has been learned from the gender-related research can be applied here. In other words, do MBAs earn more than those individuals who do not possess an MBA? Research has identified three major categories of variables which help to explain compensation levels: human capital, labor market variables, and demographics. Cognitive ability, or intelligence, has been recently investigated as an additional explanatory variable. It is important to include variables from each of these categories in order to accurately estimate the incremental impact of getting an MBA.

### Human Capital Variables

Human capital theory is the most frequently investigated explanation of worker compensation. The theory suggests that a worker's knowledge and skill generate value resulting in different levels of compensation (Becker, 1975; Ehrenberg & Smith, 2003). The value of this human capital stems from the importance the labor market attaches to these skills. While human capital research is quite broad and somewhat fragmented, education and work experience are the two most commonly investigated measures of human capital. Several studies have shown that college major is an important predictor of compensation (Brown & Corcoran, 1997; Gerhart, 1990). Work experience is also an important determinant of earnings (Loury, 1997; Mitra, 2002) and biases in estimating earnings are possible when labor force experience is not accounted for (Stanley & Jarrell, 1998). Hours worked per week are also an important determinant of overall compensation (Joy, 2003). This variable can be classified as human capital when hours worked are viewed as a function of an individual's motivation and willingness to add value; or as a labor market variable, where hours worked are determined by the demands of the job. Studies examining the impact of obtaining an MBA should control for college major, years of work experience and hours worked.

### Demographic Characteristics

In order to accurately assess the impact of obtaining an MBA, demographic characteristics should be controlled for. A number of studies have reported that marital status is positively related to compensation (Joy, 2003; Judge Cable, Boudreau, & Bretz, 1995; Kilbourne, Farkas, England, Weir, & Beron, 1994; Landau & Arthur, 1992). Race differences in compensation have been reported and thus must be controlled for (Blau, Ferber, & Winkler, 2002; Weinberger, 1998). Age has been reported to be related to compensation in studies of wage discrimination (Stanley & Jarrell, 1998), thus ignoring age may result in biased findings. This possibility is especially important when looking at the variable measuring percentage change in compensation. Older workers are likely to be receiving higher compensation when they enter MBA programs, and may not receive large increases. While including many of the aforementioned variables helps to explain gender differences in compensation, it is important to control for any unexplained variance in the differences of wages for men and women. Thus, gender must be included in any study estimating wages.

### Cognitive Ability and Success

A concern echoed by some observers is that success of business school graduates has less to do with the education received and is more influenced by the selectivity of the schools and the quality of the individuals (Godin, 2000; Pfeffer & Fong, 2002). The impact of the particular type of education that an individual receives in an MBA program has been questioned. Critics point to the fact that MBA programs tend to attract bright people. Therefore, any career success of these individuals may just as likely be attributed to "innate intelligence," rather than information gained from course work in an MBA program.

Cognitive ability has been heavily studied in the psychological literature (see Ackerman, 1999; Hunter, 1986). General mental ability or "g" has been shown to be strongly related to both educational and occupational performance and is a better predictor than any other trait (Jensen, 2000; Schmidt & Hunter, 2004). More recently, researchers in the areas of organizational behavior and human resources have investigated the relationship between cognitive ability and a variety of career related variables including career success (O'Reilly & Chatman, 1994), recruiting (Trank, Rynes, & Bretz, 2002) and search activities (Boudreau, Boswell, Judge, & Bretz, 2001). Cognitive ability is considered a strong predictor of performance across a broad variety of job categories (Gottfredson, 1986; Hunter & Hunter, 1984; Hunter, Schmidt, & Rauschenberger, 1984; Ree & Earles, 1991). With the exception of the work by O'Reilly and Chatman (1994) little research has been conducted on the extent to which cognitive ability is related to career success.

O'Reilly and Chatman (1994), using GMAT scores as a measure of cognitive ability, found no direct effect between cognitive ability and salary. However, they reported an interaction effect of cognitive ability and motivation on success. They concluded that being highly motivated might compensate for lower cognitive ability, while high cognitive ability might compensate for lack of motivation. The findings from this study may not be generalizable because the sample was collected from a "highly competitive" MBA program, where GMAT scores were not representative of the general population. O'Reilly and Chatman (1994) reported a mean of 626 on the GMAT with a standard deviation of 58 for the respondents in their study. The mean for all individuals taking the GMAT at that time was approximately 500 ($SD = 100$). O'Reilly and Chatman's (1994) sample is clearly not representative of the general population of MBA students. A more recent study by Boudreau et al. (2001) investigated the relationship between cognitive ability and job search reported that individuals with higher cognitive ability searched more intently for jobs and obtained positions with higher salaries. The sample of Boudreau et al. (2001) was comprised of high-ranking executives in 1994 that were already successful, earning an average of $165,000 per year.

The positive relationship between cognitive ability and performance as noted in the psychological literature combined with the findings of O'Reilly and Chatman (1994) and Boudreau et al. (2001) indicate the importance of including a measure of cognitive ability when studying career success. Based upon the previous discussion it is important to control for the effect of cognitive ability when investigating the impact of obtaining an MBA degree.

### Do Grades Matter?

Does performance influence income? In a perfect world we would expect this to be true. Previous research investigating the relationship between grades in an MBA program and income is mixed. Pfeffer (1977) and Dreher, Doherty, & Whitely (1985) reported that grade point average (GPA) had no effect on current income. Earlier studies by Williams and Harrell (1964) and Weinstein and Srinivasan (1974) reported a positive relationship between grade point average and starting salary. We expect that grades will not be related to salary for a variety of reasons. First, GPA is only one measure of an individual's qualifications. Second, many firms do not place an emphasis on GPA. Third, GPA is range restricted; it usually varies between 3.0 and 4.0. Students earning less than a 3.0 average are removed from MBA programs.

Based upon the previous discussion, we offer that there are numerous variables that impact compensation above and beyond obtaining an MBA degree. As noted these classes of variables include human capital, demographics and intelligence. We expect that obtaining an MBA will have an incremental effect on compensation, measured in terms of total salary and percentage change. In addition, we investigate the belief that if you cannot attend a top-ranked program there is little benefit to be gain from earning an MBA.

## METHODS

The sample for this study is drawn from the Graduate Management Admission Test Registrant Survey initiated in 1989. The overriding purpose of the initial endeavor was to gain valuable information about individuals who were considering the pursuit of a graduate degree. The survey was comprised of four separate waves of data collection starting in 1990 and ending in 1998. Approximately 250,000 individuals register to take the GMAT every year. Based on a stratified random sample of test registrants, questionnaires were sent to 7,006 individuals who signed up to take the test between June 1990 and March 1991. Completed questionnaires were received from 5,790 individuals for Wave I and 3,769 individuals in Wave IV. In order to achieve a high response rate and reduce the problem of nonresponse bias, the Total Design Method (TDM) developed by Dillman 1978 was employed. This technique is based on concepts associated with social exchange theory. Dillman explains this approach in the following way:

> The appeal of the TDM is based on convincing people first that a problem exists that is of importance to a group with which they identify, and second, that their help is needed to find a solution. The researcher is portrayed as a reasonable person who, in light of the complexity of the problem, is making a reasonable request for help, and, if forthcoming, such help will contribute to the solution of that problem. (1978, pp. 162-163)

For Wave I, in 1990, all individuals were sent a personalized cover letter, a copy of the questionnaire, prepaid return postage, and $5.00. Approximately 1 week later individuals were sent a follow-up postcard, and 2 weeks later a second questionnaire was sent to nonrespondents followed by another postcard. This approach was followed for all four waves of data collection, resulting in an average response rate of approximately 85% for each wave and an overall response rate of 54%. The current investigation focuses on information collected in Waves I and IV, conducted in 1990 and 1998, respectively. Only individuals who reported that they were working full-time in 1990 and 1998 were included, resulting in a final sample of 1602.

For the final sample representing all the individuals studied, 58% were male, 72% were married and 46% had completed an MBA degree. The average respondent had approximately 10 years full-time work experience and worked about 46 hours per week. Approximately 49% of the sample had undergraduate degrees in business administration, while 22% earned engineering degrees, 24% had degrees in the social sciences and education, and the remaining 5% had science degrees. With respect to race, 51% were Caucasian, 14% were African American, 17% were Hispanic. and 16% were Asian. A portion of our analyses focused only on those individuals who had received an MBA degree. Overall, the characteristics of the sample of MBAs were similar to the total sample. A few differences are worth noting. MBAs reported a higher current salary ($72,300), 55% were Caucasian while 11% were African American, and

25% of the MBAs had engineering degrees. There were several demographic differences between individuals who obtained a degree in a full-time MBA program versus those who attended a part-time MBA program. Individuals attending the full-time program tended to be younger (34 versus 36 years of age), were less likely to be married (66% versus 80%) and had about 2 years less work experience. In addition, 50% of the students in full-time MBA programs were non-White while only 40% of the students in part-time programs were non-White.

## Measures

### Career Success

Five measures of career success were employed in this study. Salary in current job was assessed by asking respondents to report their salary for their present job in 1998. Individuals reported their total annual salary, including bonuses and incentive payments. Percentage change in salary was measured by computing the percentage change in salary between 1990 and 1998. As noted earlier, only individuals who were working full-time in both 1990 and 1998 were included in the study. The Job Description Inventory (Smith, Kendall, & Hulin, 1969) was used to measure two facets of job satisfaction: current pay and opportunities for promotion. Cronbach alphas for current pay and opportunities for promotion are .89 and .77, respectively. Number of promotions was measured by asking respondents to indicate how many promotions they had received in the last 3 years. Return on investment (ROI) was computed by dividing the cost of MBA education by average income change in last 2 years.

### Human Capital Variables

Four human capital variables were measured in this study: college major, undergraduate grade point average, work experience, and average number of hours worked per week. We constructed dummy variables for whether the individual received an undergraduate degree in engineering, physical sciences or social sciences. Business majors served as the comparison group. Work experience was measured as the number of years working full-time. Respondents were asked to report the average number of hours worked each week.

### Demographic Variables

Marital status, age, gender, and race were included as demographic variables. Four race categories were measured: Caucasian, African American, Hispanic, and Asian. Three dummy variables were used in the analysis, with Caucasians serving as the comparison group.

*Cognitive Ability*

The GMAT was used as a measure of cognitive ability (O'Reilly & Chatman, 1994). Scores of respondents were obtained directly from the Educational Testing Service, the agency that administers the test under the auspices of the Graduate Management Admissions Council. The mean and standard deviation for the current sample was 480 and 106, respectively. The mean score for respondents from the current study is slightly lower than the mean of 492 reported for all individuals who took the GMAT in 1989. The standard deviation of the GMAT for all test takers is generally around 100.

*MBA Program Variables*

Pfeffer and Fong (2002) indicate that only individuals who graduate from a top-ranked program will experience significant economic gain. Individuals provided specific information regarding the school they attended. We matched this information with rankings obtained from *U.S. News and World Reports* to assess program quality. We created a 0,1 dummy variable to classify respondents as to whether or not they attended a "Top 25 Program." Student GPA in graduate school was measured by asking student to report their overall grade point average on a four-point scale. Respondents were asked to indicate whether they attended a full-time or part-time MBA program.

## Analyses

Hierarchical linear regression was utilized to measure the impact of receiving an MBA on the five career success variables. Demographic variables were entered first, followed by human capital variables and a measure of cognitive ability. The variable measuring whether or not a respondent received an MBA was entered last, allowing us to determine the incremental impact of receiving an MBA while controlling for the other study variables. The last analysis focuses only on those respondents who received an MBA. The final group of variables entered to assess the differential impact of MBA programs include quality of MBA program, public or private school and full-time versus part-time program.

## RESULTS

Table 1.1 shows the descriptive statistics and intercorrelations for the variables in this study. The correlations between having an MBA and the

**Table 1.1.  Correlation for Study Variables**

| | Mean | 1 | 2 | 3 | 4 | 5 | 6 | 7 | 8 | 9 | 10 | 11 | 12 | 13 | 14 | 15 |
|---|---|---|---|---|---|---|---|---|---|---|---|---|---|---|---|---|
| 1. Current salary | 67,305.67 | | | | | | | | | | | | | | | |
| 2. Percentage change in salary | 128.00 | .59 | | | | | | | | | | | | | | |
| 3. Satisfaction with pay | 2.42 | .30 | .28 | | | | | | | | | | | | | |
| 4. Satisfaction with promotion | 2.17 | .20 | .22 | .35 | | | | | | | | | | | | |
| 5. Number of promotions | 1.53 | .13 | .08 | .10 | .16 | | | | | | | | | | | |
| 6. Age | 35.75 | .04 | -.28 | -.06 | -.20 | .01 | | | | | | | | | | |
| 7. Marital status | 0.72 | .09 | .02 | .10 | .01 | .08 | .02 | | | | | | | | | |
| 8. Gender | 0.58 | .19 | .06 | .07 | .07 | .08 | .08 | .15 | | | | | | | | |
| 9. Major-engineering | 0.22 | .10 | -.08 | .07 | .01 | .06 | -.01 | .01 | .18 | | | | | | | |
| 10. Major-physical science | 0.05 | .04 | .01 | -.01 | -.04 | .03 | .04 | .00 | -.05 | -.13 | | | | | | |
| 11. Major-social science | 0.24 | -.05 | -.01 | -.04 | .02 | -.06 | .03 | -.03 | -.09 | -.29 | -.13 | | | | | |
| 12. Undergraduate GPA | 3.10 | .02 | .02 | -.00 | -.01 | .02 | -.03 | .03 | -.05 | -.01 | -.01 | -.02 | | | | |
| 13. Work experience | 10.29 | .05 | -.27 | -.05 | -.17 | .03 | .75 | .03 | .08 | -.03 | .02 | .03 | -.03 | | | |
| 14. Hours worked weekly | 46.10 | .30 | .17 | .07 | .09 | .11 | .06 | .04 | .11 | .01 | -.01 | -.05 | .05 | .07 | | |
| 15. Cognitive ability | 485.42 | .27 | .11 | .16 | .10 | .05 | -.11 | .05 | .21 | .22 | .07 | -.01 | .08 | -.11 | .07 | |
| 16. MBA | 0.46 | .14 | .09 | .08 | .09 | - | -.02 | .06 | .05 | .01 | -.02 | .05 | .04 | -.03 | .06 | .19 |

Correlations above .06 are significant at .05 level.

five measures of career success are positive and significant at the .001 level. Thus, hypothesis 1 is supported.

Table 1.2 presents the results of regression analyses for the five career success variables for the full sample. Hours worked per week and cognitive ability were the strongest predictors of current income, while age, majoring in engineering, work experience, and hours worked per week were related to percentage change in salary. The positive relationship between gender and the two income measures indicates that men earned significantly more money than the women and their income was increasing at a slightly higher rate. With the exception of respondents who earned undergraduate degrees in engineering, there was no significant relationship between undergraduate major or race and our measures of income. In fact, the income of engineering majors increased at a slower rate over the 8 years studied. The results of the regression analysis show support for a main effect of cognitive ability on current salary ($\beta = .21$,

**Table 1.2.   Results of Regression Analyses Predicting Career Success of Total Sample**

| Demographic | Current Salary | Percentage Change in Salary | Satisfaction With Pay | Satisfaction With Promotions | Number of Promotions |
|---|---|---|---|---|---|
| Marital status | .04 | .01 | .08** | .01 | .06* |
| Age | .01 | -.18** | -.04 | -.17** | .01 |
| Gender | .10** | .08** | .01 | .06** | .04 |
| African American | .01 | .02 | -.02 | -.01 | -.02 |
| Hispanic | .01 | .02 | .02 | .04 | -.01 |
| Asian | .02 | .04 | -.06* | .01 | -.04 |
| *Human Capital* | | | | | |
| Major—Engineering | .04 | -.12** | .02 | -.02 | .04 |
| Major—Phys. Science | .05* | .02 | -.01 | -.03* | .02 |
| Major—Soc. Science | -.01 | -.03 | -.03 | .02 | -.04 |
| Work experience | .05 | -.13** | .01 | -.04 | .02 |
| Undergrad GPA | | -.01 | -.02 | -.02 | .01 |
| Hours worked | .28** | .21** | .06* | .09** | .09** |
| *Cognitive Ability* | .21** | .05* | .12** | .07** | -.02 |
| MBA | .08**[a] | .05*[a] | .04 | .07** | .10** |
| $R^2$ | .19 | .15 | .04 | .06 | .04 |
| Overall *F* | | | | | |

Values are standardized regression coefficients.
[a] MBA degree accounts for an additional 2% of the variance in current salary and percentage change in salary
*$p < .05$

$p < .001$) and percentage increase in income ($\beta = .05, p < .01$). We found a significant main effort for earning an MBA on measures of current salary, percentage change in salary satisfaction with promotions and number of promotions received. There was no incremental main effect for earning an MBA on the satisfaction with pay measure.

Tables 1.3 and 1.4 present the results of separate regression analyses for full-time and part-time students, respectively. Focusing on graduates of full-time MBA programs, results in Table 1.3 show a positive effect for obtaining an MBA on current salary and percentage change in income. For graduates of part-time MBA programs (Table 1.4), there is no effect of obtaining an MBA on current income or percentage change in income. However, there is a positive effect for obtaining an MBA on number of promotions received in the last 3 years.

Table 1.5 presents the regression results of analyses examining the effect of type of MBA program, quality of the program and student performance on career success. The findings indicate that program quality is

**Table 1.3.  Results of Regression Analyses Predicting Career Success (No MBA vs. Full-time MBA)**

| Demographic | Current Salary | Percentage Change in Salary | Satisfaction With Pay | Satisfaction With Promotions | Number of Promotions |
|---|---|---|---|---|---|
| Marital status | .03 | .01 | .09** | -.01 | |
| Age | -.04 | -.18** | -.07* | -.16** | .02 |
| Gender | .12** | .09** | .03 | .08** | .02 |
| African American | -.01 | -.02 | .01 | -.05 | -.03 |
| Hispanic | -.01 | -.02 | .01 | .01 | -.01 |
| Asian | -.01 | .01 | -.04 | -.02 | -.04 |
| *Human Capital* | | | | | |
| Major—Engineering | .03 | -.12** | -.01 | -.01 | .05 |
| Major—Phys. Science | .07* | .02 | -.01 | -.01 | .02 |
| Major—Soc. Science | -.01 | -.05 | -.04 | .02 | -.01 |
| Work experience | .08* | -.12** | -.01 | -.06 | .01 |
| Undergrad GPA | -.01 | -.01 | -.02 | -.03 | .02 |
| Hours worked | .29** | .19** | .06 | .09** | .09** |
| *Cognitive Ability* | .20** | .03 | .17** | .04 | -.02 |
| MBA | .10** | .12** | -.03 | .07** | .02 |
| $R^2$ | .20 | .16 | .05 | .09 | .02 |
| Overall $F$ | | | | | |

Values are standardized regression coefficients.
* $p < .05$; ** $p < .01$

**Table 1.4.   Results of Regression Analyses
Predicting Career Success (No MBA vs. Part-time MBA)**

| Demographic | Current Salary | Percentage Change in Salary | Satisfaction With Pay | Satisfaction With Promotions | Number of Promotions |
|---|---|---|---|---|---|
| Marital status | .06* | .03 | .06* | .02 | .06* |
| Age | .03 | -.14** | -.06 | -.18** | .01 |
| Gender | .12** | .09** | .01 | .07* | .04 |
| African American | -.02 | -.04 | -.03 | -.02 | .01 |
| Hispanic | -.01 | .01 | .03 | .04 | .03 |
| Asian | -.01 | .01 | -.08* | .01 | -.04 |
| *Human Capital* | | | | | |
| Major—Engineering | .07* | -.09** | .05 | -.02 | .04 |
| Major—Phys. Science | .09* | .05 | .01 | -.04 | .02 |
| Major—Soc. Science. | -.01 | -.03 | -.03 | .02 | -.04 |
| Work experience | .06* | -.13** | .03 | .05 | .01 |
| Undergrad GPA | .06* | .02 | .01 | -.03 | .03 |
| Hours worked | .25** | .18** | .06* | .11* | .09** |
| *Cognitive Ability* | .13** | .01 | .12** | .03 | .01 |
| MBA | .03 | -.01 | .06 | .04 | .13** |
| $R^2$ | .19 | .15 | .04 | .06 | .04 |
| Overall $F$ | | | | | |

Values are standardized regression coefficients.
* $p < .05$;  ** $p < .01$

a significant predictor of current salary but unrelated to percentage change in salary. Graduates of full-time programs enjoyed a greater percentage change in salary than graduates of part-time programs. However graduates of full-time programs are less satisfied with their current pay and reported receiving fewer promotions. Grades obtained in graduate school are not related to either current income or percentage change in income. In order to examine Pfeffer and Fong's contention that only those who attend top ranked programs benefit from obtaining an MBA we constructed a measure of ROI. Findings reported in Table 1.5 show that program quality had no effect on ROI; however MBA graduates from public institutions had a greater ROI than graduates from private schools.

## DISCUSSION

The current study represents the first broad-scale attempt to address some of the concerns/statements made by Pfeffer and Fong (2002).

**Table 1.5. Results of Regression Analyses Predicting Career Success (MBA Graduates)**

| Demographics | Current Salary | Percentage Change in Salary | Satisfaction With Pay | Satisfaction With Promotions | Number of Promotions | Return on Investment |
|---|---|---|---|---|---|---|
| Marital status | .05 | -.02 | .06 | -.03 | .01 | .03 |
| Age | .13* | -.19** | -.02 | -.14* | -.06 | -.04 |
| Gender | .08* | .10* | -.01 | .05 | .06 | .06 |
| African American | .03 | .03 | -.01 | .04 | .03 | -.01 |
| Hispanic | .02 | .04 | .07 | .08* | .03 | .06 |
| Asian | -.02 | .05 | -.09* | -.02 | -.01 | -.01 |
| *Human Capital* | | | | | | |
| Major—Engineering | .02 | -.13** | .02 | -.06 | .01 | -.07 |
| Major—Phys. Science | -.01 | .02 | .04 | -.05 | .02 | -.01 |
| Major-Soc. Science | -.05 | -.05 | .01 | 01 | -.01 | -.04 |
| Undergrad GPA | -.02 | -.02 | -.03 | -.05 | .03 | -.02 |
| Graduate GPA | .02 | -.01 | -.02 | .04 | .05 | .05 |
| Work experience | -.03 | -.11* | .03 | -.06 | .03 | -.03 |
| Hours worked | .32** | .28** | .08* | .06 | .09* | .19** |
| *Cognitive ability* | .18** | .03 | .13** | .02 | .07 | .01 |
| MBA Program | | | | | | |
| Top 25 program | .19** | .03 | -.02 | .04 | -.08 | -.02 |
| Public vs private | -.01 | .01 | .08* | -.03 | -.04 | .27** |
| $R^2$ | .25 | .22 | .06 | .06 | .06 | .06 |
| Overall $F$ | | | | | | |

Values are standardized regression coefficients.

$* p < .05;  ** p < .01$

Using the same database employed by Dugan et al. (1999) this study extends the work of previous researchers. First, we use a nation-wide database containing graduates representing all types of MBA programs. Second, we include a number of control variables in an attempt to examine an independent evaluation of the impact of obtaining an MBA. Third, we investigate the impact of cognitive ability on salary. Fourth, we look at percentage change in salary to examine the relative impact ofM an MBA.

The results indicate a modest but statistically significant impact from obtaining an MBA. Controlling for demographic characteristics and cognitive ability, obtaining an MBA degree explained an additional 2% of the variance in current income and percentage change income. MBA graduates also reported receiving more promotions than did those individuals who did not receive an MBA degree.

Earlier research by O'Reilly and Chatman (1994) found no direct relationship between cognitive ability and success. These researchers questioned the emphasis placed on GMAT scores by business schools and indicated that perhaps more focus should be placed on assessing individual conscientiousness. Our findings indicate that cognitive ability, measured with GMAT scores, is a good indicator of career success. One potential explanation for the difference in findings of the two studies lies in the student samples used. O'Reilly and Chatman (1994) collected data from a top-ranked, highly competitive business school, where average GMAT scores of graduates are in the top 10% of all test takers. The profile of GMAT scores for students in the current sample is similar to the population norms of all test takers. Based on our findings, GMAT scores seem to an appropriate tool for measuring potential success of MBA graduates.

A recent study by Connolly (2003) reported that MBA graduates from a Midwestern university experienced an average rate of return of about 18.8% between 1999 and 2002. Pfeffer and Fong (2003) indicate that Connolly (2003) overstates the potential impact of the MBA degree because of the lack of a comparison group. Pfeffer and Fong (2003) argue that individuals are more likely to experience rapid wage growth early in their career. Our findings indicate that, despite being out of the workforce for a period of time or pursuing a part-time MBA, individuals who obtain MBAs do experience income growth.

Pfeffer and Fong (2002) argue the explosion of MBA programs throughout the United States has diluted the impact of an MBA degree. They indicate that only graduates from top-ranked MBA programs will experience a true benefit. Our findings present a somewhat different story. Program quality was significantly related to current income of MBA graduates, but was unrelated to percentage change in income. This indicates that, relatively speaking, there is no impact of program quality on income. In practical terms, this means that even individuals who are attending MBA programs of average quality will still benefit. Their salaries are likely to be lower when they enter the program, as are their expectations. The average MBA student is not expecting a career in consulting or investment banking. However, they are expecting some return on their investment. Our findings show that relatively speaking, the return, percentage wise, is the same regardless of the quality of the MBA program. Our results do indicate that individuals who attended full-time programs enjoyed a great percentage increase in compensation than those who attended part-time programs. This finding was expected and can be explained in a variety ways. Full-time students are typically younger on average with fewer years of work experience, and thus are making less money to start. In addition, full-time programs stress the importance of job placement services. Conversely, a large proportion of part-time students receive tuition benefits from their employers and MBA programs face concerns about sponsoring recruiting opportunities. Our findings indicate that students attending public institutions have a better ROI, in general, than students attending more costly private schools.

There are clearly a number of limitations that should be noted. Because we did not design the questionnaire and the data was collected prior to the work of Pfeffer and Fong (2002), we are not able to address all of the issues mentioned by Pfeffer and Fong. Second, the questionnaires do not contain any appropriate measures of personality or motivation. Thus, we could not directly replicate the findings of O'Reilly and Chapman (1994). However, the nation-wide sample of MBA programs allows for greater generalizability of the results. Third, the data focuses only on the early careers of MBA graduates. However, the data does allow for direct comparisons with non-MBA graduates, a clear advantage over previous research studies. Fourth, since our dataset only includes individuals who took the GMAT® exam, we do not have a complete representation of non-MBA graduates. Future research efforts should include individuals who have not considered obtaining an MBA. Finally, some of the differences noted between individuals attending full-time and part-time MBA programs may be due, in-part, to individuals changing careers. We were not able to assess the impact of career-change in the current study.

In summary, this study was not designed to address the criticisms of Pfeffer and Fong (2002) on a point-by-point basis, but rather to investigate their contention that MBA education has little or no effect on career success. Our findings show that obtaining an MBA has a moderate effect on income for MBA graduates.

## ACKNOWLEDGMENTS

We sincerely thank the Graduate Management Admissions Council, Rachel Edgington, Joseph Fox, and Mark Montgomery for providing access to and assistance with the Graduate Management Admission Test Registrant Survey and Rebecca Altschaefl for research assistance.

## REFERENCES

Ackerman, P. L. (1999). Traits and knowledge as determinants of learning and individual differences: Putting it all together. In P. L. Ackerman, P. C. Kyllonen, & R. D. Roberts (Eds.), *Learning and individual differences* (pp. 437-460). Washington, DC: American Psychological Association.

Baruch, Y., Bell, M. P., & Gray, D.(2005). Generalist and specialist graduate business degrees: Tangible and intangible value. *Journal of Vocational Behavior,* 67, 51-68.

Becker, G. (1975). *Human capital* (2nd ed.). Chicago: The University of Chicago Press.

Blau, F. D., Ferber, M. A., & Winkler, A. E. (2002). *The economics of women, men and work* (4th ed.). Upper Saddle River, NJ: Prentice Hall.

Boudreau, J. W., Boswell, W. R., Judge, T. A., & Bretz, R. D., Jr. (2001). Personality and cognitive ability as predictors of job search among employed managers. *Personnel Psychology, 54,* 25-54.

Brown, C., & Corcoran, M. (1997). Sex-based differences in school content and the male-female wage gap. *Journal of Labor Economics, 15,* 431-65.

Bruce, G. D., Edgington, R., & Olkin, J. M. (2003, Spring). Apply and demand: How the economy affects graduates' career choices. *Selections,* 5-11.

Connolly, M. (2003). The end of the MBA as we know it? *Academy of Management Learning and Education, 2,* 365-367.

Dillman, D. A. (1978). *Mail and telephone surveys: The Total Design Method.* New York: Wiley.

Dreher, G. F., Doherty, T. W., & Whitely, B. (1985). Generalizability of MBA degree and socioeconomic effects on business school graduates' salaries. *Journal of Applied Psychology, 70,* 769-773.

Dugan, M. K., Grady, W. R., Payne, B., & Johnson, T. R. (1999). The benefits of an MBA: A comparison of graduates and non-graduates. *Selections, 1,* 18-24.

Ehrenberg, R. G., & Smith, R. S. (2003). *Modern labor economics: Theory and public policy* (8th ed.) Boston: Addison Wesley.

Gerhart, B. (1990). Gender differences in current and starting salaries: The role of performance, college major and job title. *Industrial and Labor Relations Review, 43,* 418-33.

Godin, S. (2000). Change agent. *Fast company, 38,* 322.

Gottfredson, L. S. (1986). Societal consequences of the g factor in employment. *Journal of Vocational Behavior, 29,* 379-410.

Hawksley, F. (1996). In the right place at the right time. *Accountancy, 117*(1233), 44-46.

Hunter, J. E. (1986). Cognitive ability, cognitive aptitudes, job knowledge and job performance. *Journal of Vocational Behavior, 29,* 340-362.

Hondo, B. (2002). An MBA: Is it still worth it? Salaries for 2002 MBAs have shrunk. That means it will take longer to get a payback. *Business Week, 3804,* 104.

Hunter, J. E., & Hunter, R. F. (1984). Validity and utility of alternative predictors of job performance. *Psychological Bulletin, 96,* 72-98.

Hunter, J. E., Schmidt, F. L., & Rauschenberger, J. (1984). Methodological, statistical, and ethical issues in the study of bias in psychological tests. In C. R. Reynolds & R. T. Brown (Eds.), *Perspectives on bias in mental testing* (pp. 41-99). New York: Plenum Press.

Jensen, A. R. (2000). Testing: The dilemma of group differences. *Psychology, Public Policy and Law, 6,* 121-27.

Joy, L. (2003). Salaries of recent male and female college graduates: Educational and labor market effects. *Industrial and Labor Relations Review, 56,* 606-621.

Judge, T. A., Cable, D. M., Boudreau, J. W., & Bretz, R. D., Jr. (1995). An empirical investigation of the predictors of executive career success. *Personnel Psychology, 48,* 485-519.

Kilbourne, B. S., Farkas, G., England, P., Weir, D., & Beron, K. (1994). Returns to skill, compensating differentials, and gender bias: Effects of occupational characteristics of wages of white women and men. *American Journal of Sociology, 100,* 689-719.

Landau, J., & Arthur, M. B. (1992). The relationship of marital status, spouse's career status, and gender to salary level. *Sex Roles, 27,* 665-681.

Leonhardt, D. (2000, October 1). A matter of degree? Not for consultants. *New York Times, Section 32,* pp. 1-18.

Livingston, J. S. (1971). The myth of the well-educated manager. *Harvard Business Review, 49,* 79-89.

Loury, L. D. (1997). The gender earnings gap among college-educated workers. *Industrial and Labor Relations Review, 50,* 580-593.

Mintzberg, H. (2004). *Managers not MBAs: A hard look at the soft practice of managing and management development.* London: Prentice Education.

Mitra, A. (2002). Mathematics skill and male-female wages. *Journal of Socio-Economics, 31,* 443-456.

O'Reilly, C. A., & Chatman, J. A. (1994). Working smarter and harder: A longitudinal study of managerial success. *Administrative Science Quarterly, 39,* 603-627.

Pfeffer, J. (1977). Effects of an MBA and socioeconomic origins on business school graduates' salaries. *Journal of Applied Psychology, 62,* 698-705.

Pfeffer, J., & Fong, C. T. (2002). The end of business schools? Less success than meets the eye. *Academy of Management Learning and Education, 1,* 78-95.

Pfeffer, J., & Fong, C. T. (2003). Assessing business schools: Reply to Connolly. *Academy of Management Learning and Education, 2,* 368-370.

Ree, M. J., & Earles, J. A. (1991). Predicting training success: Not much more than g. *Personnel Psychology, 44,* 321-332.

Schmidt, F. L., & Hunter, J. (2004). General mental ability in the world of work: Occupational attainment and job performance. *Journal of Personality and Social Psychology, 86,* 162-73.

Smith, P. C., Kendall, L. M., & Hulin, C. L. (1969). *The measurement of satisfaction in work and retirement.* Chicago: Rand McNally.

Stanley, T. D., & Jarrell, S. B. (1998). Gender wage discrimination bias? A meta-regression analysis. *Journal of Human Resources, 33,* 947-973.

The MBA cost-benefit analysis. (1994, August 6). *The Economist,* p. 58.

Trank, C. Q., Rynes, S. L., & Bretz, R. D., Jr. (2002). Attracting applicants in the war for talent: Differences in work preferences among high achievers. *Journal of Business and Psychology, 16,* 331-345.

Weinberger, C. J. (1998). Race and gender wage gaps in the market for recent college graduates. *Industrial Relations, 37,* 67-84.

Weinstein, A. G., & Srinivasan, V. (1974). Predicting managerial success of master of business administration graduates. *Journal of Applied Psychology, 59,* 207-212.

Williams, F. J., & Harrell, T. W. (1964). Predicting success in business. *Journal of Applied Psychology, 48,* 164-167.

CHAPTER 2

# TRACKING CAREERS TO IMPROVE COMPETENCY-BASED MANAGEMENT EDUCATION

## A Longitudinal Study of Italian MBAs

**Arnaldo Camuffo, Fabrizio Gerli, and Francesca Chiara**

A number of studies have recently questioned the value and meaning of MBA programs and how effectively Business Schools provide management education and shape future business leaders. While these studies share a critical view about the current status of MBA education and the conviction that it should be reformed, there is less convergence about how to do it. This chapter presents the findings of a project that conducted a systematic longitudinal analysis explicitly aimed to evaluate the impact of an Italian MBA program on competency development of five students' cohorts, and to identify which competencies were related to rapid and successful careers. It develops the application of competency-based methodologies to MBA education applying competency-based techniques throughout all the phases of the educational process to include post-MBA career analysis.

*New Visions for Graduate Management Education,* 23–64
Copyright © 2006 by Information Age Publishing

## INTRODUCTION

A number of studies have recently questioned the value and meaning of MBA programs and, more generally, how effectively business schools provide management education and shape future business leaders (Armstrong, 2005; Augier & Teece, 2005; Connolly, 2003; Dreher & Ryan, 2004; Feldman, 2005; Fisher, 2004; Miles, 2005; Mintzberg, 2004, 2005; Mintzberg & Gosling, 2002; Pfeffer & Fong, 2002, 2003, 2004; Siemens, Burton, Jensen, & Mendoza, 2005). These studies address a wide array of issues, from the nature and quantity of learning actually taking place in such programs, to their impact on salaries and careers; from the scientific foundation and quality of the knowledge these courses teach, to the kind of skills and competencies students develop; from the capacity of MBA programs to evolve and innovate as economy and society change, to the ethical issues involved in teaching management.

While these studies share a critical view about the current status of MBA education and the conviction that it should be reformed, there is less convergence about how to do it. Among the diverse, possible ways to innovate MBA programs, the adoption of competency-based methodologies has been indicated as particularly promising (Pfeffer & Fong, 2002, 2004).

Building on the pioneering work done by Boyatzis, Cowen, Kolb, and Associates (1995) at the Weatherhead School of Management, Case Western Reserve University, and on research recently conducted in Italy (Camuffo & Gerli, 2004), this chapter further develops the application of competency-based methodologies to MBA education.

Our general point is that designing and delivering effective MBA education is not to be grounded only in the piecemeal adaptation of the curricula and teaching methodologies of the MBA programs. We believe that effective MBA education needs applying competency-based techniques throughout all the phases of the educational process, here broadly conceived beyond the traditional boundaries, to include post-MBA career analysis.

The innovative character of this competency-based approach to MBA education hinges on two focal elements: (a) the integration of all the stages of the educational process, from the assessment of the educational needs, to the identification of educational objectives to the design and delivery of the MBA program, to the evaluation of learning, to the monitoring of graduates' performances and careers on the labor market; (b) the adoption of a multiple constituency approach, which actively engage educational institutions, students/graduates and the companies that hire and employ them in the continuous fine tuning of the educational process. We also believe that academics have the responsibility to ground management education on scientific foundations, using, as much as they can, the analytical tools provided by social sciences and management studies (in our case the option is the competency tool kit).

Since the seminal work conducted by Boyatzis et al. (1995) at the Weatherhead School of Management, several studies have applied competency-based techniques to management education. Most of these, however, discuss the applications (and implications) of competency-based methodologies on only one or few components of the educational process. They do not adopt a comprehensive, integrated approach to the educational process and do not address the issue of the fit among the components of the process itself. For example, Boyatzis and Kolb (1995), Burke and Day (1986), Hansson (2001), Mulcahy and James (2000), Sala (2001), Smith (1999), Wagner and Moffett III (2000) and Warn and Tranter (2001) apply competency-based techniques to outcome evaluation, at the individual or at the collective (class/cohort) level. A little wider perspective is taken by Ballou, Bowers, Boyatzis, and Kolb (1999) and by Sluijsmans, Dochy, and Moerkerke (1999), who complement competency-based outcome evaluation with the application of competency-based concepts to the design of curricula and didactics. Sturges, Simpson, and Altman (2003) use qualitative analysis to explore the skills, knowledge and capabilities acquired by MBAs during the course. Boyatzis (1999, 2002), Kolb (1984) and Robotham (1995) develop and apply analytical competency-based methodologies to monitor the learning process.

Furthermore, rarely these studies conduct a systematic longitudinal analysis on different cohorts of MBA graduates at different points of time, with the specific aim of verifying the impact of the MBA program on their careers, assessing the relevance of what they learned, and then feeding back this information into the design process of the future editions of the course (a partial exception is the study of Boyatzis, Stubbs, and Taylor [2002]).

Our chapter investigates this relatively unexplored aspect and presents a competency-based analysis of the educational outcomes and careers of the MBA graduates of the master's program organized by the Fondazione CUOA[1] of Vicenza, one of the top business schools in Italy.

In the late 1990s, the CUOA master's program was completely redesigned according to competency-based principles (Camuffo & Gerli, 2004). Whereas the new program achieved almost immediately significant accomplishments in terms of students' competency development and of alignment among employers' competency requirements, students' expectations and course characteristics, it is now possible to assess its impact on several cohorts of MBAs and on their careers. Thus, this chapter builds on the model, methods and findings of that previous study and presents the findings of a follow-up project explicitly aimed to: (a) analyze the impact of the CUOA MBA program on competency development of several students' cohorts; (b) identify which competencies related to rapid and successful careers; and (c) feed this information back into the MBA design process so that it can better reflect labor market trends and develop the competencies that effectively support MBAs' careers.

## Theoretical Framework

This study is theoretically positioned within competency-based research (Boyatzis, 1982; Boyatzis & Kolb, 1991, 1995; Boyatzis et al., 1995; Camuffo & Comacchio, 2004; Camuffo & Gerli, 2004; Spencer & Spencer, 1993) which maintains that effective performance in managerial jobs depends on personal qualities and defines these personal qualities as competencies.

The competency literature has developed significantly in the last three decades, since the pioneering work by David McClelland (1973). He argues that intelligence testing, scholastic grades and the traditional job analytic approaches to personnel selection, fail to predict job performance. Instead, McClelland proposes testing for competency. Although controversial among applied and organizational psychologists (Atwater, 1992; Barrett, 1994; Barrett & Depinet, 1991; Sternberg & Wagner, 1986), competency-based studies and applications have gained popularity and acceptance within the human resource academic and business community through the work of McClelland and his associates, particularly Richard Boyatzis, at Case Western Reserve University (CWRU).

In his study of managers' effectiveness, Boyatzis (1982, p. 21) defines a job competency as "an underlying characteristic of a person, in that it may be a motive, trait, skill, aspect of one's self-image or social role, or a body of knowledge which he or she uses, which is causally related to the achievement of effective, or better, work performances." His definition of competency is general (and somewhat ambiguous) enough to reflect either individual or specific organizational concerns. Such ambiguity left room for subsequent research which redefined competencies as:

1. the knowledge, skills, abilities, and other attributes required to perform desired future behavior (Blancero, Boroski, & Dyer, 1996, p. 387);

2. an individual's demonstrated knowledge, skills, or abilities (Ulrich, Brockbank, Yeung, & Lake, 1995, p. 474);

3. skills and traits that are needed by employees to be effective in a job (Mansfield, 1996);

4. knowledge and skills that underlie effective performance (McLagan, 1997);
5. knowledge, skills, abilities and behaviors required for successful performance of job duties (Mirabile, 1995, p. 13);
6. "an underlying characteristic of an individual that is causally related to criterion-referenced effective and/or superior performance in a given job or situation" (Mitrani, Dalziel, & Fitt, 1992; Spencer & Spencer, 1993, p. 11);
7. a collection of observable behaviors that superior performers exhibit more consistently than average performers, grouped according to a central theme, which then becomes the competency (Klein, 1996).

Klein's definition is significantly different from the others since, instead of maintaining that competencies underlie behaviors, it suggests that behaviors underlie competency. Woodruff (1993) raises a similar issue distinguishing between competence and competency and proposing that competence is a performance criterion while competencies are the behaviors driving the competence. This is similar to Klein's (1996) argument that competencies are not psychological constructs but thematic groups of demonstrated observable behaviors that discriminate between superior and average performance. These behaviors require no inference, assumptions, or interpretation.

All these definitions, though different, share some common elements. First, most of them assume that competencies are the knowledge, skills, attitudes or other attributes that underlie effective or successful job performance. Second, these elements must be observable or measurable. Third, these elements differentiate between best and other performers. According to this perspective, we adopt a notion of competencies that defines them as those personal characteristics, that include knowledge, skills, self-image, social roles, traits and motives, "that are causally related to effective and/or superior performance in a job" (Boyatzis, 1982, p. 23), thus considering both managerial knowledge and skills, and behavioral competencies.

We already used this notion of competencies in defining the CUOA competency-based MBA education model (Camuffo & Gerli, 2004) characterized by: (a) competency-based analysis of educational needs and definition of educational objectives; (b) competency-based design of the MBA curriculum and didactics; (c) competency-based outcome evaluation of the MBA program (assessment of learning and development); (d) a multiple constituency approach that involves students, hiring companies and business schools in all the phases of the educational process.

In this chapter we enrich that model with a competency-based analysis of MBAs' careers, and use the CUOA MBA as a case study to show: (a) how a competency-based MBA program impacted on its graduates' careers; (b) how this data can feed back into MBA design (Figure 2.1). Throughout this analysis we continue to use competency-based methods and metrics consistent with a multiple constituency approach.

## Using Competency-Based Tools to Design MBA Education

In order to assess the nature and intensity of competency development of CUOA's MBAs, we adopted (and updated) the competency modeling techniques described by Camuffo and Gerli (2004). Namely, we identified a list of competencies and skills against which we assessed MBAs' development.

Our multiple constituency approach postulates that the training needs and educational objectives of an MBA program ought to be defined: (a) formally involving employers in the definition of the competencies they require and reward; and (b) identifying the competencies that lead MBAs

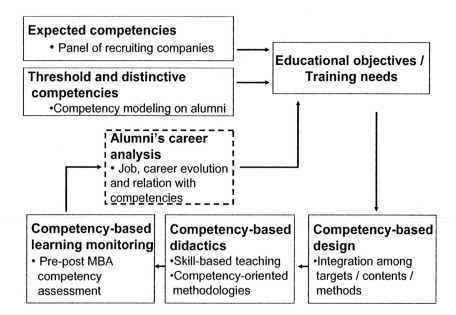

Figure 2.1.   Research framework and design.

to successful careers. In order to do that, we used two complementary sources (Camuffo & Gerli, 2004):

1. panels of recruiting companies (typically HR directors), convened at different times, aimed to identify the evolution of their expectations towards MBAs;
2. a competency model of CUOA MBAs, aimed to identify threshold competencies and top performers' differentiators.

### Expected Competencies: What do Companies Want From MBAs?

We conducted two series of panels, one in 1999 and the other in 2004. The 1999 panel (36 participants) led to the redesign of the CUOA MBA according to a competency-based approach. The 2004 panel (28 participants) allowed to check and update the set of expected competencies. Panel participants were asked to formulate their expectations (in terms of desired competencies) using two structured questionnaires. One questionnaire (defined "Managerial Skills Profile") was an adapted version of the Executive Skills Profile used by Boyatzis and Kolb (1991, 1995) and by Boyatzis et al. (1995). It included 60 managerial (cross-functional) skills clustered into 12 groups of competencies. The other (defined "Functional Skills Profile") contained 40 functional skills clustered into 10 groups, encompassing the main areas of managerial knowledge normally developed within an MBA program (e.g. skills in such areas as marketing, accounting, finance, operations, organization, HRM, etc.).

Panel participants were asked to indicate how important they considered each skill in the managerial roles typically played by MBAs in their post-MBA working experience. In other words, they were asked how important, according to their expectations, each skill in the questionnaires should be in the skills portfolio of an MBA graduate. Accordingly, two types of "expected" Skills Profiles became available: one regarding a set of managerial competencies and another regarding a set of functional competencies. Panel participants were asked to attribute a level of importance to each skill in the questionnaires, following a 7-point scale, ranging from "This skill is not required" (scale-point 1), to "This skill is absolutely necessary for work effectiveness" (scale-point 7). The human resource managers filling in the questionnaires were asked to take an abstract view of the matter: they had no specific job description to refer to; instead, they had to define the expected competencies for an MBA graduate in general terms, based on their personal experiences and referring to the jobs MBAs would typically do.

Table 2.1 presents the results of the two HR managers panels (in 1999 and 2004) reporting the standardized evaluations for both the managerial and functional skills, aggregated at the cluster level.

**Table 2.1.  Hiring Firms' Expectations
(From Human Resource Managers' Panels) in 1999 and in 2004:
Managerial Skills and Functional Skills
(Normalized Aggregated at the Skill Cluster Value)**

| Managerial Skills | 1999 | 2004 |
|---|---|---|
| Help | 70.2 | 72.2 |
| Sense-making | 77.8 | 78.7 |
| Information gathering | 67.5 | 65.2 |
| Information analysis | 67.0 | 66.7 |
| Theory | 58.5 | 66.2 |
| Quantitative methods | 50.0 | 52.2 |
| Technology | 63.8 | 61.0 |
| Goal setting | 81.5 | 80.9 |
| Action | 80.7 | 76.3 |
| Initiative | 73.2 | 77.2 |
| Leadership | 70.8 | 75.2 |
| Relationship | 81.3 | 73.4 |
| Marketing | 57.5 | 63.9 |
| Logistics | 59.0 | 55.3 |
| Operations Management | 55.6 | 56.4 |
| Accounting and Control | 62.7 | 61.3 |
| Finance | 56.7 | 55.3 |
| Organization Design & Behavior | 68.3 | 62.3 |
| Human Resource Management | 58.1 | 59.7 |
| Information Technology | 69.2 | 60.9 |
| Globalization - International Management | 48.8 | 51.2 |
| Strategic Management | 63.1 | 64.4 |

As regards managerial skills, standard evaluations were relatively high, homogenous and time consistent across the skill clusters confirming that the questionnaires were reliable and capable to capture firms' expectations (even at the single skill level, most of the skills had standardized evaluations larger than 60%). Interestingly, skills in the goal and action and in the interpersonal skill clusters were the most relevant in the 1999 panel and remained so also in 2004, with some changes in terms of intensity (e.g., leadership).

Similar considerations apply to the functional skill questionnaire, though standardized evaluations were usually slightly lower on average. HR managers' expectations towards MBAs, though slightly changing in 2004, remained clear: emphasis on marketing, performance measurement (accounting and control), IT and strategic management skills. Interestingly, as a result of globalization, international management skills have become more important over time.

### Modeling MBAs' Competencies

We also identified a competency model of CUOA's MBAs, that is, a set of threshold and distinctive competencies associated with MBAs' performance on the labor market (careers and compensation), the understanding being that these would then become the target competencies and, hence, the master's program educational objectives. We adopted the modeling procedures proposed by Boyatzis (1982), as refined by Spencer and Spencer's (1993) and by the studies conducted by scholars at CWRU and in the United Kingdom (Boyatzis, 1994; Boam & Sparrow, 1992; Ballou, Bower, Boyatzis, & Kolb, 1999; Boyatzis et al., 1995),[2] and followed these steps:

- Step 1: definition of a performance criterion. The aim of the analysis was to identify the competencies that characterize successful MBAs. By success we meant post-MBA jobs, careers and compensation. Thus, as described in Camuffo and Gerli (2004), we ran an employment and salary survey on a group of 182 MBAs (all the graduates of three latest editions—1996, 1997, 1998—of the CUOA master's program).

- Step 2: MBAs' performance analysis, ranking and classification. We used the data collected in Step 1 to rank the MBAs and classify them into two categories: best and average performers.

- Step 3: sampling and collection of data on how MBAs performed their job. We built two small samples of MBAs, comprising, respectively, 16 "best performers" and 14 "average performers." Sampling was not random in order to guarantee, within each sample, the presence of different MBAs' profiles in terms of age, gender, seniority, job/function. We interviewed the MBAs using Behavioral Event Interviewing[3] (BEI) techniques. Interviews ranged from a minimum of 100 minutes to a maximum of 260 minutes. As an introduction to each BEI, we asked the MBAs to tell us about their professional background, and their current jobs' task and responsibilities.

- Step 4: MBAs' behavior analysis. We taped and typed up all the 30 BEIs; we analyzed (thematic analysis) and coded the transcripts for frequency of occurrence (Boyatzis, 1998). We applied blind double coding to check for interrating reliability (Boyatzis, 1998; Spencer & Spencer, 1993).[4] We used the Boyatzis' codebook as an initial, main reference for coding (Boyatzis, 1982; Boyatzis et al., 1995, pp. 82-91). This codebook categorizes 22 themes of competencies that are divided into three groups: goal and action management abilities, people management abilities and analytic reasoning abilities.[5]

- Step 5:   identification of patterns (competencies/themes) within the data that differentiate MBAs' performance. We grew our statistical analysis out of the database stemming from coding for frequency of occurrence, and calculated frequency distributions for the coded competencies[6]; they provided a first summary of the behaviors and personal qualities needed to cover the analyzed role. Then, we used standard nonparametric statistical analysis to: (a) test if best performers had more and more articulated competencies than average performers; (b) identify the set of competencies causally related to outstanding performance (top performers' differentiators) (McLagan, 1997; Spencer & Spencer, 1993) as well as the set of threshold competencies. The former emerged by comparing the competency portfolio of the two subsamples of subjects (by using the Mann-Whitney U Test), one of which comprised "best performers" and the other "average performers" (referred to their "post-MBA success" as defined by the above mentioned performance criterion). The latter were defined as those competencies possessed by the average performers with a significant intensity, and not emerged as distinctive.[7]

The competency model for CUOA's MBAs (Camuffo & Gerli, 2004, p. 247) included seven distinctive competencies, or top-performers' differentiators (efficiency orientation, planning, persuasiveness, self-confidence, quantitative analysis, organizational awareness, directing) and six threshold competencies (initiative, attention to detail, use of concepts, pattern recognition, result orientation, information gathering).

As a result of these two studies (HR managers' panels and MBAs' competency model) we came to know the set of competencies hiring firms want from MBAs as well as those associated with fast careers and labor market success. Both these studies not only were the cornerstones of the CUOA master's program redesign, but also the parameter against which we evaluated both learning outcomes and hiring firms' and students' satisfaction (Camuffo & Gerli, 2004). Consequently, since 2000, the curriculum and didactics of the CUOA master's program have been reviewed according to a competency-based approach, inspired by the CWRU's experiments with competency-based MBA education (Boyatzis et al., 1995; Boyatzis, Stubbs, & Taylor, 2002), which included: (a) a comprehensive and articulated set of educational targets, i.e., pieces of knowledge, skills, and behaviors, on which to build the MBA curriculum; (b) an intimate connection among competencies, curriculum content, and teaching methods, so that each relevant competency was covered by the MBA program.

On the whole, the new CUOA master's program was consistent with the self-directed model of learning (Boyatzis, 1999; Kolb & Boyatzis, 1970; Kolb, Winter, & Berlew, 1968). Indeed, it aimed to entrust the development of the "target" competencies to all the courses of the MBA curriculum and to support competency development across courses, projects and activities using a wide array of teaching methods and learning experiences.

## Competency Development Evaluation: A Longitudinal Analysis of Five MBA Cohorts

Once identified the expected/desired/ideal competency portfolio for CUOA's MBAs, and once redesigned the CUOA master's program according to competency-based principles (the first competency-based edition was delivered in 2000), we analyzed five cohorts of students/graduates (from 2000 to 2004) with the explicit goal to assess competency development at the start and at the end of the MBA.[8]

Our evaluation scheme built on previous works on competency-based graduate management education conducted at the Weatherhead School of Management (Ballou, Bowers, Boyatzis & Kolb, 1999; Boyatzis, 1994; Boyatzis et al., 1995; Boyatzis, Stubbs, & Taylor, 2002), but introduced some significant innovations, too:

(a) It used a structured peer-evaluation process to assess managerial skills, alongside self and third party evaluation processes (Wagner & Moffett, 2000);

(b) It analyzed all the MBAs in a given cohort class, not just a sample, thus improving the reliability of the study and allowing to monitor individually the development process for each student; moreover, each student was entitled to get access to his/her record of competency assessment; this, together with individual mentoring, made students more conscious and responsible, and facilitated self-directed development in terms of definition of individual study plans and learning strategies;

(c) It allowed matching the competency profiles that represent the MBA educational objectives (as defined in the previous section) with those representing the actual learning outcomes of each edition of the CUOA MBA.

Our evaluation scheme measured competencies at the start and at the end of the MBA and consisted of three distinct processes and methodologies:

(a) self-evaluation: all the students of each cohort were asked to self-evaluate their skills at different times during the MBA using the Managerial Skills Profile and the Functional Skills Profile questionnaires (the same ones used by the panel of human resource managers in defining recruiting companies' expected competencies); the results provided pictures (for each single student and for the MBA class as a whole) at different times, of the perceived possession of skills, thus allowing the assessment of the improvement and/or decline of such skills over time. These results were also compared with the expectations defined by the recruiting companies' panel in the preliminary study stage;

(b) evaluation by a third party: a team of researchers interviewed, using BEI techniques, all the CUOA MBA students both at the beginning and at the end of the course; the initial BEI was an integrative part of the CUOA MBA admission and selection process; the final BEI represented, for each student, the formal conclusion of the MBA program and was held right before graduation; the initial and final BEIs were analyzed and coded for frequency and variety[9] of occurrence; we performed statistical analysis on the resulting data following procedures similar to those described in the previous section, and compared pre- and post-MBA competency possession, thus monitoring individual and class learning during the course; we also compared the competencies from final BEIs with those of the competency model described in the previous section, thus evaluating the correspondence between the competencies developed by the MBAs during the program and those associated with successful careers in the job market;

(c) peer-evaluation: all the students of each cohort were asked to evaluate their classmates' skills—according to a peer review process based on nominations—using the Managerial Skills Profile questionnaire; these data allowed to evaluate each student's managerial skill set as it was perceived by his/her classmates and compare this profile with the profiles emerging from self-evaluation and from firms' expectations.

These three competency-based methodologies were used to assess the outcomes of five MBA cohorts, that is, those corresponding to the CUOA MBA classes of 2000 (71 students), 2001 (63 students), 2002 (64 students),

2003 (79 students) and 2004 (68 students). More specifically, the evaluation scheme shown, for each cohort:

(a) the extent and type of competencies that have been developed during the MBA;
(b) the within and between cohort variation in competency development, also in relation to the individual characteristics of MBAs;
(c) the degree to which the competencies developed during the different editions of the MBA matched the educational targets (expected competencies);
(d) the degree of consistency of the different methods applied to evaluating competency development.

### Self-Evaluation

The students of the five analyzed cohorts were asked to self-assess their competencies on the same sets of skills that made up the profile of expected competencies assessed by the recruiting companies. Also here, we used a 7-point scale, ranging from "I do not possess this skill" (scale-point 1), to "I master this skill" (scale-point 7). Self-evaluation was carried out at different times during the program in order to link the evaluation to the contents of the curriculum (classes): managerial skills were assessed at the beginning of the course, at the end of the first semester and at the end of the course, while functional skills were assessed at the beginning of the course and at the end of the first semester only, because during the second semester the MBA class splits in different majors.

Table 2.2 shows self-evaluations at different stages during the MBA and analyzes the extent and statistical significance of competency development pre- and post-MBA.

Across the five analyzed cohorts/editions managerial skills always increased significantly (on average of approximately 35%, with a peak of 46% in the 2003 edition). Interestingly, the extent of competency development was larger in the more recent editions, probably because of learning effects in the implementation of competency-based tools (e.g., in applications' selection and didactics). Moreover, the bulk of learning seemed to be taking place in class (earlier part of the MBA) rather than during the internship (mandatory in the second part of the MBA). Finally, we observed in all the analyzed cohorts a reduction of the standard deviation of the self evaluations at the end of the MBA (compared to that of the initial ones). This can be the effect either of scaling and perceptions or of an actual homogenization of students' competency portfolios. Overall, competency development and cross-student homogenization of competency portfolios appear to be, at least in MBAs' self perceptions, the main outcomes of competency-based MBA education.[10]

**Table 2.2. Managerial and Functional Skills Profile:**
**Self-Evaluations in the CUOA MBA Classes 2000, 2001, 2002, 2003, 2004**

| MANAGERIAL SP | Class 2000; n = 71 | | | | | | Class 2001; n = 63 | | | | | |
|---|---|---|---|---|---|---|---|---|---|---|---|---|
| | Initial | Interm. | Final | A | B | C | Initial | Interm. | Final | A | B | C |
| Help | 55.3 | 58.9 | 67.7 | 5.54* | 2.09* | 4.96* | 57.5 | 66.3 | 72.0 | 3.64* | 3.04* | 5.35* |
| Sense-making | 54.7 | 60.3 | 68.1 | 5.54* | 1.51 | 5.19* | 58.7 | 65.7 | 73.2 | 3.21* | 3.93* | 5.41* |
| Information gathering | 49.4 | 58.1 | 69.3 | 5.46* | 2.77* | 6.45* | 50.3 | 63.6 | 73.5 | 5.33* | 4.62* | 6.22* |
| Information analysis | 52.6 | 61.2 | 70.2 | 5.99* | 1.60 | 6.40* | 53.9 | 65.7 | 73.2 | 4.85* | 4.05* | 6.22* |
| Theory | 52.3 | 59.3 | 67.4 | 5.61* | 2.09* | 6.19* | 54.9 | 64.0 | 71.5 | 3.98* | 3.72* | 5.57* |
| Quantitative methods | 32.0 | 54.2 | 62.0 | 6.30* | 3.35* | 6.96* | 33.0 | 55.2 | 65.4 | 6.14* | 5.40* | 6.38* |
| Technology | 37.0 | 58.8 | 73.9 | 5.96* | 4.40* | 7.11* | 46.3 | 68.4 | 77.2 | 5.53* | 4.35* | 6.28* |
| Goal setting | 54.9 | 62.7 | 69.9 | 5.37* | 3.06* | 5.82* | 53.6 | 64.1 | 73.4 | 4.45* | 4.61* | 5.99* |
| Action | 62.2 | 65.3 | 73.1 | 5.50* | 1.69* | 4.86* | 63.6 | 68.1 | 76.2 | 1.80* | 3.95* | 5.31* |
| Initiative | 55.3 | 60.6 | 68.1 | 5.71* | 2.21* | 5.55* | 60.7 | 65.4 | 75.7 | 2.39* | 4.13* | 4.88* |
| Leadership | 50.8 | 53.3 | 65.1 | 4.73* | 2.14* | 5.27* | 57.6 | 61.1 | 71.2 | 1.97* | 4.13* | 4.89* |
| Relationship | 62.9 | 68.0 | 76.2 | 5.17* | 1.62 | 5.41* | 67.7 | 71.5 | 80.1 | 2.14* | 4.09* | 4.65* |

Table continues

|  | Class 2002; n = 64 | | | | | | Class 2003; n = 79 | | | | | |
| MANAGERIAL SP | Initial | Interm. | Final | A | B | C | Initial | Interm. | Final | A | B | C |
|---|---|---|---|---|---|---|---|---|---|---|---|---|
| Help | 53.9 | 61.1 | 68.6 | 3.29* | 3.60* | 5.99* | 51.6 | 68.4 | 71.6 | 7.02* | 2.40* | 7.21* |
| Sense-making | 55.1 | 63.7 | 69.2 | 3.90* | 2.67* | 5.63* | 50.9 | 67.9 | 72.6 | 6.96* | 3.79* | 7.30* |
| Information gathering | 49.5 | 62.2 | 70.4 | 4.99* | 3.73* | 6.29* | 46.0 | 67.3 | 72.6 | 7.22* | 3.85* | 7.31* |
| Information analysis | 52.1 | 63.9 | 69.2 | 4.68* | 3.08* | 5.87* | 48.4 | 68.7 | 71.7 | 7.37* | 2.64* | 7.19* |
| Theory | 53.6 | 62.7 | 68.5 | 4.26* | 3.41* | 5.75* | 50.5 | 69.1 | 71.6 | 7.12* | 2.01* | 7.24* |
| Quantitative methods | 35.8 | 57.6 | 65.3 | 5.98* | 4.30* | 6.54* | 32.6 | 60.5 | 65.0 | 7.52* | 3.62* | 7.63* |
| Technology | 45.7 | 66.5 | 76.1 | 5.98* | 4.75* | 5.60* | 44.5 | 70.7 | 77.4 | 7.46* | 4.01* | 7.64* |
| Goal setting | 49.9 | 64.2 | 69.5 | 5.64* | 2.42* | 6.15* | 51.0 | 69.7 | 72.7 | 7.29* | 1.90* | 7.28* |
| Action | 55.6 | 66.3 | 71.8 | 4.29* | 2.56* | 5.88* | 55.0 | 71.2 | 74.5 | 7.04* | 2.67* | 7.21* |
| Initiative | 56.0 | 66.3 | 72.1 | 4.21* | 2.66* | 6.10* | 54.5 | 69.1 | 73.8 | 6.61* | 3.55* | 7.03* |
| Leadership | 53.2 | 57.8 | 65.4 | 2.34* | 3.69* | 4.75* | 49.5 | 64.5 | 67.6 | 6.50* | 1.65* | 6.91* |
| Relationship | 61.3 | 69.9 | 76.4 | 3.95* | 2.54* | 6.03* | 60.8 | 75.0 | 78.3 | 6.17* | 2.14* | 6.95* |

Table continues

| MANAGERIAL SP | Class 2004; n = 68 | | | | | |
|---|---|---|---|---|---|---|
| | Initial | Interm. | Final | A | B | C |
| Help | 54.8 | 69.9 | 73.3 | 5.54* | 2.09* | 6.49* |
| Sense-making | 57.1 | 70.6 | 73.2 | 5.54* | 1.51 | 6.25* |
| Information gathering | 53.9 | 69.5 | 74.2 | 5.46* | 2.77* | 6.39* |
| Information analysis | 54.3 | 70.2 | 73.2 | 5.99* | 1.58 | 6.69* |
| Theory | 55.4 | 70.3 | 74.2 | 5.61* | 2.09* | 6.42* |
| Quantitative methods | 38.6 | 62.0 | 68.8 | 6.30* | 3.35* | 6.89* |
| Technology | 52.5 | 71.3 | 81.4 | 5.96* | 4.40* | 6.86* |
| Goal setting | 54.0 | 69.8 | 75.3 | 5.37* | 3.06* | 6.69* |
| Action | 57.1 | 70.4 | 74.1 | 5.50* | 1.69* | 6.40* |
| Initiative | 57.3 | 72.0 | 75.6 | 5.71* | 2.21* | 6.56* |
| Leadership | 54.1 | 65.5 | 69.4 | 4.73* | 2.14* | 5.92* |
| Relationship | 63.0 | 75.0 | 76.9 | 5.17* | 1.62 | 5.59* |

Table continues

| FUNCTIONAL SP | Class 2000 | | | Class 2001 | | |
|---|---|---|---|---|---|---|
| | Initial | Final | C | Initial | Final | C |
| Marketing | 19.3 | 38.9 | 6.35* | 17.8 | 41.1 | 5.89* |
| Logistics | 13.2 | 39.7 | 6.99* | 11.5 | 43.6 | 6.36* |
| Operations management | 16.2 | 48.7 | 7.25* | 11.4 | 45.8 | 6.50* |
| Accounting and control | 24.4 | 48.5 | 6.88* | 25.2 | 49.8 | 5.75* |
| Finance | 13.4 | 37.6 | 6.70* | 11.5 | 30.4 | 5.68* |
| Organization design and behavior | 16.5 | 51.2 | 7.27* | 20.5 | 49.8 | 6.34* |
| Human resource management | 7.6 | 39.3 | 7.21* | 10.8 | 33.2 | 5.87* |
| Information technology | 18.0 | 40.3 | 6.96* | 26.3 | 45.2 | 5.85* |
| Globalization-International management | 11.0 | 36.7 | 7.03* | 11.5 | 39.8 | 6.14* |
| Strategic management | 16.3 | 46.6 | 7.14* | 12.3 | 49.7 | 6.57* |

Table continues

| FUNCTIONAL SP | Class 2002 | | | Class 2003 | | | Class 2004 | | |
|---|---|---|---|---|---|---|---|---|---|
| | Initial | Final | C | Initial | Final | C | Initial | Final | C |
| Marketing | 17.7 | 43.0 | 6.56* | 25.9 | 59.1 | 7.32* | 29.8 | 62.6 | 6.83* |
| Logistics | 17.3 | 52.6 | 6.83* | 16.9 | 49.4 | 7.47* | 20.1 | 53.5 | 6.79* |
| Operations management | 14.9 | 49.4 | 6.79* | 17.2 | 49.5 | 7.42* | 20.3 | 51.8 | 6.75* |
| Accounting and control | 21.8 | 62.5 | 6.79* | 26.3 | 66.8 | 7.61* | 30.1 | 63.9 | 6.87* |
| Finance | 11.5 | 43.0 | 6.78* | 17.8 | 49.5 | 7.27* | 18.9 | 53.6 | 6.88* |
| Organization design and behavior | 19.5 | 49.5 | 6.77* | 22.3 | 55.7 | 7.53* | 21.7 | 53.5 | 7.04* |
| Human resource management | 14.0 | 41.6 | 6.71* | 17.8 | 50.1 | 7.60* | 16.2 | 59.3 | 7.11* |
| Information technology | 32.3 | 52.0 | 6.69* | 28.9 | 51.2 | 7.32* | 32.6 | 54.4 | 6.70* |
| Globalization-International management | 12.6 | 44.8 | 6.85* | 16.4 | 47.3 | 7.51* | 18.3 | 47.7 | 6.95* |
| Strategic management | 19.8 | 57.7 | 6.74* | 21.6 | 62.4 | 7.60* | 23.7 | 61.6 | 7.05* |

Wilcoxon matched-pairs signed rank test, one-tailed: * $p < 0.05$. $A$ = initial vs interm.; $B$ = interm. vs final; $C$ = initial vs final.

Similar considerations apply to functional skills, which always increased significantly during the MBA across the five analyzed cohorts/ editions (on average of approximately 170%, with smaller values only for the 2004 cohort: 148%). Also here the standard deviation of the evaluations decreased during the MBA as the average level of possession of the competencies increased. Also in this case, the extent of competency development seemed to increase in the more recent editions.

### Peer-Evaluation

In order to get a more accurate assessment of the extent and type of competency development going on during the MBA, we introduced peer-evaluation, too.

All the students were asked to evaluate their classmates' skills, using the same set of managerial skills that were used in self-evaluation. This allowed to ascertain the possession of each student's skills as it was perceived by his/her classmates and to compare it with the results of self-evaluation and with firms' expected competency profile.

Approximately at half-course (i.e., at a time when the students would know each other sufficiently well), each student nominated four classmates that evaluated him/her; nominations and evaluations were kept confidential. The Mann-Whitney U test was used to compare the results of peer-evaluation with those of self-evaluations at midcourse and at the end of the MBA (Table 2.3).

Data in Table 2.3 show that peer evaluations were consistent with self evaluations for all the analyzed cohorts, with the exception of the third cohort (2002 edition of the CUOA MBA), where peer-evaluations were systematically higher than self-evaluations.

More in detail, while in the first two observed editions peer evaluations substantially overlapped with *final* (end of MBA) self-evaluations, in the last two observed editions they better overlapped with *intermediate* (midcourse) self-evaluations, which is consistent with the fact that the peer-evaluation process took place half-way the program.

We interpret these outcomes as the result of learning effects in the implementation of competency-based tools (e.g., in curriculum design and didactics), as well of refinements in the peer evaluation process, that led to a better accuracy in the respondents.

### Third-Party Evaluation

We complemented self-evaluations and peer evaluations with a third method of MBAs' competency development assessment: Behavioral Event Interviews (BEIs) conducted by a third party (members of the research team).[11] All the MBA students of the five analyzed cohorts were interviewed using the Behavioral Event Interview technique both before and at

**Table 2.3. Managerial Skills Profile: Peer Evaluation in the CUOA MBA Classes 2000, 2001, 2002, 2003, 2004 and Comparison With Self-Evaluations for the Managerial Skills Profile, at mid-Course and at the end of the MBA**

| | Class 2000 | A | B | Class 2001 | A | B | Class 2002 | A | B | Class 2003 | A | B | Class 2004 | A | B |
|---|---|---|---|---|---|---|---|---|---|---|---|---|---|---|---|
| Help | 64.6 | 2.66* | -1.97* | 70.1 | 1.93* | -0.86 | 76.1 | 5.67* | 3.43* | 68.4 | -0.11 | -1.44 | 66.2 | -1.89* | -3.40* |
| Sense-making | 66.1 | 2.78* | -1.24 | 72.0 | 3.50* | -0.43 | 78.4 | 5.72* | 3.86* | 70.1 | 0.89 | -1.28 | 71.0 | 0.07 | -1.28 |
| Info. gathering | 69.9 | 5.40* | -0.76 | 74.9 | 5.28* | 0.97 | 80.1 | 7.07* | 4.85* | 74.2 | 3.65* | 1.76* | 73.8 | 2.06* | -0.21* |
| Info. analysis | 69.0 | 3.79* | -1.13 | 73.6 | 4.04* | -0.18 | 78.5 | 6.19* | 4.62* | 71.9 | 0.75 | -0.57 | 72.0 | 1.52 | -0.36* |
| Theory | 66.7 | 3.72* | -0.36 | 71.2 | 3.60* | -0.09 | 78.1 | 6.50* | 4.81* | 71.5 | 1.69* | 0.49 | 72.7 | 0.87 | -0.97* |
| Quantit. methods | 62.2 | 2.89* | -0.03 | 67.5 | 4.15* | 0.73 | 75.1 | 5.38* | 3.42* | 66.2 | 1.67* | 0.06 | 70.2 | 2.66* | 0.45* |
| Technology | 67.6 | 3.29* | 2.78* | 71.9 | 1.35 | -2.34* | 81.2 | 4.38* | 2.09* | 71.4 | 0.14 | -2.22* | 74.3 | 0.48 | -3.24* |
| Goal setting | 68.5 | 2.74* | -0.97 | 72.6 | 4.42* | -0.59 | 79.6 | 6.21* | 4.47* | 72.1 | 1.49 | 0.15 | 71.6 | 0.45 | -2.74* |
| Action | 71.7 | 2.69* | -0.75 | 75.8 | 3.60* | -0.24 | 80.4 | 5.23* | 3.89* | 72.5 | 1.27 | -0.02 | 72.3 | 0.53 | -1.10* |
| Initiative | 66.1 | 2.46* | -0.54 | 72.1 | 2.75* | -1.84* | 79.5 | 5.17* | 2.92* | 70.3 | 0.62 | -1.07 | 71.9 | -0.39 | -2.21* |
| Leadership | 62.1 | 3.37* | -1.45 | 67.4 | 2.14* | -1.68* | 72.8 | 5.11* | 2.94* | 64.6 | -0.47 | -1.50 | 63.8 | -0.92 | -2.30* |
| Relationship | 73.5 | 2.39* | -1.49 | 78.4 | 3.09* | -0.69 | 83.4 | 5.25* | 3.28* | 76.3 | 1.21 | 0.00 | 74.2 | -0.47 | -0.88* |

Note: Mann-Whitney U Test, one-tailed, *$p < 0.05$.

A = z values (Peer Evaluation vs Intermediate Skills Profile);

B = z values (Peer Evaluation vs Final Skills Profile).

the end of the course (the pre-MBA BEIs were an integrative part of the admission process).

Following the procedures described in the previous section, we analyzed (thematic analysis) and coded the BEIs' transcripts for frequency and variety of occurrence and applied blind double coding to check for interrating reliability (Boyatzis, 1998; Spencer & Spencer, 1993). We performed statistical analysis on the database stemming from coding for frequency and variety of occurrence. Frequency distributions for the coded competencies provided a first summary of the competencies MBAs had before and after the MBA. Variety distributions provided an indication of the evolution of the richness of possession of each single competency at the individual and class level. We used standard nonparametric statistical analysis to test if: (a) significant competency development had taken place during the MBA; (b) the developed competencies matched with those previously identified for the CUOA MBAs' competency model. In other words, this analysis allowed us to evaluate from a different angle the evolution of individual and class learning and to compare it with the results of the competency model of the CUOA MBA graduates.

Table 2.4 (a and b) reports the results of this analysis, conducted on each of the five editions considered in this study. The following findings are particularly noteworthy.

First, both the extent of competency development during the MBA and the degree of overlapping with the "target" competencies (as identified by the model in the previous section) improved in the most recent editions. Other conditions being equal, we believe this relates to an increasing effectiveness of the program in competency development, probably due to a better implementation of competency-based didactics, a refined applications of competency-based tools and a stronger awareness and involvement of the instructors.

Second, from a strictly quantitative standpoint, the number of competencies that showed significant increases in frequency and/or variety of occurrence got larger in the most recent editions: 13 competencies improved significantly during the first examined edition (2000), 16 in the second and third ones (2001 and 2002), 19 in the fourth one (2003) and 25 in the last one (2004).

Third, if we compare *initial* (pre-MBA) frequency and variety of occurrence of all the competencies across the five cohorts, the class competency portfolio worsened (smaller frequency and variety) in the most recent years. This seems to confirm anecdotal evidence about the worsening "quality" of Italian MBA students attending Italian MBAs. Because of the globalization of the educational industry, the recent reform of the Italian University system, the higher costs of Italian MBA education, and the increased domestic competition among business schools, it is common

**Table 2.4a.   Initial (Pre-MBA) and Final (Post-MBA) Competencies in the CUOA MBA Classes 2000, 2001**

| | Class 2000 | | | | | | Class 2001 | | | | | |
|---|---|---|---|---|---|---|---|---|---|---|---|---|
| | Frequency % | | Variety % | | Z values[a] | | Frequency % | | Variety % | | Z values[a] | |
| Competencies | Initial | Final | Initial | Final | Freq. | Var. | Initial | Final | Initial | Final | Freq. | Var. |
| Efficiency orientation | 22.0 | 26.3 | 27.1 | 30.1 | 0.35 | 1.29[+] | 6.5 | 10.3 | 27.3 | 25.0 | 1.28 | 0.62 |
| Planning | 23.7 | 30.4 | 22.1 | 25.6 | 1.39[+] | 2.32* | 10.1 | 15.5 | 22.4 | 22.6 | 1.75* | 1.38[+] |
| Initiative | 11.9 | 16.4 | 35.1 | 33.3 | 1.05 | 0.89[b] | 11.3 | 26.5 | 37.3 | 44.4 | 3.04** | 3.41** |
| Attention to detail | 16.4 | 30.4 | 50.0 | 54.7 | 2.95** | 3.06** | 15.5 | 27.1 | 52.1 | 59.4 | 2.16* | 2.14* |
| Self-control | 7.3 | 8.8 | 33.3 | 35.6 | 1.04 | 0.53 | 6.0 | 9.0 | 33.3 | 35.9 | 0.28 | 0.76 |
| Flexibility | 4.5 | 5.3 | 50.0 | 50.0 | 0.85 | 0.51[b] | 1.8 | 7.7 | 50.0 | 50.0 | 2.13* | 2.07[b]* |
| Empathy | 19.2 | 14.6 | 25.8 | 29.2 | 1.23[b] | 0.79 | 11.3 | 18.1 | 29.4 | 31.7 | 2.22* | 2.05* |
| Persuasiveness | 16.4 | 19.9 | 18.6 | 20.1 | 0.43 | 1.31[+] | 10.1 | 12.9 | 19.0 | 17.5 | 0.82 | 0.78[b] |
| Networking | 5.1 | 7.6 | 33.3 | 35.9 | 1.01 | 0.98 | 6.0 | 4.5 | 33.3 | 33.3 | 0.51[b] | 0.56[b] |
| Negotiating | 2.8 | 3.5 | 33.3 | 38.9 | 1.24 | 0.49 | 5.4 | 5.8 | 33.3 | 33.3 | 0.00 | 0.21[b] |
| Self-confidence | 8.5 | 4.7 | 50.0 | 50.0 | 0.85[b] | 1.32[b] | 24.4 | 33.5 | 52.9 | 53.8 | 1.07 | 0.82 |
| Group management | 3.4 | 2.9 | 20.0 | 24.0 | 0.15[b] | 0.00[b] | 2.4 | 3.9 | 20.0 | 20.0 | 0.14 | 0.73[b] |
| Developing others | 4.0 | 3.5 | 25.0 | 25.0 | 0.25[b] | 0.63[b] | 6.0 | 5.2 | 25.0 | 25.0 | 0.41[b] | 0.00[b] |
| Oral communication | 4.5 | 6.4 | 16.7 | 16.7 | 0.98 | 0.73[b] | 2.4 | 4.5 | 16.7 | 16.7 | 0.89 | 0.80[b] |
| Use of concepts | 15.3 | 31.6 | 36.0 | 38.8 | 4.02** | 3.42** | 7.7 | 20.6 | 33.3 | 37.9 | 2.88** | 3.15** |
| System thinking | 1.7 | 4.7 | 50.0 | 50.0 | 1.58[+] | 0.89[b] | 0.0 | 2.6 | 0.0 | 50.0 | 1.83* | 1.83* |
| Pattern recognition | 12.4 | 18.2 | 25.0 | 29.3 | 2.08* | 1.60[+] | 2.4 | 9.0 | 25.0 | 26.9 | 2.12* | 2.13* |
| Theory building | 2.3 | 2.3 | 100.0 | 100.0 | 0.10 | 0.40[b] | 0.0 | 0.0 | — | — | — | — |
| Using technology | 7.9 | 15.2 | 25.0 | 26.1 | 1.92* | 1.68* | 2.4 | 27.7 | 25.0 | 28.1 | 4.91** | 4.67** |
| Quantitative analysis | 7.9 | 13.5 | 33.3 | 33.3 | 1.30[+] | 0.87[b] | 5.4 | 12.9 | 33.3 | 35.2 | 2.16* | 1.96* |
| Social objectivity | 0.0 | 0.0 | 0.0 | 0.0 | — | — | 0.0 | 0.0 | — | — | — | — |
| Written communication | 6.2 | 14.1 | 20.0 | 21.8 | 2.58** | 2.28* | 2.4 | 6.5 | 25.0 | 22.5 | 1.42[+] | 0.92[b] |

## Competencies not from Boyatzis' code-book

| Competencies | Freq % Initial | Freq % Final | Variety % Initial | Variety % Final | Z | Freq % Initial | Freq % Final | Variety % Initial | Variety % Final | Z Freq | Z Var |
|---|---|---|---|---|---|---|---|---|---|---|---|
| Result orientation | 16.4 | 20.5 | 100.0 | 100.0 | 0.00 | 14.9 | 28.4 | 30.0 | 32.1 | 3.29** | 2.66** |
| Information gathering | 17.0 | 21.7 | 100.0 | 100.0 | 0.00 | 14.3 | 15.5 | 55.0 | 52.3 | 0.79 | 0.31[b] |
| Organizational commitment | 2.8 | 4.7 | 100.0 | 100.0 | 0.00 | 0.0 | 0.0 | — | — | — | — |
| Leadership | 1.1 | 4.1 | 100.0 | 100.0 | 0.00 | 3.0 | 5.8 | 33.3 | 40.7 | 0.45 | 1.33+ |
| Customer orientation | 6.2 | 3.5 | 100.0 | 100.0 | 0.00 | 4.2 | 8.4 | 33.3 | 33.3 | 1.89* | 1.71[b]* |
| Business Bargaining[c] | | | | | | 0.0 | 2.6 | - | 33.3 | 1.83* | 1.83* |
| Team-working[c] | | | | | | 2.4 | 7.7 | 33.3 | 36.1 | 2.30* | 2.13* |

Table continues below and on page 44

## Class 2002

| Competencies | Frequency % Initial | Frequency % Final | Variety % Initial | Variety % Final | Z values[a] Freq. | Z values[a] Var. |
|---|---|---|---|---|---|---|
| Efficiency orientation | 13.2 | 17.0 | 27.9 | 30.0 | 1.07 | 2.55** |
| Planning | 9.3 | 6.6 | 20.0 | 22.0 | 1.40[b] | 0.21 |
| Initiative | 15.5 | 8.8 | 35.0 | 37.5 | 2.37[b]** | 0.50 |
| Attention to detail | 12.4 | 13.7 | 50.0 | 54.2 | 0.16 | 1.50+ |
| Self-control | 5.4 | 4.9 | 33.3 | 37.0 | 0.67[b] | 0.62 |
| Flexibility | 3.1 | 2.7 | 50.0 | 50.0 | 0.28[b] | 0.34[b] |
| Empathy | 12.4 | 14.3 | 26.6 | 31.7 | 0.89 | 2.32* |
| Persuasiveness | 10.9 | 12.6 | 20.2 | 21.0 | 0.55 | 1.66* |
| Networking | 6.2 | 6.6 | 33.3 | 41.7 | 0.30 | 1.37+ |
| Negotiating | 5.4 | 7.1 | 33.3 | 33.3 | 0.67 | 1.41[b] |
| Self-confidence | 14.0 | 8.2 | 50.0 | 50.0 | 1.86[b]+ | 0.52 |
| Group management | 6.2 | 18.7 | 20.0 | 24.8 | 3.43** | 4.26** |
| Developing others | 3.9 | 8.2 | 25.0 | 28.3 | 1.65* | 2.24** |
| Oral communication | 3.9 | 4.4 | 16.7 | 16.7 | 0.49 | 0.73[b] |
| Use of concepts | 10.9 | 15.4 | 33.3 | 37.8 | 1.36+ | 2.66** |

| | | | | | | |
|---|---|---|---|---|---|---|
| System thinking | 0.8 | 1.6 | 50.0 | 50.0 | 1.60+ | 0.91[b] |
| Pattern recognition | 7.0 | 8.2 | 25.0 | 25.0 | 0.76 | 1.24 |
| Theory building | 0.0 | 0.0 | — | — | — | — |
| Using technology | 7.8 | 18.1 | 27.5 | 25.8 | 3.27** | 3.61[b]** |
| Quantitative analysis | 10.9 | 19.8 | 33.3 | 40.0 | 2.38** | 3.45** |
| Social objectivity | 0.8 | 0.0 | 33.3 | — | — | — |
| Written communication | 9.3 | 10.4 | 21.7 | 22.1 | 0.24 | 1.40+ |
| Competencies not from Boyatzis' code-book | | | | | | |
| Result orientation | 22.5 | 13.7 | 27.6 | 29.0 | 2.29[b]* | 0.42 |
| Information gathering | 12.4 | 15.9 | 50.0 | 51.8 | 1.17 | 2.32* |
| Organizational commitment | 1.6 | 0.5 | 100.0 | 100.0 | 1.07[b] | 0.53[b] |
| Leadership | 6.2 | 7.7 | 33.3 | 38.1 | 0.35 | 1.44+ |
| Customer orientation | 1.6 | 3.3 | 33.3 | 33.3 | 1.36+ | 1.47[b]+ |
| Business bargaining[c] | 5.4 | 4.4 | 33.3 | 37.5 | 0.91[b] | 0.45 |
| Team-working[c] | 9.3 | 13.7 | 36.1 | 34.7 | 1.67* | 2.23[b]* |

Note: [a] Wilcoxon matched-pairs signed rank test, one tailed: $+\ p < 0.10$; $*\ p < 0.05$; $**\ p < 0.01$. [b] Test two-tailed. [c] Not collected in the class 2000.

**Table 2.4b.  Initial (Pre-MBA) and Final (Post-MBA) Competencies in the CUOA MBA Classes 2003 and 2004**

| Competencies | Class 2003 | | | | | | Class 2004 | | | | | |
|---|---|---|---|---|---|---|---|---|---|---|---|---|
| | Frequency % | | Variety % | | Z values[a] | | Frequency % | | Variety % | | Z values[a] | |
| | Initial | Final | Initial | Final | Freq. | Var. | Initial | Final | Initial | Final | Freq. | Var. |
| Efficiency orientation | 10.2 | 13.1 | 32.7 | 32.6 | 0.06 | 1.69^b+ | 8.3 | 18.9 | 27.8 | 29.5 | 2.59** | 3.76** |
| Planning | 14.8 | 9.5 | 23.2 | 22.2 | 1.25^b | 0.30^b | 11.9 | 14.9 | 20.0 | 22.4 | 0.41 | 2.35** |
| Initiative | 16.4 | 18.6 | 33.3 | 38.4 | 0.01 | 2.41** | 3.7 | 21.7 | 33.3 | 38.0 | 3.57** | 4.65** |
| Attention to detail | 12.5 | 23.6 | 53.6 | 57.5 | 1.74* | 3.65** | 8.3 | 29.1 | 50.0 | 55.3 | 3.79** | 4.37** |
| Self-control | 2.3 | 4.5 | 33.3 | 33.3 | 0.87 | 2.07^b* | 2.8 | 9.7 | 33.3 | 33.3 | 2.39** | 2.62^b** |
| Flexibility | 4.7 | 4.5 | 50.0 | 50.0 | 0.28^b | 0.68^b | 0.9 | 8.0 | 50.0 | 50.0 | 2.24* | 2.95^b** |
| Empathy | 6.3 | 8.0 | 28.1 | 29.7 | 0.03 | 1.67* | 6.4 | 21.7 | 25.0 | 34.3 | 3.78** | 4.72** |
| Persuasiveness | 5.5 | 6.5 | 16.7 | 19.2 | 0.46 | 1.58+ | 7.3 | 14.3 | 18.8 | 19.3 | 1.71+ | 3.35** |
| Networking | 2.3 | 6.0 | 33.3 | 41.7 | 1.68* | 2.30* | 5.5 | 13.1 | 33.3 | 34.9 | 1.20 | 2.74** |
| Negotiating | 3.1 | 3.5 | 33.3 | 33.3 | 0.06 | 0.80^b | 1.8 | 8.0 | 33.3 | 33.3 | 1.64+ | 2.64^b** |
| Self-confidence | 9.4 | 15.1 | 50.0 | 51.9 | 0.48 | 2.57** | 8.3 | 14.9 | 50.0 | 58.7 | 1.27 | 2.79** |
| Group management | 1.6 | 8.0 | 20.0 | 20.0 | 2.45** | 2.90^b** | 2.8 | 12.0 | 20.0 | 25.0 | 3.12** | 3.49** |
| Developing others | 2.3 | 2.0 | 25.0 | 25.0 | 0.17^b | 0.34^b | 2.8 | 5.7 | 25.0 | 25.0 | 0.94 | 1.71^b+ |
| Oral communication | 3.1 | 8.5 | 16.7 | 18.6 | 1.63+ | 2.62** | 3.7 | 10.9 | 16.7 | 19.3 | 1.54+ | 2.92** |
| Use of concepts | 27.3 | 39.2 | 34.3 | 41.5 | 1.42+ | 4.27** | 5.5 | 44.0 | 33.3 | 44.4 | 5.40** | 5.91** |
| System thinking | 0.0 | 1.5 | — | 50.0 | 1.60+ | 1.60+ | 0.9 | 2.3 | 50.0 | 50.0 | 0.73 | 1.21^b |
| Pattern recognition | 2.3 | 5.5 | 25.0 | 32.5 | 1.18 | 2.13* | 1.8 | 12.6 | 25.0 | 28.6 | 2.83** | 3.56** |
| Theory building | 0.0 | 0.5 | - | 100.0 | 0.00 | 0.00 | 0.9 | 0.0 | 100.0 | — | — | — |
| Using technology | 14.8 | 32.7 | 25.0 | 25.5 | 3.76** | 4.06** | 12.8 | 38.3 | 25.0 | 30.3 | 4.92** | 5.51** |
| Quantitative analysis | 5.5 | 14.6 | 38.1 | 33.3 | 1.83* | 3.17^b** | 7.3 | 30.9 | 33.3 | 37.0 | 4.26** | 5.16** |

| | | | | | | | | | | | |
|---|---|---|---|---|---|---|---|---|---|---|---|
| Social objectivity | 0.0 | 0.0 | — | — | — | — | 0.0 | 0.0 | — | — | — | — |
| Written communication | 2.3 | 5.5 | 20.0 | 25.5 | 1.02 | 2.17* | 0.9 | 10.3 | 20.0 | 25.0 | 3.46** | 3.52** |
| Competencies not from Boyatzis' code-book | | | | | | | | | | | | |
| Result orientation | 21.9 | 19.6 | 26.8 | 27.8 | 0.45[b] | 1.24 | 29.4 | 22.3 | 26.6 | 32.6 | 1.06[b] | 1.46+ |
| Information gathering | 11.7 | 34.2 | 50.0 | 51.0 | 3.98*** | 4.90** | 11.9 | 40.6 | 50.0 | 52.9 | 4.58*** | 4.95** |
| Organizational commitment | 4.7 | 15.1 | 100.0 | 100.0 | 2.40** | 1.19[b] | 2.8 | 24.0 | 100.0 | 100.0 | 4.4** | 1.09[b] |
| Leadership | 0.8 | 2.5 | 33.3 | 33.3 | 1.36+ | 1.47[b] | 2.8 | 7.4 | 25.0 | 35.9 | 2.23* | 2.42** |
| Customer orientation | 3.9 | 1.0 | 33.3 | 33.3 | 1.89[b]+ | 1.01[b] | 0.9 | 3.4 | 16.7 | 33.3 | 1.77* | 1.69* |
| Business bargaining[c] | 3.9 | 0.0 | 33.3 | — | 2.02[b]* | — | 6.4 | 0.0 | 33.3 | — | 1.20[b] | — |
| Team-working[c] | 2.3 | 10.6 | 33.3 | 33.3 | 3.19** | 3.36[b]** | 4.6 | 20.6 | 27.8 | 36.4 | 3.37** | 4.38** |

*Note:* [a] Wilcoxon matched-pairs signed rank test, one tailed: $+ p < 0.10$; $* p < 0.05$; $** p < 0.01$; $*** p < 0.01$. [b] Test two-tailed. [c] Not collected in the class 2000.

opinion that it has become increasingly difficult to recruit brilliant MBA students.

Fourth, if we compare *final* (post-MBA) frequency and variety of occurrence of all the competencies across the five cohorts, the class competency portfolio improved (larger frequency and variety) in the most recent years (with the exception of 2002). The fact that this happened while the initial (pre-MBA) class competency portfolio worsened in the most recent years seems to suggest that the application of competency-based tools to MBA education can be particularly effective. This data seem to confirm that the implementation of competency-based methods to MBA education can greatly impact on the quality of the program.

What highlighted so far is consistent with our findings from self and peer evaluations. Moreover, still similarly with results from self-evaluations, for all the five analyzed cohorts the standard deviations of post-MBA competency frequency distributions were smaller than the pre-MBA ones. In other words, even if at the individual level there can be significantly different levels and types of competency development (and competency portfolios greatly differ across individuals), at the class level it seems as if the MBA had a homogenizing effect.

There are few specific cases of significant competency reduction, limited to the third analyzed edition (three competencies showed a reduction of their frequency and two of them of their variety, but these ones presented a significant increase of their frequency as well), and to the fourth analyzed edition (two competencies showed a reduction of their frequency and two of them of their variety, but one of them increased its frequency).

As regards the type of competencies that have been developed during the five analyzed MBA editions, data in Table 2.4 suggest that:

(a) there is a core of competencies that, even if with a different intensity, have been significantly and consistently developed across the cohorts. To this core belong the following competencies: attention to detail, use of concepts, using technology, quantitative analysis, written communication, leadership and team-working;

(b) some of the competencies belonging to this core match the competencies identified as threshold competencies (attention to detail and use of concepts) and top performers' differentiators (quantitative analysis) in the CUOA MBAs competency model described in the previous section; it is worth recalling that these are the "target" competencies, since they relate to post-MBA success in terms of careers and compensation;

(c) some of these "target" competencies (efficiency orientation, planning, persuasiveness, etc.) have not been steadily developed during all the five analyzed editions of the MBA, which suggests there is more to do in order to increase the effectiveness of the program vis-à-vis its educational objectives;

(d) the MBAs competency profile looks biased toward goal and action and analytic reasoning abilities, which is consistent with hiring firms' expectations and with the post-MBA competency model previously described; the under representation of people management abilities, however, could derive from the type of managerial roles CUOA MBAs (but, more generally, Italian MBAs in Italy) are asked to cover, at least in the early stages of their careers (and our analysis is probably biased form this standpoint).

## Linking MBAs' Competencies and Careers

So far, our analysis has used a variety of competency-based tools throughout all the stages of the educational process underlying an MBA, in order to increase the quality of the program and improve its efficacy in meeting hiring firms' needs and supporting MBA careers in the labor market.

However, this analysis has been focused prevalently on the short term: for example, educational outcomes have been evaluated during and right after the MBA, with the intent to identify would-be gaps against "target" competencies and, consequently, adjust the MBA program redesigning one or more of its components.

We believe this analysis could be usefully expanded and extended adopting a longer term perspective, capable to capture the relation between the competencies developed during the MBA and the careers of MBA graduates. Thus, in this section we further expand our analysis to MBAs' careers with the explicit aim of verifying if competencies are related to rapid and successful careers. The ultimate goal of this analysis is to feed this information back into the MBA design process so that the program can better reflect labor market trends and develop the competencies that effectively support MBAs' careers.

In late 2004 the CUOA Foundation launched, with the support of the CUOA MBA Alumni Association, a survey of MBAs current employment situation. Within this survey, we carved out a narrower project geared toward investigating the jobs, firm seniority and tenure, compensation and careers of 345 CUOA MBAs, all the graduates of the classes of 2000, 2001, 2002, 2003, and 2004 (the five cohorts/editions analyzed in the previous sections). We used an online survey, posted on the CUOA Foundation's Web site. The survey was widely advertised and the CUOA MBA Alumni Association further supported it sending an e-mail message to each graduate of the target population containing detailed information about the nature and goals of the survey. Three months later, another message, asking again for the compilation of the online questionnaire, was sent to those who had not taken the survey, yet. After 6 months we gathered a total of 103 questionnaires compiled on line, corresponding to a 29,86% answer rate. The main characteristics of the sample of respondents are shown in Table 2.5.[12]

The online survey included questions about the respondents' current job, previous (post-MBA) jobs, characteristics of the employing firms (industry, size, international scope, etc.), current compensation (total annual remuneration, base salary, incentives and bonuses, benefits) and internal and external labor market mobility. This data were used to build two measures of post-MBA success: a "career index" and a "compensation grading".

The career index considered three elements: the respondent's current job (classified according to an adapted version of the Watson Wyatt Global Grading System), the characteristics of the employing firm (in terms of: sales turnover, number of employees, organizational complexity and degree of internationalization and diversification), and the "career lead time" (i.e., number of years since the end of the MBA it took to the respondent to reach the current position). The higher the grade, the more complex the employing organization and the shortest the career lead time, the higher the corresponding career index value. These values were then normalized on a 0-100 scale and the corresponding distribution classified into 4 uniform classes (0-25; 26-50; 51-75; 76-100). Using the information provided by the online survey, we assigned each respondent to his/her career class (only the first three classes were used, since no respondent could be assigned to the highest class). The result was a classification of the respondents into three career grades: (a) fast track; (b) normal; (c) slow.

The compensation indicator considered the respondents' total annual remuneration, adding up base salary, incentives, bonuses and benefits. The distribution of the respondents' total annual remuneration was divided into three classes (corresponding to the distribution tertiles).

We decided to keep these indicators separated since:

(a) not all the respondents provided complete information about their compensation (the 35% of them didn't answer the related questions);

(b) the career index was based on more objective and readily verifiable data;

(c) previous studies considered promotions and salary as dependent measures of objective career success (Heslin, 2005; Ng, Eby, Sorensen, & Feldman, 2005).

**Table 2.5.   The Sample of Respondents to
the Online Survey on MBAs' Careers**

|  | No. | % |
|---|---|---|
| *Gender* | | |
| Female | 30 | 29.1 |
| Male | 73 | 70.9 |
| *Type of Degree* | No. | % |
| Economics | 44 | 42.7 |
| Engineering | 17 | 16.5 |
| Law | 11 | 10.7 |
| Humanistic | 10 | 9.7 |
| Scientific | 3 | 2.9 |
| Other | 18 | 17.5 |
| *Job Function* | No. | % |
| Marketing/Communication | 29 | 28.2 |
| Sales | 17 | 16.5 |
| Accounting /Control | 15 | 14.6 |
| Organization/HRM | 8 | 7.8 |
| Purchasing | 6 | 5.8 |
| Operations/SCM | 6 | 5.8 |
| Finance | 4 | 3.9 |
| R&D | 4 | 3.9 |
| General direction | 2 | 1.9 |
| Other/No reply | 12 | 11.6 |
| *Job Industry* | No. | % |
| Mechanical | 22 | 21.4 |
| Food and beverage | 10 | 9.7 |
| Commerce | 10 | 9.7 |
| Banking and insurance | 10 | 9.7 |
| Fashion | 8 | 7.8 |
| Consulting | 7 | 6.8 |
| Chemistry | 5 | 4.9 |
| Other manufacturing | 3 | 2.9 |
| Wood and furniture | 2 | 1.9 |
| Utilities | 2 | 1.9 |
| Education | 2 | 1.9 |
| ICT | 1 | 1.0 |
| Other /No reply | 21 | 20.4 |
| Total | 103 | 100 |

Once graded the respondents' careers and compensation, we related them to the corresponding individual competency portfolio, as assessed at the end of the MBA. By doing this, we wished to: (a) investigate the relationship between MBAs' competencies and post-MBA success (as measured by careers and compensation); (b) feed this information back into the CUOA MBA design process; (c) come full-circle back to the original MBAs competency model.

### Findings

In order to investigate the relationship between MBAs' competencies (as measured at the end of the MBA) and post-MBA success in the labor market, we tested the alternative hypothesis that competency frequency and variety of occurrence for "fast track career" respondents larger than for "normal career" respondents. Similarly, for "normal career" respondents versus "slow career" respondents.

Besides, we disaggregated the competencies into the three clusters proposed by Boyatzis (1982): goal and action, people management and analytic reasoning abilities. For each cluster, we considered competency frequency and variety of occurrence pre-MBA (as measured by BEIs before admission to the CUOA MBA program) and post-MBA (as measured by BEIs at the end of the CUOA MBA program) and tested the alternative hypothesis that the *increase* in competency frequency and variety of occurrence for "fast track career" respondents was larger than for "normal career" respondents. Similarly, for "normal career" respondents versus "slow career" respondents.

Data in Tables 2.6 and 2.7 summarize the results of the hypothesis tests.[13] Indeed, "fast track career" MBAs had, at the end of the MBA, higher competency frequency and variety of occurrence. This is not enough to conclude that post-MBA competency portfolio/endowment is a predictor of MBAs' careers, but it supports our view that competency-based analysis can be appropriately used to drive MBA programs toward more effective outcomes. Moreover, "fast track career" respondents had a larger increase in competencies like planning, initiative, flexibility, self confidence, organizational commitment, use of concepts and oral communication.

At the competency cluster level, Goal and action, People management and Analytic reasoning abilities relate in completely different ways to careers and compensation. Fast-track career MBAs seem to be those who had better developed the goal and action competencies during the MBA (though only in terms of frequency of occurrence). People management and Analytic reasoning abilities, instead, had improved only in terms of variety of occurrence. This suggests that relational and cognitive abilities are somewhat more innate than goal and action ones. While the latter can

**Table 2.6. The Relationship Between MBAs' Competency Portfolio (at the end of MBA), Competency Development During MBA (Increase in Competency Frequency and Variety of Occurrence Measured by pre- and post-MBA BEIs), and post-MBA Career**

| | MBAs' Career | | | t Values | | |
|---|---|---|---|---|---|---|
| | Fast-Track (FT) | Normal (N) | Slow (S) | FT vs N | FT vs S | N vs S |
| End-of-MBA global competency portfolio: Frequency | 389.58 | 286.27 | 313.69 | 2.22** | 1.78** | -0.78 |
| End-of-MBA global competency portfolio: Variety | 359.48 | 299.22 | 338.12 | 1.70** | 1.66** | -1.28 |
| Increase in goal and action competencies (Freq.) | 63.54 | 22.06 | 33.44 | 2.81** | 1.34* | -2.58** |
| Increase in people management competencies (Freq.) | 38.54 | 45.59 | 23.58 | -0.28 | 0.57 | -0.88 |
| Increase in analytic reasoning competencies (Freq.) | 64.58 | 13.73 | 39.29 | 1.62** | 1.00 | -1.07 |
| Increase in goal and action competencies (Var.) | 100.52 | 28.24 | 89.86 | 2.38** | 0.37 | -2.41** |
| Increase in people management competencies (Var.) | 46.14 | 45.88 | 46.77 | 0.01 | 0.03 | -0.04 |
| Increase in analytic reasoning competencies (Var.) | 51.67 | 13.33 | 46.49 | 1.72** | 0.28 | -1.74** |

$n = 103$; $t$ test on independent samples, one-tailed, *$p < 0.10$, **$p < 0.05$.

**Table 2.7. The Relationship Between MBAs' Competency Portfolio (at the end of MBA), Competency Development During MBA (Increase in Competency Frequency and Variety of Occurrence Measured by pre- and post-MBA BEIs), and post-MBA Compensation**

| | MBAs' Compensation | | | t Values | | |
|---|---|---|---|---|---|---|
| | High | Medium | Low | High vs Medium | High vs Low | Medium vs Low |
| End-of-MBA global competency portfolio: Frequency | 346.43 | 341.35 | 284.00 | 0.11 | 1.48* | 1.57* |
| End-of-MBA global competency portfolio: Variety | 346.11 | 340.79 | 298.40 | 0.16** | 1.57* | 1.39* |
| Increase in goal and action competencies (Freq.) | 11.98 | 53.73 | 12.00 | -1.43* | 0.00 | 1.70** |
| Increase in people management competencies (Freq.) | 48.41 | 34.13 | 15.33 | 0.48* | 1.20 | 0.86 |
| Increase in analytic reasoning competencies (Freq.) | 21.75 | 72.54 | 33.33 | -1.90** | -0.44 | 1.58* |
| Increase in goal and action competencies (Var.) | 56.98 | 103.02 | 70.00 | -1.44* | -0.51 | 1.19 |
| Increase in people management competencies (Var.) | 73.02 | 38.73 | 38.07 | 1.49* | 1.70** | 0.04 |
| Increase in analytic reasoning competencies (Var.) | 34.05 | 58.57 | 27.67 | -1.29* | 0.32 | 1.69** |

$n = 67$; $t$ test on independent samples, one-tailed, *$p < 0.10$, **$p < 0.05$.

be significantly improved through an MBA (increase in frequency), the former are part of a personal endowment that can only be refined and articulated (increase in variety).

On the other hand, data show no significant relation between compensation grading and the post-MBA final competency portfolio, considered as a whole. However, disaggregating this analysis at the level of a single competency, there seems to be a positive relation between compensation and possession (at the end of the MBA) of some specific competencies, such as: planning, initiative, negotiating, persuasion and use of concepts.

Our statistical analysis also showed:

1.  A positive relation between the development of interpersonal competencies during the MBA and span of control in the current job: respondents' with the highest increase, during the MBA, in such People management abilities as empathy, persuasion, negotiation, self-confidence, oral communication and customer orientation tend to have the highest span of control in their current job.

2.  No relation between the MBAs' competency portfolio and their within-firm and cross-firm mobility; however, MBAs with the largest final competency portfolio seem to be more bound to undertake international careers in more complex organizations. More specifically, this tendency is mostly related to the development during the course of the following competencies: initiative, self-control, flexibility, result orientation, attention to detail and organizational commitment.

3.  Larger post-MBA competency portfolios (in terms of both frequency and variety of occurrence) for respondents whose current job is that of managing directors/CEOs. These respondents also had achieved, during the MBA, the largest increases in goal and action management abilities (and more in detail in planning, flexibility and self-control);

4.  Larger increases, during the MBA, in analytic reasoning competencies for MBAs that undertook careers in operations and research and development (R&D);

5.  Larger increases, during the MBA, in People management abilities for MBAs who undertook careers in HRM.

Moreover, we searched for and found no relation among the MBAs' personal characteristics (gender, age, college education type and performance, working experience) and the change in their competency portfolio, considering both each edition of the course separately and the whole population of 345 students. This is consistent with research that criticize the use of personal (cognitive, demographic, census) variables (see for example Dreher & Ryan (2004) on the use of working experience as a selection criterion) as predictors of learning and personal development.

As regards competency development, we found a positive and significant relation between competency frequency and variety of occurrence. This supports the idea that learning and personal development is not a mere quantitative phenomenon but, rather, it implies the articulation of one's competency endowment.

We found no correlation between the three different competency clusters; Goal and action management, People management and Analytic reasoning. In the different considered editions, however, there were some positive correlation between single competencies *inside* the same cluster. This can be an expression of typical behavioral patterns acted by the students: as an example, the competency "quantitative analysis" is correlated with "using technology," "use of concepts," and "pattern recognition," while "result orientation" is correlated with "information gathering" and "organizational commitment." This is consistent with the theoretical assumptions and the empirical confirmations on the independence of the different competency clusters and on the interdependence of the competencies inside a single cluster (Boyatzis & Kolb, 1995).

## Discussion and Implications

The implemented evaluation scheme serves to direct individual development toward the defined educational objectives and to monitor the extent to which they are achieved. Moving along the cohorts, self-evaluations and third-party evaluations progressively and increasingly tended to meet firms' expectations and match the competency model. This means that the program became more effective over time and that the design mechanisms worked.

The different evaluation tools that constitute our scheme led to similar, consistent results. The results obtained from self-evaluation were widely confirmed by third-party evaluation; moreover, there was a good overlap between self-evaluation and peer-evaluation. This confirms the reliability of the analysis tools and suggests that it would be possible to use them separately/modularly, with little information loss.

Our investigation of the relationship between MBAs' competencies and post-MBA success (as measured by careers and compensation) supports the view that competency-based analysis can be appropriately used to drive MBA programs toward more effective outcomes. Relating post-MBA careers to competency development during the MBA allows to close a feed-back loop, coming full-circle back to the original MBAs' competency model.

This chapter has presented several avenues to develop the application of competency-based methodologies to MBA education. Building on previous research (Camuffo & Gerli, 2004) we conducted a longitudinal analysis with the specific aim of verifying the impact of the MBA program on their careers, assessing the relevance of what was learned, and then feeding back this information into the MBA design process. Our findings allow: (a) analyzing the impact of the MBA program on competency development of several students' cohorts; (b) identifying which competencies were related to rapid and successful careers and feed this information back into the MBA design process so that it can better reflect labor market trends; (c) developing the competencies that effectively support MBAs' careers.

Overall, our analysis showed that designing and delivering innovative and effective MBA education can be grounded on the rigorous implementation of competency-based techniques, provided that: (a) all the phases of the educational process (from the assessment of the educational needs, to the identification of educational objectives to the design and delivery of the MBA program, to the evaluation of learning, to the analysis of post-MBA careers) are considered and integrated in the analysis; (b) a multiple constituency approach is adopted, that is, one which actively engage business schools, students/graduates and the companies that hire and employ them in the continuous improvement of MBA education.

Though still limited in terms of scope and depth of analysis, we believe the findings of this study pave the road to further applications and analysis of competency based tools to management education.

## ACKNOWLEDGMENTS

We thank Richard Boyatzis, Franco Ratti, Ricard Serlavos Serra, and participants at the 1st EASR Conference at ESADE, Barcelona, for suggestions and comments on earlier versions. Research funded by the CUOA Foundation and MIUR.

## NOTES

1.   Fondazione CUOA is a management school founded in 1957 and located in North-East Italy. Its founders and supporters are universities, firms, trade associations, banks and public agencies. This study was conducted on five editions of its 1-year full time MBA program (from the 42nd edition realized in 1999/2000 to the 46th edition realized in 2003/2004).

2.  Our team comprised six researchers, all previously trained in repertory grid and behavioral event interview techniques. Graduate students provided support in data analysis. Here is a synthesis of the provisions of the research protocol. Before conducting the study, we had each perspective MBA student agree on the following: (a) the study was made for research purposes only; (b) all the information collected during the study had confidential nature; (c) the research team would not provide to third parties any personal information on the interviewees and would not made them recognizable at any stage of the project. Moreover, to minimize the risk of biased interviewing and coding, neither the interviewees (MBAs), the interviewers, nor the coders knew the ranking of the MBAs and if they classify as best or average.

3.  The Behavioral Event Interview (BEI) is an adaptation of the critical-incident interview originally developed by Flanagan. McClelland (1998, p. 332) designed it as a way to discover differences between two types of incumbents: those outstanding and those typical in performing a job. The BEI is "an intensive face-to-face interview that involves soliciting critical incidents from performers and documenting what the performers were thinking, feeling and doing during the incident" (Rothwell & Lindblom, 1999, p. 94).

4.  Double coding technique was used to attain higher reliability (Boyatzis, 1998) and a percentage of agreement of more than 85% was always obtained. The same method was used in the assessment of MBAs' development, with slightly lower results in terms of reliability (81%).

5.  The Italian market for MBAs is different from the U.S. typical situation in terms of remuneration, status, job level, and so forth. This derives from the peculiarity of the Italian economic structure and, namely, from firms' size (comparatively smaller) and ownership structure (private, nonlisted family owned businesses). For these reasons, the Italian MBAs' profile is, on average, different from the U.S. one. Thus, the use of a standard codebook derived from the U.S. context seemed inappropriate. Original thematic analysis was necessary to take into account further behaviors that led to effective performances in the specific context. The result was an adapted, enriched, competency dictionary (Raelin & Cooledge, 1995).

6.  The percentage frequency of occurrence of a competency is the number of times a competency is detected out of the maximum possible number of times; for example, a 10% frequency means that a competency appears in one behavioral event out of ten. More generally, we coded for frequency of occurrence using the following measure:

$$F_i = \frac{\sum_{j}^{n} CC_{i,j}}{\sum_{j}^{n} PC_{i,j}}$$

with:

$F_i$ = Frequency of competency $i$;

$CC_{i,j}$ = Coded competencies: the number of behaviors associated with competency $i$ detected in the interview with subject $j$ (independently on the specific behavioral indicator);

$PC_{i,j}$ = Potential competencies: the maximum number of behaviors associated with competency $i$ detectable in the interview with subject $j$ (independently on the specific behavioral indicator).

7.  In order to detect the threshold competencies we considered as "significant intensity" at least a 10% in frequency.

8.  However, a more traditional system of students' evaluation and grading for each course/subject was also in place, and included exams, tests, assignments, instructors' evaluation of class participation and team projects.

9.  The variety of a competency is a measure of how many different behaviors were expressed by an interviewee among those associated to a certain given competency. It is a measure of the richness of the possession of a competency. We coded for variety of occurrence using the following measure:

$$V_i = \frac{\sum_{j}^{n} db_{i,j}}{\sum_{j}^{n} pb_{i,j}}.$$

$V_i$ = Variety of competency i;

$db_{i,n}$ = Different behaviors: the number of different behavioral indicators associated with competency i detected in the interview with subject j;

$pb_{i,j}$ = Potential behaviors: the number of different behavioral indicators associated with competency i detectable in the interview with subject j.

10.  A possible criticism could be related to a potential distortion of the self-assessment tools, deriving from the fact that those students who invest much money and efforts attending an MBA could report that they have become highly competent. The consistency among the results coming from the self-evaluation and those obtained by using peer and third party evaluation seems to suggest that self-evaluation is, at least in this case, reliable.

11.  Also in this case, our team comprised six researchers, all previously trained in behavioral event interview techniques. Here is a synthesis of the provisions of the research protocol. Before conducting the study, we had each perspective MBA student agree on the following: (a) the study was made for research purposes, but pre-MBA BEIs could be used as a selection tool to complement the admission process; (b) all the information collected during the study had confidential nature; (c) the research team would not provide any personal information on the interviewees and would not made them recognizable at any stage of the project.

12.   This sample is representative of the population. Even though among the variables/data available there were not good proxies for the propensity to take the on-line survey, we performed the Chi-square test to assess the goodness of fit of the sample to the population using some of the available variables (gender, age, type of college degree, MBA admission score/ranking, etc.). For all these variables the Chi-square test results allow to accept the null hypothesis that the sample's distribution fits the population's distribution at the 0.05 level of significance.

13.   We calculated the global competency portfolio adding the average individual frequency/variety of all the 29 detected competencies for each considered class in the test. Since the frequency/variety of a competency is expressed on a 0-100 scale, the global competency portfolio is expressed on a 0-2900 scale, and can be referred either to an individual or, as in the case of Tables 2.6 and 2.7, to a group of individuals (by computing its average value).

$$GCP(F) = \frac{\sum_i F_i}{s}$$

$$GCP(V) = \frac{\sum_i V_i}{s}$$

*GCP* (*F*) =   Global competency portfolio in terms of frequency;

*GCP* (*V*) =   Global competency portfolio in terms of variety;

$F_i$ =   Frequency of competency *i*;

$V_i$ =   Variety of competency *i*;

*s* =   number of subjects in the considered class.
The increase in competencies has been computed as the difference between final (post-MBA) global competency portfolio and initial (pre-MBA) global competency portfolio, in terms of frequency and variety.

## REFERENCES

Armstrong, S. (2005). Postgraduate management education in the UK: Lessons from or lessons for the U.S. model? *Academy of Management Learning & Education, 4*(2), 229-234.

Atwater, L. (1992). Beyond cognitive ability: Improving the prediction of performance. *Journal of Business and Psychology, 7,* 27-44.

Augier, M., & Teece, D. J. (2005). Reflections on (Schumpeterian) leadership: A report on a seminar on leadership and management education. *California Management Review, 47*(2), 114-136.

Ballou, R., Bowers, D., Boyatzis, R. E., & Kolb, D. A. (1999). Fellowship in lifelong learning: An executive development program for advanced professionals. *Journal of Management Education, 23*(4), 338-354.

Barrett, G. V. (1994). Empirical data say it all. *American Psychologist, 1*, 69-71.

Barrett, G. V., & Depinet, R. L. (1991). A reconsideration of testing for competence rather than intelligence. *American Psychologist, 46*, 1012-1024.

Blancero, D., Boroski, J., & Dyer, L. (1996). Key competencies for a transformed human resource organization: Results of a field study. *Human Resource Management, 35*, 383-403.

Boam, R., & Sparrow, P. (1992). Designing and achieving competency. London: McGraw-Hill.

Boyatzis, R. E., & Kolb, D. A. (1991). Assessing individuality in learning: The learning skills profile. *Educational Psychology, 11*(3&4), 279-295.

Boyatzis, R. E., & Kolb, D. A. (1995). From learning styles to learning skills: The executive skills profile. *Journal of Managerial Psychology, 10*(5), 3-17.

Boyatzis, R. E. (1982). *The competent manager: A model for effective performance.* New York: Wiley.

Boyatzis, R. E. (1994). Stimulating self-directed learning through the Managerial Assessment and Development course. *Journal of Management Education, 18*(3), 304-323.

Boyatzis, R. E. (1998). *Transforming qualitative information. Thematic analysis and code development.* Thousand Oaks, CA: Sage.

Boyatzis, R. E., Cowen, S. S., Kolb, D. A., & Associates (1995). *Innovation in professional education.* San Francisco: Jossey-Bass.

Boyatzis, R. E., Stubbs, E. C., & Taylor, S. N. (2002). Learning cognitive and emotional intelligence competencies through graduate management education, *Academy of Management Learning and Education, 1*(2), 150-162.

Boyatzis, R. E. (1999). Self-directed change and learning as a necessary meta-competency for success and effectiveness in the 21st century. In R. Sims & J. G. Veres (Eds.), *Keys to employee success in the coming decades* (pp. 15-32). Westport, CT: Greenwood.

Boyatzis, R. E. (2002). Unleashing the power of self-directed learning. In R. Sims (Ed.), *Changing the way we manage change: The consultants speak* (pp. 13-32). New York: Quorum Books.

Burke, M. J., & Day, R. R. (1986). A cumulative study of the effectiveness of managerial training. *Journal of Applied Psychology, 71*(2), 232-245.

Camuffo, A., & Comacchio, A. (2004). The competent middle manager: framing individual knowledge in north-east Italian SMEs, *International Journal of Innovation and Learning, 1*(4), 330-350.

Camuffo, A., & Gerli, F. (2004). An integrated competency-based approach to management education: an Italian MBA case study. *International Journal of Training and Development, 8*(4), 240-257.

Connolly, M. (2003). The end of the MBA as we know it? *Academy of Management Learning and Education, 2*(3), 364-366.

Dreher, G., & Ryan, K. (2004). A suspect MBA selection model: The case against the standard work experience requirement. *Academy of Management Learning and Education, 3*(1), 87-91.

Feldman, D. (2005). The food's no good and they don't give us enough: reflections on Mintzberg's critique of MBA education. *Academy of Management Learning & Education, 4*(2), 217-220.

Fisher A. (2004, June 6). Why an MBA may not be worth it. *Fortune, 149*(12), 56-58.

Hansson, B. (2001). Competency models: Are self-perceptions accurate enough? *Journal of European Industrial Training, 25*(9), 428-441.

Heslin, P. (2005). Conceptualizing and evaluating career success. *Journal of Organization Behavior, 26*(2), 113-137.

Klein, A. L. (1996). Validity and reliability for competency-based systems: Reducing litigation risks, *Compensation and Benefits Review, 28*, 31-37.

Kolb, D. A., & Boyatzis, R. E. (1970). Goal-setting and self-directed behavior change. *Human Relations, 23*(5), 439-457.

Kolb, D. A. (1984). *Experiential learning: Experience as the source of learning and development.* Englewood Cliffs, NJ:Prentice-Hall.

Kolb, D. A., Winter, S. K., & Berlew, D. E. (1968). Self-directed change: Two studies. *Journal of Applied Behavioral Science, 6*(3), 453-471.

Mansfield, R. S. (1996). Building competency models, *Human Resource Management, 35*, 718.

McClelland, D. C. (1973). Testing for competence rather than intelligence, *American Psychologist, 28*, 1-14.

McClelland, D. C. (1998). Identifying competencies with behavioral event interviews, *Psychological Science, 9*(5), 331-339.

McLagan, P. A. (1997). Competencies: The next generation. *Training & Development, 51*(5), 40-47.

Miles, R. (2005). Telling it like it ought to be. *Academy of Management Learning & Education, 4*(2), 214-216.

Mintzberg, H. (2004). *Managers not MBAs.* San Francisco: Berret Koehler.

Mintzberg, H. (2005). The magic number seven—plus or minus a couple of managers. *Academy of Management Learning & Education, 4*(2), 244-247.

Mintzberg, H., Gosling, J. R. (2002). Reality programming for MBAs. *Strategy and Business, 26*(1),28-31.

Mirabile, R. J. (1995). A model for competency-based career development. *Personnel, 62*, 30-38

Mitrani, A., Dalziel, M., & Fitt, D. (1992). *Competency-based human resource management: Value-driven strategies for recruitment, development and reward.* London: Kogan Page.

Mulcahy, D., & James, P. (2000). Evaluating the contribution of competency-based training: an enterprise perspective. *International Journal of Training and Development, 4*(3), 160-175.

Ng, T., Eby, L., Sorensen, K., & Feldman, D. (2005). Predictors of objective and subjective career success: a meta-analysis. *Personnel Psychology, 58*(2), 367-409.

Pfeffer, J., & Fong, C. T. (2002). The end of business schools? Less success than meets the eye. *Academy of Management Learning and Education, 1*(1), 78-95.

Pfeffer, J., & Fong, C. T. (2003). Assessing business schools: Reply to Connolly. *Academy of Management Learning and Education, 2*(4), 368-370.

Pfeffer, J., & Fong, C. T. (2004). *The business school "business": Some lessons from the U.S. experience. The Journal of Management Studies, 41*(8), 1501-1520.

Raelin, J. A., & Cooledge, A. S. (1995). From generic to organic competencies. *Human Resources Planning, 18*(3), 1-12.

Robotham, D. (1995). Self-directed learning: The ultimate learning style? *Journal of European Industrial Training, 19*(7/8), 3-7.

Rothwell, W. J., & Lindholm, J. E. (1999). Competency identification, modeling and assessment in the USA. *International Journal of Training and Development, 3*(2), 90-105.

Sala, F. (2004). *Do programs designed to increase emotional intelligence at work—work?* New Brunswick, NJ: Rutgers University, The Consortium for Research on Emotional Intelligence in Organizations. Retrieved June 28, 2005, from http://www.eiconsortium.org/research/do_ei_programs_work.htm

Siemens, J., Burton, S., Jensen, T., & Mendoza, N. (2005). An examination of the relationship between research productivity in prestigious business journals and popular press business school rankings. *Journal of Business Research, 58*(4), 467-476.

Sluijsmans, D., Dochy, F., & Moerkerke, G. (1999). Creating a learning environment by using self-, peer- and co-assessment. *Learning Environments Research, 1*(3), 293-319.

Smith, E. (1999). Ten years of competency-based training: The experience of accredited training providers in Australia. *International Journal of Training and Development, 3*(2), 106-117.

Spencer, L. M., Jr., & Spencer, S. M. (1993). *Competence at work: Models for superior performance.* New York: Wiley.

Sternberg, R. J., & Wagner, R. K. (1986). *Practical intelligence: Nature and origins of competence in the everyday world.* New York: Cambridge University Press.

Sturges, J., Simpson, R., & Altman, Y. (2003). Capitalising on learning: An exploration of the MBA as a vehicle for developing career competencies. *International Journal of Training and Development, 7*(1), 53-66.

Ulrich, D., Brockbank, W., Yeung, A. K., & Lake, D.G. (1995). Human resource competencies: An empirical assessment, *Human Resource Management, 34*, 473-495.

Wagner, S. L., & Moffett, R. G., III. (2000). Assessment methodology, context and empowerment: The ACE model of skill development. *Journal of Management Education, 24*(4), 424-444.

Warn, J., & Tranter, P. (2001). Measuring quality in higher education: A competency approach. *Quality in Higher Education, 7*(3), 191-198.

Woodruff, C. (1993). What is meant by a competency? *Leadership and Organization Development Journal, 14*, 29-36.

## CHAPTER 3

# WHEN GRADUATES ENTER THE WORKPLACE

## Trade-Offs Between Formal and Dynamic Knowledge

**Wim H. Gijselaers, Jos A. R. Arts,
Henny P. A. Boshuizen, and M. S. R. Segers**

Which kind of managerial information and knowledge is important during managerial reasoning? Our article addresses this question by drawing further on key findings from cognitive psychological research. The present article addresses how managers—as compared to novices and graduates—process and represent typical task information, identifying which cognitive knowledge units play a pivotal role during managerial reasoning of a typical task, and how managerial knowledge acquisition and use evolves from novices (business school students) to experts. Our contribution is based on a series of studies conducted at Maastricht University, the Netherlands. Our research shows that managerial experts made high quality representations of problem information by filtering out irrelevant information while processing only highly critical case information. Furthermore, experts represented this selected information in a more meaningful way while novices concentrated on superficial case aspects. The results additionally demonstrate the importance of domain-specific content knowledge during reasoning. Especially practical knowledge types such as inferences ("meaningful

*New Visions for Graduate Management Education*, 65–84
Copyright © 2006 by Information Age Publishing
All rights of reproduction in any form reserved.

interpretations"). The use of practical ("dynamical") knowledge increases linearly with growing expertise. We agree with critics on management education that the importance of formal business school knowledge is generally overemphasized. We underscore the necessity that students get sufficient opportunities to develop, explore and use managerial knowledge in the daily practice of the managerial workplace. Several explanations and implications of the results are provided for managerial problem-solving and education.

## INTRODUCTION

Business schools aim to foster development of students' managerial problem-solving skills by training them in the functions of business. It is expected that graduates are capable to demonstrate proficiency when confronted with academic or business problems. The underlying assumption is that problem-solving performance on case studies explored at business school are a good predictor for graduates' ability to do well when handling managerial situations encountered in managerial practice. For that purpose, students of business schools have spent considerable time and efforts to acquire large amounts of formal textbook knowledge, to work on assignments and to prepare presentations on business cases.

However, the question may be posed whether we really know how experienced managers approach (complex) problems in daily practice, and whether we really possess a theory of schooling that may contribute to development of managerial competencies. One may even go one step further and challenge the very idea that the management classroom helps to develop students who are capable for managerial practice. For example, recent publications in the *Harvard Business Review* suggest that graduating students are "ill-equipped to wrangle with complex, unquantifiable issues—in other words, the stuff of management" (Bennis & O'Toole, 2005, p. 1). In the same journal, Leonard and Swap (2004) analyze how management novices acquire complex managerial skills, and conclude that development of managerial expertise requires extensive training and coaching in managerial practice. They make a distinction between being competent and being a truly expert. In their view, business school graduates can never surpass the level of being competent, because becoming a truly expert requires extensive experience and continuous guided learning at the managerial workplace. Leonard and Swap (2004, p. 4) assert that:

> Chances are, if you are not just competent, but truly expert, it took ten years or more to develop that expertise,—in which time you have come across countless situations. With so many of them under your belt, you have likely

found some common ground, and discovered a few rules of thumb that usually work.

The question may be raised to what extent these authors make a case in point, and whether business education is indeed incapable of delivering competent graduates. To take it one step further, the issue is not whether experience at the workplace contributes to management learning and how management education may fail to do so, but whether we have any insights grounded in educational theory and research about how business schools can make a substantial contribution to preparing graduates for the workplace.

The purpose of this chapter is to consider how managerial problem-solving abilities develop over time, and how curriculum interventions may further the development of students' managerial competencies. Our first key issue deals with how cognitive performance varies from managerial novices (students) to those in the work place with high levels of expertise. The second main issue concerns with issues of curricular redesign and its effects on development of managerial expertise. We will explore in a critical fashion whether current debates about management education warrant their claims about the necessity of curriculum reform in business education. In the next sections we will provides an analysis about current insights on the development of (managerial) expertise, and discuss findings of a series of studies we conducted that explore how managerial problem-solving abilities develop over time. We will describe how cognitive performance varies from managerial novices (students) to those in the work place with high levels of expertise. Finally, we provide an example of a learning environment in which the aim is to foster the solving of ill-structured managerial problems. Special attention is paid to the gap between the knowledge and problem-solving competencies gained in management education and the needs at the managerial workplace. The views we express in this chapter are based on a series of recent studies conducted at the Department of Educational Development and Educational Research from Maastricht University, the Netherlands.

## CRITICISMS ON THE NATURE OF BUSINESS EDUCATION

Recently, Mintzberg (2004, p. 1) raised (again) an issue which seems to be getting a sad evergreen in business education:

Using the classroom to help develop people already practicing management is a fine idea, but pretending to create managers out of people who never managed is a sham. It is time that our business schools gave proper attention to management.

How far can one get with fundamental criticism on the nature of business education? It touches the heart of the existence of business education at institutions for higher education. Because if the only thing business education does is to pretend to creating managers, instead of delivering graduates who are competent or proficient, then why bother about the importance of business schools? In our view such criticism calls for clarification and in-depth examination through educational and empirical research.

Criticisms on the nature of business education seem to be fueled by two leading arguments (Crainer & Dearlove, 1998; Grey & Mitev, 1995; Mintzberg, 2004; Perriton & Reynolds, 2004; Stinson & Milter, 1996). First, the question is raised whether business school curricula overemphasize that management is a science and not a profession based on best-evidence practices. Authors such as Mintzberg (2004), and Bennis and O'Toole (2005) claim that business schools are overly scientific and out of touch with business realities, concentrating on research which has little to do with the needs of business world. Second, it has been argued that business graduates do not have a realistic understanding of the business world. These critics argue that graduates are not prepared to respond to work situations in ways for which employers are calling (Bigelow, 2001). They complain that graduates in management lack adequate problem-solving abilities (Boyatzis, Cowen, & Kolb, 1995; Business-Higher Education Forum, 1999), possess poor decision-making skills, and demonstrate insufficient leadership skills (Hansen, 2002).

Those who employ management graduates do not complain about a lack of specialized knowledge, rather they criticize their ability to face today's problems and to acquire new knowledge. Given their selection criteria, employers seem to prefer graduates with generic skills. A possible reason for this is that current information and knowledge has a short life-cycle and accumulates more rapidly than ever (Boshuizen, 2003). Whatever the reason for this mismatch between the qualities of graduates and the expectations of the business world, schools of management should not fall into the trap of neglecting the role of educating (scientific) managerial knowledge in their curricula. As many authors argue, generic problem-solving abilities can only be acquired through the use (application) of content knowledge (Bransford & Schwartz, 1999). In this context, Bransford and Schwartz (p. 94) warn that "A potential danger of the preparation for future learning perspective is that it could lead to claims such as 'I'm teaching for future learning, so I don't worry about mastery of content.'" Therefore, we take the view that problem-solving skills can only be acquired and developed through applying content knowledge.

Although critics do not seem to warrant a profound empirical basis in educational, pedagogical, or psychological research, they do provide food for thought about how business curricula may contribute to students' acquisition of managerial competencies. Researchers such as Isenberg (1984, 1986), Wagner (1991, 2002), and Walsh (1995) are among the few who tried to address practical aspects of managerial work, and investigated its implications for the development of managerial expertise through conducting research with a strong basis in cognitive psychology. Their research followed earlier work in professions facing similar criticisms about the perceived lack of graduates' competencies such as within the medical profession (Patel & Groen, 1991), or in other traditional and more established scientific domains such as physics (Chi, Glaser, & Farr, 1988).

In general these critics express concerns about graduates' understanding of the business world, and the problems they may encounter in everyday practice. In response to those concerns several studies haven been conducted to evaluate the degree to which management education prepares students for the management profession. Typically these studies collect interview or survey data from human resource executives, management practitioners, members of executive advisory boards, program directors, and graduates (e.g., Douglas Johnson, & King, 2002; Giannantonio & Hurley, 2002; Hansen, 2002). A consistent research finding is that about four required competencies may be identified that are needed to function adequately in managerial practice. Graduates are expected to posses (1) functional competencies (discipline specific), (2) systemic competencies (cross-disciplinary knowledge and skills), (3) personal competencies (self-management), and (4) organizational competencies (managing others). It has been found that employers put a growing emphasis on interpersonal skills such as "interpersonal communication," "team-building," and cognitive skills such as "problem solving." For example, Douglas Johnson and King (2002) conclude that human resource programs are doing an excellent job when focusing on academe's traditional functional competencies, but they underestimate the importance of developing students' personal competencies. Similar conclusions were drawn by Giannantonio and Hurley (2002) when they found that the most important issue human resource executives face is "management of change." A review by Hansen (2002) shows that more attention should be paid to the graduate's ability to combine traditional curriculum contents (academic functional knowledge) and acquired skills in creative ways that add value to their employers. In his view "substantial gaps exist between what employers seek to find, and what students believe they should be getting from these programs, if they are to be adequately prepared for ever more challenging employment opportunities" (Hansen 2002, p. 536).

Despite the development of new learning methods such as Action Learning, Case- and Problem-Based Learning, the question can be raised whether business schools are indeed capable to deliver graduates who can surpass the level of being competent. In our view, approaches to optimizing business education have often been solely driven by demands from the workplace without giving it a sufficient basis in what we know about cognition, instruction and its effects on learning outcomes. Translation of workplace demands into curricular consequences requires curricular action based on state-of-the-art insights from the learning sciences. Our skepticism is nurtured by the fact that the majority of employer studies rely on survey methods and fail to make clear in their "conclusion" or "implications for instruction" section how we should proceed in closing the gap between what is needed and how business schools can fill the gap between school and the workplace.

## CURRENT RESEARCH ON MANAGERIAL COMPETENCIES

So, if employer and graduate surveys do not provide the curricular guidelines we are looking for, what else can be done? Since the 1970s, studies on managerial problem-solving and decision making have tried to identify (knowledge-related) determinants of cognitive performance. For a long time, the nature of this research remained largely behavioral. Mintzberg's (1973) study "The Nature of Managerial Work" can be considered as a hallmark in this area, but it is a typical example of behavioral research which by its very nature relied solely on interviews and observations. This research showed that managers primarily pay attention to information that is seemingly unrelated to the decisions they are in the process of making. But Mintzberg was very well aware that even although he found consistent observable patterns in managers' behavior, he could still not develop a theoretical understanding of the cognitive processes and components underlying their behavior. Being aware that he lacked modern tools from cognitive psychology for further examination of managerial problem-solving, Mintzberg considered his own study as "sketchy."

Next to studies that relied on observations and interviews, managerial psychology tried to understand managers' cognitive performance by analyzing whether general problem-solving skills were underlying managers' problem-solving behavior. This research was based on the idea that managers can be considered as rational technicians or management engineers whose problem-solving behavior is based on the use of generic problem-solving skills (Wagner, 1991). The general idea was that someone who could manage an IT firm could also manage a soft-drink production company, because effective management was independent of the domain a manager was operating in. Business schools who adopted this view typically aimed on teaching rational, behavioral approaches to managerial problem-solving. They emphasized the training of general principles of managerial problem solving. Content or domain knowledge was considered as less important.

However, in the 1970s and the 1980s a growing skepticism rose about the power of general principles of problem solving. When researchers started to analyze differences between novices' and experts' problem-solving processes, they assumed that experts' superior achievements were based on more deep or exhaustive reasoning skills. However it turned out that knowledge structures play a central role in reasoning, and in turn facilitate information processing and decision making. General intellectual capabilities were not a sufficient condition to explain differences between experts and novices (Hakkarainen, Palonen, Paavola, & Lehtinen, 2004). Wagner (2002) points out that the capability to solve managerial problems does not especially depend on acquiring all kinds of generic, predefined heuristics or general problem-solving skills as has been assumed for a long time. To put it simple: an excellent chess player isn't necessarily a good problem solver of business cases. But excellent performance on solving business cases depends on whether someone possesses a well-organized body of business knowledge that helps her/him to make relevant evaluations and try out meaningful alternatives. In our view this is the point were we get close to Mintzberg's (2004) views on management education.

Close examination of current research on expertise development demonstrates the importance of applying theoretical knowledge to practical experiences (Alexander, 2003). Most acquired formal knowledge develops further after students have graduated and entered the workplace. In the 1980s, researchers such as Anderson (1987) developed the important view that declarative knowledge precedes procedural (or "practical") knowledge. Practice allows declarative knowledge, as acquired in schools, to transform into practical knowledge. In this paper we use the term *declarative* knowledge for formal discipline knowledge as being taught at business schools. We also define *practical knowledge* as acquired declarative knowledge in use of certain business contexts. "In use" implies that the declarative knowledge is not only *reproduced* or used to *label* situations, but is also dynamic as applied to a certain business situations. As information is meaningful interpreted and actively transformed into inferences. We refer to the production of inferences as an example of *dynamical* knowledge.

In the managerial domain, a limited but valuable number of expertise studies have been performed following methods of cognitive research (e.g., Isenberg, 1984, 1986; Lash, 1988; Wagner 2002). The Isenberg studies (1984, 1986) were among the first in the field of management sciences that researched expertise using cognitive research methods similar to those used in chess, medicine, or physics research. Isenberg showed that managers heavily rely on previous experiences and restrict their information searches, even although they knew that complete information was available. In comparing management students and experienced managers, his research showed that managers commenced action-planning sooner than students; were less reflective about how they went about performing the case analysis, and reasoned from, rather than categorized the information (Isenberg, 1986). Furthermore, experts used more causal reasoning (causal inferences) than students. Following the Isenberg studies (1984, 1986), Lash (1988) compared novices in marketing with a group of marketing managers from a large petrochemical organization. Similar to findings of Isenberg, experts typically demonstrated the ability to infer upon information by making summaries. Novices in contrast concentrated more on declarative knowledge: they recalled many facts based on management principles.

Wagner (1991, 2002) drew further upon the work of Isenberg, and conducted research on the nature of managerial expertise following the framework of cognitive studies as applied in a wide variety of other domain such as chess or medicine (for reviews see Ericsson, 2003, 2004). He was interested in the identification of key factors that contribute to the development of managerial competencies. He demonstrated that acquiring experience at the managerial workplace is more important than learning principles, facts, and problem-solving procedures from managerial textbooks. Wagner (2002, p. 44.) argues that "the book smarts approach to management, known as rational or technical management, considers problems found in the workplace to be similar to academic intelligence-type tasks." In his view it "has become clear from countless studies of problem solving, domain-specific knowledge is extraordinarily powerful for successful problem solving" (Wagner, 2002, p. 51).

In general, research supports the idea that higher levels of expertise are less demonstrative in formal knowledge types, although their reasoning power continues to grow. In contrast, it has been repeatedly found that experts demonstrate large amounts of practical knowledge such as inferences during reasoning (Patel, Evans, & Groen, 1989). The use of inferences appears to increase linearly with level of expertise (Boshuizen, 1989; Coughlin & Patel, 1987). Over time, the *length* of these inferences becomes compiled into shorter chains (Sternberg & Horvath, 1999; Van de Wiel, 1997). The overall pattern that emerges on the use of knowledge in both the managerial domain as in other areas suggests a transition from using formal declarative knowledge (knowing "what") toward using more dynamical (the capability to make inferences) and practical knowledge types ("knowing *how* procedures").

## TRANSITORY STAGES IN MANAGERIAL EXPERTISE DEVELOPMENT IN MANAGEMENT: GAPS BETWEEN SCHOOLS AND PRACTICE

When Mintzberg (2004) raised the question about what the most important characteristics are that makes one a skillful manager, he argued that formal business education produces only limited conditions for the development of managerial expertise. Especially the absence of developing practical know-how within business schools was a point of concern because this seems to be an extremely powerful learning tool for development of managerial expertise. As a consequence the question may be raised whether examination of the trajectory toward managerial expertise may help us in developing a better understanding of what the constituents of managerial expertise are, and how management education may contribute to the development of managerial expertise. Especially the interplay between school knowledge (declarative knowledge) and know-how (dynamical knowledge and practical knowledge) needs to be assessed to get a clear picture of development of managerial expertise.

The present section describes in short a series of studies addressing this issue (Arts, Gijselaers, & Boshuizen, 2000, 2006 in press). Detailed descriptions of coding procedures, and statistical analyses can be found in Arts, Gijselaers, and Boshuizen (2006, under review). We followed standard procedures as applied in cognitive research on expertise development (e.g., Ericsson & Smith, 1991).

In our studies we examined the following characteristics and parts of the trajectory toward expertise: (a) cognitive performance during formal education, (b) the initial transition from formal education to the first years of workplace experience, and (c) the final stage in which "true expertise" develops. We addressed the following research questions:

How does cognitive problem-solving performance, with respect to diagnostic and solution accuracy, vary from managerial beginners (students) to experts?

How does the use of underlying knowledge used during problem solving, vary from managerial beginners and experts, and explain differences in cognitive performance?

The studies from Arts, Gijselaers, and Boshuizen (2000, 2006 in press) were conducted to gain further understanding of problem-solving perfor-

### Text Box 3.1.   Descriptions of the
### Instruments Used in the Present Study

The materials consisted of a case description on organizational development. Two university professors in management sciences designed the case which was then verified by two expert management consultants. The materials consisted of (a) instructions, (b) the case description, and (c) blank pages for the answers of the participants. Not only was the case realistic, but the case-stories also resembled those found in typical managerial casebooks. The case contained neither interpretations nor analyses; we presented case information merely as authentic data and events. The business case began with a section in which the leading character is introduced, and the context in which he or she is working in is described. Next, we presented the reader a set of factual information about the firm (case history, employees, future goals, turnover, etc). The case contained both case-relevant and case-irrelevant cues. Irrelevant cues did not contain false information; their only purpose was to better distinguish experts from non-experts. The participants' task was to select relevant information, analyze the ill-structured situations and solve problems, which is a realistic task in professional situations.

We developed a case "answer model" in advance, that contained a description of the main problems in the case and a diagnostic explanation. In well-defined disciplines like mathematics or physics, it is relatively easy to specify criteria for assessing the number of correct steps in case answers. In an ill-structured domain as management, obtaining a consensus about the correct solution of the business problems is more difficult. Indeed multiple strategies may be acceptable. For that reason, two management experts developed several plausible case diagnoses and solution directions (the answer model).

mance of students (novices and undergraduates), of graduates who had recently entered the workplace, and of experts in the managerial field. In total 115 subjects participated, representing nine different levels of expertise ranging from younger novices to older experts with over 25 years of work experience in business administration. Subjects analyzed and solved realistic and ill-structured managerial cases in the field of Organizational Development.

We examined the development of problem-solving abilities by examining performance on the following measures: diagnostic accuracy and solution accuracy. Diagnostic accuracy covers identifying, defining and explaining case problems, in terms of sources and causes, followed by explaining and classifying the phenomena encountered. We defined solution accuracy as the ability to provide correct case solutions in terms of guidance or further action that the company should take. Our particular interest lied in examining how subjects with different levels of experience used school knowledge and dynamical knowledge.

The major findings of our studies can be summarized as follows:

1.   Successful problem-solving depended stronger on the use of dynamical knowledge than on the use of scientific managerial knowledge as taught at business school.

2. After graduation, it takes at least 7 to 10 years of experience in managerial practice before subjects showed problem-solving behavior of truly experts.

3. Experts use more dynamical knowledge (denoted by the number of inferences in the problem-solving protocols) than novices and graduates. The more experience subjects had the more significant the use of dynamical knowledge. The capability to use dynamical knowledge while working on problem situations developed continuously in a monotonic, linear way starting from undergraduate level (lowest level of using dynamical knowledge) until the higher levels of expertise.

4. Experts used significantly less time to solve the case as compared to undergraduates and graduates, but produced better diagnoses and solutions.

5. Experts differ truly from graduates and undergraduates with respect to production of case solutions (what should be done), while differences tend be smaller with respect to the production of case diagnoses (how is the present situation defined in terms of underlying causes).

We found that cognitive performance (as expressed in the production of case solution accuracy) is related with different levels of schooling and experience. Solutions accuracy refers to the capacity to provide highly correct case solutions. We defined a case solution as directions or decisions for further action. Whereas problem diagnosis requires analytic activities, offering solutions is an activity which requires insight about how action plans can work out in managerial practice. Therefore, the degree of solution accuracy represents an essential aspect of expertise. Participants with higher degrees of managerial experience showed superior performance concerning the production of accurate solutions. This finding is of course self-evident. Also the production of inaccurate solutions was hardly surprising. The more schooling students received, the lower the amount of inaccurate solutions. But the most important finding concerned the relation between experience on one hand and production of partial correct solutions at the other hand. During schooling and the first 7 to 10 years after graduation, our subjects produced more partially correct solutions than correct solutions. It took subjects 4 years of schooling at the business schools plus 7 to 10 years experience at the workplace before they produced more correct solutions than partial correct solutions. This outcome seems to confirm Mintzberg's ideas that business schools indeed do not produce business experts, but that the key for entering the stage of becoming a true expert lies in the experience one gets after school.

A close analysis of our results indicated that during time at business school improvement with respect to the production of correct solutions is small; the main gain takes place after graduation, while simultaneously the mean number of partially correct solutions decreases with comparable rate. We found that a trade-off mechanism occurred between the capability to produce correct solutions and partially correct solutions. It seemed as if students have to pass through an educational period of making incorrect solutions before developing better problem solving abilities. And apparently, after graduation participants learn to perfect their solutions, as this trade-off occurs between the number of correct and partially correct solutions. Finally, after about 7 to 10 years work experience, subjects produced more correct solutions than partially correct solution, which can be interpreted as that these subjects reached the stage of proficiency. Taken together, we found that excellent managerial performance occurs after at least 10 years of work experience.[1] This confirmed our expectations that it would take a substantial amount of work experience before graduates would perform at the level of a true expert. It also confirms ideas as expressed by Leonard and Swap (2004) who hypothesized that it takes several years before graduates move from the level of competency toward the level of being a true expert.

In trying to understand how the production of solution accuracy could be explained, we examined as well the nature of the knowledge in use while working on the cases. In particular attention was paid to characteristics of the written protocols with respect whether participants used knowledge which could be classified as inferences (dynamical knowledge) or whether they relied on factual knowledge (reproduction of literal facts as contained in the case, which can be viewed as declarative knowledge). As argued in previous sections, the capability to use inferences is typical for expert behavior. Only experience at the workplace (job experience or internships, or projects) can result in the development of dynamical knowledge.

Inferences are the most important indicator for the knowledge used while working on the cases. In comparison with management students, experts' problem-solving behavior is largely based on the use of inferences. We found that graduates and students demonstrated the possession of significant amounts of factual knowledge, but are not yet able to transform their school knowledge into dynamic knowledge. We consider this as a problem, especially when we relate this result to the weak problem-solving performances of junior experts. These findings do indeed support claims from Leonard and Swap (2004), and Bennis and O'Toole (2005) that the significance of acquiring formal knowledge and formal learning is commonly overemphasized, as our studies show that typically graduates possess large amounts of formal knowledge, while this is not enough for solving practical problems.

Our results suggest that a trade-off exists between the use of school knowledge and dynamic knowledge. A similar trade-off occurs in the production of partial correct solutions and correct solutions. Apparently, once individuals have entered professional practice, the number of correct solutions they generate grows rapidly while at the same time the number of partially correct solutions decreases sharply! Our data suggest that only after a long period—that is about 10 years of professional practice—a phase of competence is reached that equals the level of true expert. This finding confirms the general belief that it takes a substantial amount of practice before the average management graduate has acquired the ability to perform excellently. It also demonstrates that educating school knowledge is not a sufficient basis for performance at the level of true expertise.

From our research we concluded that while third and fourth year students (graduates) generated many case solutions, their diagnoses and solutions were of moderate quality, that is, not yet correct. Strong indications existed that students cannot filter out irrelevant information, and process large amounts of (irrelevant) information which can lead to many solution possibilities and many faults during reasoning. This ineffective problem-solving behavior of students can also explain why students provide so many partial correct solutions. The longer students stayed in a program the more partial correct solutions were produced. Only after graduation a substantial drop in the production of partial correct solutions was found.

Overall, our data indicated that as participants proceed from beginner to expert, our results show a shift from high quantity and low quality solutions to low quantity, high quality solutions. A possible explanation is that experts can recognize patterns and distinguish between relevant and irrelevant information, due to their experience (Arts et al., 2000; Patel & Groen, 1991). Consequently, the experts seem to have fewer solution alternatives available. Our analysis of solution quality (correct, partially correct, and incorrect) provides evidence that junior-experts encounter after graduation an "experience or practice shock" in the sense that solving workplace problems requires different thinking and different knowledge than during their time at business school. It seems that business schools tend to be strong in educating students with respect to diagnosing situations ("this is the case"), and relatively weak in teaching our students how to develop correct solutions ("this needs to be done").

## IMPLICATIONS FOR MANAGEMENT EDUCATION

Our research on how cognitive performance is related to different levels of schooling and experience, deviates from survey studies that collect data from employers and/or graduates. We investigated stages of progress toward development of managerial expertise by analyzing cognitive performance and the nature of underlying knowledge. Our research on stages of expertise was based on the contention that learners move through various but characteristic stages of knowledge organization before reaching the proficiency level that "true" experts have. Stage-like development of expertise has indeed been evidenced in the work of Alexander (2003) and Boshuizen (1989, 2003). Our main focus was whether and how subjects with different levels of business schooling and management experience make progress in cognitive performance during solving realistic problems. We tried to analyze this progress through examining how differences in cognitive problem solving could be explained by changes in knowledge structures underlying problem-solving performance. The question may be raised what the implications are for business education, and whether current teaching practices can be modified to speed up the process of expertise development. From our research the conclusion can be drawn that the key to speed up this process lies in the capability to find better ways for incorporating business practice in business education.

Recent stage models claim that individual learners go through (Alexander, 2003; Dreyfus & Dreyfus, 1986, 2005) five stages of acquiring problem-solving skills, before expertise is acquired: novice, advanced beginner, competent, proficiency-expert, and expert. Progression of one stage to a higher occurs when individuals gain practical experiences. The main dimensions of cognitive progression in the Dreyfus' model can be summarized as: (1) reasoning on problems, and (2) use of knowledge during problem-solving. Concerning reasoning, it is argued that the development progresses from ineffective to effective, quick, and unconscious reasoning. Knowledge use develops from acquiring facts and rules toward using the rules in a context (Dreyfus et. al., 1986, 2005). It is claimed that proficiency only seems to develop if experience is assimilated in the learner's knowledge base. Alexander (2003) adds to this model that beginners typically focus on the acquisition and reproduction of domain knowledge, covering the "breadth" of knowledge: the underlying concepts and principles of a field. Competency is marked by quantitative and qualitative changes in the knowledge base. Experiences lead to a deeper form of subject-matter knowledge. In the final proficiency or 'true expertise' stage, individuals extend their capabilities beyond their learned knowledge since they are able to derive new and personalized inferences and knowledge when encountering problems in practice. Typical for this stage is that a trade-off occurs between (diminishing) surface-level strategies and (emerging) deep processing strategies.

So how can business education gain from these insights? The obvious approach would be to reduce the gap between theory and practice by incorporating business practice through cases, problems, projects etc. But as Ball (2006, this volume) puts forward, curricular reform visions are for the most part content based (what should we teach?), with a second concern over pedagogy (how en when should we teach?). We agree with Ball and therefore we will discuss some alternate educational approaches that focus on the curricular form and not on content, showing how this can help students in bridging the gap between theory and practice.

One framework for narrowing the theory-practice gap is the situated-learning theory (Williams, 1992). Situated learning theory emphasizes the importance of a situation (problem context) in which students are learning, and it questions the idea of separating learning from practical situations. An implication of this theory is that we should either send students more to practice (e.g., apprenticeships), or that we should bring more "practice" into education. As such this theoretical framework is in line with the ideas of Mintzberg (2004) or Bennis and O'Toole (2005). But the differences lie in the way practice can be brought to the classroom.

Examples of concrete solutions for the aforementioned knowledge-transition problems that we have identified include "dual learning" and "action learning." Dual learning implies that students divide their time between school and work such that knowledge acquired in a school context can be readily applied to a professional situation, and vice versa. Action learning involves real-life structured projects in organizations ("learning by doing") rather than performing projects in traditional classroom settings. Such approaches can circumvent the time delay between (a) knowledge acquisition in formal educational settings and (b) knowledge application in practical (workplace) settings. Of course, dual learning and action learning are not always realistic options for formal education. Another approach is to "bring the workplace" in the context of professional curricula, for example by enhancing the authenticity of assignments and of the learning environment (e.g., Arts, Gijselaers, & Segers, 2002, 2006; De Grave, Boshuizen, & Schmidt, 1996). These studies have shown that it is possible to stimulate development of managerial problem-solving expertise.

The example in Text Box 3.2 shows that is possible by integrating practice with theory—even in undergraduate business education—manage-

### Text Box 3.2.   Example of a Modified PBL Approach in Marketing Management

Arts, Gijselaers, and Segers (2002, 2004, 2006) showed in a series of studies that it is possible to adapt the instructional design of an undergraduate business course in such a way that students develop advanced problem-solving skills. By implementing a coherent set of changes in an undergraduate marketing management course, we aimed to improve student's learning. Our study was based on a comparative, research design. Students were randomly assigned to an "experimental condition" (the redesigned course) and a "control condition" (the current course version).

The first important element in our redesigned course was that students worked with small team settings of four students that have the characteristics of cooperative and professional teams. The small team setting was used for brainstorming on the initial analysis of a problem and to perform a thorough analysis. Next, in groups of 14 students a discussion of the different team results and solution(s) of the problem was performed. Second, we used a variety of cases with case information consisting of problem descriptions together with raw ("authentic"), critical and less critical company data. Third, we used a structured form guiding the steps for students to (a) take in the initial analysis of the problem, (b) assure the feedback by the tutor and (c) foster the discussion of issues addressed by the students. For measuring the cognitive effects of this redesign, we used similar indicators for measuring expertise development in management as discussed in the previous section: the use of an organized knowledge base, reasoning directionality, diagnostic ability, and quality of solutions.

We found that students participating in the experimental version used significantly more inferential knowledge while working on an authentic case. On the other hand, the results of our research indicated that within both conditions no differences were found with respect to the amount of formal managerial knowledge concepts. This is was (again) an indication that differences in managerial expertise are not explained by mastery of business school knowledge, but whether students develop the capability to build inferential knowledge (dynamical knowledge).

Concerning the quality of diagnoses and quality of case solutions, we found that students in the experimental condition from outperformed the control condition. Interestingly, no differences were found for the quantity of diagnoses and solutions. Overall, our research results indicate that the combination of all the changes in the design facilitated the acquisition of a more advanced level of knowledge and skills in problem solving. Our studies showed that students gained increased understanding of the marketing domain, and became better prepared to approach authentic task situations as may be found in this particular domain.

ment courses can foster student's development toward managerial expertise. In a way the example illustrates how critics of management education may go wrong and how they can be right at the same time. Our expertise studies confirm the notion that practice is indeed the key for developing experts in management practice. It goes wrong when business schools are chastised for their lack of opportunities to do so. Our example in Text box 3.2 shows that through radical redesign of management courses, one can alter management education in such a way that it meets the needs of practice in a better way.

## WHERE DOES THIS LEAVE THE BUSINESS EDUCATOR?

First, it must be recognized that recent debates by Mintzberg (2004), and Bennis and O'Toole (2005) do have their value. As our studies show, their criticisms provide indeed a case in point. But, when business schools claim that they aim to produce proficient management experts it seems unlikely they can hold their claims in the light of research findings as provided by Isenberg (1986), Wagner (2002), expertise studies (Ericsson, 2003), or our own work. We agree with Mintzberg (2004), and Bennis and O'Toole (2005) that business schools overemphasize the importance of management as science or principled framework. However, we do not draw the conclusion that it is a matter of changing curricular contents only. We argue that educational research should form the basis for developing instructional methods that may guide our efforts to improve management education through modifying form as well. Unfortunately, so far the empirical basis for realigning management education has been restricted to relatively few studies. Business schools do have a weak tradition to question their own assumptions about their own production processes (for example as compared to medical or science education). The good news is that a great deal of debate has taken place between some leading management experts resulting in the identification of some serious issues that need to be addressed. The bad news is that business schools have not developed sufficient empirical and theoretical underpinnings of one of their primary processes: teaching business.

Having said this, what can be said about a research agenda for the near future? It is clear that experts possess a superior, substantial body of knowledge and practical experience. And of course this may all be brought to bear on the solution of a managerial problem. Sure, we need to train our students in acquiring this body of knowledge. We do not deny that we need to teach around a database of practical examples. This idea is not new, in fact Harvard Business School is famous for this approach. However, what is new that students should be enabled to actively engage in the process of problem-solving. This engagement should be developed through collaborative learning methods. Next we should work on the teacher's awareness—or maybe even more important to develop a sense of critical reflection on curriculum development among academic leaders —that students should receive sufficient exposure to pedagogical relevant cases. Also, it deserves recognition that teaching business functions in business curricula is one way to develop understanding of business practice, but it is "practice, practice, practice" which counts to reach levels of mastery associated with expertise. Unfortunately, keeping in touch with practice is where business schools lost their way. We should not rely on our intuition when designing curricula, but apply the same academic scrutiny on our curriculum thoughts as we do in business research. We hope this chapter was written in this spirit.

## NOTE

1.  More information about statistical analyses, description of procedures, and limitations of our analyses can be found in Arts, Gijselaers, & Boshuizen (2006, under review).

## REFERENCES

Alexander, P.A. (2003). The development of expertise: The journey from acclimation to proficiency. *Educational Researcher, 32*(8), 10-14.

Anderson, J.R. (1987). Skill acquisition: Compilation of weak-method problem solutions. *Psychological Review, 94*, 192-210.

Arts, J. A. R., Gijselaers, W. H., & Boshuizen, H. P. A. (2000, April). *Expertise development in managerial sciences: The use of knowledge types in problem-solving.* Annual meeting of the American Educational Research Association, New Orleans, Louisiana. (ERIC Document Reproduction Service No. ED 440276)

Arts, J. A. R. Gijselaers, W. H., & Boshuizen, H. P. A. (2006, in press). Understanding managerial problem-solving, Knowledge use and information processing: Investigating stages from school to the workplace. *Contemporary Educational Physchology.*

Arts, J. A. R. Gijselaers, W. H., & Segers, M. S. R. (2002). Cognitive effects of an authentic computer-supported, problem-based learning environment. *Instructional Science, 30*, 465-495.

Arts, J. A. R., Gijselaers, W. H., & Segers, M. S. R (2004). Fostering managerial problem-solving. In H. P. A. Boshuizen, R. Bromme, & H. Gruber (Eds.), *Professional learning: Gaps and transitions on the way from novice to expert* (pp. 97-119). Dordrecht, the Netherlands: Kluwer Academic.

Arts, J. A. R., Gijselaers, W. H., & Segers, M. S. R. (2006). From cognition to instruction to expertise: Measurement of expertise effects in an authentic, computer supported, and problem-based course. *European Journal of Psychology of Education, 21*(1), 71-90.

Bennis, W. G., & O'Toole, J. (2005, May). How business schools lost their way. *Harvard Business Review,* 1-9.

Bigelow, J. D. (2001). *Preparing undergraduates for organizational situations: A frames/problem-based approach.* Unpublished manuscript, Boise State University.

Boshuizen, H. P. A. (1989). *The development of medical expertise: a cognitive-psychological approach.* Unpublished doctoral dissertation, University of Maastricht.

Boshuizen, H. P. A. (Ed.). (2003). *Expertise development: The transition between school and work.* Heerlen, the Netherlands: Open University Press.

Boyatzis, R. E., Cowen, S. S., Kolb, D. A. (1995). *Innovation in professional education: Steps on a journey from teaching to learning.* San Francisco: Jossey-Bass.

Bransford, J. D., & Schwartz, D. L. (1999). Rethinking transfer: A simple proposal with multiple implications. *Review of Research in Education, 24*, 61-100.

Business-Higher Education Forum. (1999). *Spanning the chasm: A blueprint for action.* Washington DC: Author.

Chi, M. T. H., Glaser, R., & Farr, M. J. (Eds.). (1988). *The nature of expertise.* London: Erlbaum.

Coughlin, L. D., & Patel, V. L. (1987). Processing of critical information by physicians and medical students. *Medical Education, 62*, 818-828.

Crainer, S., & Dearlove, D. (1998). *gravy training. inside the shadowy world of business schools.* Oxford, England: Capstone.

DeGrave, W. S., Boshuizen, H. P. A., & Schmidt, H. G. (1996). Problem-based learning: Cognitive and meta-cognitive processes during problem analysis. *Instructional Science, 29*, 321-341.

Douglas J. C., & King, J. (2002). Are we properly training future HR/IR practitioners? A review of the curricula. *Human Resource Management Review, 12*, 539-554.

Dreyfus, H. L., & Dreyfus, S. E. (1986). *Mind over machine: The power of human intuition and expertise in the era of the computer.* New York: Free Press.

Dreyfus, H. L., & Dreyfus, S. E. (2005). Expertise in real world contexts. *Organization Studies, 26*(5), 779-792.

Ericsson, K., & Smith, A. J. (1991). Prospects and limits of the empirical study of expertise: an introduction. In K. A. Ericsson & J. Smith, (Eds.), *Toward a general theory of expertise, prospects and limits* (pp. 1-38). Cambridge, MA: Cambridge University Press.

Ericsson, K. (2003). The acquisition of expert performance as problem solving: Construction and modification of mediating mechanisms through deliberate practice. In J. E. Davidson & R. J. Sternberg (Eds.), *The psychology of problem solving* (pp. 31-86). Cambridge, MA: Cambridge University Press.

Ericsson, K. (2004). Deliberate practice and the acquisition and maintenance of expert performance in medicine and related domains. *Academic Medicine, 10*, S1-S12.

Giannantonio, C., & Hurley, A. (2002). Executive insights into HR practices and education. *Human Resource Management Review, 12*, 491-511.

Grey, C., & Mitev, N. (1995). Management education: a polemic. *Management Learning, 26*(1), 73-90.

Hakkarainen, K., Palonen, T., Paavola, S., & Lehtinen, E. (Eds.). (2004). *Communities of networked expertise: Professional and educational perspectives.* Amsterdam: Elsevier.

Hansen, W. L. (2002). Developing new proficiencies for human resource and industrial relations professionals. *Human Resource Management Review, 12*, 513-538.

Isenberg, D. J. (1984). How senior managers think. *Harvard Business Review, 62*(6), 80-90.

Isenberg, D. J. (1986). Thinking and managing: A verbal protocol analysis of managerial problem solving. *Academy of Management Journal, 4*, 775-788.

Lash, F. B. (1988, April). *Problem solving and the development of expertise in management.* Paper presented at the annual meeting of the American Psychological Association. Atlanta, GA.

Leonard, D., & Swap, L. (2004, September). Deep smarts. *Harvard Business Review,* 1-12.

Mintzberg, H. (1973). *The nature of managerial work.* New York: Harper Row.

Mintzberg, H. (2004). *Managers not MBAS.* London: Prentice Hall

Patel, V. L., Evans, D. A., & Groen, G. J. (1989). Reconciling basic science and clinical reasoning. *Teaching and Learning in Medicine, 1,* 116-121.

Patel, V. L., & Groen, G. J. (1991). The general and specific nature of medical expertise: A critical look. In A. Ericsson & J. Smith (Eds.), *Toward a general theory of expertise: Prospects and limits* (pp. 93-125). Cambridge, MA: Cambridge University Press.

Perriton, L., & Reynolds, M. (2004). Critical management education: From pedagogy of possibility to pedagogy of refusal? *Management Learning, 35*(1), 61-77.

Sternberg, R. J., & Horvath, J. (Eds.). (1999). *Tacit knowledge in the professions.* Mahwah, NJ: Erlbaum.

Stinson, J., & Milter, R. G. (1996). Problem-based learning in business education: curriculum design and implementation issues. In L. Wilkerson & W. H. Gijselaers (Eds.), *Bringing problem-based learning to higher education: Theory and practice* (pp. 33-42). San Francisco: Jossey-Bass.

Van de Wiel, M. (1997). *Knowledge encapsulation. Studies on the development of medical expertise.* Unpublished doctoral dissertation, Maastricht: University of Maastricht Press.

Wagner, R. K. (1991). Managerial problem solving. In R. J. Sternberg & P. A. Frensch (Eds.), *Complex problem solving: Principles and mechanisms* (pp. 159-184). Hillsdale, NJ: LEA.

Wagner, R. K. (2002). Smart people doing dumb things: The case of managerial incompetence. In R. J. Sternberg (Ed.), *Why smart people can be so stupid* (pp. 42-63). Yale, CT: Yale University Press.

Walsh, J. P. (1995). Managerial and organizational cognition: Notes from a trip down memory lane. *Organizational Science, 6,* 280-321.

Williams, S. M. (1992). Putting case-based instruction into context: Examples from legal and medical education. *Journal of the Learning Sciences, 2,* 367-427.

# Part II

## DESIGNS FOR GRADUATE MANAGEMENT EDUCATION

CHAPTER 4

# BRIDGING THE GAP

## A Model for Graduate
## Management Education

### Stephen R. Ball

Calls for change in the education of business leaders have recurred regularly for the past 100 years. Calls come from a variety of influencers, including accreditation agencies (such as The American Association of Collegiate Schools of Business (AACSB), as cited in Ryan, 1999), professional organizations (von Brachel, 1996), and a variety of faculty and administrators in business programs (Gunz & McCutcheon, 1998; Hamalainen, Whinston, & Vishik, 1996; Pearce II, 1999a; Stewart, Felicetti, & Kuehn, 1996). They cite a variety of reasons why change is needed. The foci of change are varied and include the content of the curriculum (Gunz & McCutcheon, 1998; Stewart et al., 1996) and instructional resources (Hamalainen et al., 1996). The current calls for change by Mintzberg (for instance, Mintzberg & Lampel, 2001) and Pfeffer and Fong (2002) are the latest in an arc of compelling calls. Extensive literature reviews show a lack of organization to these changes or calls for change, especially on the part of faculty in business education programs. Models developed empirically in the field of higher education have the potential to help business faculty organize their thinking about their curricula. One model (Stark & Lattuca, 1997) is particularly useful in this effort. This chapter reviews the history of calls for business education change over the last century to set the context, critiques this "academic

*New Visions for Graduate Management Education*, 87–106
Copyright © 2006 by Information Age Publishing
All rights of reproduction in any form reserved.

plan" model for graduate business education, and discuss ways that business faculty can use it to broaden their thinking about curricular improvements.

## INTRODUCTION

Business programs continue to account for at least one in every five undergraduate degrees conferred nationally, according to the National Center for Education Statistics. Systematic study of business programs is important, since improved understanding of the curriculum would be expected to yield efficiencies in achieving intended learning outcomes and in planning and implementing change. Yet there is little evidence that authors in business education literature are aware either of research conducted over the past decade into the nature of the higher education curriculum, or research conducted on professional programs in particular. As a result the suggestions for improvements tend to be less holistic than they might be, and have limited usefulness beyond the unique culture of the authors' institutions (often based on qualitative study methods in one or two courses, which findings cannot be generalized broadly). This paper explores the history of calls for change in professional management education in order to give a firmer grounding in the current issues and introduces a model from higher education research (Stark & Lattuca, 1997) that has potential to help faculty with program improvement efforts. Through this I hope to bridge the gap between higher education researchers, who extensively study curricula and programs, and MBA faculty who are largely unaware of this body of research. Increased use of curricular models can increase the understanding of MBA faculty about some less understood elements of their programs, moving beyond the two popular questions MBA faculty tend to ask: What should we teach (content) and how should we teach it (pedagogy and technology)?

## CALLS FOR CHANGE: VOICES FROM THE PROFESSION

Many authors, typically faculty who teach in business programs, have written about program or curricular change throughout the twentieth century in a variety of business education and other journals. However, a majority of articles that purport to offer curricular change ideas are actually focused on course-level changes, often written by the faculty who initiated the described change in their own course(s). The calls for change in business education during the 1990s are rooted in the history of calls for program reform, which are presented below. The treatment of the history becomes increasingly detailed as the time period moves toward the 1990s, arguably an extension of the history, since those later developments are believed to have more influence on the period of study than the earliest history. The historical context is important to provide an overall sense of the debates about the business curriculum, many issues of which have been remarkably stable (that is to say, unresolved) for over 100 years. Taken together these establish the socioeconomic backdrop, and the calls for change are synthesized into key movements or issues. They provide an early framework for understanding the 1990s, which will be useful when we consider a model for graduate management education.

## A HISTORY OF CALLS FOR CHANGE: 1880s-1990

The increasing use of machinery as a result of the Industrial Revolution in the mid-1700s allowed for more efficient, larger organizations, which required people with a knowledge of business who could exercise judgment (AACSB, 1966). This was a requirement largely unknown before the nineteenth century (Daniel, 1998; Haynes & Jackson, 1935). As the nineteenth century drew to a close, manufacturing and production workers made up one-third (up from one-quarter) of the workforce; agricultural workers had dropped to one-third from one-half.

Faculty and administrators eventually responded to these new economic pressures with new programs and individual innovations (Hearn, 1996). Business education is remarkable for its unprecedented rise to prominence in higher education. No other discipline grew from "small and random beginnings" in the 1880s to positions of prominence in their institutions in only 4 decades (Daniel, 1998, p. 148). By the 1920s, business programs had emerged from small, disorganized efforts to become important programs in colleges and universities nationwide. During their meteoric growth from the late nineteenth century to the mid-twentieth century (Daniel, 1998), these programs have been characterized by debate: over their purposes and philosophies, what should be taught (e.g., the mix of social sciences and quantitative content), methods of teaching and research, qualifications of faculty, types of students who should attend, the proper relationship the programs should have with business and professional associations (e.g., the mix of practical and theoretical foci), the role of business education in society, and, indeed, if it was even possible to teach business (Barzun, 1968; Crainer & Dearlove, 1999; Daniel, 1998; Gordon & Howell, 1959; Jones, 1913; Pierson, 1959; Ridgeway, 1968).

## Early Calls for Change: 1880s-1930s

An influential set of three principles and seven propositions (Jones, 1913) seemed to sum up what little could be agreed upon in the early years (1880s-1930s; Daniel, 1998). Jones's first principle was that business schools needed to define the *type of student* they intended to train, and *what careers are intended* (entry or senior management, entry into business or enhancing the skills of those in midcareer). Second, they needed to ensure that a *systematic foundation* was offered in the curriculum to achieve a sound understanding of the ways of business. Third, a *liberal education* must be a part of the business curriculum. The first of his seven propositions was that business schools should seek to train people in managerial functions such as accounting, finance, distribution, and policy, and to develop those sciences. Second, core subjects should include administration, corporate finance (including accounting), and the theory of distribution. Third, economics is a foundational science, but he felt new sciences are also needed. Fourth, all business sciences should be grounded in the scientific method. Fifth, "liberal culture" (Jones, 1913, p. 192) should be included in the curriculum. Sixth, the curriculum should primarily be taught in undergraduate programs, except for a "few necessary graduate schools" (p. 193). And, seventh, the teaching of business, and investigation into its sciences, should be considered a "high calling" (p. 194) by those involved.

A later study (Bossard & Dewhurst, 1931) identified five problems with business management training: (a) programs were unreasonably bound by tradition; (b) there was a general neglect of research; (c) it was difficult to involve businesses in curriculum design (impeding practical training); (d) attention to educational purpose was pulled away as schools coped with rapid growth; and (e) an inadequate attention to the philosophy of education. Several trends were also reported: (a) more fundamental business studies were being added to curricula; (b) less specialization in subject matter (fewer courses in the catalog) but more attention to regional industries' problems; (c) improved courses and teaching methods; (d) more of an analytic ("engineering") viewpoint and an application of scientific methods; (e) more objective curricular decisions; and (f) more interdisciplinarity.

In summary, the purposes of business education in this period were unclear, such as what mix of business topics and the liberal arts was needed for a proper business education (Donham, 1935; Heilman, Keikofer, Ruggles, Sharfman, & Marshall., 1928). The major focus of calls for improvements in management education (Gilbreth, 1935; Heilman et al., 1928; Heiss, 1935; Johnson, 1932; Lyon, 1932; Marshall, 1917; Morgan, 1935) was for a variety of specific course contents. Common were calls for statistics, accounting, marketing, "a good English style" (Marshall, 1917, p. 84), history, government, social and physical sciences, foreign languages, economics in business topics, and "the geographic control of economic affairs" (Johnson, 1932, p. 22). The Great Depression saw calls for more social involvement content (Heiss, 1935; McCrea, 1935). Largely missing from the discourse of the time were the topics of student or faculty quality, learning resources or methods,[1] how the learning material should be sequenced, and suggestions for implementing change.

## Midcourse Correction: World War II-Middle 1960s

The end of WWII brought about a surge of enrollments, thanks in part to the G.I. Bill. Three topics that would become more important were of lesser concern at the time: small enrollments of women in business programs, needs of small businesses, and internationalization (Daniel, 1998).

### Calls for Change

The year 1959 was important for business education: The Ford Foundation and the Carnegie Corporation separately issued important critiques of business schools (Gordon & Howell, 1959; and Pierson, 1959; respectively). These critiques were negative and critical of business programs, garnered sensational national media attention, and were influential enough to continue to be cited into the present age (Calkins, 1961; Daniel, 1998; Commission on Graduate Management Education of the Graduate Management Admission Council, 1990; Committee for Economic Development, 1964; Crainer & Dearlove, 1999; Porter & McKibbin, 1988). First, a larger proportion of mediocre students were being admitted to business schools than to the traditional college fields (Gordon & Howell, 1959; Pierson, 1959). Second, extremely specialized courses were still plentiful, even though programs publicly prided themselves that their curricula were based on broad fundamentals of business (Gordon & Howell, 1959).

Third, it was quite common that business faculty held degrees in mathematics, statistics, economics, psychology, and sociology; many had no interest or experience in business (Gordon & Howell, 1959; Pierson, 1959). Only 40% of faculty held the doctorate degree. The situation would become worse, given that student enrollments would more than double in coming years, and the production of business PhDs would remain flat (Daniel, 1998). Fourth, there was relatively little research production of any kind within these programs (Gordon & Howell, 1959; Pierson, 1959). The research being conducted was largely descriptive and focused on the needs of a narrow group of businesses important in the school's region. Rarely was research focused on finding general principles that could be tested in a scientific manner. Gordon and Howell (1959) claimed that nonbusiness departments at the university, such as psychology, statistics, economics, and sociology, had made more significant research contributions than business program faculty. A fifth and final criticism lay in the form of a question: Should graduate programs of business be restricted to students who already held an undergraduate business degree, or should it be restricted, as it was at Harvard and Stanford, to those who had studied widely in the humanities or sciences? Many of the charges leveled in these reports had been recurring debates since the beginning of collegiate schools of business. Many of these concerns continue to the present time in one form or another (Crainer & Dearlove, 1999).

## Into the Present Era: Late 1960s-1990

In the social unrest of the 1960s business school enrollments declined, although minority student enrollments increased due to increased school recruiting efforts and government loan programs. Enrollments rebounded in the 1970s, however, for a variety of reasons. America had grown tired of the excesses of the antiwar protestors, other professions (e.g., teaching) were becoming overcrowded, women's enrollment in business programs grew at a faster rate than men's, and minority and international student enrollments continued to climb (Daniel, 1998). Curricular innovation was common in this period. Programs experimented with offering programs on-site at corporate offices for their employees. International programs and entrepreneurial studies grew. Schools developed joint programs with other professional schools. Hiring demand for MBA graduates increased for a variety of reasons. The curriculum, from program purpose to individual courses, was swinging toward practicality, a movement reflected in the rise in competency-based programs.

Programs that were shaken into innovation in the late 1960s and early 1970s soon settled into complacency as a result of continuing high enrollments. In the early-1980s public opinion swayed to criticism once again, perhaps in part due to the programs' phenomenal successes as well as criticisms of MBAs on the job. Subject matter, teaching methods, evaluation, lifelong learning, and the role of the business school in society were now thought to be dynamic, unlike earlier times, and in need of constant review and active management.

More recently a 1980 survey of leaders in business and business education (Hunger & Wheelen, 1980) revealed that business leaders wanted closer contacts with business faculty so they could influence curricular decisions. They also wanted more focus on teaching communication skills, more use of field projects for experiential learning, and a higher emphasis on practical application of theory than business schools then provided. Hunger and Wheelen (1980) offered three overall suggestions for improvements: to develop better career counseling strategies that reconcile the divergent views of practitioners (i.e., nonfaculty business leaders) and academics; move toward less specialization in keeping with practitioners' beliefs; and find ways in general to get business leaders more involved in business education.

At about the same time the Business-Higher Education Forum (Business-Higher Education Forum, 1985) argued for more student choice in elective courses; more emphasis on communication skills; for the study of people skills as rigorously as the study of quantitative skills; and more joint ventures, both inside and outside of the academy. Business leaders were urged to join schools' boards of trustees and advisory boards, provide more financial support, and join in innovative joint projects.

Porter and McKibbin's (1988) survey found complacency and self-satisfaction within business schools, which they attributed to the recent high enrollments and high starting salaries of graduates, and which they felt was stifling innovation. Practitioners reported wanting more practical and behaviorally-oriented content, while maintaining the current emphasis on analytical skills. Practitioners reported a perception of improved relations with business programs in the past decade, but paid little attention to whether the school was AACSB accredited. Program content was not well integrated across functions, not enough attention was paid to managing people or international studies in the curriculum, and graduates often had inflated opinions of their worth in the job market. Younger faculty members were too narrowly trained and all faculty lacked real-world business experience. Research was self-serving for academics and of little use to business and faculty did not interact with the business community enough.

A series of recommendations (Porter & McKibbin, 1988) called for more innovation in mission and curriculum overall (contrary to the conservative view that most schools took, to avoid difficulties with AACSB and its rigid accreditation standards). Other specific recommendations included: (a) more breadth in the curriculum beyond the typical core, (b) more focus on external organizational environments and international studies in the curriculum, (c) more focus on a service-oriented (rather than manufacturing) and information-based economy, (d) integrating studies across functional areas, and (e) more emphasis on interpersonal skills.

Two years later the Graduate Management Admission Council of the Graduate Management Admission Council (Commission on Graduate Management Education, 1990) built upon Porter and McKibbin suggesting three significant trends that business schools would have to incorporate in their plans: (a) accelerating rates of change and the complexity of technology; (b) globalization of markets, communication, and human resources; and (c) increasing demographic diversity. The report called for more outward-looking collaborations, within and outside of the university and internationally. In an important new contribution, the report acknowledged that the century-old debate of theory versus practice was really one of balance between theory and practice. The report called for improving student quality, suggesting that all students should have (a) certain prior knowledge before entering their programs, (b) intellectual curiosity, (c) a management point of view, (d) respect for diversity and individuals, (e) self-motivation, and (f) an understanding of the consequences of one's actions on others.

## Synthesis of Calls for Change: 1880s-1990

This review of calls for change during the first century of formal management education programs shows some common topics, and points to a rich history of debate. Who will teach, what topics; who will be taught, how; why do these programs exist are questions that remain important topics of discussion for business faculty. Yet, an extensive review of the suggestions of business program faculty in the 1990s for improving their programs showed that business faculty overwhelmingly see their curricula as primarily *content* (what will we teach?), *pedagogy* (how will we teach?), and sometimes *sequencing* (in what order will the content be taught?) (Ball, 2000). Other important curricular elements are generally shortchanged. As a result graduate management curricular reforms are often cosmetic at best. Given the steady, strong enrollments for several decades in these programs there is little financial incentive to improve or innovate. Yet other pressures provide reasons to pay more attention, such as increasing global competition. We need to focus on deep and substantive improvements, clearly beyond recent efforts. To help us broaden our thinking we can look to the work of our colleagues researching higher education curricula, work that very rarely is cited in the many studies by business faculty in talking about their programs throughout the 1990s. Bridging this gap between the business and higher education disciplines has great potential for graduate management curricular reforms.

## A MODEL FOR GRADUATE MANAGEMENT EDUCATION

Several models for higher education curriculum design are available, but they are largely missed by business faculty writing about their curricula (Ball, 2000). Perhaps the most useful model for graduate management education is a comprehensive analysis provided by Stark and Lattuca (1997). This "academic plan" model is the synthesis of years of work by Stark and several of her colleagues (Francis, Mulder, & Stark, 1995; Hagerty & Stark, 1989; Lattuca & Stark, 1994; Lattuca & Stark, 1995; Purdue & Stark, 1998; Stark, 1988; Stark, 1998; Stark & Lattuca, 1997; Stark & Lowther, 1988; Stark, Lowther, Bentley, Ryan, & Martens, 1990a; Stark, Lowther, & Hagerty, 1986a; Stark, Lowther, & Hagerty, 1986b; Stark, Lowther & Hagerty, 1987a; Stark, Lowther & Hagerty, 1987b; Stark, Lowther, Hagerty, & Lokken, 1988a; Stark, Lowther, Hagerty & Orczyk, 1986c) who have published extensively on the nature of professional education.

Faculty in graduate management programs can improve their effectiveness by approaching curricular change more holistically. As I have shown, faculty think of their curriculum as being the content they teach, the pedagogies they use, and—less frequently—the sequencing of content. This approach is too narrow; important elements (e.g., characteristics of students in their programs) are underrepresented in curricular plans. Through my discussion of the Stark and Lattuca model I hope to provide a structure for faculty conversations for the improvement of graduate management education at their institutions.

## ACADEMIC PLAN ELEMENTS: THE FOCI OF CHANGE

Stark and Lattuca (1997) suggest a systematic approach to program design in which eight elements are integrally related. No elements can be ignored; synergistic approaches to change are needed. Their discussion of curricular elements, which forms "the core of an emerging theory of curriculum" (p. 10), is much more complete than the calls for change I found in the 1990s business education literature. These eight elements include curricular purpose, content, the learners, instructional resources, sequence of presentation, instructional processes, and evaluation of outcomes. They go on to note that "relationships among them have not yet been explored" (p. 10), with two exceptions: linkages are suggested between (a) purpose and content and (b) content and sequence. These linkages emerged from Stark's and others' earlier research (Stark et al., 1988b; Stark et al., 1988c), which were based on faculty interviews.

## Purpose

The purpose of the business curriculum is to transmit the knowledge, skills, and attitudes (KSA) of the profession to new members. These are the intended learning outcomes of the program, reflect the collective beliefs of the faculty about what is important to be learned, and often engender heated debate among faculty (Stark & Lattuca, 1997). They note six purposes, commonly-held faculty beliefs, that differ by discipline. These include (a) societal improvement, (b) effective thinking, (c) providing a set of knowledge and skills for a career, (d) personal enrichment, (e) understanding great discoveries and knowledge of the past, and (f) helping students to develop a strong belief and value structure (Stark, Lowther, Bentley, Ryan, & Martens, 1990). Stimuli for changing a program (Stark et al., 1990b) include strong program leadership who develop a shared vision for excellence and achieving mission. The 1990s literature reported little on purpose for business education, other than three content-related topics; values development as a purpose was largely absent. This is particularly worrisome as a lack of purpose will permeate other curricular elements.

## Content

Subject matter content is interdependent with program purpose (Stark & Lattuca, 1997). Calls for more attitude content, adaptability in new professionals, and social context issues were largely absent from the 1990s business education literature. Present were calls for new ways to address technology; calls for more communication, conceptual, and technical skills; and for integration of theory and practice in new professionals. In the recent business education literature, however, faculty rarely reported collaborating with outside experts in offering their (rarely empirically-based) conclusions (Ball, 2000).

Decisions on what content to teach can be largely self-serving (faculty teach what we like to teach, all things being equal) as there is no strong professional group providing oversight of graduate management education, unlike law, nursing or accounting. There are no state board exams managers must pass to join the profession and, given the lack of agreement on what constitutes the management canon, this is unlikely to develop. (Until recently, AACSB established a canon of sorts with its requirements for accreditation. But they have moved to a "mission centered" approach that no longer rigidly specifies content.) So curricular content is influenced at least in part by the pressures of the marketplace: what students find interesting and are willing to buy (and for which their companies are willing to reimburse tuition). This leads to an economic discussion of how graduate management programs exist in a monopolistic competition world, with its never ending quest for defining a niche market that each school can "own." The benefits and problems of this is a topic for another paper, however. It is enough to say here that decisions on program content are made at the local level, largely driven by the desires of the faculty since there is no coordinated oversight from a professional body.

## Sequencing

Sequencing of the curricular content refers to the structure of the content in order "to facilitate the learner's contact with it" (Stark & Lattuca, 1997, p. 13). Sequencing can include chronological versus thematic presentation, inclusion of practice to support theory, connectedness to prior learning in the program, relevance to students' lives and their communities, and broad versus narrow focus. Four themes offered by Stark and Lattuca (1997) are based on their analysis of calls for general reform of higher education, not specific to business education. First, they note a general movement to decrease student choice. On this, the business education literature has swung back and forth; the 1959 reports called for less choice but more recent literature calls for more choice. A second theme calls for deliberately planning content sequence to emphasize interrelationships between courses. This was occasionally seen in the 1990s literature in calls for more integration within the business school and with liberal arts disciplines. A third theme has students more involved in the debate on sequencing, a theme not present in the 1990s literature. A fourth theme linking professional and general education early in the student's career and reinforcing this linkage throughout the college experience is seen repeatedly in the 1990s literature.

Disciplinary differences affect sequencing decisions within a program, and these are in turn affected by outside influences. Options for sequencing include systematically working through increasingly difficult material, typically found in chemistry programs, as well as the more student-choice approach often found in sociology (Stark & Lattuca, 1997). The arrangement of courses in professional fields is influenced more by the realities of practice, in efforts to design the program to anticipate the work environment students will encounter as professionals. The business literature recently shows evidence of debate over sequence and structure. A debate in the first half of the twentieth century over the placement of general education, before or after business education, has settled into the now

ubiquitous BBA program design, in which students start their professional training as juniors.

## Learners

Students, or learners as Stark and Lattuca (1997) refer to them (I use
the terms interchangeably), bring their own goals, needs, prior preparation, motivation, and effort into their program of studies. Stark and
Lattuca, and others (e.g., Vogelstein, 1999), assert that faculty often
overlook these factors in designing their programs and that more attention to these learner issues in the planning phases is needed. They
found "that direct expressions of student needs received minimal attention" (Stark & Lattuca, 1997, p. 92), findings that are consistent with
my review of the 1990s literature. Earlier calls for reform noted the
poor quality of business students, but these have not continued into the
present day.

Faculty opinions of students are developed through faculty impressions
of their ideal student and their contacts with current students. Stark and
Lattuca (1997) review some of the current literature on student characteristics that they feel could be useful for faculty to consider in program
planning: cognition and cognitive influences, intelligence and ability,
cognitive styles (such as Kolb's learning styles), learning strategies, motivation and motivational influences, goals, and interest and involvement.
Goals and motivation can be incorporated through increased communication between faculty and students, using the "Student Goals Exploration"
instrument (Stark & Lattuca, 1997, p. 198; Stark, Lowther, Shaw, & Sossen, 1991). Some 1990s works did address learning styles, but these were
not comprehensively integrated into programs.

## Instructional Processes

Instructional processes, or pedagogy, are often associated with particular disciplines and can influence, and be influenced by, the purposes and
content of the curriculum (Stark & Lattuca, 1997), although they do not
show this relationship in their model. They assert that decisions about
pedagogy are frequently left to the individual faculty who design and
implement their own courses, and are rarely included in the program-
level planning. Historically, instructional process has not enjoyed a deliberate and central focus in curricular debates. In the last two decades, however, Stark and Lattuca (1997) note that attention has "increased
dramatically" (p. 94). At the program level, the discussions about instruc-

tional processes include limits on class size, and the inclusion of seminars, laboratory experiences, internships, capstone courses, and/or senior theses (Stark & Lattuca, 1997). Discussion of teaching methods was a popular topic in the 1990s business education literature.

Stark and Lattuca (1997) postulate that internal influences of faculty, students, disciplinary structures, program mission, and leadership are more likely to influence instructional process than are organizational or external influences. They claim that instructional processes in professional programs are influenced by field-specific accreditation agencies (AACSB for business), professional associations, and employers. Stark and Lattuca provide over a dozen suggestions for improving instructional processes (Stark & Lattuca, 1997), implying a connection between learner and instructional process that is not shown on their model.

## Instructional Resources

Instructional resources include both the materials and settings in which instruction takes place, according to Stark and Lattuca, although I expand this to include faculty. I include faculty in this element mainly because the business faculty do not talk about themselves in recent calls for change. Yet this is a huge area for curricular discussions. For instance, the Chronicle of Higher Education has reported for years on the trend to using more and more adjunct faculty as current full-time professors retire, very pronounced in specialized schools of business (Ball, 2005). These schools increasingly use "practitioner faculty," that is, MBAs with years of successful management practice who teach in night school or online programs. Yet little attention has been paid to the effects on program outcomes of this shift in human resource strategy, even though it seems reasonable to conclude that this shift has some effect.

Commonly, textbooks and syllabi are thought of in this category, although the physical layout of classrooms and laboratories, technology, the quality of faculty, and the supportive infrastructure (including financial resources) provided to the program by the institution can all be considered instructional resources (Stark & Lattuca, 1997). One outside influence on resources is the increasing "packaging" of instructional materials, encouraging a tendency on the part of faculty to arrange their course sequencing according to the layout of the text. Stark and Lattuca (1997) note that new computer and telecommunications technologies, as well as the selection of field settings for service learning experiences are emerging instructional resource issues. Stark and Lattuca feel that organizational resource influences act most strongly upon instructional resources (1997, p. 213). Technology was a significant topic of the 1990s literature, as the Internet has become more pervasive in society. Otherwise, this literature was largely silent on the resources issues Stark and Lattuca identified.

## Evaluation: Adjusting Academic Plans

Professional education such as graduate management programs is typically focused on two major types of outcomes: professional competencies (i.e., knowledge and skills) and professional attitudes (Stark et al., 1986b). In their review of the literature, Stark and her colleagues (Stark et al., 1986b) developed categories of competency and attitude outcomes common to professional preparation programs, owing to these programs' common focus on training new members for professional practice. Competencies include (a) understanding the *conceptual* and theoretical foundations of the profession, (b) ability to perform *technical* professional tasks, (c) understanding the social *context* of the profession, (d) written and oral *communication* ability, (e) ability to *integrate* theory and technical skills in practice, and (f) the ability to anticipate and *adapt* to changes in the profession over time. Attitudes include (a) *career_marketability*, (b) *professional_identity* (internalizing of professional norms), (c) development of *ethical standards* common to the profession, (d) *scholarly concern for improvement* of the profession through research, and (e) the development of a *motivation for continued learning*. These competencies provide a good starting point for faculty to talk about purpose and philosophy of their programs, which brings us back full circle in the academic plan.

Evaluation occurs through the assessment (formal or informal) of students' achievement of the intended learning outcomes and, less frequently, through periodic program review. Faculty view evaluation as separate from the curriculum, yet believe it has a natural connection to the purpose and goals of the program. They push for (a) more of a focus on the students' goals in evaluation, rather than focusing solely on the educator's goals and encourage systematic assessment programs; (b) faculty training in assessment techniques; (c) use of assessment as a teaching tool; and (d) increased involvement of accreditation agencies to hold institutions accountable to assess the success of their programs. Purpose, content, and evaluation seem to be seldom adjusted; resources, sequencing, and instructional process are often adjusted; and that evaluation and instructional process are increasingly being adjusted (Stark & Lattuca, 1997).

## Educational Process and Outcomes

Finally in our discussion of Stark and Lattuca's model, we step back a bit for a bigger picture of overall educational process and outcomes. Unlike the constant, incremental changes that individuals make to their courses, program changes require effort by groups of faculty, who are not "experts on student needs, learning theory, or pedagogical alternatives" (Stark & Lattuca, 1997, pp. 124-125). These are often politically charged and undertaken sporadically. Major changes occur as a result of significant external or organizational influences, subject to the many pressures of stakeholders throughout the institution, from management professionals outside the school, and from societal voices at-large. Faculty tend to have a lower personal involvement in program planning, unlike their high interest in their own courses. This contributes to program changes that are shortersighted and less synergistic than they might otherwise be.

This lack of attention to broader program issues generally means faculty pay less attention to bigger trends; one example is the shift to for-profit institutions in professional management education. The University of Phoenix (UOP) came from a small, failing institution in the 1970s to become a powerhouse, enrolling hundreds of thousands of students and having a stock market capitalization of $10.6 billion by the end of 2005 (Smith, 2006). They have shaped Internet-based distance learning, with the Department of Education recently dropping the "50% rule" (no federal monies for programs offering more than 50% of their programs online). UOP, with its centrally planned curricula that use faculty tangentially in the process (relying on professional curriculum designers, Himelhoch, 2002), operates largely outside of the sight of faculty at more traditional institutions. So these trends will not be seen by traditional faculty until there is little we can do to shape the conversation.

## BRIDGING THE GAP: A NEW PATH FORWARD

Stark and Lattuca (1997) propose a basic framework consisting of four elements from their academic plan that would be most helpful to business faculty, untrained in curricular research as most business school faculty members are, to create or adjust programs: (a) purpose of the program, (b) sequencing of program content, (c) relationship of material to the student's world, and (d) appropriate evaluation methods.

The gap in this title is an interdisciplinary one between business school faculty and higher education researchers. With 20% of undergraduate degrees conferred in a business field each year (National Center for Education Statistics, 2006), the largest discipline in academe, business school faculty have an excellent opportunity to learn from the psychological and sociological traditions of higher education research into the complexities of the human learning process. Not only do most business faculty have little profit-and-loss experience in business (a repeated criticism of business faculty throughout the twentieth century), it is the rare business professor who has been trained extensively in how to teach well—including how to design effective programs. Faculty support efforts usually center around pedagogy, the day-to-day activities in the classroom. Course design receives less attention and program design usually none at all. We should not be surprised that graduate management education comes under repeated criticism; we might wonder why it works as well as it does in this environment.

Faculty conversations about graduate management curricular planning that are organized around the elements of the academic-plan model presented here will yield more holistic programs with better alignment of all elements, leading to better outcomes. This would be most effective starting with broad discussions on program philosophy and purpose, and by consciously giving more weight to under-studied elements such as characteristics of students and faculty. In particular, repeated and deep discussions about the purposes of our programs would yield substantial benefits, as we air our private thoughts about the curriculum, discover our colleagues have different views, and work to reconcile these into cohesive missions. A second area that needs conversation surrounds the characteristics of our students, what they are and what we think they should be. It is hard work to gather meaningful information from students. Quantitative studies are limited by the quality of questions asked, and qualitative studies are time-consuming. And it is easier to design programs that we, the faculty, "know" are the right mix of content, and so forth. (What do students know, after all? They don't have advanced degrees in management.) Yet students, especially the midcareer, middle-aged student that describes many of our students, have extensive experience on the practical side of management. This expertise is a valuable and often untapped resource for faculty in their program design deliberations.

I will end with a challenge to us from ourselves for the next 10 years: Explore general curriculum models from higher education research and use them to move toward broader thinking in program planning for graduate management education. Stark and Lattuca provide an excellent model, as I have shown here. Different faculty groups may find others in the course of their conversations. And, as a service to the profession, research on the effectiveness of this model would be a logical next step. Qualitatively, a single or multiple site case study (along the lines of Boyatzis, Cowen, & Kolb, 1995) of examples that used the academic plan model would be illustrative. A handful of these qualitative studies would point to suggested adjustments that may pertain to this profession. From those quantitative studies (e.g., path analysis) testing the relationships of the academic plan elements and the extent to which they explain student learning outcomes would be most useful in furthering knowledge.

## NOTE

1.  In one notable exception (Arben, 1997), Harvard adapted the case study method of teaching, which is still commonly used today, from its use in the law school.

## REFERENCES

Arben, P. D. (1997, March-April). The integrating course in the business school curriculum, or, whatever happened to business policy? *Business Horizons, 40,* 65-70.

Ball, S. R. (2000). *Making sense of recent calls for change in business professional preparation programs.* Unpublished manuscript, The University of Michigan at Ann Arbor.

Ball, S. R. (2005). *The role of organizational culture in innovation adoption: Teaching through the Internet in specialized schools of business.* Unpublished manuscript, The University of Michigan at Ann Arbor.

Barzun, J. (1968). *The American university: How it runs, where it is going.* New York: Harper and Row.

Business-Higher Education Forum. (1985). *America's business schools: Priorities for change.* Washington, DC: Author.

Bossard, J. H. S., & Dewhurst, J. F. (1931). *University education for business.* Philadelphia, PA: University of Pennsylvania Press.

Calkins, R. D. (1961). The problems of business education. *Journal of Business, 34*(1), 1-9.

Crainer, S., & Dearlove, D. (1999). *Gravy training: Inside the business of business schools.* San Francisco: Jossey-Bass.

Boyatzis, R. E., Cowen, S. S., & Kolb, D. A. (1995). *Innovation in professional education: Steps on a journey from teaching to learning.* San Francisco: Jossey-Bass.

Commission on Graduate Management Education of the Graduate Management Admission Council. (1990). *Leadership for a changing world: The future role of graduate management education.* Los Angeles: Author.

Committee for Economic Development. (1964). *Educating tomorrow's managers. The business schools and the business community.* New York: Committee for Economic Development.

Daniel, C. A. (1998). *MBA: The first century.* Cranbury, NJ: Associated University Presses.

Donham, W. B. (1935). The relationship of business education to government and industry. *Journal of Educational Sociology, 8*(9), 562-567.

104 S. R. BALL

Francis, M. C., Mulder, T. C., & Stark, J. S. (1995). *Intentional learning: A process for learning to learn in the accounting curriculum, 12*. Sarasota, FL: Accounting Education Change Commission and American Accounting Association.

Gilbreth, L. M. (1935). What do we ask of business education? *Journal of Educational Sociology, 8*(9), 549-554.

Gordon, R. A., & Howell, J. E. (1959). *Higher education for business.* New York: Columbia University Press.

Gunz, S., & McCutcheon, J. (1998). Are academics committed to accounting ethics education? *Journal of Business Ethics, 17*(11), 1145-1154.

Hagerty, B. M. K., & Stark, J. S. (1989). Comparing educational accreditation standards in selected professional fields. *Journal of Higher Education, 60*(1), 1-20.

Hamalainen, M., Whinston, A. B., & Vishik, S. (1996). Electronic markets for learning: Education brokerages on the Internet. *Association for Computing Machinery, 39*(6), 51-58.

Haynes, B. R., & Jackson, H. P. (1935). *A history of business education in the United States.* Cincinnati, OH: South-Western.

Heilman, R. E., Keikhofer, W. H., Ruggles, C. O., Sharfman, I. L., & Marshall, L. C. (1928). Collegiate education for business. *Journal of Business of the University of Chicago, 1*(1), 1-59.

Hearn, J. C. (1996). Transforming U.S. higher education: An organizational perspective. *Innovative Higher Education, 21*(2), 141-154.

Heiss, C. A. (1935). Readjustments in education for business management. *Journal of Educational Sociology, 8*(9), 534-541.

Himelhoch, C. R. (2002). *The influence of faculty characteristics on their perceptions of worklife quality in centralized and decentralized curriculum planning environments.* Unpublished manuscript, The University of Michigan at Ann Arbor.

Hunger, J. D., & Wheelen, T. L. (1980). *An assessment of undergraduate business education in the United States.* Charlottesville, VA: McIntire School of Commerce, The University of Virginia.

Johnson, E. R. (1932). Collegiate education for business. *Journal of Business of the University of Chicago, 5*(4), 17-28.

Jones, E. D. (1913). Some propositions concerning university instruction in business administration. *Journal of Political Economy, 21*,185-195.

Lattuca, L. R., & Stark, J. S. (1994). Will disciplinary perspectives impede curricular reform? *Journal of Higher Education, 65*(4), 403-426.

Lattuca, L. R., & Stark, J. S. (1995). Modifying the major: Discretionary thoughts from ten disciplines. *The Review of Higher Education, 18*(2), 315-344.

Lyon, L. S. (1932). A ten year look ahead in business education. *Journal of Business of the University of Chicago, 5*(4), 123-132.

Marshall, L. C. (1917). A balanced curriculum in business education. *The Journal of Political Economy, 25*(1), 84-105.

McCrea, R. C. (1935). The collegiate school of business in our American economy. *Journal of Educational Sociology, 8*(9), 520-528.

Mintzberg, H., & Lampel, J. (2001, February 19). Do MBAs make better managers? Sorry, Dubya, it ain't necessarily so. *Fortune, 143*(4), 244.

Morgan, J. E. (1935). Readjustments which need emphasis in business education. *Journal of Educational Sociology, 8*(9), 555-561.

National Center for Education Statistics. (2006). *Bachelor's degrees conferred, by field of study, 1971-2002.* U.S. Department of Education. Retrieved June 28, 2006, from http://nces.ed.gov/programs/digest/d03/tables/dt252.asp

Pearce II, J. A. (1999). Faculty survey on business education reform. *The Academy of Management Executive, 13*(2), 105-109.

Pfeffer, J., & Fong, C. T. (2002). The end of business schools? Less success than meets the eye. *The Academy of Management Learning & Education, 1*(1), 78-95.

Pierson, F. C. (1959). *The education of American businessmen.* New York: McGraw-Hill.

Porter, L. W., & McKibbin, L.E. (1988). *Management education and development: Drift or thrust into the 21st century?* New York: McGraw-Hill.

Purdue, H. H., & Stark, J. S. (1998. May). *Quality management for the postsecondary classroom.* Paper presented at the AIR Forum, Minneapolis, MN.

Ridgeway, J. (1968). *The closed corporation: American universities in crisis.* New York: Random House.

Ryan, C. (1999). Trends in business curricula: The view from AACSB. *Business Communication Quarterly, 62*(1), 91-95.

Smith, R. (2006). *Fools want to know: With Apollo Group.* Retrieved June 28, 2006, from http://www.fool.com/news/commentary/2006/commentary06010405.htm

Stark, J. S. (1988). [Review of the book Contesting the boundaries of liberal and professional education]. *Journal of Higher Education, 60*(4), 482-484.

Stark, J. S. (1998). Classifying professional preparation programs. *The Journal of Higher Education, 69*(4), 353-383.

Stark, J. S., & Lattuca, L. R. (1997). *Shaping the college curriculum: Academic plans in action.* Needham Heights, MA: Allyn & Bacon.

Stark, J. S., & Lowther, M. A. (1988). *Strengthening the ties that bind: Integrating undergraduate and professional study.* Ann Arbor, MI: The University of Michigan, Professional Preparation Network.

Stark, J. S., Lowther, M. A., Bentley, R. J., & Martens, G. G. (1990a). Disciplinary differences in course planning. *Review of Higher Education, 13*(2), 141-165.

Stark, J. S., Lowther, M. A., Bentley, R. J., Ryan, M. P., Martens, G. G., Genthon, M. L., Wren, P. A., & Shaw, K. M. (1990b). *Planning introductory college courses* (89-C-003.0). Ann Arbor, MI: The University of Michigan, National Center for Research to Improve Postsecondary Teaching and Learning.

Stark, J. S., Lowther, M. A., & Hagerty, B. M. K. (1986a). Faculty roles and role preference in ten fields of professional study. *Research in Higher Education, 25*(1), 3-30.

Stark, J. S., Lowther, M. A., & Hagerty, B. M. K. (1986b). *Responsive professional education: Balancing outcomes and opportunities.* Washington, DC. Association for the Study of Higher Education.

Stark, J. S., Lowther, M. A., & Hagerty, B. M. K. (1987a). Faculty and administrator views of influences on professional programs. *Research in Higher Education, 27*(1), 63-83.

Stark, J. S., Lowther, M. A., & Hagerty, B. M. K. (1987b). Faculty perceptions of professional preparation environments–testing a conceptual framework. *Journal of Higher Education, 58*(5), 530-561.

Stark, J. S., Lowther, M. A., Hagerty, B. M. K., & Lokken, P. (1988a). *PLUSS: Professional/liberal undergraduate self-study.* Ann Arbor, MI: University of Michigan, Professional Preparation Network.

Stark, J. S., Lowther, M. A., Ryan, M. P., Bomotti, S. S., Genthon, M. L., Haven, C. L., & Martens, G. G. (1988b). *Reflections on course planning: Faculty and students consider influences and goals* (88-C-002.0). Ann Arbor: The University of Michigan, National Center for Research to Improve Postsecondary Teaching and Learning.

Stark, J. S., Lowther, M. A., Hagerty, B. M. K., & Orczyk, C. (1986c). A conceptual framework for the study of preservice professional programs in colleges and universities. *Journal of Higher Education, 57*(3), 231-257.

Stark, J. S., Lowther, M. A., Shaw, K. M., & Sossen, P. L. (1991). *Student goals exploration: User's manual (Institutional research guide; classroom research guide).* Ann Arbor, MI: University of Michigan, National Center for Research to Improve Postsecondary Teaching and Learning.

Stewart, K., Felicetti, L., & Kuehn, S. (1996). The attitudes of business majors toward the teaching of business ethics. *Journal of Business Ethics, 15*(8), 913-918.

The American Association of Collegiate Schools of Business. (Ed.). (1966). *1916-1966.* Homewood, IL: Richard D. Irwin.

Vogelstein, F. (1999, December 6). Wanted: MBAs to work for six figures. *U.S. News & World Report, 127,* 67.

von Brachel, J. (1996). Reinventing the CPA. *Journal of Accountancy, 182*(5), 49-51.

# CHAPTER 5

# A PRACTICE-CENTERED APPROACH TO MANAGEMENT EDUCATION

## Mark Fenton-O'Creevy, Peter Knight, and Judith Margolis

In this chapter we argue for a practice-centered approach to post-graduate management education. We set our arguments in the broader context of the nature of professional learning and expertise, and begin by considering the nature of professional knowing, the nature of professional expertise and the ways in which professionals learn. To sustain our arguments, we draw on our research on the learning of other professional groups such as teachers and financial traders in investment banks.

In particular, we argue that designing learning environments and experiences should replace the current emphasis on organizing curriculum 'content. To illustrate one way that a practice-centered pedagogy might be approached we describe a portion of the post-graduate management curriculum at the Open University and the way in which the program learning design revolves around a series of dialogues: between different disciplinary perspectives on management; between theory and practice; and between participants different experiences of the world.

We conclude with some proposals for a practice-centered teaching and research agenda

*New Visions for Graduate Management Education,* 107–127
Copyright © 2006 by Information Age Publishing
All rights of reproduction in any form reserved.

## THE ISSUE

Recent critiques of MBA curricula and teaching pay particular attention to a disconnection between the formal knowledge and analytical techniques conveyed in MBA programs and the messy, ambiguous nature of management practice. Mintzberg, for example, argues that:

> The practice of management is characterized by its ambiguity. ...Most work that can be programmed in an organization need not concern its managers directly; specialists can be delegated to do it. That leaves the managers mostly with the messy stuff – the intractable problems, the complicated connections. And that is what makes the practice of management so fundamentally 'soft' and why labels such as experience, intuition, judgment and wisdom are so commonly used for it. (Mintzberg, 2004, p. 13)

How can MBA programs support effective, mindful management practices? We are looking for an approach that avoids stale dualisms, such as those between situated and generalized cognition, between practice and academe, between affect and cognition. We argue that managers' work is too diverse to be captured by such dichotomies. Cognition is situated and general; the tacit and implicit knowings of practice need to stand in relation to the codified knowledge of academe; and it is widely accepted that skilful managers have emotional intelligence, or something like it (Bar-On & Parker, 2000).

We propose an approach that sets up effective dialogues between theory and practice, between different disciplinary perspectives, and between the different experiences of program participants. We use an example from the U.K. Open University's postgraduate management education curriculum to illustrate the feasibility of this approach.

To be persuasive, our argument has to do more than tell the story of what the Open University Business School does; it has to start by addressing some vexed questions about professional knowing and learning.

### Professional Knowing and Professional Learning

Knowledge is not homogenous. There is a long tradition in philosophy of differentiating between different forms of knowledge and there is a corresponding range of psychological investigations. Philosophers and psychologists cut knowledge in many ways, distinguishing, for example, between theoretical and practical, explicit and tacit and implicit, propositional and procedural knowledge. Knowing, practice, and identity are interwoven, and there is a distinct emotional element to the development of professional expertise (Dreyfus & Dreyfus, 2005).

However fine grained the analysis of knowledge, it is clear that it is not homogenous and that professional practice lies at the confluence of many different types of "knowings."[1]

Take school-teaching as an example. The 1980s saw a strong interest in trying to bridge the "theory-practice" gap by reconceptualizing the knowledge teachers need. Shulman (1986) introduced the idea of "pedagogical content knowledge" to bring subject matter and educational knowledge together; soon after he described seven forms of teaching knowledge (Shulman, 1987).

Eraut (1994) showed that professionals draw on different types of knowing according to the amount of time they have to act. Fast actions use different knowings and instantiate different mental process than do more leisured ones.

More recently, Cheetham and Chivers (2005) argued that Schön's (1983) depiction of "reflection" was neither as coherent nor as robustly based as those who put it at the heart of professional knowing and learning assume. They produced interview and survey data showing that its contribution to the initial learning of 452 informants in 20 professions "received a modest rating" (p. 138); and made the case for there being 12 general learning processes in professional learning, of which only one is "reflection." Mintzberg (2004, p. 266) also had reservations about reflection, although he called for "experienced reflection," which needs to be understood as a social, not individual, practice.

Whatever conceptual set is preferred—metacognition, experienced reflection or reflection—our point is that it will not come about by happenstance. Professional programs need to be designed to stimulate, support and sustain these deliberative processes. We claim that good postgraduate management education should be founded on professional learning processes that support the continuing formation of diverse forms of knowing.

## Professional Learning

However, just as "knowledge" is multiformed, so too is learning. We make the point through two figures, each of which we treat lightly in order to make our major point, namely that multiformed knowledge needs multiple learning approaches and diverse pedagogies. Consider the replacement for Bloom's (1956) taxonomy of learning outcomes, shown in a modified form in Table 5.1.

Clearly, the learning needed in the top left region of the chart—the learning needed to remember information, for example—is markedly different from learning needed in the bottom right region—learning

**Table 5.1.   A Taxonomy for Learning, Teaching, and Assessment**

| | The Cognitive Dimension | | | | | |
|---|---|---|---|---|---|---|
| The Knowledge Dimension | *1*<br>*Remember* | *2*<br>*Understand* | *3*<br>*Apply* | *4*<br>*Analyze* | *5*<br>*Evaluate* | *6*<br>*Create* |
| *Metacognitive knowledge* | | | | | | |
| *Propositional knowledge:*<br>*"Knowing that"* | | | | | | |
| *Procedural knowledge:*<br>*"Knowing how"* | | | | | | |

*Note:*   (after Anderson & Krathwohl, 2001, p. 28).

about one's own creative processes for example. Both kinds of knowing are important to practitioners in many domains, including management. We argue that they arise from a differentiated programme that blends together a variety of learning affordances—of engagements or opportunities.

The point is developed in Table 5.2, which says that learning may be intentional or nonintentional and it may arise in formal or nonformal settings. The outcomes of formal, intentional learning may often differ from those of nonformal, nonintentional learning.

Our claim, that some learning may be intentional and under control but much is not, is supported by work on professionals' learning (Becher, 1999; Eraut, 2000), which has shown that people in different professions reported that nonformal and informal[2] learning played a much greater role in their practice than did their formal learning.

## Teachers' Professional Learning

In 2004 Knight collected survey data from some 2,600 Open University faculty. Data were complemented by interviews. His strongest finding was that the 2,401 part-time teachers[3] who responded (a 32% response rate) said that nonformal and social learning practices had dominated their professional formation. Formal educational development provision had been much less significant. Interestingly, this is consistent with interview data collected from high school teachers learning to implement a new national curriculum in the mid-1990s (McCulloch, Helsby, & Knight, 2000). Although there was no shortage of formal provision to help them adopt the new curriculum, they said the most important learning was local, often unplanned, sometimes in the pub, sometimes through hallway conversations.

**Table 5.2.   Intentional and Nonintentional,
Formal and Nonformal Learning**

| Type of Learning Intentionality | Nonformal | Formal |
|---|---|---|
| Intentional | Processes: reflection, self-directed reading groups, mentoring. No preset curriculum. | Processes: Learning that follows a curriculum. May involve instruction and certification. |
| | Outcomes: Formation of explicit understandings of achievement often associated with an intention to build upon them. | Outcomes: greater or lesser mastery of curriculum objectives. |
| Nonintentional | Processes: learning by being and doing in an activity system. | Processes: learning from the "hidden curriculum" (Hargreaves, 1993, chapter 1)—learning about the logic-in-use (as opposed to the espoused logic of the prescribed curriculum). |
| | Outcomes: unpredictable. In some cases, settings have become so familiar that learning has stopped and unlearning may take place. | Outcomes: unpredictable. |

The part-time higher education teachers were also asked to say whether they wished that they had had more engagement with any of 21 means of professional learning. Roughly half of them wished there had been more conferences and workshops; a similar proportion said that they would have liked more social learning in the form of guidance from a mentor; and nearly 40% wished there had been more conversations with subject colleagues; again the message is that nonformal, social learning was significant.

Full-time higher education staff were asked the same questions, although their response rate did quite not reach 20% and so numerical data are not supplied, lest they give an unwarranted impression of precision and certainty. However, the pattern of responses is compatible with the data from the part-time staff and is broadly similar to Knight's 2005 data from interviews with 33 part-time teachers in other U.K. universities.

If this picture is credible, then it has powerful implications for the design of professional programs. For example, it challenges the assumption that professional learning comes through formal learning. Instruction, in its North American sense, is a powerful means to bring about some forms of learning and a powerful ingredient in many rich learning blends. By itself, it is patently insufficient for the formation of many forms of knowing. Indeed, we are implying that some important learning achievements are, in the first instance, products of the learning environment (Pascarella & Terenzini, 2005) and "hidden curriculum."

This means we need to create environments that evoke the sorts of learning that professionals need. Note the word "evoke": we can improve the probabilities of certain learning happening but we cannot guarantee it, and the more complex the learning, the less certain the outcomes. Note also the point that learning, especially complex learning, is evoked by environments (Pascarella & Terenzini, 2005). This is a fundamental challenge to the module-based approach to learning design; program-based approaches are better and environment-based ones are desirable.

## Traders' Professional Learning

But are Knight's data about the professional learning of teachers generalizable? After all is it not possible to argue that the teaching work task is so focused on the interpersonal that "soft" skills will necessarily dominate? So we turn to evidence on the learning of professional traders in investment banks, a group with some claim to have even greater need for "hard" analytical skills than managers. Fenton-O'Creevy, Nicholson, Soane, and Willman (2004) carried out a detailed multimethod study of 118 traders in four London investment banks. One of the questions they addressed to their informants concerned what it takes to be a high performing trader.

The most common responses concerned "flair," "intuition" and "gut feel." For example:

> Flair is anticipating the market, showing intuition, having a contrary, different view of events; not going with the herd, not following the market trend.

> Having a feeling is not the same as experience, it's like having whiskers, like being a deer ... you need a certain type of intelligence, but it's more about intuition.

While it was clear that a good level of analytical skill was a basic requirement to trade effectively, it was neither sufficient nor a differentiator in traders' performance. Typically new traders had a highly numerate background (PhDs in engineering or theoretical physics were common) and engaged in formal classes on markets and financial economics as part of their initial training. However, formal academic learning was not sufficient to trade well or even competently. For example:

We have two people on the desk at the moment, both of whom started at the same time, from relatively similar backgrounds and one of them has just hit the ground running and he's gone right up the curve,... The other trader has actually failed miserably and is miserable in himself. He is really struggling with the whole issue of what the market means to him. Yet academically they are very similar.

This study found that while traders relied on formal knowledge about financial markets—"theories of how the world works"—they also learned and constructed informal theories concerned with exceptions to the general rules and how to exploit them—"theories of how to work the world" (Fenton-O'Creevy et al., 2004). While the former provided conceptual scaffolding it was the latter which provided a basis for action. Further, these theories of how to work the world were often tacit, highly situated and protected as a basis for individual advantage.

To acquire competence, traders go through an apprenticeship process:

New traders need a clear understanding [of their role]. So they sit on the desk, learn and repeat what they are hearing. We ask a lot of challenging questions. Most will have come through training with a broad understanding of trading. We challenge them to understand what they are looking at while they still have formal lectures etc. Finally, we let them make mistakes and give them a certain amount of freedom.

First, you watch what other people are doing, follow and react.... Secondly, you understand what is going on, you can predict the price action, you begin to realize that you predict it right more than you predict it wrong but you haven't yet discovered the appetite of putting money at risk.... It is only the transition into the third phase where you put money at risk that really determines in my mind whether that [learning] curve develops. This can take three months, three years or never happen for some people.

It is through something akin to "legitimate peripheral participation" (Wenger, 1998) that novices begin to construct their identity as traders and engage in the use and construction of "work the world theories" It is through engagement with peers and mentors in a community of practice that they gain expertise.

Dreyfus and Dreyfus (2005) in a critique of the expert system literature point out that gaining expertise is not a process of proceeding via experience from the particular to constructing mental models of greater and greater generality. On the contrary, what distinguishes the expert from the novice or "merely competent" is the expert's vast repertoire of situational discriminations (p. 787): theory driven action is characteristic of the novice not the expert.

For the traders in this study it was clear that while their formal academic learning provided conceptual scaffolding, that expertise as a trader was built through reflective practice. As the Dreyfus brothers note:

> If one asks an expert for the rules he or she is using, one will, in effect, force the expert to regress to the level of a beginner and state the rules learned in school. Thus, instead of using rules he or she no longer remembers, as the knowledge engineers suppose, the expert is forced to remember rules he or she no longer uses. … No amount of rules and facts can capture the knowledge an expert has when he or she has stored experience of the actual outcomes of tens of thousands of situations. (Dreyfus & Dreyfus, 2005, p. 788)

For the traders in this study, an important aspect of their learning as they made the transition from novice to fully fledged trader was the increase in their own repertoire of situational discriminations, not just though experience but via the shared experiences of mentors and peers.

## Environments for Professional Learning

Insofar as MBA programs are a contribution to skilful professional practice, we need MBA environments that evoke complex outcomes. For example, studies of what employers look for in new graduate hires (e.g., Brennan Johnstone, Little, Shah, & Woodley, 2001) or in more established managers (Boyatzis & Associates, 1995) place a lot of emphasis on "non-academic" achievements, attributes or assets—on so-called "soft skills" Of course, much nonformal learning will already have contributed to the development of the soft skills that MBA participants bring with them.

However, experience lies behind misconceptions just as much as it evokes better conceptions. Part of the task for professional programs is to challenge all of the products of nonformal learning that new participants bring with them. The better-based ones will be affirmed and, where effective learning opportunities abound, the less robust ones will be displaced.

Challenging established, taken-for-granted practices and their ganglions of beliefs is hard because they have become enmeshed in networks that are, in some measure, emotionally charged and implicated in professional identities. The psychological literature on concept and attitude change coincides here with the sociological literature on activity systems: changes to one facet are difficult and, if apparently successful, are still liable to be swamped by unchanged knowings, concepts, identities, or aspects of the workplace.

This is not a quick process. Many of the complex learning outcomes that MBA programs intend to foster develop slowly, across a program, rather than across a single module. As Boyatzis and Associates (1995) show, this has significant implications for curriculum design and integration.

Nor can we assume that changes in understanding shown on a program of study are transferred to other settings: this is notoriously difficult to achieve. For example:

> Transfer has proven to be difficult even within school context ... learning how to solve problems often does not help participants solve other problems that look different but can be solved in the same way.... Classroom studies also indicate that despite the claim that thinking skills courses improve intellectual ability, they fail to reveal convincing evidence [of] ... general transfer of learning to new types of problems.... Field studies also reveal that problem solvers commonly fail to apply school-taught mathematics procedures to solve mathematics problems they encounter out of school. (Tuomi-Gröhn, Engeström, & Young, 2003, p. 2)

The assessment of learning is central to a program's success in general and, in particular, to the formation of a disposition to transfer knowing. The habit of setting "tame" tasks and "cleaned-up" case studies does little to encourage transfer and a lot to encourage the discovery of the operational rules of an artificial game with slight transfer value. Mismatches between the published espoused curriculum and the realized curriculum, as defined by procedures for the assessment of learning, will be resolved in favor of the realized curriculum.

Heeding these points, powerful learning environments will include activities such as:

- Engaging participants in coconstruction of the curriculum
- Collaborative learning about practice
- Extended workplace investigations
- Learning through social engagement
- A cross-disciplinary approach to learning design
- Fostering independent learning

An increasing range of MBA programs have adopted approaches which include such activities. For example, several programs use an action learning approach: participants make interventions in real world problems and work in facilitated learning sets to generate both learning and action: see, for example, Rickards, Hyde, and Papamichail's account (2005) of the Manchester Business School approach in the United Kingdom. Other programs have adopted a service learning approach. Student projects in not for profit and community organizations are used as a basis for learning about management: see, for example, Van der Voort, Meijs, and Whiteman's account (2005) of service learning at Erasmus University in Holland.

The approach taken at the U.K.'s Open University is detailed in the following section. We preface our discussion with the comment that we assume that MBA study should not be available to people without prior relevant work experience. In England the national benchmark statement says that, "the MBA is defined as a career development generalist program for those who have significant post-graduation and relevant work experience on which the learning process should build" (The Quality Assurance Agency for Higher Education, 2002).

## A Practice-Focused Approach at the Open University

The Open University, established in 1969, is a British university, which teaches via distance learning.[4] With over 200,000 participants, it is one of the world's largest universities. It was recently ranked in the top five British universities for teaching quality and came top in a government run national poll of student satisfaction. The Open University Business School was established in 1983 and has grown to be one of Europe's largest business schools, with students in around 40 different countries. It is accredited by all three major international accrediting bodies (Association of MBAs, European Quality Improvement System, and the Association to Advance Collegiate Schools of Business.

## The Professional Diploma in Management

The Professional Diploma in Management is a 1-year part-time program (at masters level) that forms the first stage of the Open University MBA. As with all Open University programs it is taught via distance learning. It is intended to provide a good foundation in general management. The program was the first to be accredited under the European Foundation for Management Development's Certification of e-Learning scheme. Participants are practicing managers who study alongside their work. Participants' age and experience varies considerably, but the median age is 35. The program is founded on four assumptions:

- Program participants are practicing managers who jointly bring to the program experience of business and management in diverse settings;
- The artificial division of management theory into disciplines (marketing; finance; organizational behavior etc.) is a convenience for faculty members who have narrow disciplinary bases. It is not the most effective way of preparing managers for the richness and complexity of the worlds in which they operate.
- Learning happens most readily when participants are exposed to experiences which challenge their existing assumptions and when they are invited to grapple with the tensions set up between multiple perspectives on the same problem;
- There is no unitary body of knowledge. Each participant will encounter a different curriculum which they create from the program tools and frameworks they find useful, their own learning history, their learning encounters in their own organization, and ideas and management practice from fellow participants. Assessment should reflect this assumption.

## A Learning Episode

We first describe the structure of a learning episode in the diploma program before unpacking the approaches to teaching and learning that it embodies.

The diploma program is not divided up into discipline-specific modules, but is constructed around a series of themes. The theme of the first module is "Understanding Performance," the second "Improving Performance" the third "Managing Projects and Change" The final module "Investigating Performance and Change" is an extended investigation into a management problem in the participants' own organizations.

The first study session[5] of the diploma program starts by problematizing the notion of performance. Participants are invited to consider a local school that they know well. They approach the question "what is good performance for this school?" by reflecting on and debating the answers that might be given respectively by a parents, a pupil, a teacher, a local shopkeeper, a business employing school leavers, a university accepting entrants from the school, and so on. The principal aim here is to help participants to take a wide perspective and grapple with some of the complexity of performance in a real world setting. The program does not suggest any "right" answers but does encourage participants to think as widely as possible about the question and to grasp that there are many possible understandings of what constitutes "good performance"

Subsequent sessions introduce the participant to a series of disciplinary perspectives on performance in organizations. A session on "The Market-Led Organization" provides one set of frameworks for thinking about performance from a marketing perspective. Next, two study sessions "Understanding Operations" and "Managing Operations Performance" approach performance from an operations perspective, followed by sessions which take a human resources perspective, "Managing Performance through People" and then an accounting perspective, "Accounting in an Age of Empowerment." Substantial linking material between sessions asks participants to engage in activities that consider the tensions and relationships between perspectives.

As participants work through these program materials and activities, they also engage in an extended assignment, which requires collaboration with peers. Each participant first writes around 600 words explaining how performance is understood in their own organization (or their part of it if it is a large organization). Each posts this contribution to an online asynchronous conference shared with four or five other participants. Using these initial contributions as a starting point, they engage in an extended online discussion (over about 2 weeks) and reflect on similarities and differences while trying to understand what may lie behind them. Each participant then pairs with another in order to exchange information in more detail and write an assignment. The assignment requires participants to compare different understandings of performance in their two organizations and reflect on how this understanding might be usefully enriched. Each part of the assignment, including contribution to the online discussion, is assessed to signal the importance of engagement with the task.

## A Dialectical Approach

The notion of reflective practice lies at the heart of our curriculum. Reflective practice encourages the integration of formal, tacit and self-regulative forms of expert knowledge. Effective reflective practice requires several forms of dialogue: between management frameworks and theories and the participant's own work practice and experience; between participants, in order to expose similarities and differences in practice and to conceptualize those differences and similarities in terms of program frameworks; between the participant and members of their own community of practice in the workplace and elsewhere. It also requires participants to work with the tensions between different disciplinary and functional perspectives on management problems. Much of this reflection is structured through assignments and through online collaborative work. Dialogue with faculty also has a role here, although it is important to note that in this program model the tutor role is more that of a facilitator than an instructor.

The approach we describe above (in the diploma program) has at its heart the notion of learning as a dialectical process. The notion of a dialectical approach to learning goes back at least to Socrates: learning advances through questioning and dialogue.[6] In the dialectical approach, learning happens as a consequence of experienced dissonance. The learner is challenged to reconceptualize the world as they encounter tensions between their existing mental models and the evidence and ideas presented to them.

The structure of the program creates several forms of dialectical exchange: between disciplinary perspectives; between theory and practice and between the different learning histories of the participants. We unpack each of these elements in turn below.

### Setting up a Dialectic Between Disciplinary Perspectives

The program is organized around themes rather than disciplinary perspectives. Participants do encounter study materials within a single disciplinary perspective at the level of the study session (about 2½ hours work). However, much of the learning is in the activities and materials that link these sessions. These activities and materials are designed to help participants explore the tensions between perspectives and the implications each perspective may have for the other.

Examples include:

- An activity to surface the different assumptions about human motivation and behavior implicit in a range of financial control systems and a commitment focused approach to human resource management.

- An activity to examine the implications of different value propositions for how operational performance should be understood.

- Using the order management cycle and balanced score card as examples of narrative devices to frame links and tensions between different perspectives on performance.

- Using a case study of a premium hotel to examine tensions and relationships between different aspects of performance.

- An extended case study of the use of the balanced scorecard in a banking organization and the debates it caused about the 'primacy' of financial performance.

- Activities which encourage participants to surface and share the tensions and connections between different performance perspectives in their own organizations.

### A Dialectic Between Theory and Practice

Just as von Clauswitz observed that "no plan survives the first encounter with the enemy" no management theory survives unscathed from an encounter with the messy realities of management practice. For the most part the theories and frameworks we teach in management schools are heuristics and idealized representations of the world which oversimplify in the process of providing a sufficiently abstract representation to apply to many different contexts. There is an inevitable tension between theory and practice, between the general and the specific.

We certainly do not mean to reject management theories as valueless; they provide important conceptual scaffolding on which expertise can be built. Rather we suggest, first, that applying them in a critical and reflective fashion is nontrivial and needs to be an important concern for any management education program. Second, no less important than this conceptual scaffolding, is the body of experiences (one's own and others') which allows participants to expand their ability to recognize, discriminate between and respond to different situations.

Thus an important element in the program we describe is the continual dialectic between the theory and practice of management. The program invites participants to apply their own experience and the experience of fellow participants to a critique of program ideas and to apply program ideas reflectively to their own practice. By engaging in this cycle of theorizing practice and particularizing theory, participants are encouraged to develop their capacity to generalize about their own experiences and to translate ideas and learning into their own situation.

The role in the curriculum of participants' own practice and that of their peers is reflected in the assessment. Their study guide tells them that:

> Through the tasks in the study guide, you will build up a body of knowledge about the practice of management in your own organization and those of other participants You will be asked to draw on this work to answer both [assignments] and exam questions.

As the program proceeds participants engage in a series of activities that involve gathering information in their own organizations and constructing their own "case" to which they are invited to apply program ideas and to reflect on their learning from the process. Where, as is usual, program ideas and practice do not come together neatly participants are invited to critique the ideas. For example, in engaging with the balanced scorecard metaphor, participants are invited to consider how Kaplan and Norton's (1992) framework might need to be modified to be relevant to their own context; to account, for example, for a wider range of stake-holders.

### A Dialectic Between Different Experiences of the World

We have emphasized the importance to learning of the experienced dissonance that arises out of a dialectical approach to teaching. However, personal cognitive schema are often robust and participants are able to employ a range of strategies to preserve existing world views: "of course that is all very well in theory but in the real world …"; "whoever wrote that obviously doesn't understand healthcare/the oil business/retailing/" and so on.

On a full-time face-to-face teaching program with a relatively young group of participants there is an initial process of deskilling as partici-pants find themselves in a novel environment. This provides a window of opportunity to challenge fixed views and assumptions. However, with a program cohort typically in their mid-30s, with a significant level of management experience and actively engaged in the practice of man-agement, existing assumptions, and understandings are often difficult to disturb. This does, though, happen more readily in peer-to-peer relationships. In the learning episode described above, some of the most profound learning happens in the online conference as partici-pants encounter each other's very different understandings of perfor-mance and how it is managed in their different cultures, sectors, and organizations.

## Evaluating the Program

Table 5.3 summarizes responses from end of program evaluation sur-veys for both the current diploma and its predecessor program. The pre-decessor program was more conventionally divided into study modules with a disciplinary focus, rather more didactic in approach and did not employ online collaboration as a principal learning approach.

As can be seen from the table, the new program demonstrates signifi-cant improvements in overall participant satisfaction and achievement of learning objectives including reflection on learning and application of knowledge. A further measure of effectiveness was a decline in participant dropout rate on the program.

The third author carried out an internal evaluation of the program (with colleagues). As part of this evaluation, they tracked the activities of

**Table 5.3.   Comparative Participant Evaluation of Professional Diploma Program**

|  |  | Diploma (2004) | Predecessor Program (2000) |
|---|---|---|---|
| Survey sample $N$ = |  | 86 | 176 |
| Overall satisfaction with program quality | very | 55.3%[a] | 28.0% |
|  | fairly/very | 98.8%[a] | 79.4% |
| Would you recommend the program to another participant | yes | 95.2% | 85.8% |
| Program achieved stated objectives | very | 60.2%[a] | 27.4% |
|  | fairly/very | 98.8%[a] | 85.7% |
| Extent to which you can use the skills learned in own work | very | 48.2%[a] | 30.1% |
|  | fairly/very | 87.9% | 82.7% |
| Developed ability to apply knowledge | very | 51.8%[a] | 21.5% |
|  | fairly/very | 95.2%[a] | 82.0% |
| Developed critical analysis | very | 38.8%[a] | 21.5% |
|  | fairly/very | 85.8% | 77.3% |
| Developed problem solving skills | very | 26.6% | 19.4% |
|  | fairly/very | 79.7% | 75.9% |
| Developed independent learning skills | very | 48.2% | 39.4% |
|  | fairly/very | 91.7%[a] | 80.0% |
| Developed reflection on own learning | very | 35.6%[a] | 18.8% |
|  | fairly/very | 88.1%[a] | 71.2% |
| Developed specialist knowledge | very | 38.1%[a] | 14.8% |
|  | fairly/very | 83.3% | 71.6% |

a - Diploma different to predecessor at $p > 0.95$.

150 program participants in the online conferences over a period of 6 weeks (a period which spanned activity on two assignments); examining both the patterns of participation and the content of discourse in the conferences. [7]

Participants were typically highly engaged in the online activities. The number of postings per working group (of four or five participants) ranged from 204 to 406. One group posted 156 messages in 4 days. These were not just postings for the sake of it—they were substantive and highly articulate discussions of the issues in hand. In reviewing participant postings they were struck by the thoughtful and reflective quality of the postings and the challenging nature of the questions participants posed each other. Tutor intervention was useful in the early stages to motivate discussion and provide structure. However, many participants quickly became adept at weaving together others' contributions, building on them and providing summaries of the discussion so far. Thus they began quickly to structure their own online conversations and learning.

## A Practice-Centered Agenda for Teaching and Research

In this chapter we have argued for necessary modesty about the role of academic knowing and for a more effective understanding of the strengths and limits of practice knowing. In concluding we want to emphasize this approach.

On the one hand, we suggest that many of the assumptions of the academic community about intellectual engagement at master's level are rooted in a model of the master's degree as a preparation for doing research rather than as an enhancement of professional practice. This has led to a dysfunctional approach to understanding the nature of professional postgraduate intellectual engagement in higher education.

This view is shared by Bennis and O'Toole (2005), who argue that:

What professors study, and the way they study it, directly affects the education of MBA candidates. As research-oriented business professors come to dominate B school faculties, they assume responsibility for setting the MBA curriculum. Not surprisingly, they tend to teach what they know.... They are ill at ease subjectively analyzing multifaceted questions of policy and strategy, or examining cases that require judgment based on wisdom and experience in addition to—and sometimes opposed to—isolated facts.... The dirty little secret at most of today's best business schools is that they chiefly serve the faculty's research interests and career goals, with too little regard for the needs of other stakeholders. Serving the business community by educating practitioners and generating knowledge they can use may exist as secondary functions at those institutions, but such objectives are honored mainly in speeches made by deans seeking donations. (Bennis & O'Toole, 2005, pp. 101,103)

On the other hand, we argue that it would be unhelpful to construct a curriculum, purely dominated by practice knowing. The most effective learning experiences for managers will be those that subject their existing understandings to challenge and widen their repertoire of perspectives. Many of us have heard participants or executives preface a claim to understanding with the phrase, 'of course in the real world" As Weick (2001) has argued, the role of the academic is often to challenge such unitary perspectives.

Much of the heat in discussions about bridging the relevance gap comes from the infamous real world. Practitioners who chide academics for their naiveté regarding the "real world" are sometimes people who want *their* real world to be treated as if it were *the* real world. That is not the academic's job. The academic's job is to understand how an idiosyncratic individual world comes to be seen as a universal world and how vested interests work to convey this definition of universality.... [I]f the university continues to stand for wisdom rather than a vocation, character rather than technicalities, and mindfulness rather than rationality, then it will remain a strong partner in a [practice focused] alliance and foster a richer definition of the "context of application. (Weick, 2001, p. 74)

We suggest that the challenge for management educators is to pay attention to both practice relevance and to providing appropriate challenge to program participants' perceptions of the real world.

We have suggested that the route to achieving this combination of relevance and challenge is to see management education as a process of designing learning environments and experiences, not as a process of transmitting a body of knowledge. We have suggested that program participants' previous, current, and shared experiences are a rich resource for learning and argued that rich learning often comes out of the collision between different experiences or "real worlds"; between different perspectives, theories, and practices.

However, such an approach confronts us with some significant challenges. The first challenge might be summarized as "How do we teach what we don't know?" If the job of the management educator is no longer to transmit a body of knowledge contained in their field of expertise then we might expect to hear this question frequently voiced. Rephrasing the question helps. If instead we ask the question "How do we help program participants learn what we don't know?" then we can understand that the answer lies in the nature of the learning environments and experiences we construct for them, or construct with them. Ideas and frameworks from our fields of expertise do not disappear from the learning mix. However, now, rather than being the sum of what is to be learned, these ideas and frameworks provide scaffolding for the learning process.

A second challenge is that as management educators we need a much greater appreciation of the practice of learning design. This implies both personal development (as individual educators develop their own practice knowledge), organizational development (as we understand the institutional supports such approaches require), and development of the field (as we jointly engage in developing our understanding and competence in practice-relevant management education).

We have outlined some parts of the Open University management curriculum, which represent some steps in the direction of practice-focused pedagogy. We believe we have more to learn as we develop our practice further and that this learning should be informed by good research.

There is much more to be understood about the nature of management expertise and how it is developed. There is scope here to draw on some of the excellent existing research on the workplace learning of managers. We should also look to build on ideas from research into other professions and create extensive and well-conceptualized accounts of the mindful practices of management and of ways of learning to be expert in them.

There would be much value in collaborative practitioner learning research in which business schools, and employers sponsoring executive MBA participants, work together to understand how program participants relate program learning to the workplace.

We also need good pedagogic research that examines the realized curriculum, as opposed to the formal curriculum, in a range of management education settings. We need ways of better understanding the gap between what we intend to teach and what is learned.

Finally, we recognize that an important implication is that the realized curriculum will vary from participant to participant. If teaching is about constructing learning environments and experiences, then what is learned is not within the direct control of faculty. Indeed, developments in the use of web technologies mean that, even if universities fail to personalize the curriculum to any great extent, participants can personalize their own learning to an unprecedented and growing degree. This poses interesting challenges for assessment. What is to be assessed and how are standards to be judged? Although one of us is addressing some of these questions (Knight, 2006), we believe there is a need for more research that examines how effectively and usefully to judge the achievements of program participants following a practice-focused curriculum.

We are addressing issues that have considerable intellectual interest and that bear fundamentally on the contribution universities can make to the economic and social well-being of practitioners in for-profit and not-for-profit enterprises. We hope that many more schools will join with us in considering how best to promote high-quality, practice-focused learning that benefits all concerned.

## NOTES

1. We prefer "knowings" on the grounds that "knowledge" is too static and too reified to capture three features: it is provisional, in the sense that it changes; knowing is colored by the settings in which it is active; the interplays between these provisional and dynamic knowings change. "Knowings" better captures these provisional, situated and dynamic elements.

2.  The European Commission (Rennie & Mason, 2004) distinguishes between formal, nonformal, and informal learning. There is no need here to do more than distinguish between formal and nonformal learning.

3.  The Open University makes considerable use of adjunct faculty to support its more than 200,000 geographically dispersed students.

4.  The Open University uses the term "supported open learning" rather than "distance learning" to denote a particular approach to distance learning which commonly includes local support and a high degree of contact between students and tutors.

5.  Each study session is designed to contain about 2½ hours of study with a further 1 to 1½ hours of activities which make links to other sessions and often involve gathering information in participants own organizations or online discussions with other participants

6.  Our use of the idea of dialectic though is perhaps closer to the Hegelian notion of dialectic as a process of dialogue which proceeds through making contradictions and polarities explicit and resolving them through synthesis.

7.  Half of these participants were on the diploma program, the other half were on a precursor certificate program. Typically participants were working in online groups of four or five.

## REFERENCES

Anderson, L. W., & Krathwohl, D. R. (2001). *A taxonomy for learning, teaching and assessment*. New York: Addison Wesley Longman.

Bar-On, R., & Parker, J. (2000). *The Handbook of Emotional Intelligence*. San Francisco: Jossey-Bass.

Becher, T. (1999). *Professional practices: Commitment and capability in a changing environment*. New Brunswick, NJ: Transaction.

Bennis, W. G., & O'Toole, J. (2005). How business schools lost their way. *Harvard Business Review, 83*(5), 96-104.

Bloom, B. S. (1956). *Taxonomy of educational objectives, Handbook 1: Cognitive domain*. London: Longman.

Boyatzis, R. E., & Associates. (1995). *Innovation in professional education*. San Francisco: Jossey-Bass.

Brennan, J., Johnstone, B., Little, B., Shah, T., & Woodley, A. (2001). *The employment of UK graduates: Comparisons with Europe and Japan*. London: The Higher Education Funding Council for England.

Cheetham, G., & Chivers, G. (2005) *Professions, competence and informal learning*. Cheltenham, England: Edadrw Elgar.

Dreyfus, H., & Dreyfus, S. (2005). Expertise in real world contexts. *Organization Studies, 26*(5), 779-792.

Eraut, M. (1994). *Developing professional knowledge and competence*, London: Falmer Press.

Eraut, M. (2000). Non-formal learning and tacit and implicit knowledge in professional work. *British Journal of Educational Psychology, 70*, 113-136.

Fenton-O'Creevy, M. Nicholson, N., Soane, E., & Willman, P. (2004) *Traders: Risks, decisions and management in financial markets.* Oxford, England: Oxford University Press.

Hargreaves, D. (1983) *The challenge of the comprehensive.* London: Routledge and Kegan Paul.

Kaplan, R. S., & Norton, D. P. (1992, Jan/Feb). The balanced scorecard—measures that drive performance. *Harvard Business Review, 70*(1), 71-79.

Knight, P. T. (2006). The local practice of assessment. *Assessment and Evaluation in Higher Education, 31*(4), 435-452.

McCulloch, G., Helsby, G., & Knight, P. T. (2000). *The politics of professionalism.* London: Cassell.

Mintzberg, H. (2004). *Managers not MBAs: A hard look at the soft practice of managing and management development.* San Francisco: Berret-Koehler.

Pascarella, E. T., & Terenzini, P. T. (2005). *How college affects participants: A third decade of research* (Vol. 2). San Francisco: Jossey-Bass.

Rennie, F., & Mason. R. (2004). *The connecticon: Learning for the connected generation.* Greenwich CT: Information Age.

Rickards, T., Hyde, P., & Papamichail, K. N. (2005). The Manchester method: A critical review. In C. Wankel and R. DePhillipi (Eds.), *Educating managers through real world projects* (pp. 241-254). Greenwich, CT: Information Age.

Schön, D. A. (1983). *The reflective practitioner.* New York: Basic Books.

Shulman, L. (1986). Those who understand: Knowledge growth in teaching. *Educational Researcher, 15,* 4-14.

Shulman, M. (1987). Knowledge and teaching foundations of the new reform. *Harvard Education Review, 57*(1), 1-22.

The Quality Assurance Agency for Higher Education. (2002). *Masters awards in business and management.* Retrieved June 28, 2006, from www.qaa.ac.uk/academicinfrastructure/benchmark/masters/mba.pdf

Tuomi-Gröhn, T., Engeström, Y., & Young, M. (Eds.). (2003). *Between school and work: New perspectives on transfer and boundary-crossing.* Amsterdam: Pergamon.

Van der Voort, J. M., Meijs, L. C. P. M., & Whiteman, G. (2005). Creating actionable knowledge: Practicing service learning in a Dutch business school context. In C. Wankel & R. DePhillipi (Eds.), *Educating managers through real world projects* (pp. 149-180). Greenwich, CT: Information Age.

Weick, K. (2001). Gapping the relevance bridge. *British Journal of Management 12*(S1), S71-S75.

Wenger, E. (1998). *Communities of practice. Learning, meaning, and identity.* Cambridge, MA: Cambridge University Press.

CHAPTER 6

# INTERNATIONAL MASTERS PROGRAM IN PRACTICING MANAGEMENT

## Pedagogy of Experienced Reflection and Phenomenon of *Refraction* in Management Learning

**Tunç D. Medeni**

In today's knowledge economy and learning society, learning to be reflective is of great importance for managers. In response to this challenge, Mintzberg and his colleagues have proposed the International Masters Program in Practicing Management (IMPM), which is a next-generation management development/education program based on the innovative pedagogy of "experienced reflection" and managerial mindsets. This chapter is grounded on the perspectives and findings of Mintzberg and his colleagues with IMPM. The incorporation of the phenomenon of "refraction" into the pedagogy of experienced reflection and managerial mindsets is suggested. Managers' learning reflective and refractive mindsets is put forth as a new vision of graduate management education. The interesting implications for management knowledge and knowledge management are discussed such as developing managers who are better at cross-cultural/

*New Visions for Graduate Management Education,* 129–189

contextual communication and knowledge transfer, as well as managing in a more critical and creative manner.

## INTRODUCTION

Generally speaking, one ironic fact about most of the existing graduate management education programs is that the practicing managers who participate in these programs know better than anyone else what they actually do, thus trying to educate them about management would not be very useful, if not actually useless. Most of what is taught in these programs is either highly specific to a context or function, which may or may not be similar to that of the participants, or about issues that make the participants become aware that as practitioners they know these better themselves. These teachings are thus destined to remain just as taught information, but not learned knowledge for the participants. What would be useful enough to take back to their practice could be then learning to make better use of their valuable personal knowledge for the development of their own practice. The aim of a management development/education program would be to show managers "how they should develop a frame of mind that is always learning from the experience of thoughtful action and careful observation, rather than to teach clever ideas and techniques to take them back home" (Gosling & Westall, 2006, p. 1), in other words to "encourage true wisdom rather than information" (Lao Tszu) (Mintzberg, 2004).

This frame of mind for learning, knowing and acting "wisely" is to be highlighted for the so-called knowledge economy and learning society of our times, which, for many, point out to a paradigm change in our ever-evolving civilization (Blunt, 2001; Gamble & Blackwell, 2001; Little, Quintas, & Ray, 2002; Organisation For Economic Co-operation and Development, 2000, 2001). Managers of today face complex problems that come with this paradigm change, or simply change in times, however you would like to see it. They have to deal with new problems or look from a new perspective at existing problems about their environment, employees, structures, and relationships. To complicate matters further, too often they are given only simple solutions to their complex problems. These simplistic solutions usually focus on fragmented parts of an organization rather than the whole, taking little account of any ongoing or possible interaction. While they promise a panacea-like quick fix, one best remedy for all circumstances, such solutions often fail, making the matter even more difficult. Besides, the education typically offered to managers is less about general, real management practices than about out-of-context, separate, specific functions of business. This traditional discipline-based education model is consonant with most of the research undertaken in business schools and the unilateral learning model used in many higher education institutions, which arguably stress the scientific, analytical aspect of management practice in the expense of the craft, practical, as well as artistic, visionary aspects. Individual students are offered a set of standardized courses that, taken together, characterize a particular degree or program, which often is no more than a vague signal to companies recruiting employees. No matter what, in general, the individual and organizational actors in both the demand and supply side of management/business education seem to be comfortable with the current situation (Coghlan, Dromgoole, Joynt, & Sorensen, 2004; Cunha, Cunha, Cabral-Cordoso, 2004; Jackson, 2003; Mintzberg, 2004).

As a sound, viable alternative to the currently available offerings, the IMPM will be the subject of our discussion in this chapter. Proposed as a next-generation management development/education program, the program is based on the innovative pedagogy of managerial mindsets and "experienced reflection." After a summary of the overall IMPM approach, the pedagogical underpinnings of the program will be developed with the introduction of a mindset for refraction beside reflection for management learning and practice. Later, some theoretical and practical implications of this new reflective and refractive mindset will be discussed in the chapter, which will be concluded with comments for future research. As a part of this stimulating book for the new visions of graduate management education, based on our IMPM experience, we specifically have aimed for the development of a conceptual framework that contributes to bridging classroom learning in formal education and actual doing in real practice. Although it may not represent a fully orthodox way of writing, we hope the resulting work will provoke thought and discussion about graduate management education and management learning—or for the education, training, and development of managers (Fox, 1997) in general.

The research about the IMPM case that has resulted in this chapter is a 5-year research project conducted in England and Japan. While the former half in Lancaster University in England has contributed significantly to the presentation of not only the overall framework of the IMPM and management learning but also the development of the conceptual framework about reflection and refraction, the impact of the latter half in JAIST (Japan Advanced Institute of Science and Technology) in Japan can mostly be found in the conceptualizations about knowledge creation and management as well as the most recent practical insights and highlights about the program. In our research of the IMPM case, interviews with not only participants and graduates, but also tutors, who have taken part in the design and delivery of the IMPM, are supported by participant observations, IMPM documents, and literature reviews. Since our findings have been from diverse sources spread over time, we have been careful to use different, compatible methods and data sources in order to be able to triangulate and work on these findings.

Lancaster University is considered to be among the five best management research programs in the world and is well-known, among other things, for its soft systems research, organizational and management learning, leadership, and critical studies. On the other side, JAIST is considered to be the first and only university in the world that has a school for knowledge science that does research on social knowledge science and knowledge systems science. In just one laboratory of this school, research on religion, tourism, community development, disabled or elderly people, university management, and wine production can be found going on together within the comprehensive framework of knowledge management. The school encourages the integration of knowledge science with relevant social sciences and natural sciences. These two universities certainly have their own dominant approaches to knowledge, management, learning, and other concepts as a combination of these three. The integration of these two dominant perspectives from two different cultures has been itself a challenging research task, which, we think, also fits well within the "visions" of this book.

A framework that can integrate different, related but separate fields in social and natural sciences, as well as clarify and unify the different understandings and approaches within the fields of management learning and knowledge management has always been implicit in our research. The abundance of discussions that explain different issues with the same terms or similar issues with different terms, and the absence of satisfactory explanations for some other issues in multidisciplinary fields have been a reason for us to look for concepts from various fields that have more explanatory power, and use them as metaphorical conceptualizations in our discussions for developing a clarifying and unifying framework. These metaphorical conceptualizations also have been in accordance with our research findings, since the program participants and tutors of the IMPM have been benefiting from related metaphors to explain their opinions in the same fashion. One of these metaphors is using a mirror, a physical object, to explain reflection, an individual and social process and outcome. We also will use this metaphor to discuss the reflective mindset in the IMPM, even improve it to argue refraction in nature in order to highlight the importance of creativity, critical thinking, and cross-contextual knowledge transfer, which are crucial concepts in knowledge creation, management, and organizational learning. To support the use of these metaphors, and analogies developed from them, we provide numerous visualizations, as well. These metaphors and visualizations make more possible and visible the incorporation of different social and natural sciences issues into the same picture.

## INTERNATIONAL MASTERS PROGRAM IN PRACTICING MANAGEMENT

In this section, we will discuss the IMPM, providing first a summary of the overall program, while highlighting the unique characteristics like the pedagogy of experienced reflection and managerial mindsets, among others, and then more specific information about the two mindsets, which we have been actively involved in the research of. We hope this discussion will give the reader a good idea of what the IMPM approach is and us a suitable base to further this approach in the following section.

### The Overview of the Program

The IMPM is a collaborative effort by more than five major business schools—Lancaster University in England, McGill University in Canada, Indian Institute of Management in India, INSEAD in France, Hitotsubashi University, JAIST, and Kobe University in Japan and KDI School of Public Policy and Management in Korea—and more than 10 major corporations around the world, including Fujitsu, Matsushita, LG, EDF and Gaz de France, Lufthansa, and The International Federation of Red Cross and Red Crescent Societies. It is

> designed to be the "Next Generation" Masters Program, combining management development with management education. IMPM is a degree program that focuses directly on the development of managers in their own contexts—their jobs and their organizations. The IMPM is therefore deeper than conventional management development programs and more applied than traditional degree programs

(http://www.impm.org/overview.htm). Developed by a worldly consortium of universities and companies, IMPM strikes a good balance between practical and academic implications (Mintzberg, 2004; Pfeffer & Fong 2002; Reingold, 2000).

Detailed information about the program can be found on their Web site (http://www.impm.org). "The IMPM seeks to break the mold of the functional 'silos' so common in management education"—production, marketing, finance, organizational behavior, human resources, strategy, information technology, and so on. Instead, the program is structured around integrated, managerial "mindsets," one for each module:

> Opening in Lancaster with Managing in general and the reflective mindset in particular, the program moves to McGill, where attention turns to Managing Organisations and the analytic mindset. Bangalore follows with Managing Context, the worldly mindset. In Japan and Korea, we take up Managing Relationships, the collaborative mindset. The Program closes at INSEAD with Managing Change, the action mindset.... The Program is spread over a year and a half, encompassing ten weeks in the classroom and two separate weeks on a managerial exchange with a fellow participant. The classroom activity takes place in modules of approximately two weeks at each of the participating schools.... For those participants who wish to receive ... the Masters Degree grows out of the modular program. Papers submitted in the course of the program, including reflections on each of the modules and reports on the Managerial Exchange and the Venture, constitute the main body of work. Degree candidates also prepare a major paper after the final module. This paper can evolve from the experiences of the IMPM, including the Venture in the participating organizations. (Figure 6.1, http://www.impm.org/overview.htm)

According to Mintzberg (2004), pedagogy of experienced reflection can be used in graduate management education programs to help practicing managers make best use of the program. According to this, in the classroom the faculty introduces concepts, and the managers bring their experience, so that learning, and thoughtful reflection at both the indi-

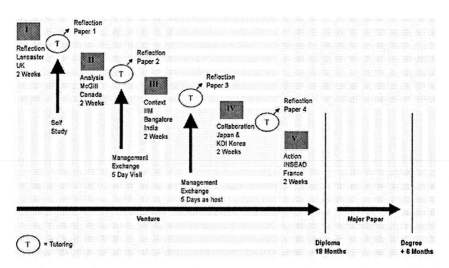

Figure 6.1.   Overview of IMPM.

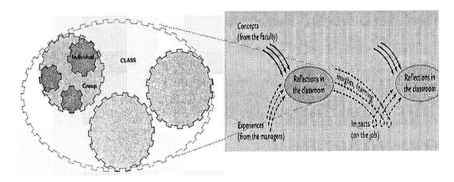

Figure 6.2.    Pedagogy of experienced reflection, adapted from Mintzberg (2004, pp. 256, 265).

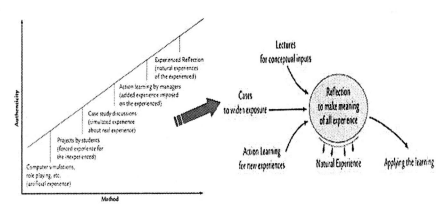

Figure 6.3.    Blending pedagogies for management learning, adapted from Mintzberg (2004, pp. 266, 267.)

vidual and group levels occur where the two meet, which, in return, would presumably generate some beneficial impact in the participants' organizations, as well as future development/education programs (Figure 6.2).

Relying on first-hand reality and reflection on this reality, experienced reflection is claimed to be more effective for management learning than the other existing pedagogical methods as such simulations, projects, case studies, and action learning, ordered respectively with regard to the authenticity level of each method. IMPM proposes to blend these different pedagogies with the natural, real experiences of the managers, which should take central place in the learning process (Figure 6.3).

Ultimately, learning has to be responsive and customized comments Mintzberg.

> It has to be ... blended into a stream of discovery—much like managing itself, where experiences, concepts, and reflections blend together as the manager goes along. And so should this be true of management education, back and forth between the classroom and the job. (Mintzberg, 2004, p. 268)

Besides,

> Close learning (so-called "distance learning," but here labeled from the perspective of the participant) is used to increase the efficiency of the educational process, particularly for learning those aspects of "the language of Management" that can be done in self-study. (http://www.impm.org/innov.htm)

As another innovation of the program, "the seating arrangement in the classroom is designed so that participants can switch easily into instant workshops, allowing discussion of the material presented from the company or other small group point of view." As a result, the educator can take advantage of facing six/eight clusters of people, and not just 25/35 individuals.

The group discussions, and morning reflection sessions at each module enable the practice and development of the introduced mindset. Each participant also spends one week of the program on a managerial exchange observing a fellow participant at work, in as different a setting as possible. That visit is returned, so that each participant acts as both host and guest. Training during the modules prepares everyone to learn about themselves and others through observation. Moreover, all participants work on a venture throughout the program, an activity designed to bring about some substantial change in their organization. Each participant is also provided with a book in which to record insights relating to classroom discussions and reflections on their work. This book is used as a vehicle to share the learning with the class. Finally, between each module participants prepare individual reflection papers (http://www.impm.org/overview.htm, Mintzberg, 2004). These are all important tools for individual and collective reflection that contribute to learning and knowledge creation.

Generally, companies that wish to send four or five participants to a class apply to the program. Entrepreneurs who wish to apply as individuals also are encouraged. Proposals for industry clusters, in which different companies each send one or two participants to make up a group of five are welcomed as well. Normally participants are people in the 35-45-age range destined for positions in senior management.

In IMPM, the reflection, analysis, context, collaboration, and action mindsets of a manager (Gosling & Mintzberg, 2003) together offer a holistic perspective on the practice of management. According to a participating organization, IMPM's design for considering management issues from these five different angles is a unique and effective methodology to enable managers to come to grips with their personal, cultural, and professional identities, which are important for "worldly" managers. As a result, participants deepen their insights on themselves and interact and collaborate with other participants from various countries (Purves, 2006, p. 6), which cannot be effectively facilitated in other management development programs established by companies or universities. This holistic perspective of managerial mindsets also fits well with the principles and practices of organizational learning and knowledge management. The participating managers, for instance, get the chance to learn how to get knowledge and take action with this knowledge for continuous individual and institutional development. Regarding this, reflection helps managers externalize practical experience for the benefit of future action, as well as internalize learning from past action.

As it is commonly stated, the IMPM program gives the participating practitioner "a 'mirror' that lets you see yourself" (Mintzberg & Gosling, 2002), providing a chance to "reflect about yourself as an individual and the way in which you relate to others" (Liu, 2001, Appendix D: "IMPM Personal Appraisal"). In IMPM, if the Lancaster module can be considered to be about looking inward, where individuals get the chance to turn their attention into themselves and reflect upon the outcomes of this personal unfolding experience, then McGill is about looking outward, and Bangalore is about looking outward to see inward (Mintzberg, 2004), and perhaps Kanazawa is about looking inward to see outward. In general, IMPM provides a "playground" for the participants, as one faculty member expresses (Medeni, 2001), where they can take a break from the ongoing life of business and busy-ness, and experience and learn the art of reflection. In this playground, participants get the chance to reconsider their life and think about their career, from past to present and future. Consistently, most participants regard the program as a valuable, even a "life-changing experience" that has had impact beyond their workplace, in their personal and family lives.

An important benefit not only for the individual but also for the organizational participants is "learning to ask the right questions" rather than simply looking for answers to given questions; in other words, as one participant put it (Purves, 2006, p. 8), learning how to catch fish rather than simply getting a caught fish. Kaz Mishina stresses this issue of questioning the taken for granted, and challenging the given or extant as well:

> Before participation, executives tended to regard their organisation as a given. After the intense immersion in each module, they were newly motivated to put what they felt and thought in to practice in the context of their own jobs. As we selected middle management to send to IMPM, they had to grasp the challenge of changing the organisation, as well as influencing upper management. Even during the 16 months of the program, they spent most of the time in the workplace. As a result, they were forced to be reflective about their job and its context. (Purves, p. 6)

The importance of having the opportunity to ask and receive good questions is also highlighted in the comments about "field studies," visits to the local operations of the companies represented in the class, which are not passive tours but active investigations on a subject related to the module. "Participants from the companies frequently praise the insightfulness of their colleagues' comments, while people interviewed back in the companies often comment on how much they learned simply from the questions they were asked." For instance, "Why don't we ask each other those simple questions?" was the remark of a manager (Mintzberg, 2004, p. 298). The ability to ask the right questions highlights the potential for the transfer of learning, and change (Belfer, 2004), and developing this capability is crucial for not only the individual but also the organization in order to leverage human capital within a strategic human resource management and development framework.

The ventures and theses of the participants are especially important in facilitating knowledge transfer between the education program and the company, as well. For instance in a participating company, a company executive sponsor works with the participants and the IMPM tutor in the venture and thesis, linking the learning to the company's "burning strategic themes." However, not all companies have been satisfied with their performance for integrating individual and organizational development after the program (Purves, 2006). This dissatisfaction can be found in the comments of the individual participants like Jane McCroary, as well: "The biggest criticism of the IMPM is the shortfall on behalf of the companies. The companies hadn't worked out what to do with the participants on their return" (McCroary, Chinwalla, & Guthrie, 2006, p. 7). IMPM and the companies together continuously look for ways to enhance the "impact" after the program, for instance by using organizational and technological tools to enable the interaction of program participants and graduates with each other and with people connected to the program or their companies (Mintzberg, 2004; Purves, 2006). Specific situations where participants thought the impact of the IMPM has been realized also can be found in Jane McCroary comments: "Of all the companies who were involved, I would say the Japanese companies did the best job. For example, one company created a knowledge institute in which the IMPM learning could be shared." (McCroary, Chinwalla, & Guthrie, p. 8) Still, on the other side, for instance, a Japanese graduates we have talked acknowledges that it is not easy to apply what has been learned in the IMPM to the workplace and real life after the program. At the end, in general, it would be true to note that, when asked, graduates and participants agree on the general usefulness of the program, or confirm program's usefulness for their personal development; however, their responses are less positive about the direct benefits of the program for organizational development, improvements in workplace practices.

## The Reflective and Collaborative Mindsets—Managing Self and Relationships

Having provided general information about IMPM and the mindsets, now we would like to give some more specific information about the two of these mindsets and the modules they are taught that we have studied closely. Among these two, the reflective mindset module in Lancaster is more associated with organizational learning and can be seen to be the core of the Mintzberg's propositions for management development and IMPM provided above. The other one, the collaborative mindset module is more associated with knowledge management, reflecting Japanese concepts like organizational knowledge creation and "*ba*," which will be discussed as the following.

### The Reflective Mindset

Reflective Mindset—Managing Self, the first module of the IMPM program in the U.K. functions effectively to build the basics of the program. It encourages the participating manager to think about and question themselves as well as their jobs, relationships, organizations, and society. The Lancaster module brings together the spiritual, historical, cultural, and commercial elements of the contextual content for experiencing and learning the art of reflective practice (Mintzberg, 2004). A theater workshop to appreciate the nature of spontaneous interaction, when creative and open-ended objectives are sought; "pilgrimage" to a pagan site, a Buddhist monastery, and a Christian Church; visits to a cotton mill, and knowledge-intensive-firm; trip to Lake District and its beautiful gardens all contribute to this experience and learning. The theoretical and practical content, educational methods, and supports provided by the module become a significant experience for participants to trace the currently evolving knowledge economy and society back to its roots in preindustrial times, enabling them to investigate the circumstancing conditions for their work, identity and life—their place in the given context.

When the program moves on, the reflective mindset also continues to be practiced and developed in the other modules. For instance, when in Japan for the collaborative mindset module, Kenrokuen Garden (Kanazawa's Garden of Six Sublimities) and the 21st Century Museum of Contemporary Art, Kanazawa are two good places, where participants can discover traditional and contemporary Japanese conceptualizations of reflection, as one of the many dualities and dialects that distinguish Japan.

Traditional Mediterranean-and-Asian-oriented belief systems include in their teachings (such as the humanistic mysticism and sufism of the thirteenth-fourteenth philosopher and poet, Yunus Emre, 1989, http://www.turkishculture.org/philosophers/yunus_emre_humanism.html and http://www.lightmillennium.org/2006_17th/thalman_yemre_p1.html), that what is created in nature is the reflection of the creative force. Another way to explain this is finding the macrocosmos in the microcosmos. Accordingly created one can become one with the creating one. Through reflection at a deeper, more spiritual level, that is, looking inward to see outward or outward to see inward through meditation and contemplation, feeling as a part of the collective existence and realizing how one's self is related with the bigger scheme of events would be possible. A relaxing walk in Kenrokuen is also a suitable way to experience the search for this finding and realization (Hendy, 2001). On the other side, the 21st Century Museum of Contemporary Art provides a special, *state-of-the-art*, space for a reflective mindset in a new society and economy, which, we believe, deserves a closer look.

### 21st Century Museum of Contemporary Art, Kanazawa, a "device" for Reflection

Established in 2004, 21st Century Museum of Contemporary Art, Kanazawa is designed to be a "device" that transcends its function as a museum space to offer a range of information and program experiences to stimulate and engineer visitors' awareness. The design of the museum space integrates with the program so that the museum design itself *"reprograms"* individual experiences into something unique.

Circular in form, the museum building has no front or back, leaving it free to be explored from all directions. The design that "allows the visitor to decide on the route that he/she is going to take through the museum, combined with the flexible gallery rooms that can adapt to every type of media," and the "transparent corridors that offer a clear view of the entire museum space, encourage 'coexistence' in which individual visitors

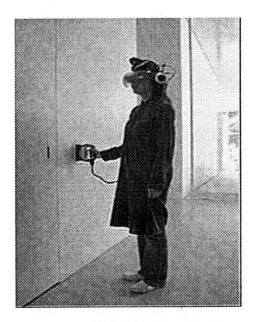

Figure 6.4.    SYS017 (Mathieu Briand).

remain autonomous while sharing personal space with others." This is "open art" for a

> co-creative relation in which viewers participate not only in the creative process but also in the production of meaning.... The works spill out from one exhibition space to another and scatter, expanding out into the encompassing circular space.... Within this circuit, the spatial orientation such as front and back, above and below, and linear progression of time, and even, gravity are all lost. Instead, an unknown sensibility will be extracted.... At the end, every visitor would utter a different story, a different experience. (21st Century Museum, 2004, p. 11)

The programs would provide opportunities for every visitor to not only deconstruct the perception of "self" but also encounter his or her "unknown self."

Figures 6.4, 6.5, 6.6, and 6.7 are chosen examples of works incorporated into the building itself, designed to contribute to this unique reflective encounter. In Leandro Erlich's "Swimming Pool," the visitor can see what lies below the surface by walking down the stairs located in another section of the gallery. A mock pool is installed in the light court just inside the entrance. The layer of water covers a sheet of glass, while the pool below the glass is empty. In this work, those standing below the pool and

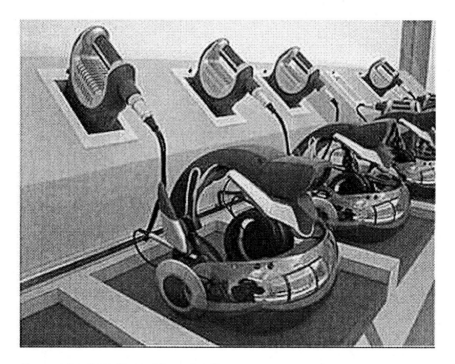

Figure 6.5.    SYS017 (Mathieu Briand).

those looking down at the pool encounter each other through the surface of the water (Figures 6.6, 6.7). Mathieu Briand has produced "SYS017" a futuristic work featuring visual communication. Visitors wear headsets of the sort seen in animation, and experience each other's perceptions by manually plugging and unplugging jacks (Figure 6.4, 6.5).

The 21st Century Museum of Contemporary Art, Kanazawa *dreams* of a time when anyone can become a curator, a time when anyone can decide on what is of value and show works based on their own criteria. The resources of the museum would become a device that can transcend a non-Western perspective focusing on values that are different from twentieth century Western modernism, driven by the three M's of "Man," "Money" and "Materialism" instead committing to a deep and strong involvement with society and the world at large while continuing to generate different values—with the replacement of these three M's with the three C's of "Consciousness," "Collective Intelligence" and "Co-existence." "The museum is an enormous catalytic 'device,' the purpose of which is to convey the 'psychological products' of these three C's to visitors, to ensure their effect and to revitalize everyone that comes into con-

Figure 6.6.   Swimming Pool (Leandro Erlich).

tact with the museum." For further information about this interesting museum in Kanazawa, where the collaborative mindset module is actually held, interested readers also could visit the museum Web site (http://www.kanazawa21.jp/en/). In Kanazawa, Japan, the main focus is for the learning of the collaborative mindset; however, the module could significantly contribute to the learning and practice of the reflective mindset, as well.

### The Collaborative Mindset

The collaborative mindset that participants learn for managing relationships in Japan and Korea is the fourth module of the IMPM program, interchangeably called the collaborative mindset or managing relationships module. Associated with a collaborative mindset, thus the relational aspects in management practice and development also need to be emphasized. On an organizational level, this emphasis mainly results from the increasing recognition that business processes are becoming more interorganizational and that competition is more network based than individual firm based. As organizations become more intercon-

Figure 6.7.   Swimming Pool (Leandro Erlich).

nected, they also become more cross-functional and cross-cultural, which also has implications at the individual level. It is suggested that individual managers need the necessary skills to connect upper and lower hierarchical levels, as well as to understand their peers, managers of other functional areas. They also should learn how to relate the matters they deal with to others and consider the impacts of their actions on other parties. The Japanese term *ba*, the shared space/context, which could be real, virtual or mental, for relationship building and knowledge creation (Von Krogh, Ichijo, & Nonaka, 2000), care, trust, and the tacit knowledge embedded in the social context and relations are perhaps the most important elements for comprehending and explaining the collaborative mindset for managing relationships in organizational and social life (Nonaka, Toyama, & Konno, 2000).

In June 2005, around 25 IMPM participants came to Japan to learn about Japanese management, and knowledge management practices as well as the traditional and contemporary aspects of Japanese culture. They learned about the unique characteristics of Japanese companies like Toyota and Honda that make them successful in their own special KM way. Through lectures and field studies, participants also got the chance to learn about innovative practices in other Japanese companies that are smaller, operate in the service sector, or in rapidly-changing markets, and about still other companies whose developed products are not doing as well as their competition.

This year, participants also visited a newly established office of a participating company to see some of the major points of Japanese academicians and practitioners in practice. This new office provides a new way of working in which a nonterritorial working environment, supported by state-of-the-art information and security technology, enhances knowledge-based collaboration for better customer service and company performance. According to this new work style, there are no personal spaces like desks or cubicles, but all the employees share a common space where all the facilities necessary for working individually or collectively are ready for use. Thus the whole building can be imagined as a fascinating example of a big physical *ba* (although whether the provision of the physical and technological infrastructure would be sufficient for cultivating the necessary conditions for successful strategic knowledge management is another question). Furthermore, some important aspects of the original concept have been developed by a leading manager while he was participating in one of the development programs of the corporate university, to which also IMPM belongs. Thus this is also a good example of the organizational development as a result of knowledge transfer from a management development program.

There are other interesting cases in which company practices and academic concepts about collaboration, organizational development, and knowledge creation also could contribute significantly to the individual and organizational learning of participating individuals and their companies. One participant interviewed pointed out the stimulating interlink between the pyramid of knowledge hierarchy (data→information→knowledge→wisdom) and the pyramid of organization hierarchy (management trainees and apprentices→lower level managers→middle managers→top managers), and he was going to suggest to his company that it could benefit from this interlink to improve their management development programs. This means managers at different organizational levels should learn about the management of the knowledge type relevant to their management level.[1]

Japanese companies are especially good at seeing how *ba* works well within organizations. When the program moves to Korea, the focus of the module also moves to learning about interorganizational *ba*. In fact, *ba* has been one of the most important themes for the fourth module (Mintzberg, 2004). Kanazawa City in Ishikawa Prefecture, Japan, where Kitaro Nishida—the Japanese philosopher who proposed this concept—used to live, and where his teachings still live, provides a good *ba* for IMPM. The concepts introduced and organizations visited, complemented by the experiences of onsen (hot springs), karaoke and "nomination" (socialization occasions for drinking and communication—*nomi* means drink in Japanese) help participants appreciate the complex collaborative relations that exist in Japanese culture. Kenrokuen Garden (Kanazawa's Garden of Six Sublimities) and the 21st Century Contemporary Art Museum are also two good places to visit as a part of the module.

Generally speaking, this is a striking experience for participants coming from Western cultures.

> It has long been the case that if you give a non-Japanese with experience of Japan an opportunity to talk about the Japanese they will always do so. For some reason, Japan has always been a particularly illuminating mirror in which to contemplate cultural difference. And as a one-time resident of Japan I suspect the Japanese quite enjoy this look-you role. The participants (Japanese and non-Japanese) were also eager to contribute their observations. (McCroary, Chinwalla, & Guthrie, 2006, p. 12)

For Japanese, it is a chance to step back, stand aside from their usual practice, and reflect as an outsider about what they are normally immersed in. Some interesting comments about Japanese participants and Japan from other participants follow.

> In Japan, it may be the opposite, but on the program they were just like you and me, but in the corporate setting they are very different, the environment puts a lot of pressure on them.

> The Japanese derived a lot benefit given their closed structure.

> For the Japanese it was almost like a vacation. It was a big relief for them from all that rush and sense of duty and they just took advantage of this time to themselves.

All the participants are exposed to real Japanese practices as much as possible, following the pathways of "breathing the local air," "seeing is believing," or embodied knowledge. In general, recognizing the importance of tacit, collective, contextual knowledge in addition to explicit, individual knowledge is an important outcome of the module. Furthermore, the facilitated interaction between tacit and explicit knowledge is what makes knowledge creation occur in practice, as a result of not only individual but also group, organizational or interorganizational processes (Nonaka & Takeuchi, 1995). New knowledge is created through the synthesizing interplay between these dialectical dualities, tacit↔explicit, individual↔social, action↔cognition and others. Finally, *ba* is a good place to facilitate this knowledge-creating process as a collective, shared context among individuals within a company or an education program (Nonaka & Teece, 2001; Nonaka, Toyama, & Konno, 2000). Lectures from academicians and practitioners, reflection sessions, and field studies facilitate the participants' learning of these principles and practices.

According to one participant; "perhaps *ba* best describes IMPM, and most IMPM participants would nod in agreement, comfortable and confident in doing so," (McCroary, Chinwalla, & Guthrie, 2006, p. 14) This description also matches well with the relationship-cultivating and building aspect of *ba*. It is also realized that "communication is not only through language, and not only about explicit items of knowledge" but also tacit aspects, sharing the same context (Baker, Jensen, & Kolb, 2002), "using the 'here and now' experience of joining the programme as learning material and building the learning community" (Gosling & Westall, 2006, p. 3). In fact the *communities of practice* (Wenger, 1998) and *learning* complements well the *ba* created in the IMPM and the collaborative mindset module, since the dynamic interaction between tacit and explicit knowledge, or the interplay between knowledge and knowing (Cook & Brown, 1999) can be matched well with the mutual existence of learning and practice, or the duality of *reification* and *participation* in communities of practice (Medeni, 2005).

For interested readers, further information about the content and dynamics of the module can be found in Mintzberg's book *Managers Not MBAs* (2004) and IMPM Web site (http://www.impm.org/overview.htm). However, in this chapter what we would like to do next is furthering the core reflective mindset by incorporating our own perspective of reflection, and a complementing concept of "refraction" for management learning and knowledge (Burgoyne & Reynolds, 1997; Fox, 1997; Griseri, 2002).[2]

## CONCEPTUALIZING AND COMPREHENDING REFLECTION AND *REFRACTION*, MOVING TOWARD A "REFRACTIVE MINDSET?"

We can define the art of reflection as the act of contemplating and articulating otherwise tacit past experience and future purpose for present practice that is perceived within a context shaping and shaped by the individual or collective actions. We should try to reflect on what (including how, why, etc.) we are doing at present in our relationships with others, with a perspective on both the past and the future (Medeni, 2001, 2004; Mintzberg, 2004; Schön, 1983; Usher, 1985; Weick, 1995). This section explains in more detail the definition of reflection we have developed as a result of our research, and then offers a complementing refractive mindset, mostly using natural phenomena as metaphors to explain social phenomena. A model development to use the enriched reflective mindset to explain management learning will also be proposed for consideration, which will be followed by some theoretical and practical implications.

## Reflection

Some explanation of how learning about a reflective mindset could be influential as such can perhaps be found in the conceptualization of reflection, within management learning and the IMPM. Reflection is a significant concept for making sense of, learning about, knowing, acting; creating, and transferring knowledge. This vast range of conceptualizations also makes different interpretations and derivations of the concept possible. The comprehension of reflection can come from sources as various as psychoanalysis, physics, religion, and social movement theories, as well as from different levels, from intraindividual to intersocial.

Briefly, we have discussed about the spiritual and religious perception of reflection above, and will discuss the emancipatory nature of reflection, which can move societies, when we discuss refraction. However, now looking at Figure 6.8 (http://www.liverpoolmuseums.org.uk/walker/collections/20c/Waterhouse.asp), we can provide an easy explanation about the physical reflection, which we commonly come across in our daily lives, such as the image of the young man on the surface of the water. However, there is more to this, if we recognize this picture as "Echo and Narcissus" painted by John William Waterhouse (1849-1917). While a mirror image is a reflection we perceive with our eyes, an echo is a reflection we perceive with our ears. Furthermore, according to the myth: Narcissus falls in love with his self, his own reflection on the water; and finally dies, trapped by an obsession with his own beauty; where he dies, narcissus flowers grow. Finding their roots in such mythological stories or other works of the classical age, psychology and psychoanalysis make use of reflection as well, such as in the works of Lacan, or in transactional analysis. Similar links between the natural world and the social world provide rich sources of metaphorical relations to explain and use the concept of reflection, such as in the picture by Javad Alizadeh (Figure 6.9, http://www.javad.8m.com/photo.html). With regard to this, in the IMPM, one of the important aspects of the reflection concept is that it is not limited to past experience. Together with past one can reflect on future, for instance about one's purposes or plans to reach these purposes. By reflecting past and future, then present experience can be "unfolded," with respect to the original meaning of the word, "re-flect."

Management of self-knowledge through reflection is important and there are personal ways to reflect on our own selves. For instance, to use a

Figure 6.8.    Echo and Narcissus.

physical metaphor, consider a person inside a room looking out from a glass window at twilight. As it gradually gets dark the window glass turns into a mirror, reflecting the person together with the surroundings, rather than what exists outside. In daily life, keeping a diary, a morning run, taking time off for a trip to a place that has not been visited before or for a long time, or a relaxing shower can all contribute to personal reflection. Similarly, field trips, reflection papers, insight books are among the tools that are used in IMPM for personal reflection. Furthermore, it is also important to consider reflection as a collective act that includes other people. This inclusion of others can be at different levels such as considering self-knowledge in relation with others, or assuming social responsibility for contributing to the reflective act of others and learn from their reflections. In the same sense, we can also reflect on ourselves using another person as a mirror. In the story of Echo and Narcissus, Echo, who falls in love with Narcissus does not hesitate to assume the role of the reflected image of the man she loves and echoes back what Narcissus tells to his beloved image in order to win his heart. The same logic applies using another context as a mirror to reflect upon our own context, as when, for instance, we visit a different place or the same place at different times. Reflective debriefing discussions or the Management Exchange program are very good examples of this collective reflection, when, using

Figure 6.9.   Future and past are relative.

other persons as mirrors, participants get the chance to reflect on themselves and others.

## Reflection and Refraction

In general, reflection and reflective mindset is a useful concept for management learning and professional/practitioner development and training (Moon, 1999, 2004; Taylor, 2006), but there are other related issues that can be better explained with the concept of refraction beside reflection. For instance, we previously said that in general, one of the most important things that participants learn from the IMPM is how to ask the right questions, which can be linked with critical and creative skills for problem solving, being able to think out-of-box or nonlinearly

Figure 6.10.   Refraction in
water.

where "everyone else" thinks in-box or in a linear fashion. And, this
nonlinear, critical, and creative thinking associates more with refraction
than reflection. Thus, a closer look at refraction would be helpful to
understand issues related with reflection. To explain refraction we would
like to give two examples, again from the physical world.

First, if we look at Figure 6.10, the human perception of a break in the
straw in a glass of water is a good example of being able to see nonlinearly. This could be interpreted as the ability to think in a nonlinear but
rational fashion through refraction. The other interpretation, the ratio-
nalized misperception of something actually linear, is another issue. Our
mind has the tendency to simply perceive the course of light in a linear
fashion, even if the course of light passes through different contexts. As a
result, we mistakenly see a break in the straw. This simple misperception
based on linearity is common in our thinking and decision making. Figure 6.11 shows us a natural phenomenon we observe in optical prisms,
the refraction of sunlight. Just as white light turns into different colors as
it travels through and out of the prism, refraction can help individuals to
think colorfully and creatively, to become able to see the true different
colors that construct the white, among others who can see only the visible
white. Another optic instrument can then be used to convert the split col-

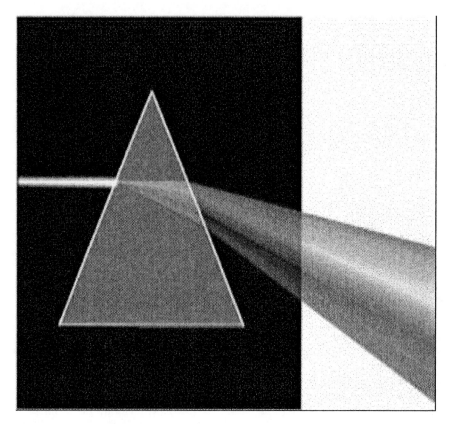

Figure 6.11.   Refraction in prism.

ors into one, maintaining the continuity of the phenomenon without reducing it into separate pieces, unless this separation would be done deliberately, for, for instance, analytical purposes. In fact, by nature, reflection and refraction exist together, and can be conceptualized with respect to each other, with their special cases, such as the total internal reflection as an "ideal" refraction in fiber optics, as well as practical complications, an everyday example of which is seeing our reflection when we walk by a store window. Thus, reflection can be understood better by considering refraction, and we should use both of these concepts together.

We suggest that beside reflection, refraction is also an important concept for management learning. Reflection and refraction together can play an important role in the transfer of learning and knowledge from one context to another. Here temporal and spatial concerns are very important, together with human perceptions and misperceptions, which are exemplified by the above examples of the prism and the straw in a glass of water. When we deal with the transfer of data and information, a simple linear understanding of reflection and refraction can be sufficient, as in fiber optics, but when it comes to the creation and transfer of knowledge from one context to another, the situation becomes more complex and chaotic, necessitating a nonlinear, multidimensional explanation resembling perhaps a continuous spiral as in the knowledge-creation model of Nonaka and Takeuchi (1995), butterfly flapping of Lorenz's Attractor, or the infinity symbol. The IMPM program also recognizes the necessity of dealing in the right way with the complex nature of knowledge transfer and, to a certain extent, facilitates the transfer of knowledge, learning, and experience of participants from workplace to the program and then back again to the work. Theses and ventures are important examples to facilitate the knowledge transfer between the education program and the organization. For instance, as discussed above, in participating organizations, an executive sponsor works with the participants and the IMPM tutor in the venture and thesis, linking the learning to the company's strategic priorities, or "burning strategic themes" (Purves, 2006, p. 11).

Besides, reflective and refractive interactions are equally important, when we consider individuals as agents and actors in their actual work and personal life, or members of their respective communities of practice, or of work groups and other social formations. Moreover, the free and creative thinking associated with reflection and refraction coincides with the "emancipatory" nature of the term, as an important social dimension. This stresses being critical and evaluative towards an outcome that is transformative and liberating in effect, not only for the individual but also for society (Habermas, 1973, 1972; Mezirow, 1990; Reynolds, 1998). That critical aspect of reflection is also encouraged in the reflective mindset at the IMPM, although there is contradictory evidence about whether the program is able to produce successful results on this (Liu, 2001).

To what extend is the IMPM successful for the learning of reflection, and how the pedagogy of experienced reflection can be improved are also issues of discussion for the faculty and researchers of the IMPM. For instance, IMPM's "Management Exchange" program, in which participants pair up and spend a week at each other's work place, provides an enabling tool for personal and collective reflection. Within this program, each individual acts as a mirror for the other. In this way, one gets the chance to see one's own experience through the eyes of another. The faculty (Western & Gosling, 2006) identifies three stages within this reflective learning experience: (1) "Acquiring Knowledge," (2) Reflective Thinking," and (3) "New Mindsets." The flow of learning in the Management

Exchange leads to emergent thinking, imagination and creativity in the third stage, although not all the participants manage to cross the boundary between the reflective thinking and this emergent thinking, and reach the higher part of the evolving new mindsets. Furthermore, Liu (2001) and Medeni (2001) argue that a more critical and creative perspective could be developed for a reflective mindset, which then could be incorporated into the philosophy and practice of the IMPM program and its reflective mindset module.

One of the reasons of this contradictory evidence, and discussions can be found in the conceptualization of the IMPM reflective mindset that does not make an explicit distinction between reflection and refraction, while incorporating some of the discussions about refraction into those of reflection. In the same fashion, in general, it is unusual to have discussions about refraction, when we talk about a reflective mindset or reflective learning and practice, although refraction is an important concept for management learning, beside reflection. Refractive issues either remain unnoticed or incorporated into the conceptualizations of reflection. Examples of this can be found in Moon's classification of Best Possible Representation of Learning (1999); or in the title of an e-Portfolio Conference (2004), "Reflection Is Not a Mirror, It's a Lens," which works by refraction. On the other hand, the two concepts can be distinguished, for instance by associating reflection with being able to see things as they are, while refraction with seeing things differently, both of which are important. Nevertheless, it would be useful to consider reflection and refraction together, and complementing each other in order to make our general point and develop our discussion for management learning and reflective mindset. What is next in our discussion will be the development of a model based on the above conceptualization of reflection (and thus refraction).

## Model Development for a Reflective and Refractive Mindset

We continue our discussion with the development of a conceptual modeling for reflection and refraction that are seen as the bridging dynamic between practice and learning. In order to do this, we will introduce different elements of the model one by one, and then combine all these elements in the overall model.

For the development of the model, first metaphorically we will use the geometric characteristics of an ellipse. Forming around the interplay and the duality of concepts like practice and learning, we visualize an ellipse that is drawn over two center points of practice (or action) and learning (or knowing), as in Figure 6.12. This visualization is in contrast to a circle, which is drawn over one center, and used for the formulation of various models about learning, learning by doing (or doing by learning), management pedagogy and practice (Kolb, 1984). Following a bifocal approach and placing the learning, and practice as the two locus points of an ellipse metaphorically exhibits the inseparable, equally important roles they play in relation to each other. In the ellipse, the sum of the distances between any point on the plane curve and the fixed points is constant. In our ellipse of practice and learning, this also means that whatever is done in reality always consists of some action and some learning, although their ratio could be different[3] (Medeni, 2005).

Second, we will benefit from the geometric representation of the relationship between an independent variable such as time and dependent variable as such outcome in order to visualize the process, and the product of this process for both the practice and learning. The main point of such 2 x 2 representation would be that both process and product could be attainable at the same time.[4] The process as well as outcome of practice, and learning is important (Figure 6.13).

Third, we use the organizational knowledge creation model of Nonaka and Takeuchi (1995). According to this model, the continuous and dynamic interaction between tacit and explicit knowledge that happens at the individual, group, organizational, and interorganizational levels can be significant for the sustainable development of any social setting. Nonaka and Takeuchi follow the distinction of Polanyi (1966) between tacit and explicit knowledge: Tacit knowledge is personal, context specific, and therefore hard to formalize and communicate. Tacit-explicit knowledge interaction is identified as the epistemological aspect, while the interactions among the different levels (individual, group and organization, interorganizational) correspond to the ontological aspect of the model. When the authors first introduced their model; at the epistemology level they identified four distinctive interactions between tacit and explicit knowledge: socialization, externalization, combination, and internalization. Socialization is the process of creating tacit knowledge from tacit knowledge, whereas externalization is that of articulating tacit knowledge into explicit concepts. Combination involves the process of systemizing concepts into an explicit knowledge system. Internalization is a process of embodying explicit knowledge into tacit knowledge (Figure 6.14).

Finally, between practice and learning we will draw a border-like object that allows transfer between each side in the form of reflection or refraction, such as a special lens or membrane. Then, when we integrate all the

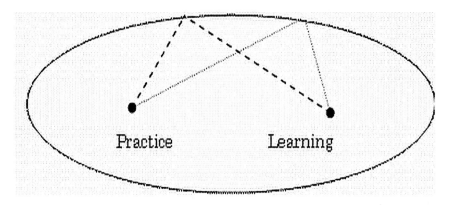

Figure 6.12.   Practice and learning ellipse.

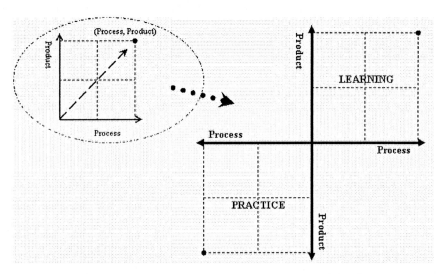

Figure 6.13.   Process and product of practice and learning, adapted from Medeni (2001).

above components, the result is a reflective (and refractive) mindset, which is shown in the Figure 6.15.

The resulting figure provides a useful expression for the role of reflection and refraction in constructing the continuous, unbreakable bond and interaction between learning and practice that is established through knowledge creation. Moving along the practice and learning ellipse, which underlines the inseparable roles of action and learning in real life, means to get involved with the process of learning or practice,

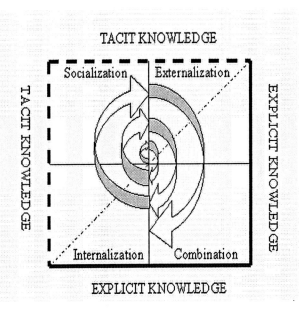

Figure 6.14.   Model of tacit explicit knowledge conversion and knowledge creation spiral, adapted from Nonaka and Takeuchi (1995).

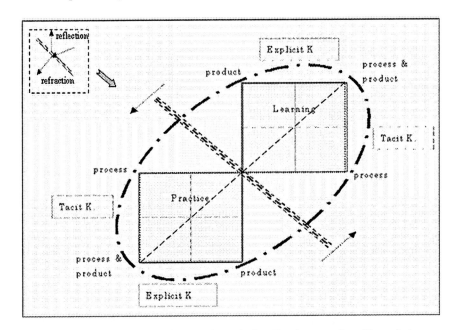

Figure 6.15.   A reflective and refractive mindset for the transfer of knowledge between practice and learning, adapted from Medeni (2001).

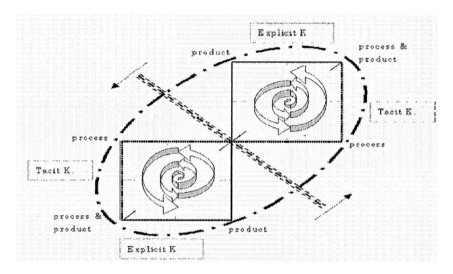

Figure 6.16.   The two knowledge spirals in the reflective and refractive mindset.

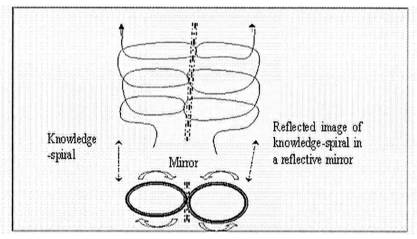

Figure 6.17.   Knowledge-Creation spiral and its reflection as a 3D and 2D image.

as a process of knowledge creation, which, at first stage, is tacit. Then, ideally the products come out of these processes of learning and practice, while tacit knowing and knowledge are externalized into more explicit, tangible forms. Later, even if the processes of learning and practice end, their products are retained. Finally, these products are/can be transferred with a reflective and refractive object to be included into the processes of each other., which completes one turn of the movement along the ellipse and restarts a second turn for establishing the knowledge transfer between practice and learning through reflection and refraction. In fact, what is behind the establishment of this movement and interaction continuity is the existence of two knowledge creating spirals on the two sides of the reflective/refractive object, as seen in Figure 6.16.

### The Role of Reflection (and Refraction) in the Interaction Between the two Knowledge Creation Spirals

As we have seen above, there are two knowledge-creating spirals, interdependent of each other, one for learning and the second for practice. Their interdependence is constructed by reflection and refraction, which enables the transfer of knowledge from learning to practice or vice versa. From another perspective, the knowledge spirals could be the reflection and refraction of one another.

For instance, Figure 6.17 exhibits the conceptualization of one knowledge spiral as a simple reflection of the other in a reflective object like mirror (Medeni & Medeni, 2004). The upper part of Figure 6.17 is a 3D visualization, while the bottom part is a 2D projection on a plain surface. The upward spiral in 3D looks like an endless cyclic movement in 2D. Finally, the cyclic movement in the left spiral/circle is *clockwise*, whereas in the right spiral/circle, it is *anticlockwise*, which together creates a continuous horizontal-8 figure, resembling the infinity symbol, in 2D. This figure in fact recalls the image shown in Figure 6.9, which exhibits past and future relative to, and as a reflection of each other. What is also worth noting is that the conceptualization of reflection here is not only the reflection of a physical object, but the metaphorical reflection of a knowledge-creating process that proceeds in time and produces an outcome, as well, as we have discussed above. Accordingly, if the clockwise move symbolizes the natural proceeding of time from past to present and future, then its reflected image, the anticlockwise move, symbolizes the reversed flow of time from future to past, while reflection plays the role of establishing the link between these two flows, that is, making use of the reversed flow in order to make sense of the real flow, which could be one interpretation of reflection. Leaving this interpretation aside, what the above figure implies is that the two knowledge-creating spirals of practice and learning are simply conceptualized as one knowledge-creating spiral and its reflected image, while their interdependence is the mere result of an exact, one-to-one reflection. However, such reflection would exhibit a simplified or ideal case, as it is more realistic to think that the reflection would be mostly

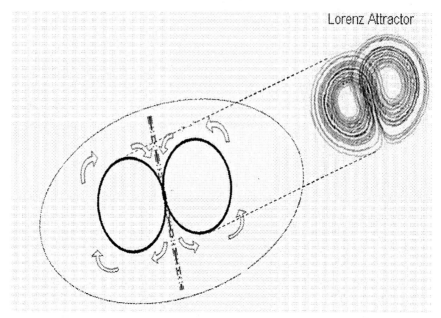

Figure 6.18.   The resemblance of reflected knowledge-spirals of learning and practice with Lorenz Attractor.

refracted, and these refracted reflections would replace any exact linear correspondence with more dynamic, nonlinear approximations.

### Reflective and Refractive Mindset as a Chaotic System

In our modeling, reflection and refraction construct the practice-learning link and interaction, which includes concerns like what we learn from practice, how we apply our learning into action, or how we construct our knowledge, and accumulate our experience. These concerns highlight that how we reflect and refract is not simple, but a lot more dynamic, and chaotic; and a modeling about reflection and refraction should address this creative chaos. In fact, the inclusion of refraction within the conceptualization of reflection is an initial premise for such a nonlinear, more dynamic modeling. Then, considering learning and practice as two interdependent knowledge-creating spirals that are reflected and refracted on each other is a stepping-stone that can be used to establish a complex system of reflective and refractive mindset. In fact, interestingly, the reflected (and refracted) knowledge spirals of learning and practice resemble the butterfly flaps of the Lorenz Attractor, as an indicator for the existence of such a chaotic system for a reflective and refractive mindset (Figure 6.18).

With respect to this, a reflective and refractive mindset is modeled as a chaotic system, whereas learning and practice are conceptualized as the two attractors, to which the system evolves after a long enough time. Within this system, reflection and refraction establishes the link and the continuity between the two knowledge-creating spirals that over time converge to their chaotic attractors of learning and practice.

### Refraction for Management Learning and Knowledge Creation

We would like to conclude our discussion with one final remark for distinguishing the concept of refraction so that we can emphasize the contribution of this concept to the fields of management learning and knowledge creation. This arises from the need to not only clarify but also enrich the reflection concept, comparing and contrasting it with a complementing concept as such refraction.

As we have mentioned before, while reflection can be interpreted as seeing reality as it is, refraction can be understood as seeing it differently. This reflective ability can be associated more with the holistic purpose of comprehending the reality, while dealing with the existing knowledge. The refractive ability, on the other side, can be associated more with the specific purpose of changing the reality, while creating new knowledge. Although we acknowledge that both reflection and refraction are important in their own right for knowledge creation and management learning, we also claim that in order to be creative, we need to be refractive. The extant, which would otherwise continue as it is, and be destined to remain the same, can diverge and then converge for change and creativity by refraction. From another viewpoint, in fact, the extant itself is refracted: what is seen is not the real one but distorted images. And thus, in order to comprehend, and change the reality we also need to be refractive. As a result, in addition to creativity, refraction can also play a significant role in the critical thinking to surface hidden assumptions, tacit power relations.

It is important to consider the reflective and refractive interaction for knowledge creation and management learning as bilateral rather than unilateral, distinguishing the two sides of learning and practice as two different contexts. Such bilateral interaction across different contexts relies more on refraction than it relies on reflection, since refraction, not reflection, is the phenomenon that occurs when the context changes, which also generally requires a change in course of interaction, while reflection happens when the interaction remains in one context, although it can still converge, diverge or bounce back as it is. In contrast to reflection, refraction enables to pass through the borders and transfer our knowledge across contexts. This is why, refraction would be more crucial for maintaining the continuity of the interaction between the two knowledge-creating spirals that occur at the attractors of learning and practice, as well as would be more useful for the understanding and development of knowledge transfer. As the existing literature in management learning is extensively based on the conceptualization of reflection, we also have developed our argument on this conceptual base, however from now on, it could be better to consider refraction for management learning and knowledge creation, as well.

The transfer of knowledge from educational context to the workplace is a very problematic concern in the real world. In the IMPM, in spite of the findings that knowledge acquired in the program is transferred to the workplace through ventures, reflection papers and so on, still there is evidence that what is learned in the education program cannot help much in the workplace, after the participant returns. How to learn to be refractive so that the learned knowledge, which is mostly internalized, thus tacit, and specific to social environment, can be converted into useful knowledge that reflects the characteristics of real life, and accommodate various conflicting, contextual issues related with education, company and personal life is a good question to ponder upon and research for academicians and practitioners. Improving our conceptualization of knowledge transfer with the incorporation of refraction could prove to be useful for addressing this problem. Recognition and incorporation of refraction into our conceptual frameworks could also help to clarify and develop our understanding and use of reflection, which has been associated with too many issues.

Even in the IMPM, which is a very good example of how reflection can be learned and practiced, it is pointed out that in the Management Exchange program, different stages for learners' reflective experience are identified, but not all participants can reach to the certain stage that leads to emergent thinking, imagination and creativity, as we have discussed above. One suggestion regarding this could be that, instead of trying to correspond all these stages with one-and-all-encompassing framework of reflection, treating and targeting these different stages differently by relating the higher stages with refraction rather than reflection could be useful for not leaving to the individual efforts but systematically supporting at an organizational level the pursuit of this ultimate learning experience. Arguably, some refractive aspects are found already in different parts of the existing program such as the IMPM Management Exchange program, reflective and catalytic mindset. Similarly, knowledge transfer, critical thinking and creativity features can be found in all five mindsets of the IMPM, as well as other management education / development programs in different ways. However, these refractive aspects and features can be more systematically identified and incorporated into the program curriculum design and delivery. Besides, again, when we suggest learning of refraction, we by no means undervalue the learning of reflection; participants should learn refraction in relation to reflection, while these two concepts are distinguished and the interrelations between them are identified, such as considering refraction as critical and creative reflection and highlighting its role in knowledge transfer.

With this final remark, we complete our discussion for the model development of a reflective and refractive mindset, as well as the conceptualization and comprehension of these two concepts. Next, we would like to further what we have discussed so far with some more theoretical and practical implications

## IMPLICATIONS OF A REFLECTIVE AND REFRACTIVE MINDSET FOR MANAGEMENT LEARNING AND KNOWLEDGE CREATION

In the previous parts of this chapter, initially we introduced the IMPM program and approach to management learning, underscoring the managerial mindsets and experienced reflection pedagogy as important innovations of the program. Meanwhile, we also noted some limitations of the program such as about the learning of a creative and critically reflective mindset and the transfer of the learning to the workplace. In response to these problems with all participants' achieving higher stages of reflection and transfer of knowledge we have introduced the concept of refraction, as an important phenomenon in management learning that is mostly ignored or ineffectively included in the conceptualizations of reflection. Later, we have proposed a model development for reflection and refraction.

In this model, we consider management practice and learning as both a process and a product of this process. We also associate the tacit and explicit knowledge with process and product, which fits well with competing discussions of process and product views of knowledge management, as well as helps us explain both action and learning as knowledge-creation for their own sake. Besides, moving beyond the perception of the previous circular models about learning and practice, an ellipse with its fixed points labeled as practice and learning is conceptualized in order to emphasize the equally important roles that both practice and learning play together in reality. Finally, a bordering reflective/refractive object that facilitates the transfer of knowledge from learning to practice or vice versa is conceptualized and visualized. The resulting framework is a chaotic knowledge-creating system of learning and action that relies on reflection and refraction in order to maintain the sustainability of the system by the mobility of knowledge within and between learning and action. Such a conceptual framework would be especially useful for addressing issues like creativity, critical thinking, knowledge transfer and utilization, which are important issues for the theory and practice of knowledge creation, management learning and the IMPM.

Having introduced our conceptualization of refraction and reflection, now we would like to discuss in more detail about some interesting implications of our conceptualization. The implications we will highlight are about knowledge and systems sciences, reflection, spirituality, and of course, manager and practitioner learning, and the IMPM, which will be discussed within the following subsections, although they should be considered as interrelated with, rather than totally separated from each other.

## Implications for Knowledge and Systems Sciences

As we have discussed before, in our model there are two knowledge-creating spirals that correspond to learning and practice, and these two knowledge-creating spirals together generate a chaotic knowledge-creating system. The existence of two knowledge-creating spirals contributing to the generation of a knowledge-creating system provides a major explanatory power to our model, which develops the existing knowledge creation and management theories such as the knowledge-creating spiral model of Nonaka and Takeuchi (1995) in return.

Nonaka and Takeuchi's conceptualization is a generic model, which makes it difficult to apply. However, our model proposes knowledge-creation as a chaotic system that relies on two attractors, which have their own knowledge-creating spirals. Two sets of knowledge conversions occur based on these attractors, and complementing each other, together these knowledge conversions generate a chaotic system of knowledge creating. As a consequence, the conceptualization of knowledge creation as a chaotic system makes the original generic modeling of knowledge creation more applicable to practice, since mathematical modeling of knowledge-creation based on systems science becomes possible.

Nonlinear dynamical systems that exhibit mathematical chaos are deterministic and thus orderly in some sense, while the cases of most interest arise when the chaotic behavior takes place on an attractor, since then a large set of initial conditions will lead to orbits that converge to this chaotic region. "Sensitive dependence on initial conditions" is the essence of chaos. The meaning of this statement about chaotic systems in Wikipedia for us is the confirmation of what Nonaka and Takeuchi discuss that there is order in chaos, which is a significant characteristic of knowledge-creation. By defining the relevant parameters regarding the attractors of learning and action, and the phenomena of reflection and refraction, we could model and demonstrate a knowledge-creating system in reality.

According to this, not a knowledge-creating spiral itself but the system that is generated through the interaction of two knowledge-creating spirals is what really makes knowledge-creation happen. An important aspect of this statement is the conceptualization of both learning and practice as knowledge-creating spirals, which diverge from and converge to the two locus points of an ellipse, as well as equal contributors to a chaotic system of knowledge-creation based on these two spirals, which individually do not represent any systemic behavior. Within the general chaotic knowledge-creating system, the knowledge creation that happens in one of practice and learning also enhances the knowledge creation as in each other, which is in accordance with the understanding in knowledge, education, and cognitive science that learning (knowledge) and action (knowing) should not be considered separately.

The system also helps the conceptualization of knowledge-creation and learning that happens at different individual and organizational levels within the same framework. For instance, our original aim has been to provide a conceptual model that contributes to bridging classroom learning in educational organizations and actual practice at workplaces, which are normally assumed to be separate from each other with their own characteristics. However, our framework can also capture and explain the inseparability of the learning, knowledge, knowing and action from each other, which is important in real life for both individuals and organizations. In addition to this, highlighting the importance of individual or organizational relations with social context or environment, we can expand the framework to include the concept of *ba*. The two interacting knowledge-spirals could represent the physical and virtual or mental aspects of *ba* that should always be considered together. Similarly, they could correspond to the mental activities in a human mind and bodily activities in actual life, or a model on personal experience that is based on action, learning and knowledge. In summary, the creation of knowledge relies on the systematic interaction between two knowledge-crating spirals, which represent the education at school and practice at office at different times, or the occurrence of learning and action together at one time for individual or organizational entities.

## Implications for Reflection (and Refraction)

According to our experience and research, the way in which management and organizational learning is interconnected to knowledge creation and management varies significantly. In fact there is an important discontent about the interrelation between learning and knowledge. As the simple basis of the argument, for many (like Peter Senge and his followers), knowledge creation is a part of learning, whereas for others (like Ikujiro Nonaka and his followers) learning is a part of knowledge creation, as well. At least, one side believes that the other side thinks like that. Nevertheless, this difference in the understanding of learning and knowledge also influences the perception and conceptualization of the reflection.

In the knowledge-creation system that we have formulated within this chapter, while we base the role of reflection on a common ground of the existing conceptualizations in management learning, we develop the concept with the incorporation of refraction. If we distinguish the roles that reflection and refraction, which complement each other; reflection plays an important part in individual knowledge-creating spirals that develop at the two attractors of learning and practice, whereas refraction facilitates the interaction between the two knowledge-creating spirals. We have imagined a reflective and refractive bordering object, which, depending on the parameters and dynamics within the system, either reflects the knowledge inwardly to develop the knowledge-creating spirals that are based on the attractors or refracts the knowledge outwardly to facilitate the cross-boundary connection and interaction between the two knowledge-spirals that together generates the chaotic knowledge-creating system. With this border-like reflective/refractive object, the explicit product knowledge of learning or practice is refracted in such a way that it becomes the part of the contextual tacit process knowledge of the other. In this way, the transfer and utilization of the rich experience and knowledge gained from learning or management practice becomes possible. As a result, the education or development program can not only channel individual past work experiences for the benefit of personal and collaborative learning in the program but also transfer the knowledge acquired or created within the program back to the workplace for organizational learning.

The chaotic system model for knowledge-creation can also be used for specifically developing applications for reflection and refraction. Based on the basic conceptualization of this chaotic system and the role of reflection and refraction in this system, mathematical modeling that could lead to simple prototype technologies can be developed to simulate reflection/refraction and evaluate its effectiveness (KMRP Seminar, Monash University, March, 2006).

## Spiritual Implications of Knowledge Creation and Reflection

Together with technological, managerial, social, personal aspects, and so forth, a spiritual dimension could also be considered, when a new conceptualization for knowledge creation and reflection is developed. Initially this could seem odd, but in fact knowledge creation and reflection have important links with spiritual issues, some of which are worth highlighting.

As we have discussed above, faith systems that emerged in the Mediterranean and Asia throughout history include in their teachings that what is created in nature is a reflection of the creative force, which can be also explained as finding the macrocosmos in the microcosmos. Accordingly, created one can become one with the creating one. Again, learning and practicing reflection and contemplation (*tefekkür*) is an important way to reach the creator and become one with the collective mind/being, the unity, or God. For instance, "Nirvana" in Buddhism and "Fenafillah" in Islam is the state of "annihilation of self within the loved one" (Çelebi, 2001). Besides, according to a different type of story for knowledge and creation, the sinful snake offered the forbidden fruit of the knowledge tree in Heaven to Eve, who was, together with Adam, thrown out of Heaven to the Earth, having learned to distinguish good and bad.[5] It is a continuous discussion then whether we, as humans, create new knowledge or just discover existing knowledge, which was already created by the Creative Force.

Moreover, various systems and knowledge science studies try to integrate personal, social, technological, spiritual aspects, and so forth, into one framework that has both theoretical and practical use. For instance, the concepts of *ba* and *ma* serve for a similar integrative purpose. As the "place" the shared context for relationship building and knowledge-creation, *ba* does have a physical, a relational, and a spiritual dimension. (Nonaka, Toyama, & Scharmer, 2001). *Ma* is the "interval" that conveys both time and space as a conceptual and perceptual unity. It is a tension between things allowing for different patterns of interpretation, a constant flow of possibilities, awaiting or undergoing transformation by the availability of physical components and potential uses. Moreover, it is expected to be recognized in relationships, as degree of formality is articulated by measuring *ma* in place, time, social position, and age (Hayashi,

2004; Kerkhove, 2003). The concepts of *ba* and *ma* are important concepts in knowing and designing, as acts of creation, which has not only business or scientific but also spiritual connotations.

Recently, there are authors that suggest the use of ba as a space for reflection at work (Boud, 2006), while Nonaka, Toyama, and Scharmer argue (2001) that more attention should be given to the spiritual and relational aspects of ba. The IMPM also includes the spiritual dimension in the conceptualization of its reflective mindset. We also think that the inclusion of spiritual issues strengthens the conceptual foundation and the implications derived from this conceptualization. For instance, after all our model relies on the dialectical and dual interdependence between two creative dynamics, and such interdependence matches well with the Asian philosophy of the natural attraction between dualities as the source of creative power, which can be perceived in the symbol of Yin-Yang. However we would not go that far to claim that a chaotic system for knowledge-creation and reflection, which is based on the two attractors of micro and macrocosmos, would also simulate the reflection and creation from a spiritual perspective, which, for instance, has an important place in the existing faith systems!

## Implications for Manager and Practitioner Learning, and the IMPM

In addition to the implications discussed above, our conceptualization about the chaotic knowledge-creating system, and the role of reflection and refraction in this system, has some of its most important implications for the learning of managers and development of practitioners. First of all, such a chaotic system addresses the nonlinear, dynamic, even chaotic and complex nature of management practice and learning. Besides, reflection and refraction are very important phenomena for learning and practice of management, or of any other profession or practice, which is directly related with the main point of our paper: managers' learning to practice a reflective and refractive mindset. In order to make our point, we have proposed a conceptual framework, according to which reflection and refraction can be used to link practice and learning, transfer and utilize knowledge, and think creatively and critically, which are very important for today's *knowledge workers*, or *practitioners and managers*. However, to explain the reason of this importance better, first we should discuss more about knowledge management and its relevance for management knowledge.

### *Knowledge Managers, Knowledge Management (KM), Management Knowledge, and a KM Mindset*

In today's knowledge socioeconomy, knowledge-intensive companies, knowledge work and knowledge workforce, management is increasingly understood and explained as knowledge management (Newell, Robertson, Scarborough, & Swan 2002). Management by knowledge, if not management of knowledge, is said by some to have become the essence of management. Supplying knowledge to determine how existing knowledge can be best applied to produce results is, in effect, what is meant by management. In addition, we must take a systematic and purposeful approach to define what new knowledge is needed, whether it is feasible, and what has to be done to make it effective. A manager is responsible for the application and performance of knowledge, the essential resource (Drucker, 1998). Moreover, managing both one's self and relations becomes increasingly important.[6] As Peter Drucker and Henry Mintzberg consistently discuss the individual manager should have self-knowledge, and manage his/her self well. The knowledge of one's self in relationship to others, the knowledge and management of individual and organizational relations, and managing these relations are equally crucial. On the other side, knowledge without managed action does not mean much. Unless what managers learn is put into practice it remains information and never becomes knowledge. At the end, the results of an individual manager's knowing and actions are outside the person, but in society and the economy or in the advancement of knowledge itself. In summary, where and when management is understood and explained as knowledge management, it would not be wrong to consider all managers as knowledge managers, as well.

However, both knowledge and management—thus, knowledge management—have existed through history, although what is understood by these terms has been different at different times. When we talk about knowledge management, we see this bilateral interaction between knowledge and management in *knowledge* management. As a result, on one side, there is "management of knowledge" that addresses issues about the creation, sharing and utilization of knowledge. On the other side, there is "knowledge of management" that addresses issues about practice and learning of management. Both of these partial aspects generate their own problems, which can be properly dealt with a holistic "knowledge-management" mindset. Management learning with a "knowledge management" mindset (as well as KM education with a "management" mindset) can help to overcome some of the frequently experienced problems related to "knowledge of management" and "management of knowledge". This would make a lot of sense in today's world where a manager is now responsible for the application and performance of knowledge.

Then, we can define a KM mindset with respect to two equally important, interacting components, Management Knowledge and Knowledge Management (Figure 6.19). Management Knowledge is a historical and critical appreciation of specific and general knowledge about management. Specific management knowledge is related to the actual practice and context of the practicing manager with all its complexity. A critical reflection on this contextual and practical knowledge should be accompanied by general, conceptual and theoretical knowledge about management itself.[7] On the other side, knowledge management is the management by or of knowledge that is embedded or created within management practices in interaction with others. In short, it captures the creation and management of knowledge in organizations. Then, a KM mindset is build upon the interaction between knowledge management and management knowledge, rather than just knowledge management itself. Managers or management educators/ researchers with a KM mindset should have a critical comprehension of management, they should know management, and should manage this knowledge, or better to say, should know about managing knowledge well. They should have the wisdom to rely on the experience or information they have, and skills to convert this tacit and explicit knowledge into new useful knowledge or practice for the benefit of their own selves, their work and all others. Reflection and refraction are among those skills that knowledge workers, practitioners and managers need most for managing knowledge and knowing management within this KM mindset. The abilities to learn from practical experience, question the reality critically, create new knowledge for problem solving and innovation, apply the learned knowledge into real practice, and etc. are getting increasingly important in today's knowledge economy and learning society. In summary, a KM mindset that relates management knowledge and knowledge management also highlights the importance of reflection and refraction for knowledge workers, practitioners, and managers, which brings the discussion back to the point, where we left in the development of our ideas about the implications for manager and practitioner learning. As a result, once again we can stress the importance of learning reflection and refraction in management development and education. This importance of learning reflection and refraction then leads us to make some specific suggestions for the IMPM.

### Suggestions for the Improvement of the IMPM

Although there are other management education/development and knowledge management education programs that incorporate the learning of reflection, with its experienced reflection pedagogy, the IMPM is

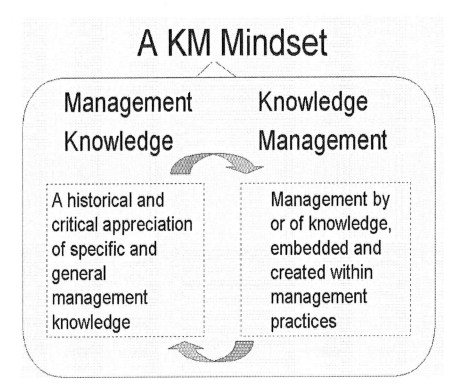

Figure 6.19.   KM mindset.

the leading edge in management development and education. Still, the integration of refraction into the curriculum, which would be supported by the application of new learning methods and technologies for reflection and refraction, can improve the program considerably.

For instance, the 21st Century Museum of Contemporary Art, Kanazawa, which we have introduced previously, can be useful for learning reflection and refraction. With its unique characteristics of concept design, the museum can be used as an open space and time, or ba and ma (which are also discussed above,) for participants to experience various aspects of reflection and refraction that can be considered from different epistemological and ontological perspectives (such as technological, natural, spiritual, social, individual, or intergroup, intragroup (interpersonal), and intrapersonal). From the loss of spatial orientation, linear progression of time, and gravity, each participant can extract a different sensibility previously unknown to him/her. In the mean time, the assumptions of modernity such as man, money and materialism, can be challenged and replaced by consciousness, collective intelligence, and coexistence. Moreover, in Leandro Erlich's "Swimming Pool," participants can ask themselves how it is like to be at the other side of the water surface, while they stand below the pool or look down at the pool (Figures 6.6, 6.7). Or, they can see in the eyes of others, wearing Mathieu Briand's futuristic headsets, which feature visual communication, and manually plugging and unplugging jacks (Figures 6.4, 6.5).[8] The philosophical, conceptual, architectural and technological offerings of this new museum can be better integrated into the IMPM so that a useful *ba* and *ma* for reflection and refraction can be provided for the practicing managers that participate in the program.

Besides, although he proposes an architecture and technology (used in general terms) for the learning of reflection, Mintzberg (2004) suggests that being low-tech and analogue in contrast to high-tech and digital works better for the facilitation of reflection and its learning. However, we think that even some simple digital technologies (used mostly in terms of specific computer and communications technology) can be very effective for the learning of reflection and refraction. For instance, not only computer-mediated collaborative learning or asynchronous communication tools (such as blogs, e-mail, discussion forums) are supportive of reflective interaction and learning; but fantasy role-playing and creative story writing in digital environments or virtual communities can contribute considerably to the practicing and learning of reflection and refraction, as well. The virtual environment provides a reflective and refractive filter and can be used as a way to express a different side of personalities, escape the social constraints of real life, or experiment and find out what kind of person one wants to be in real-life (Medeni & Medeni 2005; Techsoap, 2005 Twist, 2004). In the learning of reflection and refraction, while we can benefit from effective analog and low-tech methods (such as storytelling in real life), this should not prevent us from using some appropriate digital methods and technologies, even trying the development of new ones (such as story-telling and story-writing in virtual life).[9, 10] The combination of appropriate digital and analog methods for reflection and refraction again would be supported by the *ba* concept that has both physical and virtual aspects. The artificial, or virtual, experience of role-playing could also complement the forced experience of project work, the simulated experience of case study, the added experience of action learning, and the natural experience of experienced reflection, in accordance with Mintzberg's suggestion for blending different pedagogies for management (Figure. 6.3). As virtual experiences are increasingly becoming a part of our real lives, hybrid digital environments to have both virtual and natural experiences can be used more extensively and purposefully for the pedagogical practice of experienced reflection, for instance. To sum up, while we by no means undervalue the learning of reflection in the

IMPM, we suggest that a refractive mindset should be incorporated more systematically into the curriculum design of this leading edge management program.

For the learning and practice of management, even if concerns about creativity, critical thinking, and transfer of knowledge from the educational context to the work context can be addressed with refraction (together with reflection) in theory at school as such the IMPM, these are still problematic concerns to put into practice in the real world. Reflecting purposefully for creative or critical thinking would be always easier to do in theory than in practice. Similarly, the characteristics of the education/theory and work/practice contexts are so different that the knowledge refracts significantly during the in-between transfer, making it very hard to deal with the actual knowing for both the learning at school and the management at work for different individual and organizational purposes.

Distinguishing the context and circumstances of an educational program from real life, for instance, as more *sheltered*, brings up other relevant issues and questions, as well. Previously it was mentioned that the IMPM was considered as a "playground" where participants get a chance to take some time off from their real-life—for a certain period of time, until they return to work. If it is such a playground, then to what extent should the participants be expected to bring what they acquire with them back to real life, when they return.... What if it is seen just as a "playground" with which organizations reward some high-flyers.... Since these participants are high quality, clever, capable people, whatever they do will be successful anyway, then how the impact of the program on their success can be determined.... In general how the performance of such a (graduate management) education program can be measured better.... Such concerns are in the minds of people we researched and in ours as well. What is learned in the program, how well it is learned, how it is learned, and whether it is good enough or not can still be argued, in addition to how it can be put into practice. Pedagogically, how information is converted to individual and then organizational knowledge and action can be evaluated. These issues about the evaluation and evolution of the IMPM, not only as a pioneering management education program, but also as a normal management education and education program are to be the subject for further research, as they are important for realistically identifying the value and characteristics of the program more so that they can be furthered and diffused to other education or development programs.[11] Nevertheless, this research did not specifically aim to make an overall and thorough assessment of the IMPM. The five mindset modules and other program activities should be studied individually in order to reach such a general conclusion.

Whether it is successful at the transfer (utilization, or application) of knowledge from education to practice, or simply provides a playground for participants or not, the IMPM is an important case for highlighting the interaction between individual, organization and the education program itself, as the program tries to get the involvement of the company into the learning of the individual participant, and tailor itself to address the concerns of the individual and organizational participants. The interaction among these three parties also can be considered within a unifying knowledge creation and management mindset, where we can think and discuss about knowledge-creating individuals, companies, and organizations.

### Knowledge-Creating Schools, Companies, and Individuals

Our discussion here is a further implication of the KM mindset, which we have proposed above. In accordance with this KM mindset, education program suppliers such as universities or schools (including their faculty) and the organizational demanders of the education programs such as companies or managers are all considered as knowledge-creating entities.

Management practice and management learning should not be seen as separate but as mutually complementing entities that continuously reinforce each other. Both the practice of management and education of managers take place on three levels: individual, organizational, and social. In other words, (1) the teaching of faculty, (2) the learning of individuals who participate in the educational programs and then work as managers in companies, and (3) the actual practice of working in companies are the three cornerstones for building up a proper structure for theory and practice. In addition to this, all three of these cornerstones: teaching, learning, and doing can be considered as knowledge-creating activities. It can be suggested, then, that a knowledge-creation frame allows for the conceptualization of these three cornerstone activities together. This provides a new interpretation of the interrelated roles and responsibilities of faculty, individual participants, and employing organizations.

For business schools and their faculty, meeting the needs of today's complex business issues and challenging management matters is more demanding than ever. This requires ways that should complicate our understanding about management matters rather than simplifying it. Recognizing this fact, higher education institutions (HEIs) and business schools (BSs) already have initiated discussions or actions towards becoming knowledge-creating entities, claiming to become more capable of managing, as well as improving their knowledge (Hargreaves, 1999; Steyn, 2002). However, for our own interests we would like to emphasize the following specific points among other aspects of knowledge management and knowledge creation in HEIs and BSs.

First, many management educators no longer assume that they teach only individuals who belong to a firm; they realize they also have responsibility to provide support for the organizational learning of the companies that these individuals work for. As we have begun to see in corporate "universities" (Prince & Stewart, 2002), both the schools and firms (meaning both the companies that individuals work for and the agencies that provide them training), as well as their faculty members and trainers have to understand their individual and organizational clients well enough to offer them tailor-made programs. For these purposes, the faculty have to spend more time not only on coordination and collaboration, but also on teaching individuals. Finally, faculty members no longer merely deliver research-based teaching or facilitate learning for the participants in their classes. Rather, they should assume a more active, practical role in their *students'* companies, somehow similar to consulting (Lorange, 2002). The teaching, coordinating, and practical roles of educators also affect the faculty members' involvement with their research. While they might have less time for research, the insights and information they can get from their involvement in companies can generate fruitful research.

We also need pioneering, multidisciplinary education programs that can support the new generation of imaginative and creative generalists, which leads our discussion to the perspective of learners. For learners, then, mastering synthesizing skills, which can be more useful in real life contexts than abstract analyzing skills, should be the target for their education. To realize the inherent potential of their creation and imagination, they should be taught about the universal process of invention, as well as about intuitive and imaginative skills (Bernstein-Root & Bernstein-Root, 1999). With this background, these learners can be considered knowledge-creating managers, who have the potential to improve the community of practice or *ba* through socialization (meaning both knowledge sharing and becoming a member of the community) and to improve their personality, work, and personal life through personal and interpersonal reflection and refraction. Besides, with their creative skills, they can contribute significantly to the strategy formulation, problem solving, (process, product, or service) innovation, and technology creation systems that their companies depend on in the knowledge economy. Accordingly, these practicing managers are equipped with skills that can support them to internalize, externalize, and act upon knowledge, recognizing its merits not only in the explicit and individual form, but also in the tacit and group form. To facilitate the development of such individuals, it can be recommended that the participants of education programs be somehow representative of their companies or sectors and, if possible, participate as a group. Besides, education (both general and management) programs also should be able to provide a setting that can facilitate the refraction and reflection of the participants' learning experience in the same manner. Later these managers, in their companies, should be able to assume roles as action researchers, for their knowledge-creating skills easily can be compatible with other core competencies like problem solving abilities or social skills (Coghlan et al., 2004). The roles these learners play can include different types of administrative, managerial, or supervisory work, while they also fit very well for entrepreneurship or intrapreneurship initiatives. They know that if they can express out their tacit knowledge well enough to be seen or heard, they will be paid attention to, and get support for accomplishing their aims, even if they may not originally possess the necessary resources themselves.

The companies themselves, as learning organizations, are an embedded, inseparable part of the education process of their managers. This point basically reinforces our previous remarks, (1) Management education in HEIs or BSs and management practice in companies should not be seen as separate but as mutually complementing entities, (2) The faculty should provide support for the organizational learning of the companies that the learning individuals work for. Regarding (2), for instance, there are already innovative interactions resulting from two-way learning networks, "valleys" established between corporations and HEIs and also among corporations themselves as discussed by Lee, Miller, Hancock, and Rowen (2000) for Silicon Valley. These networks should be continuously cultivated and developed.

Having recognized the importance of knowledge as the most precious resource of a sustainable strategic advantage, academicians, and practitioners are increasingly paying more attention to organizations, and networks as knowledge-based systems, and knowledge-creating institutions (Petrides, 2002).[12] With respect to this, knowledge-creating organizations should also be able to consciously make use of the educational program as a suitable context and tool for knowledge exchange and creation. While they support the efficacious sharing of general and specific knowledge through carefully designed activities, they can develop institutional means to benefit from the tacit and explicit knowledge created from these activities. Such means include (1) regular informal or formal meetings for participants, and real or virtual community gatherings for members, (2) projects that can provide occasions to work on responding to a real issue in the organization or participating in a shadowing or mentoring relationship, (3) links with the career development of newly recruited or returning managers.

In fact there are already available organizational means like project reports and regular meetings, or technological means like information/databases and communication systems that could be useful for knowledge-creation and management, together with reflection and collaboration. However, their value may not be well regarded without an approach from the perspective of a KM mindset, and thus their use may need to be revitalized with the learning and application of a KM mindset. In addition, new means like *ba*, Communities of Practice (CoPs) and After Action Reviews (AARs) can be cultivated, again for collaborative and reflective practice (Collison & Parcell, 2004). Furthermore, applying innovative and creative means such as new spatial and temporal tools (as *ba* & *ma*, the Japanese terms for sharing place and time) for collaboration and reflection; while considering also refraction and echo (relying on sound for reflection), could be another alternative. Finally, each company or individual can develop its own specific, unique—simple or complex—options and offer them as solution to their own realities. All these can contribute to developing a collaborative and reflective culture, in accordance with the collaborative and reflective mindsets of the IMPM.

We must acknowledge that this discussion about knowledge-creating organizations (education and business or nonprofit institutions, communities) and individuals (teaching faculty and practicing managers) should be seen as a direct derivation from our previous discussions about the KM mindset, the chaotic knowledge-creating system, which conceptualizes learning and practice as knowledge-creation, and the transfer of knowledge between learning and practice, which represents only one of the approaches to learning and knowing, as among others (Paavola, Lipponen, & Hakkarainen, 2002). The furtherance of these previous discussions by conceptualizing the "three cornerstones of teaching, learning and practice" as knowledge creation thus reflects a simple, limited line of argument, as there are many other modes and models of learning apart from teaching and practice. Besides, the understanding about how we relate knowledge-creating entities and interactions to real work practices does not need to be limited to the teaching/learning at schools, and could be extended to include the employees, customers, suppliers, and so forth.

### Practicing and Learning a KM Mindset

Applying a knowledge-creative, reflective, and refractive KM mindset for individual managers, organization management, and management education/development can provide suitable tools for managers and management educators/developers to bridge the gaps that currently exist among different functions of management practice, education and research. Furthermore, such a mindset can play an important role to address the dialectics in management practice, knowledge and learning including, body↔mind, individual↔collective, school education↔company practice, local↔universal, rigor↔relevance, doing↔knowing, knowledge↔knowing, and theory↔practice. A reflective and refractive

KM mindset to address these dialectics for creation and management knowledge is important in today's knowledge economy and society.

One consequence of this statement is to suggest learning principles and practices of KM in management education. Currently graduate management education like MBA programs, which are based on business functions, generally position KM only as a separate course into their curriculum. However this research perceives KM as an embedded, inseparable part of business functions and processes, and suggests that graduate management education incorporate this view of KM in their core curriculum design. Every management function does rely on effective use of its functional knowledge and they would benefit from learning the effective management of knowledge with all its strategic, technological, organizational, and personal aspects. Knowledge creation and management acts as a bridging mindset for management practice above all individual functions. Faculty of finance, accounting, information systems and technology, human resources, marketing, operations, and others could provide a perspective for this KM mindset in the teaching of their own specializations.

Since we are talking about graduate programs, it is right to expect students to have had some previous experience. Then, students participating in such programs can learn about the effective externalization of their tacit knowledge, experience, and skills; and use their knowledge when they return to the work force. Graduates from MBA programs that successfully incorporate a KM mindset, for instance, can better learn how to make use of their acquired knowledge in workplace for the strategic goals and business success of their company through the use of technological tools, refractive methods, reflective and collaborative practices. As a result, they also become better equipped with competencies that match business needs and transferable skills that would surely help their career prospects. In general, various authors recognize that KM and KM competencies are increasingly becoming important for human resource and management development (Davenport & Prusak, 1998; Iles, Yolles, & Altman, 2001; Leibowitz, 2002; Nonaka & Takeuchi, 1995; Raub, 2002).

Another contribution of KM could be for the management of the education programs themselves, which could be considered as knowledge-creating, knowledge-based, or knowledge-intensive organizations. As a core aspect of administration and curriculum, the KM mindset also can be incorporated into graduate management education in institutions of higher learning. While an integrative KM model applied to the administration of education can also help to correct current problems of management education, our focus here is the KM mindset as a part of the curriculum of the education programs.

As KM is experiencing significant growth, it is beginning to be taught in educational institutions, first as individual courses, but now as formal training and degree programs. For instance, as a pioneering institution in KM education, Nanyang Techonological University offers a Master of Science in Knowledge Management to cover "management, technology and information topics essential for meeting the demand of employers in Singapore and the region for well-rounded knowledge professionals" (http://www.ntu.edu.sg/sci/graduate/knowledge.html). Besides, the University of Melbourne's Knowledge Management program, which is "one of a kind worldwide," "draws on expertise from three distinct fields (Information Technology/Information Systems, Management, and Organizational Learning), from three different faculties (Education, Economics/Commerce and Science)" (http://www.edfac.unimelb.edu.au/futurestudents/courses/postgraduate/Courses/knowlegdemanagement.html). Often the target of these programs is to educate or develop knowledge managers, although what these institutions understand about KM and, thus, knowledge managers differs substantively and sometimes conflicts with each other (Saito, Medeni, Marcelo, & Umemoto, 2004). According to these different understandings, for instance, a knowledge manager could learn how to manage her knowledge workers in her knowledge-intensive firm, a human resource manager could assume roles and responsibilities as a KM specialist in his organization, or any middle manager could be developed as a KM generalist by the company training or education program.

### Knowledge Management Education Programs

Our previous research and analysis on the contents of the existing graduate KM education programs has identified four perspectives that are dominant in the subject and teaching of KM: (1) Business-Strategy perspective, (2) Organization-People perspective, (3) Technology perspective, and (4) Knowledge-Information perspective (Figure 6.20). In reality, all four of these perspectives overlap and are much less clearly bounded than the distinguished quadrants, however none of the programs provides a comprehensive curriculum that covers all. Thus, we see that these four perspectives together provide an ideal case as a unifying umbrella for KM and its education that leads the way toward a KM mindset.

While these four perspectives of KM can be seen as conflicting or competing with each other (Hansen, Nohria, & Tierney, 1999; Koenig & Srikantaiah, 2000; Nonaka & Takeuchi, 1995), we believe that they provide some interesting points for management practice and the teaching of management practice. First of all, the inclusion of knowledge in management is very important. Providing such a philosophical ground for management is an important step toward equipping managers with useful skills for their work (Mintzberg, 2004). Secondly, KM can be seen as an attempt to integrate different functions of business and administration into a management mindset. Strategy, people, and technology are all

| Business / Strategy perspective<br>Purpose, Environment, Resources | Knowledge / Information perspective<br>Categories, Activities, Value |
|---|---|
| • Knowledge economy and society, new business models, innovation<br>• Competitive advantage, competitive intelligence<br>• Knowledge strategy, knowledge policy<br>• Collaboration, inter-organizational KM<br>• Knowledge evaluation, intellectual capital<br>• Ethics in KM, KM legal issues | • General concepts and typologies on knowledge, epistemology<br>• Knowledge life-cycle, knowledge activities, knowledge architecture<br>• Organization of information, taxonomies, knowledge mapping<br>• Systems theory, systems science<br>• Information policy, knowledge protection<br>• Cognitive science, learning |
| **Organization / People perspective**<br>Culture, Structure, Processes | **Technology perspective**<br>Applications, Infra-structure, Methods |
| • Organizational learning, organizational behavior, culture, power and leadership<br>• Organizational analysis and design, change management, project management<br>• Knowledge of management, management science<br>• Communities of practice, team management, group creativity<br>• Knowledge organizations, knowledge professional, knowledge entrepreneurship | • Knowledge repositories, document management, corporate portals<br>• Knowledge discovery and data-mining, business intelligence, decision support systems<br>• Knowledge engineering, knowledge representation<br>• Intelligent agents, neural computing, case-based reasoning<br>• Collaborative environments, virtual communities<br>• Systems development, KM systems development |

Figure 6.20.   KM education programs, adapted from Saito, Medeni, Machado, and Umemoto (2004).

combined under the umbrella of KM. This is particularly astonishing, if we recall that strategy, organizational behavior, human resource management, and management information systems all have been expected to play integrative roles within the management silos, but so far they have not been very successful in doing so. Finally, it is important to see that all these different, conflicting views can be brought together under one big umbrella of knowledge management and creation. This umbrella can provide a fresh, rich source of interpretation for management, especially if we see KM as embedded in all business processes and functions. Then, this can be seen as one specific interpretation of a KM mindset for management.

As a part of this KM mindset interpretation, it is possible to recognize and make use of knowledge as a strategic resource. Potential participants also can learn to learn from their experience and apply this knowledge to their work for better results through the culture, structure and various processes of the organization. Self-knowledge becomes important on one side, and on the other the ability to make use of technology; managers with a KM mindset should do both. They can get simple training about how to identify and find useful knowledge in a large storage system, overloaded by various kinds of information and data. They can also get training about how to extract knowledge from within themselves, from their interactions with others, or from their contexts, such as learning to listen to their inner voice or communicate with other people. They can learn to make decisions under the circumstances of excessive or scarce and partial knowledge. Finally, a philosophical conceptualization, a systematic inquiry for thinking and questioning, which could provide perspectives about ethics, the environment, and so forth, could also do wonders. These all work with the same principles that can be gathered within a KM mindset.

Most of the KM education programs we have studied are not close to such an ideal KM mindset. Their approach to KM is partial in one way or another. The graduates of these programs will best function as specialists in these partial perspectives. However, the sum of these program perspectives helps us come closer to a general, ideal KM mindset that can be used to educate KM generalists, which fits well to the characteristics of management practice. Meanwhile, for the education of the KM generalists, the IMPM provides a real case to study. The reflection, analysis, context, collaboration, and action mindsets of the IMPM approach, which are associated with the most important aspects of management and embedded in general practice, can be gathered around a unifying mindset of KM. The IMPM provides generalist knowledge that every management practitioner would need to know, while providing specific knowledge for learning how to acquire knowledge and take action with the knowledge acquired, while it does not provide specialized management knowledge on, for example, certain technological tools. Although it can be argued that some general technological aspects still can be incorporated into the program, the IMPM, as an already established program, seems to be closer to the realization of a management education based on a unifying KM mindset.[13]

## CONCLUSION

As a sound, viable and visionary alternative to the currently available offerings of the graduate management education programs, the IMPM has been the subject of our discussion in this chapter. After a summary of the overall IMPM approach, which is based on the innovative pedagogy of managerial mindsets and experienced reflection by Mintzberg and his

colleagues, the reflective mindset has been developed with the incorporation of refraction phenomenon. Later, some interesting implications of
this new reflective and refractive mindset have been discussed, such as in
knowledge management and management knowledge. With our discussion about reflection and refraction in this chapter, we have tried to provide stimulating suggestions for bridging the gap between practice/action
and learning/knowledge, which is identified as a major problem in management.

As the IMPM advocates, the ability/skill/competence/art of reflecting
on self-knowledge for practice, which plays a crucial role in learning,
knowing and managing, can be, and needs to be, learned by managers
and practitioners of today's knowledge economy and learning society.
In addition, the concept of reflection can also be refined and improved
with the recognition of refraction that happens in reality, and the consecutive revision of the theory and its relevant implications. Depending
on the level of difference between the characteristics of the interacting
entities or contexts, reflection or refraction occur at the interface of the
cross-boundary interaction, which can be taking place among individuals, organizations or cultures. The reflection, which does not pass
through the boundary but bounces back, can be what we can learn
about ourselves as a part of this experience with entities that stand outside our boundaries. The refraction is what moves across, on the other
side, as the boundary interface refracts the interaction in order to adjust
to the conditions of the moved context. Managing the boundary interface can help us determine the nature of the interaction across different contexts, facilitating, for instance, to refract so that we can develop
a beneficial relation among different parties such as school and workplace, consultancy firms and clients, bridge conflicting paradigms and
world views, make sense of the true nature of the reality around us,
change our thinking from in-box to out-of-the-box, solve complex problems, deal with chaotic situations, be more critical and creative, or
develop a visionary leadership.

A recent survey conducted by Koys and Gundry (2002) highlights the
critical and creative thinking (followed by the use of information technology, communication, teamwork and leadership, decision making,
ethics and social awareness, technical and analytical skills, and global
awareness) as the most important competence needed by the graduates
of management education. For developing critical and creative thinking, the learning and practice of reflection and refraction is very important, which should not be left only to individual efforts but facilitated
institutionally by education, research organizations, and workplaces.
Further research can contribute to the development of models, systems,
pedagogies, organizational practices, and technologies that support the

knowledge work of reflective and refractive practitioners. Among the important issues that are left for further research, the in-depth study for the understanding of the boundaries that function as reflective and refractive interfaces hold a profound place. A related concern would also be finding or building these boundary interfaces to enable reflection and refraction for a chaotic knowledge-creating system based on the attractors of learning and action. Besides, mainly this knowledge-creating system is based on the conceptualization of knowledge as process and product, which necessitates an expansion of the framework to include the conceptualization of knowledge as power, as well (Paechter, Preedy, Scott, & Soler, 2001). Moreover, there is much to be explored about the relation between knowledge-creation, creativity, reflection and refraction. As a result, terms we use as such knowledge transfer, knowledge diffusion, knowledge utilization, as well as creation, reflection and refraction should be better clarified.

All these research can contribute to what we have done so far for the development of a theory of reflection and refraction that can be applied for bridging practice and learning, as well as knowledge and systems science. We also hope that another bridge that the theory can construct is going to be for the different intellectual traditions of West and East, both of which have their own merits. With the positive impact of these bridges, for instance, among others, it would be interesting to think and discuss about knowledge-creating managers, refractive practitioners, virtual, and augmented realities for experienced reflection.

## ACKNOWLEDGMENTS

The research is supported by 21st COE (Center of Excellence) Program "Technology Creation Based on Knowledge Creation" of JAIST, funded by the Ministry of Education, Culture, Sports, Science and Technology (MEXT, Japan). The author is grateful to his professors, Umemoto Sensei, Toyama Sensei, Sharon, and Oliver, and colleagues, Andre, Marcelo, and Simon in JAIST and Lancaster University for their invaluable guidance and comments.

## NOTES

1. which is in accordance with Nonaka and Takeuchi's (1995) assertion that highlights the *middle* managers' role in the organizational *knowledge* creation and management.
2. An expression that captures management practice, development, and education as well as practical and academic research

3.   In addition to conceptualizing an ellipse with its fixed points labeled as practice and learning in order to emphasize the equally important roles that both practice and learning play in reality, we can use this kind of metaphorical approach to help us solve some problems related to the different taxonomies of learning and action, benefiting from other characteristics of ellipse, such as eccentricity.

4.   Such visualization also could be seen to represent well discussions about both soft systems, which are more interested in the process, and hard systems, which are more interested in the products, highlighting that both could be considered at the same time (Checkland & Scholes, 1999).

5.   The interaction between Adam and Eve could be considered to result in the first *meme* of the human history, borrowing the term of Richard Dawkins!

6.   The management of self-knowledge in relationships and with respect to others outside the self is crucial. For instance, as Drucker states in various works (see references), the individual manager must have self-knowledge, ("how do I perform, how do I learn, in what relationships do I work well with people"): this is who she is. Successful careers are the "careers of people who are prepared for the opportunity because they know their strengths, the way they work and their values." Then, asking " 'What is my contribution?' means moving from knowledge to action." Thus, in the education of managers, "the individual manager needs an opportunity to reflect on the meaning of his own experience ... also ... on himself and learn to make his strengths count. He needs development as a person even more than he needs development as a manager.... Managers are action-focused..., unless they can put into action right away the things they have learned, the things they have considered and reconsidered, the course will not "take." It will remain "information" and never become "knowledge' "(Drucker, 1993, p. 421). Thus, we should aim to "convince participants that the capacity for reflection on themselves and their environments is valuable and can add understanding that can lead to a different level of creativity in management." Mintzberg also provides supporting discussions on these issues, which is discussed specifically in the respective parts of the chapter.

7.   For instance, a manager should have an idea about where *management* comes from, being aware of the word's association with hand and the handling of horses in Italian culture in history, and where it is going in the future.

8.   Seeing in the eyes of others is what managers would need in order to appreciate other viewpoints, which could be all different refractions of the reality, and not to fall into the trap that once upon a time Narcissus had fallen: Falling in love with one's own reflections, which would mean not only the physical mirror images but also thoughts and their expressions!

9.   In general, options in the form of online role-playing games, virtual communities of avatars can be used, as well as virtual "swimming pools" (simple photo-realistic rendering technology combined with immersion into virtual reality for realizing how reality is refracted moving across different contexts), or visual communication headsets (Head Mounted Displays or context-based information browsers within an augmented reality for seeing in the eye of others, witnessing the construction of others' experiences,

and the actual refraction of reality) can be developed, if we count on some of the available digital technologies that are increasingly becoming part of our real life.

10. These technologies could be useful for learning to become not only reflective and refractive, but also more collaborative. In other words, reflective and refractive learning should be facilitated for becoming (better) critical, creative and collaborative.

11. There are already diffusions of the IMPM innovations such as the EMBA RoundTables, McGill-McConnell Master of Management for National Voluntary Sector Leaders, BAE Strategic Leaders Programme, Advanced Leadership Program (Mintzberg, 2004).

12. The interaction between firms and schools can be considered as an interorganizational, creative and collaborative knowledge-based system in which both business firms and educational institutions are interdependently knowledge-creating entities.

13. Still, since the search for a big umbrella or grand narrative would seem rather reductive in today's world, a counter argument could be made for not trying to distill five mindsets into a common framework, or a unifying mindset!

## REFERENCES

Baker, A. C., Jensen, P. J., & Kolb, D. A. (2002). Learning and conversation. In D. A. Kolb, A. C. Baker, & P. J. Jensen (Eds.), *Conversational learning: An experiential approach to knowledge creation* (pp. 1-14.) Westport, CT: Quorum Books.

Belfer, K. (2004). *Reflection for transfer learning. e-Portfolio Conference: Reflection Is not a mirror, it's a lens.* Retrieved June 28, 2006, from https://www.elearning.ubc.ca/home/DirCMSSiteContent/documents/eport2004/eport2004_KarenB.pdf.

Bernstein-Root M., & Bernstein-Root R. (1999). *Sparks of genious: The 13 thinking tools of the world's most creative people.* New York: Mariner Books.

Blunt, R. (2001). *Knowledge management in the new economy.* New York: Writers Club Press.

Boud, D. (2006). Creating the space for reflection at work. In D. Boud, P. Cressey, & P. Docherty (Eds.), *Productive reflection at work* New York: Routledge.

Burgoyne J. G., & Reynolds, M. (Eds.). (1997). *Management learning: Integrating perspectives in theory and practice.* London: Sage.

Checkland, P., & Scholes, J. (1999). *Soft systems methodology in action.* Chichester, England: Wiley.

Coghlan, D., Dromgoole T., Joynt P., & Sorensen P. (2004). *Managers learning in Action.* London: Routledge.

Collison, C., & Parcell, G. (2004). *Learning to fly: Practical knowledge management from leading and learning organizations.* Chichester, England: Capstone.

Cook, S., & Brown, J. (1999). Bridging epistemologies: The generative dance between organizational knowledge and organizational knowing. *Organization Science, 10*(4), 381-400.

Cunha, M. P., Cunha, J. V., & Cabral-Cordoso, C. (2004). Looking for complication: Four approaches to management learning. *Journal of Management Education, 28*(1), 88-103.

Çelebi, C. D. (2001). *Sema: Human being in the universal movement.* Retrieved June 28, 2006, from http://www.mevlana.net/sema.htm

Davenport, T. H., & Prusak, L. (1998). *Working knowledge: How organizations manage what they know.* Boston: Harvard Business School Press.

Drucker, P. F. (1998). From capitalism to knowledge society. In D. Neef (Ed.), *The knowledge economy: Resources for the knowledge-based economy* (pp. 15-34). Boston: Butterworth-Heinemann.

Drucker, P. F. (1993). *Management: Tasks, responsibilities, practices.* New York: Harper Business.

Emre, Y. (1989). *The drop that became the sea* (K. Helminski & R Algan, Trans.). Boston: Shambhala.

E-Portfolio Conference. (2004). Retrived June 28, 2006, from https://www.elearning.ubc.ca/home/index.cfm?p=main%2Fdsp_eport_event_20041119.cfm

Fox, S. (1997). From management education and development to the study of management learning. In J. Burgoyne & M. Reynolds (Eds.), *Management learning: Integrating perspectives in theory and practice* (pp. 21-37). London: Sage.

Gamble, P. R., & Blackwell, J. (2001). *Knowledge management: A state of the art guide.* London: Kogan Page.

Gosling, J., & Mintzberg H. (2003). The five minds of a manager. *Harvard Business Review, 81*(11), 54-63.

Gosling, J., & Westall O. (2006). *Managing self: The reflective mindset.* Retrieved June 28, 2006, from http://www.impm.org/goslingwestall.pdf

Griseri, P. (2002). *Management knowledge: A critical view.* New York: Palgrave.

Habermas, J. (1973). *Border crossings.* Boston: Beacon Press.

Habermas, J. (1972). *Theory and practice,* London: Heinemann.

Hargreaves, D. H. (1999). The knowledge-creating school. *British Journal of Educational Studies. 47*(2), 122-144.

Hansen, T. M., Nohria, N., & Tierney, T. (1999). What's your strategy for managing knowledge. *Harvard Business Review, 77*(2), 106-116.

Hayashi, T. (2004). Captured nature and Japanese way of tolerance. *MAJA Estonian Architectural Review.* Retrieved June 28, from http://www.solness.ee/majaeng/index.php?gid=44&id=453

Hendy, J. (2001). *Zen in your garden: Creating sacred spaces.* Boston: Tuttle.

Iles, P., Yolles, M., & Altman, Y. (2001). HRM and knowledge management: Responding to the challenge. *Research and Practice in Human Resource Management, 9*(1), 3-33.

Jackson, M. C. (2003). *Systems thinking: Creative holism for managers.* Wiley.

Kerkhove, D. D. (2003). Intervals-ideas-initiatives. *NextD Journal: ReRethinking Design Issue Two, Conversation, 2*(3). Retrieved June 28, 2006, from http://www.nextd.org/02/pdf_download/NextD_2_3.pdf

Koenig, M. E. D., & Srikantaiah, T. K. (2000). The evolution of knowledge management. In T. K. Srikantaiah & M. E. D. Koenig (Eds.), *Knowledge manage-*

*ment for the information professional* (pp. 23-36). Medford, NJ: Information Today.

Kolb, D. (1984). *Experiential learning as the science of learning and development*. Upper Saddle River, NJ: Prentice Hall.

Koys, D., & Gundry, L. (2002). Knowledge and skills needed by management graduates. In A. Bentzen-Bilkvist, W. H. Gijselaers, & R. G. Miller (Eds.), *Educational innovation in economics and business: Educating knowledge workers for corporate leadership: Learning into the future* (Vol. 7, pp. 93-112) London: Kluwer Academic.

Lee, C -M, Miller, W. F., Hancock, M. G., & Rowen, H. S. (Eds.). (2000). *The Silicon Valley edge: A habitat for innovation and enterpreneurship*. Palo Alto, CA: Stanford University Press.

Leibowitz, J. (2002). The role of the chief knowledge officer in organizations. *Research and Practice in Human Resource Management, 10*(2), 2-15.

Little, S., Quintas, P., & Ray, T. (Eds.). (2002). *Managing knowledge: An essential reader*. London: Open University Press and Sage.

Liu, J. (2001). *Fostering critical reflection in management education—A case study of the reflective module of IMPM*. Unpublished dissertation presented for MA in management and organizational learning, Lancaster University.

Lorange, P. (2002). *New vision for management education: Leadership challenges* Oxford, England: Elsevier Science.

McCroary, J., Chinwalla, T., & Guthrie J. (2006). *Reconfiguring conversations about the IMPM*. Retrieved June 28, 2006, from http://www.impm.org/williams.pdf

Medeni, T. (2005). Tacit-explicit and specific-general knowledge interactions in communities of practice. In E. Coakes & S. Clarke (Eds.), *Encyclopedia of communities of practice in information and knowledge management* Hershey, PA: Idea Group.

Medeni, T. (2004). Reflective management learning practice model. *Proceedings of BAI 2004 International Workshop on Business and Information in Taiwan*.

Medeni, T. (2001). *Reflections on IMPM Reflective Mindset Module*. Unpublished dissertation presented for MA in Management and Organizational Learning, Lancaster University.

Medeni, T., & Medeni T. (2005). Virtual role-playing communities, "wold" and world. In E. Coakes & S. Clarke (Eds.), *Encyclopedia of communities of practice in information and knowledge management* Hershey, PA: Idea Group.

Medeni, T., & Medeni T. (2004). An experience-based tacit-explicit knowledge interaction model of action and learning. *Proceedings of the New Information Technologies in Education Workshop, Turkey*.

Mezirow, J., & Associates. (1990). *Fostering critical reflection in adulthood a guide to transformative and emancipatory learning*. San Francisco: Jossey-Bass.

Mintzberg, H. (2004). *Managers not MBAs: A hard look at the soft practice of managing and management development*. San Francisco: Berrett-Koehler.

Mintzberg, H., & Gosling, J. (2002). *Reality programming for MBAs*. Retrieved June 28, 2006 from http://www.cl-network.com/meetingdocs/11-03/ Reality%20Programming%20for%20MBAs%20(S+B%20Q4%202002).pdf

Moon, J. (2004). *A handbook of reflective and experiential learning: Theory and practice*. London: RoutledgeFalmer.

Moon, J. (1999). *Reflection in learning and & professional development: Theory and practice*. London: Page.

Newell, S., Robertson, M., Scarborough, H., & Swan, J. (2002). *Managing knowledge work*. New York: Palgrave.

Nonaka, I., & Takeuchi, H. (1995). *The knowledge creating company: How Japanese companies create the dynamics of innovation*. New York: Oxford University Press.

Nonaka, I., & Teece, D. J. (Eds.). (2001). *Managing industrial knowledge: Creation, transfer and utilization*. London: Sage.

Nonaka, I., Toyama, R., & Konno, N. (2000). SECI, Ba and leadership: A unified model of dynamic knowledge creation. *Long Range Planning, 33*, 5-34.

Nonaka, I., Toyama, R., & Scharmer, O. (2001). *Building Ba to enhance knowledge creation and innovation at large firms*. Retrieved June 28, 2006, from http://www.dialogonleadership.org/Nonaka_et_al.html

Organisation For Economic Co-operation and Development. (2000). *Knowledge management in the learning society: Education and skills*. Paris: Author.

Organisation For Economic Co-operation and Development. (2001). *Science, technology and industry scoreboard: Towards a knowledge-based economy* Paris: Author.

Paavola, S., Lipponen, L., & Hakkarainen, K. (2002). Epistemological foundations for CSCL: A comparison of three models of innovative knowledge communities. In G. Stahl (Ed.), *Computer support for collaborative learning: Foundations for a CSCL community* (pp. 24-32). Mahwah, NJ: Erlbaum.

Paechter, C., Preedy, M., Scott, D., & Soler, J. (Eds.). (2001). *Knowledge, power and learning*. London: Paul Chapman and Open University Press.

Petrides, L. A. (2002). Organizational learning and the case for knowledge-based systems. *New Directions for Institutional Research, 113*, 69-84.

Pfeffer, J., &. Fong C. T. (2002). The end of business schools? Less success than meets the eye. *Academy of Management Learning & Education, 1*(1), 78-95.

Polanyi, M. (1966). *The tacit dimension*. London: Routledge and Kegan Paul.

Prince, C., & Stewart J. (2002). Corporate universities: An analytical framework. *The Journal of Management Development, 21*(10), 794-811.

Purves, S. (2006). *The IMPM: What the companies wanted, and what they got*. Retrieved June 28, 2006, from http://www.impm.org/purves/index.html

Raub, S. (2002). Communities of practice: A new challenge for human resources management. *Research and Practice in Human Resource Management, 10*(2), 16-35.

Reingold, J. (2000). You can't create a leader in a classroom. *Fast Company*, 40, 286. Retrieved June 28, 2006 from, http://www.fastcompany.com/online/40/wf_mintzberg.html

Reynolds, M. (1998). Reflection and critical reflection in management learning. *Management Learning, 29(2)*, 183-200.

Saito, A., Medeni, T., Machado, M., & Umemoto, K. (2004). Knowledge management education: A framework towards the development of a comprehensive degree program. *Proceedings of the Knowledge and Systems Science Conference, Japan*.

Schön, D. A. (1983). *The reflective practitioner: How professionals think in action*. San Francisco: Jossey-Bass.

Steyn, G. M. (2002). Harnessing the power of knowledge in higher education. *Education, 124(4)*, 615-631.

Taylor, B. J. (2006). *Reflective practice: A guide for nurses and midwives* New York: Open University Press.

Techsoap. (2005). *Asynchronous communication for online learning and collaboration* Retrieved June 28, 2006 from http://www.techsoup.org/ fb/index.cfm?forum=2008&fuseaction=forums.showSingleTopic&id=58245

21st Century Museum of Contemporary Art, Kanazawa. (2004). *Press release of September 25, 2004*. Kanazawa, Japan: 21st Century Museum of Contemporary Art. Retrieved June 28, 2006, from http://www.kanazawa21.jp/en/12press/pdf/ 0925PressRelease9.pdf

Twist, J. (2004). *Virtual gamers reveal themselves*. Retrieved June 28, 2006, from http://news.bbc.co.uk/1/hi/technology/3683260.stm

Usher, R. S. (1985). Beyond the anectodal: Adult learning and the use of experience. *Studies in the Education of Adults, 7*(1), 59-74.

Von Krogh, G., Ichijo, K., & Nonaka, I. (2000). *Enabling knowledge creation: How to unlock the mystery of tacit knowledge and release the power of innovation*. Oxford, England: Oxford University Press.

Weick, K. E. (1995). *Sensemaking in organisations*, London: Sage

Wenger, E. (1998). *Communities of practices: Learning, meaning, and identity*. Cambridge, MA: Cambridge University Press

Western, S., & Gosling, J. (2006). *Learning from practice: Management exchange*. Retrieved June 28, 2006, from http://www.impm.org/westerngosling/ westerngosling.pdf

CHAPTER 7

# INSTILLING THE LEADERSHIP DEVELOPMENT MINDSET

## Moving Beyond Concepts and Skills

### Peter G. Dominick and John C. Byrne

This chapter discusses courses that go beyond just the transmission of academic knowledge regarding leadership and management. A key theme is that for leadership education to be meaningful it must of course, relate the topic to the nature of today's work and work relationships (e.g., stress how leadership and interpersonal skills will help one to be effective) but it must do more. It should encourage students to adopt a "leadership development mindset." This means helping students understand and apply the process of personal skill development, and instilling the view that mastery of this process is every bit as fundamental to management as are the principles of finance, accounting and marketing. Making this happen in the classroom requires that educators embrace their own roles as leaders committed to the personal development of others.

### INTRODUCTION

Leadership education is certainly not a new topic. To make our point, go online and do a quick search using the terms leadership development or

*New Visions for Graduate Management Education*, 191–226
Copyright © 2006 by Information Age Publishing
All rights of reproduction in any form reserved.

leadership education. You will find many sites with interesting and useful information, assessment tools and even coaching services; not to mention the countless books and articles. In terms of graduate management education, we were able to identify thirty five institutions that offered degree concentrations relating to leadership and 26 that offered leadership as a minor or subemphasis. We also identified 30 business schools that provided leadership education in the forms of particular courses, programs and or specialized centers devoted to the topic. You will find these schools listed in the appendix to this chapter. This list is based upon our personal knowledge as well as information obtained from the Association of Accredited Business Schools International (AACSB) and from a listing previously reported by Doh (2003). Even still, our list is not exhaustive and we did not consider related curriculum pertaining to topics like work teams, interpersonal effectiveness or ethics. Nonetheless, this list helps to make the point that at many schools, leadership is viewed as an important aspect of management education.

That is great news. So why are we writing about it in a book whose focus is New Visions for Graduate Business Education? First, while automation and technology in general have dramatically changed the nature of work, the essence of managing organizations will always center on getting things done with, through and for other people. This fact alone means that any discussion of new visions for business education needs to keep leadership development front and center.

Second, in spite of its perceived value, we are also aware that organizations struggle with leadership development (e.g., Griffin, 2003). A Hewitt Associates' survey of CEOs and human resources executives representing 240 major U.S.-based, multinational companies found that relatively few felt their leadership development programs were successful (Gandossy & Effron, 2003). According to the survey, those companies at the top in terms of leadership development had the financial results to justify their efforts. The report based upon this survey also stressed that the population of key leaders between the ages of 35-44 will drop 15% by 2015. They argue that this trend makes the capacity to develop leadership talent even more critical. This is not to say, however, that individuals and organizations are not already devoting considerable time and money to this process. Consider for instance that annual spending on executive coaching in the United States is estimated at one billion dollars and many regard coaching to be a profession that is still in its infancy (Sherman & Freas, 2004). Academic institutions can play a prominent role in enhancing the benefits organizations derive from their leadership development initiatives. They can do so not so much by changing what organizations do in this regard but by helping to shape the mindsets of those who go on to become organizational members.

Leadership development courses represent the kind of shift in perspective and curriculum design that is stressed by contemporary critics of masters degrees in business administration (MBA). For instance, in their critique of MBA programs, Bennis and O'Toole (2005) stress that many programs have lost their way by overemphasizing academic disciplines and abstract science at the expense of applied research and the development of business professionals. In their critique they quote Thomas Lindsey, the former provost of the University of Dallas:

> Business education in this country is devoted overwhelmingly to technical training. This is ironic because even before Enron, studies showed that executives who fail-financially as well as morally- rarely do so from a lack of expertise. Rather they fail because they lack interpersonal skills and practical wisdom; what Aristotle called prudence.

Also consider recent findings from The Wall Street Journal/Harris Interactive Business School Survey which is based on the opinions of over 3 thousand MBA recruiters (Alsop, 2005). During the 5 years the survey has been conducted, recruiters' priorities in hiring MBAs have remained quite consistent. Among the attributes recruiters said they cared most about were interpersonal and communication skills, teamwork orientation, and personal ethics and integrity. The survey also found that companies are most interested in students who have accumulated significant work experience involving leadership and teamwork. Consider also that the top ranked school in 2005, (Dartmouth's Tuck School) recently implemented a leadership development program that entails individual coaching, self-assessment exercises and feedback from fellow students.

In this chapter we will discuss how graduate leadership education can play an important role in addressing Lindsey's prescient lament and the needs expressed by those who are hiring new business professionals. Central to our approach is the notion that for leadership education to be meaningful it must, instill a leadership development mindset. We'll introduce some strategies and tactics for conveying this theme and also describe how leadership education can play an important role in helping students develop additional points of view that are relevant to the nature of managerial work.

## The Leadership Development Mindset

Following Mintzberg[1] and Gosling's (2002) approach of teaching mindsets, the leadership development mindset is an action oriented point of view. It is rooted in helping students understand that they are responsible for their own development. It stresses that while leadership may be positional it is also something we bring forth and perhaps most importantly is something that can be developed (Doh, 2003).

The mindset is meant to do more than teach people *about* leadership skills. Adopting the leadership development mindset includes applying the process of personal skill development. In our view, mastering this process is every bit as fundamental to managerial success as are mastering the principles of finance, accounting and marketing.

The leadership development mindset builds upon the experiential (versus cognitive) approaches to teaching management skills that have been evolving over the past 20 years. For instance, Cameron and Whetten's (1984) general assessment, learning, analysis, practice, and application (ALAPA) model, further developed by Quinn, Faerman, Thompson, and McGrath (1990), is generally recognized for having initiated the competency based trend (e.g., Bigelow, 1991, 1995) to leadership education.

Wright and Taylor's (1994) microleadership approach emphasized the importance of breaking skills areas into component parts so that people could recognize relationships among general skills and better develop their capacity to use them. For example, their approach helps students recognize how goal setting is a microskill relating to both problem solving and conflict management. Helmer, McKnight, and Myers (1999) introduced more inductive models that called for the introduction of theory after students had contemplated managerial and interpersonal problems.

More recently, Hunt and Sorenson (2001) built upon both of these ideas in describing the learned behavior approach. This approach has students attempt to perform a skill before reflecting upon it or being introduced to the conceptual frameworks about its relevance to management. They argue that putting context and experience first enriches reflection and ultimately allows for more meaningful internalizations of constructs (Kolb, Rubin, & McIntyre, 1984).

In a 1999 review, Bigelow et al. described five management skills courses that drew upon concepts like those described above. To varying degrees, each of these courses stressed personal reflection, behavioral practice of discrete skills, situational learning through simulations, and personal development planning. In most cases, the courses included laying the groundwork for continuous self-improvement as a key learning objective. It is this particular kind of objective that we are trying to highlight by introducing the leadership development mindset. Before describing this mindset in more detail we also want to stress two key perspectives on leadership that are relevant to our point of view.

### Self-Awareness

As Kouzes and Posner (2002) noted, leadership development *is* self development. They stress that since the instrument of leadership is the self it only makes sense to develop our capacity for reflection. The process of self-exploration, they argue is the basis for among other things conveying values, articulating a vision and being able to act with credibility and conviction.

Self-awareness also features prominently in the construct of emotional intelligence (EI) which includes the cognizance of and the capacity to regulate one's emotions and interpersonal behavior (e.g., Goleman, 1998; Mayer & Salovey, 1997). In one recent study, Campbell, Clark, Callister, and Wallace (2003) reported that management skills education led to improvements in students' overall EI. The least impacted EI facet, however, was intentionality, an aspect of one's capacity to self regulate. They noted that this finding was not wholly surprising given that management skills courses typically focus more on interpersonal than personal skills such as self-regulation. One reason for introducing the leadership development mindset is to encourage greater emphasis on helping people master self-regulation/management, or in other words, the process of development.

Consider also how self-awareness fits into cognitive perspectives on behavior change and development. For instance from the perspective of control theory (e.g., Carver & Scheier, 1981), people have to first be aware of a discrepancy between how they are acting or feeling and some desired goal state. Therefore, mechanisms which enhance this awareness are a critical motivator of behavior.

Providing students with a framework for gaining personal insight is an important part of instilling the leadership development mindset. Our approach is to stress levels of analysis that include personal values, traits, attitudes, behaviors, interests and aptitudes. At the same time, we recognize that prompting self-awareness can be threatening. Therefore, helping students adopt a leadership development mindset includes assisting them with the challenges of processing feedback, interpreting it in context and developing their analytical and problem-solving skills.

### Leadership as a Shared Influence Process

While leadership is frequently vested in a formal position it is also a diffused process occurring naturally within a social system (Yukl, 2005, p. 3). This view characterizes leadership as a dynamic enterprise and that dynamicism has important implications for understanding leadership development as a mindset. First, it suggests that in order to develop, aspiring leaders must be cognizant of how context shapes behavior and relationships. Second, it helps to stress that leadership development itself is an ongoing process. Third, it highlights the fact that influence occurs at all levels. Campbell and Dardis (2004) for instance, define leadership as interpersonal influence over and above that influence originating from a person's positional authority. To the extent that leadership is defined as interpersonal influence, students are lead to understand that there is no time like the present to start developing their leadership skills. Finally, because interpersonal skills are the basis for the ability to influence, they are intertwined with leadership development.

Figure 7.1 offers a model for how the leadership development mindset translates into action. It describes what we want students to know (concepts) and more importantly do (action). By concept, we are referring to things people can know *about* leadership and skill development. The concepts we have listed in Figure 7.1 are meant to be illustrative rather than absolute. Action refers to what people should do in the pursuit of personal development, in other words, the ways in which they can apply concepts.

Our model stresses five actions, the first of which is, *Understanding the Self*, the capacity to understand and acknowledge how one's own disposition, outlook and behavior relates to leadership. Relevant concepts that help students organize their understanding include theory and research on leadership traits and behaviors, and content perspectives on motivation such as learned needs theory (McClelland, 2001) as examples. *Understanding the environment* centers on recognizing how the unique constraints, challenges, and opportunities of one's social or organizational context shape his or her capacity to influence and develop as leaders. Situational and contingency leadership theories are useful tools for helping people gain this understanding. Various other models from social and organizational psychology are also relevant such as an appreciation for how cultural norms shape behavior (e.g., Cameron & Quinn, 2000). *Defining direction* involves one's capacity to articulate the overarching reasons behind the efforts they make and development initiatives they will pursue, or to put it in other terms, the capacity to articulate a personal purpose. Relevant leadership concepts include transformational leadership (e.g., Bass, 1985; Burns, 1978) which emphasizes the motivational affects of a clearly articulated vision and mission. Frameworks for describing personal values (e.g., Kim & Shim, 2003) and ethical standards are also relevant. *Personal planning* involves establishing meaningful goals and objectives for capitalizing on strengths, and developing in other areas, all in ways that are aligned with one's personal direction. Related concepts include goal setting, control theory and self-management principles (Latham & Frayne, 1989) because they help people master the process of establishing clear plans and objectives. *Performance monitoring* involves putting development plans into action. Here again, process ori-

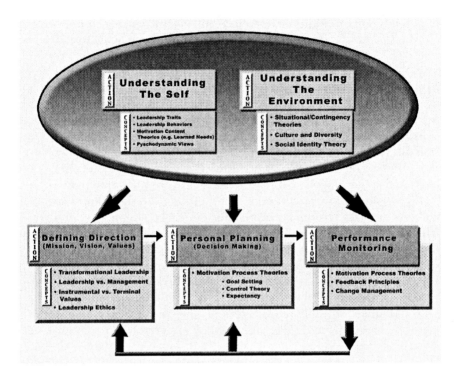

Figure 7.1.   Framework for leadership development planning.

ented theories of motivation are helpful because they highlight relation-ships between effort and performance. An understanding of the role feedback plays in personal development is another relevant concept as is an appreciation for change management as a dynamic process.

Taken together these five actions are the manifestation of the leader-ship development mindset and represent a metaskill set that forms the basis for developing particular leadership and interpersonal skills. While the leadership course we will describe is meant to help people develop in relation to specific skills its broader objective is to help people learn the process of development.

## Course Organization

We offer two graduate level versions of our leadership course both of which are delivered during a fourteen week semester. One version is a required course within our project management concentration and emphasizes how leadership skills apply to a project manager's role. The other version is required within our executive MBA degree program. This version ties course material to the broader issues of technology management and supports a team leadership thread that runs through the entire curriculum. For instance, students in this program work with the same team members on various assignments throughout their matriculation. Students in both programs tend to be working professionals. The average age of those taking the project management version of the course is 32. Students in the executive masters program have an average age of 38 and average 14 years of work experience.

Both courses are built upon the same conceptual framework that includes three overlapping components. The first component of the course stresses self-awareness and assessment. Various assessments of traits, attitudes, and behaviors encourage students to understand their own interests, skills, and behaviors when it comes to leading and managing. We rely in part, upon the conceptual model developed by Whetten and Cameron (2005), which stresses that core aspects of the self include understanding personal values, attitudes towards change, interpersonal needs, and learning style. There are, of course, other models around which to organize self-awareness. For example, Be, Know, Do (Campbell & Dardis, 2004) is another popular model developed for leadership education at West Point.

A second component stresses skills practice. This portion also includes opportunities for assessment and reflection but our focus is on exposing people to normative models of interpersonal effectiveness in relation to communication, conflict management and problem-solving for example. The third component offers frameworks for considering contextual influences on leadership effectiveness. For example, we introduce situational and contingency models of organizational leadership, utilize systems perspectives on team behavior and performance, and discuss particular leadership challenges that relate to boundary spanning roles.

There is however, a fourth component consisting of two core assignments.[2] Represented by the overlapping area in Figure 7.2, these two assignments are the vehicle for recognizing and applying the leadership development mindset. The first assignment stresses reflection and analysis and most closely relates to three of the actions in our model of the leadership development mindset; understanding the self, understanding the environment, and defining direction. Using a corporate annual report as a metaphor, we ask students to write, a skills analysis paper. Their submissions must include a statement of their mission, vision, and values, followed by a comprehensive review of their leadership skills— areas of strength and for development. Our role as instructors is to guide

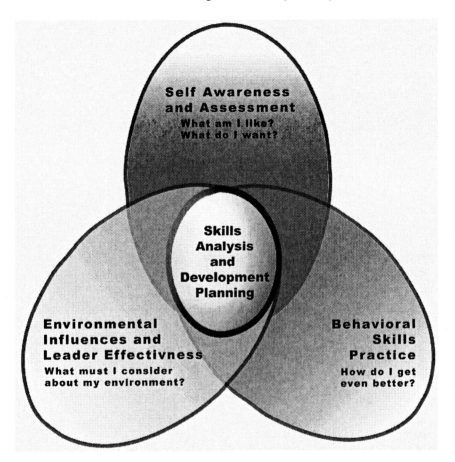

Figure 7.2.   A content framework for leadership development courses.

students in applying leadership and management concepts to themselves. The best papers are integrated analyses, ones that do more than just describe but are also able to integrate concepts and explain how they relate to one's mission, vision and values. One of the things we most enjoy each semester is hearing a common refrain from many students, "This was one of the toughest papers I have ever written, but also one of the most useful."

The second assignment is a skills development paper. It most closely relates to the actions of personal planning and performance monitoring. Based upon conclusions from their skills analysis paper, this second paper describes their efforts to improve at least two skills. The first part of the paper details efforts at developing a skill where they felt they could achieve meaningful short-term results (e.g., within the second half of the semester long course). The second part describes their initial efforts to develop a skill that is likely to require long-term, sustained attention (e.g., 6 months to a year).

Both of these assignments draw upon principles of self-management training (Latham & Frayne, 1989) and together are designed not just to help people develop particular skills but also to experience the process for pursuing ongoing development. This framework for self-management consists of several elements. Self-assessment involves systematic data gathering about the behavior(s) one wishes to modify and provides a means of interpreting and changing behavior. This element is largely accomplished through the skills analysis paper. The skills development plan is essentially a written contract with oneself and calls upon students to implement other elements of the self-management approach. In addition to articulating specific goals their plans must describe how they will engage in self-monitoring, the process of tracking progress toward their goals. They must also describe what they will do in terms of self-evaluation by specifying how they will reward themselves for achieving their goals. They address issues of maintenance/relapse prevention by identifying common problems and pitfalls they might encounter and thinking about ways around them.

## Moving Beyond Functions

Mintzberg and others (Bennis & O'Toole, 2005; Mintzberg, 2004; Mintzberg & Gosling, 2002) noted that management education has overemphasized functional knowledge at the expense of helping people develop their capacity to manage (and lead). Functional expertise should not be discarded, but they assert that we should be organizing management education around the nature of managerial work. Mintzberg and Gosling (2002) in particular, stress that this can be done by considering how a curriculum relates to five key mindsets for managing. These are the reflective mindset, the analytic mindset, the worldly mindset, the collaborative mindset, and the action mindset. Our description of leadership development as a mindset was inspired by the perspective they articulated. Therefore, using the course we have developed as an example, we will next discuss how engaging in the process of leadership development draws upon and helps to develop these other mindsets.

## Leadership Development and the Reflective Mindset

Each semester several of our leadership development sections are taught off-campus, at hotels and or corporate sites. Every so often these classrooms have mirrors on their walls. When they do, we frequently begin the semester by asking students to take a good look at their reflections. "You are looking," we tell them, "at the subject matter for this course." Encouraging a reflective mindset in relation to one's own leadership and interpersonal skills includes providing students with the right assessment tools and experiences. It also involves helping them develop their abilities to give and receive feedback and to deal with the discomfort that can frequently accompany self-awareness and reflection.

In writing their skills analysis paper, students work toward answering several related questions derived from the framework for leadership development in Figure 7.1. In relation to defining direction the key questions they must consider are, "What am I trying to achieve?" "What impact do I want to have?" Understanding the self involves exploring, "What am I like?" "How do I act?" The question derived in relation to understanding my environment is, "How does my environment impact my development?"

*What am I trying to achieve?* We ask people to deal with this question by articulating a personal statement of their mission, vision, and values. In describing a mission statement the main question we are asking them to consider is, "Why are you doing what you are doing (in life, not merely in graduate school)?" To provide a *vision* statement we ask students to articulate a mental picture of where they are going and what they will be doing 5 or 10 years down the road. In describing values we ask them to reflect on principles that govern their behavior and also to consider how and why the particular principles are important to them.

In our experience, these are not easy questions to answer and it helps to provide students with conceptual material about how to formulate a personal mission and also to identify behavioral principles and values. There are of course, no right or wrong responses and we are often impressed with the variety of ways in which students convey what is important to them. Table 7.1 lists some examples of mission statements we have reviewed over the years. These examples illustrate the sort of reflective thinking that comes from exploring one's personal mission, vision for the future and or values.

Some students also assert that they do not have a personal mission, vision or even value framework. Our role however, is to engage their reflective muscles. By posing reflective questions we can often help peo-

**Table 7.1.   Student Mission Statements**

"My mission in life is to be successful in whatever I lay my hands on, to positively impact all the peoples whose paths I cross, and to be happy and be at peace."

"My mission is to enjoy a rich and deep life experience whereby I delve into new experiences, challenges and endeavors in the interest of tasting as much of the world's offerings as I can while maintaining a balance of work, home and family."

"From day to day, I challenge myself to be a better person than I was the day before. From month to month, I make every effort to develop and maintain healthy relationships with other individuals who are a part of my life. From year to year, I work hard to be part of successful companies and organizations that directly contribute to society's needs. And throughout my life, my mission is to continuously make a positive impact on people's lives with the end result of making the world a better place to be."

"This is not the first time I have attempted to decipher my own puzzle, called "life," or try to evaluate myself. When writing about the meaning of my life, the fundamental question I always have trouble answering is consistent; why am I doing what I'm doing, and what ends are implied in such activities?... I've always associated this philosophical question with Plato's thinking on the aim of life; "... since we all wish to be happy, and since we appear to become so by using things and using them rightly, and since knowledge is the source of rightness and good fortune, it seems to be necessary that every man should prepare himself by every means to become as wise as possible." However, "to know is not to be wise. Wisdom is the right use of knowledge. Many men know a great deal, and are all the greater fools for it. There is no fool so great a fool as a knowing fool. But to know how to use knowledge is to have wisdom." Therefore, it is only fair to say that my mission in life is to become wiser so I can use that knowledge to better understand myself and therefore to become a righteous and successful person."

ple look more deeply into what might be a basis for articulating guiding principles and or direction. Examples of these kinds of reflective questions include:

- Think about some times when you felt inspired or excited.
  - What were you doing?
  - With whom were you doing it?
  - Try to describe your feelings in more detail?
  - What were some of the results from these activities?
- What are some people, places and/or things that you consider to be really important?
  - Why are they important?
  - What do you do to nurture and develop them?
  - How would you feel if you no longer had them in your life? Why?

- What are some of your personal achievements about which you feel most proud? Why?
- What are some things you most and least like about your job?
- What do you need to feel effective?
- Where in the world do you feel best about yourself?
- What is the best feedback you can get from someone?
- If you could change one or two things from your past, what would they be? Why?
- What kinds of changes would you like to help bring about?
  - Within your personal life
  - Your professional life and or workplace
  - Society in general
- What is your favorite era in history and what qualities of that time appeal to you?

One of our colleagues encourages her students to reflect upon high and low self-esteem times in their lives (P. Burke, personal communication, April 20, 2006) as a way help to help them identify underlying themes upon which to construct mission, vision and values statements. She has also used visual exercises like asking them to draw a tree and describe its parts in terms of specific aspects of their current or ideal life. There are a growing number of Web-based resources too. Franklin-Covey for instance offers a useful online tool (www.franklincovey.com/mission-builder). One can also glean interesting questions for reflection by visiting TAI Resources and the Actors Institute (www.tairesources.com) whose approach stresses that one's mission and vision are extensions of the unique ways we each see the world. It is important for people to realize that personal mission and vision statements are evolving concepts. We stress that these statements are likely to change over time. Once written down they become a benchmark for future reflection and modification.

There are other activities that also promote reflective thinking about direction and impact. For instance having students write their own eulogy calls for them to articulate ambitions and goals and to reflect on what needs to occur in their future. However, one reason we require personal mission and vision statements is because they are more generally recognized as important leadership tools. For example, the ability to convey an engaging vision and mission are essential components of transformational leadership (e.g., Avolio & Bass, 1988; Bass, 1985). Helping students to see how these tools can enhance personal effectiveness also enhances their appreciation for how these same tools can affect others who they lead and manage.

**Table 7.2.   Examples of Individual Difference Assessments**

| Traits and Personality | Leadership Inventories |
|---|---|
| NEO-FFI | Situational leadership |
| Myers-Briggs | Multifactor leadership questionnaire |
| California personality inventory | Leadership practices Inventory |
| Learning styles (various assessments exist) | Fiedler's least preferred coworkers |
| *Interpersonal Style and Needs* | Assessment |
| Personal profile system (DISC) model | |
| FIRO-B | *Emotional Intelligence Inventories* |
| *Attitudes and Behavior* | Emotional competency inventory (ECI) |
| Self-monitoring | Emotional quotient (EQ) |
| Locus of control | |
| Tolerance for ambiguity | |
| Type A personality | |
| Self-Awareness | |

*What am I like and how do I act?*   Providing students with a framework for exploring how their traits, attitudes, and behaviors relate to their leadership effectiveness also contributes to the development of a reflective mindset. We will not delve into the lengthy body of literature documenting relationships between individual differences and leader effectiveness. It is worth stressing, however, that any leadership development course needs to devote time to these topics and should include assessments that span all three levels (traits, attitudes and behaviors). Table 7.2 lists some examples of popular assessments and inventories that can be incorporated into a leadership development course depending upon time and resources.

As a measure of underlying personality traits we prefer using assessments of the Big Five because of this framework's empirical rigor (e.g., Barrick & Mount, 1991). Other key assessments that we use include, tolerance for ambiguity, locus of control, and the Fundamental Interpersonal Relations Inventory (FIRO-B) (Whetten & Cameron, 2005).

At the behavioral level useful tools include various self-assessments of particular skill areas such as conflict management, active listening, and so forth, in class role-plays and also in-basket simulations (Schor, Smither, & Seltzer, 2004). A key assessment feature of our leadership courses includes the use a of multisource feedback tool developed by Smither and Seltzer (2001). This Managerial Skills Questionnaire (MSQ) was designed around the topics covered in the text by Whetten and Cameron (2005)

Multisource feedback is generally acknowledged to be an effective tool for promoting behavior change (e.g., Smither, London, & Reilly, 2005). Our approach involves having students distribute surveys to colleagues in their work place who return the completed surveys directly to us via

MANAGERIAL SKILLS QUESTIONNAIRE FEEDBACK

| NAME: JOE SAMPLE | 6 RESPONDENTS | | |
|---|---|---|---|
| Questions | Mean | Std. Deviation | Norm |
| Self-Awareness | | | |
| 1.   Asks others for feedback to help uncover his or her blind spots. | 3.0 | 0.8 | 3.40 |
| Time Management | | | |
| 2.   Manages his or her time effectively by focusing on important tasks rather than unimportant but "urgent" tasks. | 3.3 | 0.5 | 3.91 |
| Problem Solving | | | |
| 3.   Generates several alternative solutions to problems before judging the viability of any single alternative. | 2.3 | 0.5 | 3.75 |
| 4.   Uses objective criteria to systematically evaluate alternative solutions to problems. | 2.5 | 0.6 | 3.83 |
| 5.   When solving problems, considers possible side effects that may occur from implementing alternative solutions. | 2.3 | 0.5 | 3.80 |

Figure 7.3.   Excerpt from multisource feedback survey.

email. We then process feedback reports for our students that summarize how others perceived them in relation to the leadership behaviors described in the survey.

By processing the reports ourselves we ensure the confidentiality of respondents thereby adding to the overall perceived fidelity of the information. In addition, advances in technology, for example, e-mail and survey sites on the Internet, are making it increasingly easy to administer multisource feedback programs. We are strong advocates of including them in academic leadership development programs because they provide several benefits. First, the content of the surveys themselves provides a prescriptive model and this alone promotes behavioral improvement (Van Velsor & Leslie, 1991). The surveys also provides a way for students to involve colleagues, subordinates, and bosses in their learning experience, thereby helping to strengthen the relationships between their academic learning and what they do on the job.[3]

Furthermore, unlike most other assessments, which stress self-perceptions, multisource feedback also provides the students with information on how others see them. This is important because most research on self-assessment suggests that self views and assessments tend to be biased, usually with an inclination toward seeing our behavior more positively than others see it (e.g., Bass & Yammarino, 1991; Dunning, Heath, & Suls, 2004).

Because leadership is a dynamic process between leaders and followers, it is important to understand how others see us, as well as how we see ourselves. On the other hand, although organizational literature extols the merits of feedback, making it happen constructively in the workplace is easier said then done. This is due in part to poor skills at delivery, such as being too late (e.g., Larsen, 1989), too infrequent (e.g., Ashford, 1989) or the tendency to sugarcoat (Dunning et al., 2004). It can be viewed as threatening to our self images or future outcomes in the workplace (Kluger & DeNisi, 1996).

Nonetheless feedback is essential to developing a reflective mindset and helps to target change efforts. We devote considerable class time to helping students understand and process the information they receive in their multisource feedback reports. This includes guiding them in how to interpret means and standard deviations, how to consider normative data and thoughts on how to integrate their multisource feedback with other assessments. We also provide tools (e.g., worksheets) to help students summarize their feedback information. For instance, we require them to identify the behavioral ratings that were most surprising to them, rank order personal strengths based upon feedback from others and self-assessments, and also to summarize key reactions to the written comments that are part of their feedback reports. We also make ourselves available for one-on one coaching discussions with students.

A key benefit of leadership development in an academic setting is that it provides a less threatening setting in which to reflect upon feedback from others and also in which to engage in candid self-assessment. To help students feel less defensive or threatened by their feedback we sometimes share negative feedback we receive from manuscripts submitted for publication. Our goal is to encourage acceptance (if not agreement) by demonstrating that negative feedback is a common part of development. Other themes we stress include points like the following:

- We all have strengths and areas for development. That is part of the human condition.
- It is also natural to feel a bit defensive or resistant to some of the feedback and other assessment information you receive. That is natural and human too.
- The most effective leaders understand themselves well and recognize how they impact others. This does not mean they do not have shortcomings but by stressing self-awareness they manage them and look for ways to continue their development
- You may not always agree with the feedback you receive from others but accept it as reality for someone. In that sense it is at least information that you can work with.
- The various assessments used to understand your traits, attitudes and behavior are at their core just information. You don't have to agree with all of it but take the time to consider it carefully. Look

for relationships amongst the data you have and also consider how it relates to other experiences in your life. Personal honesty and willingness to address development areas are essential to leadership development.

- You will always be developing; you don't have to have yourself "fixed" by the end of the semester. Developing the ability to be introspective and to engage in ongoing development planning are some of the most important things to take from any leadership development course.

Still, as with any skill area, students vary in their ability and willingness to be open to feedback. In addition, there are times when holding students accountable for performance can conflict with their efforts to engage in reflection. For instance, one student with poor attendance during the semester wrote a thoughtful development plan for improving his time management skills. We were glad to see he recognized this area as one for development but nonetheless gave him a low mark for participation which ultimately lowered his overall course grade. He protested the lower grade citing his efforts to develop time management. To us, the more important leadership lesson was that efforts at development and reflection do not preclude someone from being accountable for results.

*What is my environment like?*   The reflective mindset also must extend beyond the self to an examination of how one's environment relates to leadership development and effectiveness (Avolio, 2005). Every semester we have some students who claim they do not have time to lead, "I'm just trying to get things done." Others assert that their bosses will not let them lead. In response we stress that organizational life is indeed difficult and that this is all the more reason why it is important to develop your interpersonal and influence skills, a sort of resilience. In other words we retort, "You don't have time not to lead" and "You don't need permission to be a leader." On the other hand, helping people get past these constraints (be they self-imposed or not) also involves helping them reflect on the context in which they are working and developing. Leadership development also involves understanding where and how external influences provide opportunities and obstacles to overcome.

One way we encourage this reflection is by using a "customer base" as a metaphor. Within their skills analysis paper we encourage them to describe the key people, groups, or organizations that are interested in their skills. Typically, students will respond by identifying their companies and clients. We encourage them to consider family, friends, colleagues, fellow students and sometimes even us as "customers." We also ask them to describe their "product line." This includes exploring the extent to which they are creating a "product line" that offers a sustained competitive advantage (in the career marketplace, on their jobs or else-where) or adds unique value. Likewise, we ask that they consider their product line to be more than the services they provide for their employer. By using customer base and product line as metaphors we are asking people to consider their skills and future development in a particular context that is meaningful for them.

Students' skills development papers also call for them to consider context. In writing their plans they must include discussions of potential obstacles they need to address, potential development opportunities, the assignments or experiences they need to seek out, as well as an exploration of useful resources at their disposal.

On another level, we often find that some of the best discussions on leadership occur when people are able to reflect on what is and is not occurring within their own organizations. Examples include discussion of how senior leaders did or did not help organizational members deal with emerging uncertainties, such as pending mergers or cutbacks, the ways in which managers foster innovation, or examples of how political processes shape performance and opportunities. This kind of reflection helps to make discussions of theoretical perspectives on leadership more meaningful. We also find that these discussion help students obtain a better perspective on challenges they are facing. Sometimes they are bolstered by knowing that others are dealing with similar issues. At other times, it helps to hear that not every workplace is as difficult as theirs.

Examples of the kinds of questions that can help students engage in reflective discussion about contextual influences include the following:

- What are some sources of change and uncertainty within my work environment?
- How do I respond to them?
- Are there some ways I can affect change rather than just react to it?
- What are some changes I need to make around me in order to continue my development?
- How is technology impacting what we do and how we do it?
- Can I describe the key mission and vision for my organization or unit? How does it align with my own vision and mission? How do my own skills and current level of ability relate?
- What are some of the core values that characterize behaviors and action in my organization? How do they relate to my own?
- What is leadership development like in my organization?
- Who are potential mentors for me? Why?

- What are some positive and negative examples of leadership and influence that I can learn from?
- What kind of power does my current position provide?

## Leadership Development and the Analytic Mindset

We are always pleased when students are able to describe themselves relative to the array of assessments they experience, (e.g., "I have an internal locus of control," "I have high tolerance for ambiguity," "My average rating for communication skills was 3.4 on a five point scale"). This suggests to us that they have a good understanding of concepts, how to interpret their assessment scores and that they could probably pass a knowledge test. Description however, is not analysis and without analysis, their development efforts are likely to remain shallow. In terms of our leadership development framework (Figure 7.1), an analytic mindset helps students transform their reflections (self, environment, and direction) into personal plans for development.

Boyatzis (2004) for instance, stresses that simply having a student complete a series of surveys and then pointing out where she differs from the norm is of little value unless she also considers the broader context of her experiences and environment. As an example, consider the construct tolerance for ambiguity. The measure helps people gain insight to their attitudes toward dealing with change and uncertainty. Normative information on this assessment can help provide useful perspective. However, one can obtain a more nuanced understanding of this construct by exploring what their environment demands of them and how they react to those demands. In this sense the assessment results serve as a springboard for helping people analyze their behavior in particular situations on one hand and on the other hand, to identify emergent themes across situations. It is this level of analysis (rather than mere numeric comparisons) that form the basis for constructive development planning.

Recall, that earlier in this chapter we subscribed to the view that leadership is a dynamic process. An understanding of process requires looking at relationships and in terms of leadership development this is where an analytic mindset becomes important. Bruce Avolio (2005) stresses this point in his recent book, *Leadership Development in Balance*. He writes:

> when we judge the leadership of a person, we can do so by evaluating attributes such as honesty, trustworthiness, intelligence and energy. Yet in isolation and without reference to others, these concepts have little meaning, except to describe that individual. (p. 13)

Therefore, in writing their skills analysis papers we challenge students to use conceptual information covered in class to look for themes and relationships. For example, we sometimes encourage students to consider how their assessments and experiences relate to the two fundamental activities of managing work and managing relationships. Efforts at analysis are also reflected in the ways people establish relationships between who they are (traits and behaviors) and their aspirations and ideals (e.g., mission, vision, and values).

Deeper understanding also comes from analyzing the ways in which trait-based assessments relate to behavioral assessments and by elaborating on assessment results through descriptions of work-or personal experiences. Such an integrated analysis might include descriptions like the following:

> My NEO results suggest that I am highly agreeable. My FIRO-B scores were also highest in the areas of inclusion and affection. I also received multisource feedback indicating that I am a good listener and that people feel they can count on me. In retrospect I have a hard time saying no to others' requests for help and am quick to compromise or accommodate others in conflict situations. In one recent situation.

The example above illustrates how exploration across levels of analysis helps people recognize relationships between strengths and areas for development. Doing so requires that they apply higher-order analytic skills such as decomposition, integration and synthesis and ultimately deepens their capacity for implementing the leadership development mindset. This point was conveyed in a recent comment from one of our students, when he stated, "I have taken feedback surveys in the past, however, I never really came to any convincing conclusions (about myself). Writing this paper enabled me to strongly identify what I need to do to grow successfully."

Not long ago, another of our students noted the similarities between the personal development planning he was doing in his leadership course and the principles he was learning about in his strategic planning course. Since students are required to take both courses during the same semester he wondered if we had placed them together because of their similarities. While we would have liked to have taken credit for being so forward thinking we could not. Nonetheless, his observation was very astute. Successful leadership development and successful strategic thinking both require looking past the numbers to identify themes, relationships, and opportunities as they exist in our real environments. In other words, both require that we adopt an analytic mindset.

## Leadership Development and the Worldly Mindset

Exposure to others brings insight to our own and thereby helps us become worldly wise (Mintzberg & Gosling, 2002). This is the essence of a worldly mindset. Such experiences are invaluable because they help us to develop perspective which in turn promotes the kind of adaptability needed to work with and across cultures (e.g., Ernst, 2004). The 14 week leadership development program we have been describing does not provide international experience but it can play a role in helping people develop what Bruce Avolio (2005) refers to as perspective-taking capacity. It does so by helping people, on one hand to recognize and value the differences we find in others (Whetten & Cameron, 2005) and on the other hand to acknowledge, if not challenge, implicit cultural assumptions that shape and drive one's own behavior. For instance, in their skills analysis papers students frequently reflect upon the ways in which their ethnic, cultural and religious backgrounds have shaped their core values and ideals. While we cannot assure that this recognition leads to adaptability it is an important first step in developing one's perspective-taking capacity.

We found leaderless group discussions can be useful tools for helping people recognize the ways in which their cultural biases and assumptions impact their thoughts and actions. One such exercise requires students in teams of 5-7 to assume the role of a board of directors for an airline company (Seltzer, 1997). Their task is to select a chief executive officer from a list describing seven candidates. Each candidate has strengths and weaknesses and they have varying personal backgrounds and experiences. The interaction is videotaped and played back for discussants to review. During the playback session people get to observe their interpersonal behaviors. They also get to see how their implicit assumptions about others' backgrounds shape individual and group decisions. In some cases a candidate is chosen because of a non-job-related characteristic, often gender or race or a candidate is not considered due to age.

On a more tactical level, Prince and Hoppe (2004) stress that effectively working with people from other cultures requires that we tune into the discomfort the experiences produce within us. We may need to modify our communication style, they point out, when for instance, another's behavior makes us feel uncomfortable or their reaction seems confusing to us; when we jump to assumptions about who is right and wrong, when we start to generalize and stereotype or when we are inclined to exclude someone because understanding and being understood seems too difficult. Their suggestions highlight the fact that introspection and self-awareness are an important part of adopting a worldly point of view.

At the same time there is a behavioral component to the worldly mind-set. Having the interpersonal skills to constructively engage others can help people thrive in and grow from international experiences. Examples include developing communication skills, especially active listening and also mastering principles of constructive conflict management. Implicit in both of these skill sets are the importance of demonstrating empathy and an understanding of others' points of view (though not necessarily agreement) both of which can go a long way toward building trust and bridging cultural distinctions.

The backgrounds of students themselves are, of course, another important means for promoting a worldly mindset and for that reason we are proponents of considering factors like ethnic and cultural diversity as part of the admission process. In addition, many of the students in our course work for multi-national companies. Encouraging them to discuss and apply their own cross-cultural work experiences enriches the learning experience for all, including us.

In closing it helps to realize that developing a worldly mindset is an ongoing and evolving process. One of us has a colleague with an unusual collection of credentials and experiences. Besides an advanced degree in finance, this fellow is conversant in several languages, Indian (born and raised in India) and is an Orthodox Jew. A single leadership course (or for that matter an entire management degree) will not instill this kind of worldly perspective but by enhancing self-awareness and interpersonal effectiveness it can provide some foundational tools that contribute to adopting a worldly mindset.

## Leadership Development and the Collaborative Mindset

Implicit within any description of a leader is that to be one, you must have followers, which in effect, tells us that leaders are defined at least in part by those they lead. In other words, managerial success or failure is due to a significant degree on our relationships with others. To the extent that a collaborative mindset involves establishing and maintaining relationships, thoughtful leadership development must help nurture this capacity.

In fact, we stress that interpersonal relations are one of the core aspects of the self (Whetten & Cameron, 2005) and as a result include assessments that help people explore this aspect of their managerial outlook. FIRO-B is one particularly useful tool because it helps people gain some insight regarding the needs and desires they bring to relationships (e.g. inclusion, affection and control) (Schutz, 1958). It is also an excellent tool for helping people to appreciate the ways in which they differ. For this purpose we often have people form groups to calculate compatibilities based upon these results. There are of course other assessments such as measures of interpersonal style, like the personal profile system and also facets of personality as measured through NEO-FFI, IPIP or even Myers Briggs.

We also think it is important to encourage reflection on a person's capacity to stand alone (e.g., to make the tough leadership decisions that might alienate them from others or to offer alternative perspectives that are the basis for change.) As others have noted (e.g., Zaleznik, 1992) leading also implies having a sense for the ways in which one stands apart from the groups to which they belong. Therefore, we typically encourage reflection on a person's need for and comfort with using power. Reflecting on FIRO-B control needs can help in this regard and we also rely upon learned needs theory (e.g., McClelland, 1966) and especially need for power (McClelland & Burnham, 1976) to help people gain personal insight.

Skill modules on topics like interpersonal communication, conflict management, team leadership, and problem-solving allow people to consider how the collaborative mindset translates into behavior. Our approach stresses introduction of principles, the use of behavior modeling and cases followed by skill practice and feedback.

As mentioned earlier, the version of our leadership course residing within an executive master's program is integrated with a team-thread running through the entire curriculum. Team projects are built into all courses in the program and students work on the same teams throughout their matriculation. The leadership course which occurs in the second semester of this program includes having each team consider the individual difference data of its team members to identify collective strengths and challenges and also requires them to establish team working agreements. Interpersonal skill modules have also been incorporated into other courses in ways that stress their relationships to functional activities. For instance, a course on strategic planning has a module on feedback and a course on entrepreneurialism and innovation contains a module on negotiation skills as they might apply to seeking venture capital. In addition to multisource feedback from their workplaces, students in this program also complete a peer feedback instrument at roughly the midpoint and final semester of the program.[4]

As you might expect, students' collaborative experiences are not always pleasant or even successful. Moreover, we have found that using a team-thread stretches our own management and facilitation skills. In spite of the challenges these experiences pose, students consistently recognize this aspect of the program as being a valuable part of their education.

Thus far, we have stressed how a leadership development course contributes to instilling a collaborative mindset. The reverse is also true. A collaborative mindset enhances leadership development. An important value underlying a course like the one we have been describing is that improvement is largely the learner's responsibility (Whetten & Cameron, 2005, p. 20). This means instructors and fellow students are collaborators in any given individual's efforts. For example, effective experiential learning requires that people open themselves to feedback from others and be willing to provide candid and constructive feedback. As instructors we need to reinforce this kind of interdependence. Our efforts include modeling this ideal by making feedback a priority in interactions with students and also by coaching others on their feedback skills. Promoting dialogue and discussion plays a key role in shaping the classroom culture (not to mention saving everyone from the monotony of lectures). In spite of how knowledgeable we like to think we are, when it comes to collaboration it is often more important to hold back so that students can explore and respond to others' comments and inquiries.

Diversity is another important collaborative value. As we have stressed throughout this chapter, understanding oneself and appreciating what makes others unique go hand in hand. Yes, there are concepts to master in academic leadership development course such as ours but mastering the process of self-discovery and personal improvement are even more important. Moving down that path is much more meaningful (and enjoyable) when done in collaboration with others.

## Leadership Development and the Action Mindset

The action mindset involves putting reflection and analysis into practice (Mintzberg & Gosling, 2002) and is a perspective shared by proponents of action learning in general (e.g,. Noel & Charan, 1988). A major reason for writing this chapter is to stress that action learning can and should be an integral part of academic leadership development education. Recall that the leadership development mindset includes acknowledging that one need not be in a position of formal authority to influence and shape direction. That is why we are always pleased when in the midst of the course; students tell us that they are already applying what they have learned. They frequently describe situations they encounter at work but their examples often include other settings. For instance, one student recounted how he used recently learned principles of conflict management to diffuse a potential confrontation on a New York City subway. A few have also stressed how what they have learned helped them to be better spouses. The point is that opportunities for applying leadership and interpersonal skills abound and when students can describe their recent efforts to do so they have embraced an action mindset.

Promoting action is why, in completing their skills development papers, we have students document and describe their development efforts for one of their two goals. However, transforming awareness of a development need into an action-oriented plan is not always straightforward. It helps to begin this process with some coaching and support. A typical problem is the tendency for students to define their development goals too broadly, (e.g., I want to develop leadership skills). Some students will articulate goals to develop their functional skills like financial analysis or their ability to utilize a certain technology. We remind them that while such goals are worthy pursuits, for the purposes of this course, they need to think in terms of leadership and interpersonal effectiveness. In some cases, we are able help them redefine their functionally oriented goals in terms of how they relate to personal power.

Others find it difficult to articulate plans for monitoring and evaluating their performance in relation to softer skills like effective listening. One solution we offer is for them to define their goals in terms of the frequency with which they attempt a certain behavior in a given context such as one-on-one meetings with colleagues. We encourage them to keep logs and notes based upon what they attempted and their perception of the effect it may have had. Their records are then submitted as part of their skills development paper. A similar strategy can be helpful with regard to a skill area like stress management, when the most meaningful measures of success might have more to do with how someone feels than with feedback they can get from others.

Not every plan we review is ideally formed by the end of the semester. Many however are quite effective and most students, we would assert, are better off for having made the effort to develop and begin implementing their plans. The quotes below illustrate times where students seemed to have recognized that they are learning about the development process:

I have already used some techniques when attempting to solve problems, manage stress and conflict. Once again, thanks for a great course. It helps me understand more about myself and about **how** to work towards improving some of the skills that need improvement.

As I discovered while writing my skills development paper, this class not only helped me discover areas that needed development, but, also provided relevant information on **how** to develop them.

## SUMMARY AND CONCLUSIONS

In this chapter we have argued that the process of leadership development is itself a fundamental skill that management students must learn. We also stressed that helping people engage in this process supports development of other broader mindsets that transcend functional disciplines. We would like to close by offering some thoughts on the challenges and opportunities that come from teaching such courses.

Teaching leadership development requires adopting and applying the leadership development mindset. To put it in terms of transformational leadership, idealized influence is a key catalyst (Bass & Avolio, 1996). We are more effective in the classroom when we are keeping our own mission and development objectives in mind. From time to time it helps for someone teaching a leadership development course to personally consider questions like the following:

- Why am I teaching this course? How does it fit in with my current vision and mission?
- How will I use my strengths to be effective?
- What are some of my personal limitations about which I need to be mindful?
- Is there anything about my own skills or development that I want to share with my students? What kind of effect do I want this information to have on them?
- What impact do I want to have on my students this semester? What will I be looking for to let me know I'm having an impact?
- Are there ways for me to get my students involved in helping me learn?
- What are some challenges I'll have to contend with? (e.g., organizational resource issues, other demands on my time). What am I willing to do to overcome them?

One benefit of this kind of reflection is that it promotes personal involvement, an attribute others have acknowledged is critical to leadership (e.g., Bossidy & Charan, 2003; Kouzes & Posner; 2002). Executive coach, Marshall Goldsmith, for example stresses to his CEO clients, "To help others develop, start with yourself!" (Goldsmith, 2004). We know we fall short in the face of limited time, resources, energy and our own reluctance but demonstrating a commitment to the process conveys credibility and raises efficacy for students.

The learning model we propose does not lend itself to a large class size. In fact, although our leadership courses are required we are very careful to control section sizes, sometimes to the chagrin of our administrators. In response to this challenge, consider that there are ways to use other resources. For instance, we have discussed establishing a leadership development community within our Institution by drawing upon human resources students, psychology students, even others from the business community to serve as coaches and mentors. Ideally it would be helpful to extend coaching support beyond just the duration of the semester in which the course is offered.

Our courses take advantage of the fact that most of our students are working professionals. This fact facilitates our ability to offer an applied, action-oriented course experience. Although we regularly have full-time students in the classroom, some aspects of our course would need to be modified if the majority of students were not in the workforce while enrolled. For example, thread experiences that require people to assume team leadership roles are one way full-time programs could provide students with a more enriched context for leadership development education.

While students' papers call for them to engage in the various actions of the leadership development mindset, their submissions must also demonstrate efforts to work with course material and apply concepts correctly. Having to formally grade this kind of introspective work is a double-edged sword. On one hand, assigning grades helps to promote accountability. On the other hand, the grading process leads some students to focus more on offering what they think are correct responses, rather than on development issues that are personally meaningful. However, we also use their submissions as a basis for a coaching dialogue, and frequently encourage students to further develop their papers and resubmit them.

Organizational culture also shapes leadership development (Bal & Quinn, 2004). We cannoy significantly shape the cultures within our students' respective organizations. However, academic leadership development courses do not exist within vacuums. Management programs will be more likely to succeed in this area when they are cognizant of how the values and mindsets reflected in their leadership courses align with the overall curriculum. For example, leadership development features prominently in the project management concentration within the W. J. Howe School of Stevens Institute of Technology. A key tenet of this program is that successful project management requires a strategic perspective (Shenhar, Dvir, Levy, & Maltz, 2001). This broader strategic perspective in turn calls for project managers to embrace their roles as leaders thereby highlighting the relevance of leadership development and it relationship to one's overall management education.

Advances in technology represent another set of issues that relate to the meaning and nature of leadership development education. While the fundamental challenges of leading and managing remain intact, a growing base of knowledge workers and the proliferation of virtual/distributed work environments suggest that the context for leadership and leadership development is evolving (e.g., Kayworth & Leidner, 2001-2002). Key issues include bridging cultural, temporal and socioeconomic divides, conveying enthusiasm, creating structure, and even demonstrating empathy via a keyboard, a computer screen or videoconference, all at an accelerated pace.

These changes call for us to consider ways of addressing this evolving context in the classroom. We do offer an online version of the leadership development course discussed in this chapter. Keeping leadership development personal requires that we spend more time reaching out to students than we might otherwise do in a face-to-face setting. The course also calls for more attention to creating structure for weekly interaction. Overall, because our course model stresses personal development planning it does work in an asynchronous online environment. We are still able to provide students with one-on-one feedback about their individual work and can also provide feedback to them on how well they handled virtual team leadership responsibilities that are rotated amongst them on a weekly basis. This is not saying we view virtual classrooms as the preferred method for leadership development education. However, web-based curricula are becoming an increasingly significant part of the higher education landscape.

We appreciate having the opportunity to write this chapter because we are convinced that regardless of how technically complex work and the workplace becomes, leadership and interpersonal skills will always matter to the practice of management, especially if we expect business to have a positive impact on society overall. We have by now, worked with hundreds of students. Not all of them leave the course enlightened but we can candidly say that most do. A next step for us is to investigate the longitudinal effects of what they have learned and experienced. We are interested in knowing for instance, the extent to which longer term development plans were implemented and to see if colleagues still note positive behavioral changes—have they become better managers and leaders? We also want to know more about how organizational settings impact efforts started in the classroom and if there are key individual difference factors that play a role in sustaining development efforts. These are important questions that can help us improve the way we develop future business professionals and we encourage others to pursue them as well.

## ACKNOWLEDGMENTS

We would like to thank James Smither, LaSalle University, Veona Martin, Sanofi-Aventis Corporation, and our anonymous reviewers for their invaluable insights and critiques. Thanks also go to our colleagues who have helped to develop the course model described and to our students, whose reflections on their learning experiences have helped shape this chapter.

### Appendix A:
### Institutions Offering Concentrations/Majors in Leadership

| Institution | Degree Type | Concentration Description |
| --- | --- | --- |
| Claremont Graduate University (Drucker School) | MBA | Leadership concentration |
| Cleveland State University | MBA | Management and leadership |
| College of Mount St. Joseph | Other | Leadership |
| Copenhagen Business School | MBA | Leadership, knowledge, and innovation |
| DePaul University | MBA | Leadership and change management |
| ESCP European School o Management | Other | Innovation, entrepreneurship, leadership |
| George Washington University | Exec | Global leadership program |
| IMD, International Institute for Management | MBA and EMBA | Leadership; Leadership, and Strategy |
| Marquette University | MLS | Organization and leadership major |
| Michigan State University (Eli Broad School) | MBA | Leadership concentration |
| Minnesota State University, Mankato | MBA | Leadership |
| Naval Postgraduate School | MS | Management in leadership education and development |
| Nova Southeastern University | MSM | Leadership |
| Santa Clara University | MBA | Leading people and organizations |
| SDA Bocconi (Italy) | Other | Human resource leadership |
| St. Bonaventure University | MS | Professional leadership |
| Syracuse University | MBA | Entrepreneurship, innovation, and global leadership |
| Texas A&M University, (Lowry Mays School) | EMBA | Leadership concentration |
| Texas Christian University | Other | Master in educational leadership |
| The University of Auckland | Other | International strategy and leadership |
| The University of Manchester | Other | Healthcare leadership and management |
| University of Baltimore | MBA | Leadership and organizational learning |
| University of Canterbury | Other | Organizational Leadership And Development |

| | | |
|---|---|---|
| University of Chicago | MBA | Leadership effectiveness and development (LEAD) |
| University of Delaware | MBA | Museum leadership and management |
| University of Denver | IMBA and MBA | Values Based Leadership |
| University of Guelph | MA | Leadership |
| University of Missouri-Kansas City | MBA | Leadership and change in human systems |
| University of Missouri-Kansas City | MPA | Early childhood leadership |
| University of San Diego | Other | Leadership |
| University of San Diego | Other | Business leadership development |
| University of St. Thomas | MBA | Executive management and leadership |
| Washington University in St. Louis | MBA | Organizational leadership |
| Webster University | MA | Leadership and management |
| Yale School of Management | MBA | Leadership concentration |

## Appendix B:
## Institutions Offering Leadership as a Minor/Areas of Subemphasis

| Institution | Degree Type | Concentration Description |
|---|---|---|
| Butler University | MBA | Leadership |
| Copenhagen Business School | EMBA | Leadership |
| Dartmouth (Tuck) | MBA | Leading organizations |
| Emory University | MBA | Leadership |
| Georgia Institute of Technology (Dupree) | MBA | Leadership and organizational change |
| MIT (Sloan) | MBA, SM | Leadership and change in organizations |
| Northern Arizona University | Other | Educational leadership |
| Pepperdine University | MBA | Leadership and managing organizational change |
| Queensland University of Technology | MBA | Leadership |
| Rochester Institute of Technology | MBA | Management and leadership |
| Rockhurst University | MBA | Health care leadership |
| Royal Roads University | MBA | Leadership |
| SDA Bocconi (Italy) | Other | Self-assessment and leadership development |
| Simon Fraser University | MBA | Leadership and organizational change |
| Universidad Peruana de Ciencias Aplicadas—S.A.C. | EMBA | Leadership |
| University of Chicago | MBA | Business leadership in changing Times; The practice of leadership |
| University of La Verne | MBA | Management and leadership |
| University of Michigan | MBA | Leadership |
| University of Nebraska-Lincoln | EMBA | Executive leadership |
| University of Richmond | MBA | Strategic leadership |

| | | |
|---|---|---|
| University of South Florida | Other | Leadership and organizational effectiveness |
| University of Southern California | MBA | Leadership and organization |
| University of Washington | Exec. | Leadership in organizations |
| University of Wisconsin-Milwaukee | MBA | Leadership |
| Vanderbilt (Owen) | MBA | Leading Teams and organizations |
| Virginia Polytechnic Institute and State University | MBA | Executive leadership |

## Appendix C:
## Institutions With Specialized Leadership Courses, Programs, or Centers

| *Institution* | *Description(s)* |
|---|---|
| Babson College | The Center For Women's Leadership Leadership courses and mentoring integrated in program |
| Dartmouth (Tuck) | William F. Achtmeyer Center for Global Leadership Specialized leadership courses and seminars in curriculum. |
| Duke University( Fuqua) | Fuqua/Coach K Center for Leadership and Ethics |
| Harvard Business School | Program for Global Leadership |
| Indiana University (Kelley) | Leadership Research Institute |
| University of Maryland | James MacGregor Burns Academy of Leadership |
| LaSalle University | Leadership course integrated in curriculum |
| Michigan State University | Collaborative Leadership Center; Michigan Political Leadership Program; Multi Unit Leadership Training Initiative |
| MIT (Sloan) | MIT Sloan Fellows Program in Innovation and Global Leadership |
| Cornell (Johnson) | Specialized fully supported MBA fellowship focused on leadership |
| Southern Methodist University (Cox) Global | Global Leadership Program |
| Stevens Institute of Technology (W.J. Howe) | Leadership courses in project management and executive masters programs |
| Tampa University (Sykes) | TECO Energy Center for Leadership; Leadership course in curriculum |
| University of Georgia (Terry) | Institute of Leadership Advancement |
| Texas A&M, | Annual Women's Leadership Forum |
| Tufts University | Institute for Global Leadership; Leadership courses integrated in multiple programs |
| University of Buffalo | Center for Entrepreneurial Leadership; Center for International Leadership; Leadership courses integrated in multiple programs |
| University of California—Berkeley (Haas) | Executive Leadership Program and Leadership course integrated with program |
| University of California—Irvine | Leadership and Management Program for Scientists and Technology Professionals (LAMP) |
| University of Colorado, Boulder | Student Leadership Institute |
| University of Dayton | Center for Leadership and Executive Development |

| University of Iowa (Tippie) | Leadership courses integrated in multiple programs |
| University of Nebraska-Lincoln) | Gallup Leadership Institute |
| University of Pennsylvania (Wharton) | Center for Leadership and Change Management |
| University of Pittsburgh | David Berg Center for Leadership and Ethics |
| University of Southern California (Marshall) | Leadership Institute |
| University of Washington | The Center for Educational Leadership; The Center for Institutional Change |
| Vanderbilt (Owen) | Integrated course; The Cal Turner Program for Moral Leadership |
| Yale School of Management | The Yale Chief Executive Leadership Institute |

## NOTES

1. We note that Mintzberg in his book *Managers not MBAs* (2005) does not differentiate between managers and leaders. Nonetheless, we will discuss characteristics and traits that may be more typically aligned with one or the other so one may be able to focus on its development.

2. Our colleagues James Smither and Joseph Seltzer of La Salle University first developed these assignments in their leadership course and allowed us to adapt them for our own.

3. While not all students are employed when they take our course, most are and even when they are not almost all can identify people outside of the classroom who can provide meaningful feedback

4. The assessment tool we use contains twenty items related to two dimensions: team facilitation and team leadership (Reilly, 2003). In the past 2 years that we have been tracking peer feedback data we have been able to report statistically significant positive changes in peer ratings between the first and second administrations of the assessment.

## REFERENCES

Alsop, R. (2005, September 21). The wall street journal guide to the top business schools: A special report. *Wall Street Journal* (Eastern Edition), p. R4.

Ashford, S. J. (1989). Self-assessments in organizations: A literature review and integrative model. In B. M. Staw & L. L. Cummings (Eds.), *Research in Organizational Behavior, 11*, 133-174.

Avolio, B. J., & Bass, B. M. (1988). Transformational leadership, charisma and beyond. In J. G. Hunt, B. R. Baliga, H. P. Dachler, & C. A. Schrieshiem (Eds.), *Emerging leadership vistas* (pp. 29-50). Lexington, MA: Lexington Books.

Avolio, B. J. (2005). *Leadership development in balance*. Mahwah, NJ: Erlbaum.

Bal, V., & Quinn, L. (2004). The missing link: Organizational culture and leadership development. In M. Wilcox & S. Rush (Eds.), *The CCL guide to leadership in action* (pp. 163-171). San Francisco: Jossey-Bass.

Barrick, M., & Mount, M. (1991). The Big Five personality dimensions and job performance: A meta-analysis. *Personnel Psychology, 44*, 1-26.

Bass, B. M. (1985). *Leadership and performance beyond expectations*. New York: Free Press.

Bass, B. M., & Avolio, B. J. (1996). *Multifactor leadership questionnaire manual*. Palo Alto, CA: MindGarden.

Bass, B. M., & Yammarino, F. J. (1991). Congruence of self and others' leadership ratings of naval officers for understanding successful performance. *Applied Psychology, 40*, 437-454.

Bennis, W. G., & O'Toole, J. (2005, May). How business schools lost their way. *Harvard Business Review*, 96-104.

Bigelow, J. D. (1991). *Managerial skills: Explorations in practical knowledge.* Newbury Park, CA: Sage.

Bigelow, J. D. (1995). Teaching managerial skills: how do they stack up? *Journal of Management Education, 19,* 305-325.

Bigelow, J. D., Seltzer, J., van Buskirk, W., Hall, J. C., Schor, S., Garcia, J., & Keleman, K. (1999). Management skills in action: Four teaching models. *Journal of Management Education, 23*(4), 355-376.

Bossidy, L., & Charan, R. (2003). Seven essential behaviors. *Executive Excellence, 20(11)* 12-13.

Boyatzis, G. (2004) Presentation to Metropolitan New York Association of Applied Psychology, New York.

Burns, J. M. (1978). *Leadership.* New York: Harper and Row.

Cameron, K. S., & Quinn, R. E. (2000). *Diagnosing and changing organizational culture.* Reading, MA: Addison-Wesley.

Cameron, K. S., & Whetten, D. A. (1984) A model for teaching management skills. *Organizational Behavior Teaching Journal, 8,* 21-27.

Campbell Clark, S., Callister, R., & Wallace, R. (2003) Undergraduate management skills courses and students' emotional intelligence. *Journal of Management Education, 1*(27), 3-23.

Campbell, D., & Dardis, G. (2004). Be know do. *Human Resource Planning, 2*(27), 26-39

Carver, C. S., & Scheier M. F. (1981). *Attention and self-regulation: A control theory approach to human behavior.* New York: Springer-Verlag.

Doh, J. (2003). Can leadership be taught? perspectives from management educators: Interview and commentary. *Academy of Management Learning and Education, 1*(2), 54–67.

Dunning, D., Heath, C., & Suls, J. (2004, December). Flawed self assessment, Implications for health, education and the workplace *Psychological Science, 5*(3).

Ernst, C. (2004). Global managing: Mastering the spin of a complex world. In M. Wilcox & S. Rush (Eds.), *The CCL guide to leadership in action* (pp. 82-93). San Francisco: Jossey-Bass.

Gandossy, R., & Effron, M. (2003). *Leading the way: Three truths from the top companies for leaders.* Hoboken, NJ: Wiley.

Goldsmith, M. (2004). To help others develop start with yourself. *Fast Company Magazine, 80,*100.

Goleman, D. (1998, November-December). What makes a leader? *Harvard Business Review,* 93-102.

Griffin, N. S. (2003, March). Personalize your management development. *Harvard Business Review,* 3-8.

Helmer, T., McKnight, M., & Meyers, P. (1999). *An alternative science of organizational behavior: the science of experience.* Paper presented at the 26th annual Organizational Teaching Conference, Las Cruces, NM.

Hunt, J. G., & Sorenson, R. L., (2001). A learned-behavior approach to management skill development. *Journal of Management Education, 25*(2), 167-190.

Kayworth, T. R., & Leidner, D. E. (2001-2002) Leadership effectiveness in Global Virtual teams. *Journal of Management Information Systems, 18*(3), 7-40.

Kim, H. -S., & Shim, S. (2003). Gender-based approach to the understanding of leadership roles among retail managers. *Human Resource Development Quarterly, 14*(3), 321-342.

Kluger, A. N., & DeNisi, A. (1996). The effects of feedback interventions on performance: A historical review, a meta-analysis, and a preliminary feedback intervention theory. *Psychological Bulletin, 119*, 254-264.

Kolb, D. A., Rubin, I. M., & McIntyre, J. M. (1984). *Organizational psychology: An experiential approach* (4th ed.) Englewood Cliffs, NJ: Prentice Hall.

Kouzes, J. M., & Pozner, B. Z. (2002). *The leadership challenge* (3rd ed.). San Francisco: Jossey-Bass

Larsen, J. R., Jr. (1989). The dynamic interplay between employees' feedback seeking strategies and supervisors' delivery of performance. *Academy of Management Review, 14*, 408-422.

Latham, G. P., & Frayne, C. A. (1989). Self-management training for increasing job attendance: A follow-up and a replication. *Journal of Applied Psychology, 74*(3), 411-416.

Mayer, J. D., & Salovey, P. (1997). What is emotional intelligence? In P. Salovey & D. J Slutyer (Eds.), *Emotional development and emotional intelligence* (pp. 3-31). New York: Harper-Collins.

McClelland, D. C. (2001). Achievement motivation. In W. E. Natermeyer & J. T. McMahon (Eds.), *Classics of organizational behavior* (3rd ed., pp. 73-80) Long Grove, IL: Waveland Press.

McClelland, D. C., & Burnham, D. H. (1976, March-April). Power is the great motivator. *Harvard Business Review, 54*(2), 100-109.

Mintzberg, H. (2004). *Managers not MBAs: A hard look at the soft practice of managing and development.* San Francisco: Berrett-Koehler.

Mintzberg, H., & Gosling, J. (2002). Educating beyond borders. *Academy of Management Learning and Education, 1*(1), 64-76.

Noel, J. C., & Charan, R. (1988). Human resource management in action: Leadership development at G. E.'s Crotonville. *Human Resource Management, 27*(4), 433-447.

Prince, D. W., & Hoppe, M. H. (2004). Getting the message: How to feel your way with other cultures. In M. Wilcox & S. Rush (Eds.), *The CCL guide to leadership in action* (pp. 73-82). San Francisco: Jossey-Bass.

Quinn, R. E., Faerman, S. R., Thompson, M. P., & McGrath, M. R. (1990). *Becoming a master manager—A competency framework.* Chichester, England: Wiley.

Reilly, R. R. (2003) *Team helper peer feedback survey.* New York: Learning Bridge.

Schor, S., Seltzer, J., & Smither, J. (1994). SSS software: An in-basket for the 90s. *Proceedings from the 29th annual meting of the Eastern Academy of Management, Albany, NY.*

Schutz, W. C. (1958). *FIRO: A three dimensional theory of interpersonal behavior.* New York: Holt, Rinehart, & Winston.

Seltzer, J. (1997). *AIROSPAC: Decision exercise.* Philadelphia: La Salle University.

Shenhar, A. J., Dvir, D., Levy, O., & Maltz, A. C. (2001). Project success: A multidimensional strategic concept. *Long Range Planning, 34*, 699-725.

Sherman, S., & Freas, A. M. (2004, November). The wild west of executive coaching. *Harvard Business Review, 82*(11), 82-89.

Smither, J., London, M., & Reilly, R. R. (2005). Multisource feedback: Validity evidence, meta-analysis of performance change, and a theoretical framework and research review of conditions for change, *Personnel Psychology, 58*, 33-66.

Smither, J., & Seltzer, J. (2001). *Managerial skills questionnaire*. Philadelphia: La Salle University.

Van Velsor, E., & Leslie, J. B. (1991). *Feedback to managers: A review and comparison of 16 multirater feedback instruments* (Vol. 2). Greeensboro, NC: Center for Creative Leadership.

Whetten, D. A., & Cameron, K. S. (2005). *Developing management skills* (6th ed.) Upper Saddle River, NJ. Prentice Hall.

Wright, P. L., & Taylor, D. S. (1994). *Improving leadership skills: Interpersonal skills for effective leadership*. Englewood Cliffs, NJ: Prentice Hall.

Yukl, G. (2006). *Leadership in organizations* (6th ed.). Upper Saddle River, NJ: Prentice Hall

Zaleznik, A. (1992, March-April). Managers and leaders: Are they different? *Harvard Business Review., 70*(2), 126-135.

# Part III

## NON-U.S.A CENTRIC MODELS OF GRADUATE MANAGEMT EDUCATION

CHAPTER 8

# BREAKING THE MBA MOULD

## Business Education for Innovators and Entrepreneurs

**Howard Armitage and Rod B. McNaughton**

The relevancy of MBA programs, especially in developing innovative leaders for new ventures, is questioned by some leading business educators and is a theme in recent surveys of business leaders and government studies of innovation and productivity. One alternative to the MBA model is differentiated niche programs. An example of this approach is the Master of Business, Entrepreneurship, and Technology (MBET) degree developed at the University of Waterloo. This chapter documents the development and outcomes of this strongly differentiated program that offers an "education adventure" to innovators and entrepreneurs. The program provides students that have an entrepreneurial focus and technological background with the business knowledge, soft skills and networks they need to commercialize their ideas. Innovative aspects of the program, including measurement of progress toward program objectives using a balance scorecard, are described.

*New Visions for Graduate Management Education,* 229–245
Copyright © 2006 by Information Age Publishing
All rights of reproduction in any form reserved.

## INTRODUCTION

MBA programs dominate formal educational opportunities to develop the knowledge base, skills, and attitudes required of successful leaders and managers in the contemporary business environment. Yet firms, the business press, and some business educators question the effectiveness of the typical MBA program in developing the required skills and attitudes in graduates. Pfeffer and Sutton (2000) and Bossidy and Charan (2002) focus on the inability of MBA graduates to transform knowledge into action, while others raise more specific concerns about problems with the MBA approach to business education (e.g., DeAngelo & Zimmerman, 2005; Gartner, 2005; Mintzberg, 2004a, 2004b; and Pfeffer & Fong, 2002, 2004). Among these is the idea that MBA programs are not effective catalysts of innovation and entrepreneurship.

The Canadian context provides an example of this concern. Canada's record is weak on managing entrepreneurial and technological opportunities to create commercially viable products and businesses (Canadian Manufacturers and Exporters Association, 2001; Conference Board of Canada 2001, 2002, 2004; Government of Canada, 2002; and Martin & Porter, 2000). A common theme in these reports is that Canadian business leaders and managers have not adequately shifted their thinking toward entrepreneurial activities and, when they do, lack the managerial, marketing, and financing skills to bring innovations to commercial success. Nixon, cited in Little (2005), bluntly argues, "Canadian business leaders—in small, medium and large companies—lack the culture of innovation to take their companies to the next level."

A survey by the Financial Post and Compass (2001) of leaders in small, medium and large corporations and among executives of the local and national Chambers of Commerce indicated dissatisfaction with MBA programs and the skills of their graduates. Larry Tapp, former Dean of the Ivey School of Business, questioned the need for 39 MBA programs in Canada. He argued that the high number of similar MBA programs explains the trend toward mediocrity and replication in business education, and that there is a need to move away from the generalist MBA model toward differentiated niche programs (see Pitt, 2003).

This chapter presents the case of developing the 12-month long Master of Business, Entrepreneurship and Technology (MBET) program at the University of Waterloo (UW). MBET is a response to the perceived problems with MBA curricula and programs, especially as catalysts of successful innovation and entrepreneurship. The MBET program was developed during 2002, launched in 2003, and now has its third cohort of approximately 35 students. The curricula and program structure were developed during a series of retreats with faculty and members of an advisory council consisting of successful entrepreneurs. Aspects of the program were trialed with focus groups of potential students. The retreats and focus groups identified issues of concern to the business community, students and faculty. These were addressed in the program design.

The outcome is a unique "education adventure" that is strongly differentiated from existing graduate business programs in Canada and internationally. The program adopted a new venture lifecycle model to structure the curriculum into eleven courses that each extend over 12 months, and deliver knowledge "just-in-time" during seed/concept, product development and market expansion stages. The goal is to provide entrepreneurial students who have a technological background with the business knowledge, soft skills, and networks they need to commercialize their ideas. The following sections describe the process used to develop the MBET program, and innovations in curriculum design and program assessment.

## A Focused Program for a Focused University and Community

The success of an academic program designed to enhance innovation and entrepreneurial achievement depends on the reputation, resources, and competitive advantages of the host university. In this respect, the MBET program fits well with Waterloo's distinctive strengths. High quality students, cooperative education, technology transfer, research partnerships at local, national and international levels, and an innovation model where property rights to new ideas remain with the individual, are all part of the Waterloo brand. The University of Waterloo does not have a business school, but is renowned for its success in starting new ventures. A significant number of all commercial spin-offs from Canadian universities in the past decade have come from UW. Additionally, the reputation survey conducted annually by *Macleans Magazine*, ranked UW as the most innovative among 47 universities across the country for 13 consecutive years. Waterloo is also consistently rated first in the "Highest Quality," and producing "Leaders of Tomorrow" categories.

The focus on encouraging innovation also fits well with the strength of the local business community. The Waterloo Region (which encompasses the cities of Waterloo, Kitchener, and Cambridge in southwestern Ontario) is one of Canada's most important breeding grounds for leading technology companies. It is the birthplace of Research In Motion and its BlackBerry e-mail device, and home to Open Text Corporation, Com Dev International Ltd., and Dalsa Corporation, to name a few of the publicly traded technology companies based in the region.

University administrators, key faculty in several disciplines, and community supporters were all convinced that a differentiated program like MBET would succeed well in this innovative culture. UW's defining traits —connections to industry, research on advanced technologies, focus on innovation and entrepreneurship, exceptional students and the reputation for producing leaders of tomorrow—were identified as powerful magnets that would draw students to this new program. The Centre for Business, Entrepreneurship and Technology (CBET) was created to develop and manage the MBET program and future entrepreneurship related initiatives. The Centre lies outside the traditional faculty-based governance structure of the university, ensuring a multidisciplinary and entrepreneurial approach.

## Vision and Program Strategies

Discussions with key faculty and members of an advisory board composed of successful entrepreneurs and community leaders resulted in the formation of an MBET mission/vision statement:

> To be an entrepreneurship program of local and international renown, where the exceptional talents of graduates, and an international community of committed stakeholders, leverage technology to create breakthrough opportunities that result in new, market-leading businesses.

The proposition of the MBET program is that by attracting entrepreneurial students ("E") with technological backgrounds ("T") and providing them with a unique set of business skills, hands on networking opportunities and a nurturing environment ("B"), it will supply the leaders who will create and guide tomorrow's technology businesses.

Transforming the vision into reality was accomplished by developing a strategy map that the program designers used to convey the key stakeholder, financial, internal processes, and renewal strategies needed to achieve the vision. Strategy maps have become popular in both the private and public sectors (Kaplan & Norton, 2004) because they represent a visual model of how an organization can successfully execute its strategies. Above all, they are communication tools that help to tell the organization's "story" to insiders (faculty, staff, current students, administrators) and outsiders (senior university officials, prospective students, donors, alumni). Figure 8.1 shows the MBET map which begins with its vision, the key themes that program designers felt would differentiate the program and then, for each of four perspectives, provides a desired goal and a set of strategies that will accomplish the goal. Each strategy "box" can be

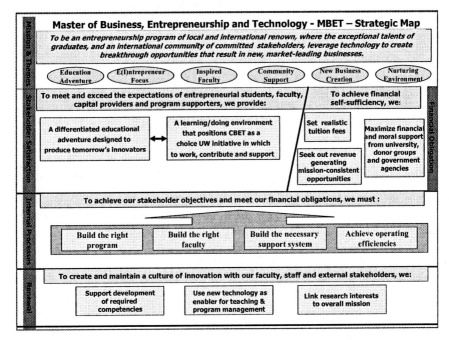

Figure 8.1   The MBET strategy map.

drilled into to obtain more detail. As an example, a stakeholder strategy is to develop "a differentiated educational adventure designed to produce tomorrow's innovators." Figure 8.2 decomposes this key stakeholder strategy into a value proposition that incorporates the input received from student focus groups and members of the advisory council as to what would truly differentiate the program. The key elements—providing an "education adventure," "unique design," "uncommon experiences," "inspiration," "industry participation" and a "nurturing environment"—provided the basis for developing the MBET curriculum.

## Curriculum Development

The MBET curriculum shown in Figure 8.3 builds on the strategy map by simulating the entrepreneurial process—concept/seed, product, and market development. Designed to address both the academic and practical aspects of an entrepreneur's education, the curriculum has both "knowing" and "doing" elements taken concurrently throughout the program.

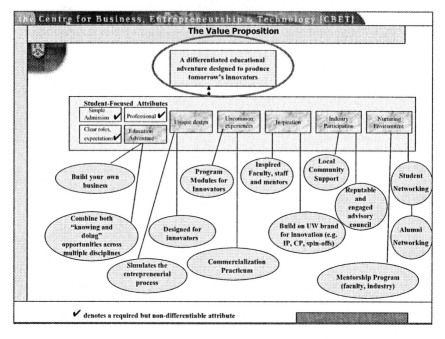

Figure 8.2.   A drill down inside the MBET strategy map.

### *"Knowing" Component*

In the "knowing" component, material in each subject area is presented in modular fashion and supports the actual entrepreneurial effort by introducing subject matter, not in a traditional discipline centric or term-by-term fashion, but as it is required for a particular phase in the entrepreneurial process. This is a significant departure from most educational paradigms. We include two examples—the accounting and marketing courses—to describe the difference between the MBET program and typical graduate business degrees.

*The accounting course.*   In almost all accounting courses offered at the MBA level, students are first introduced to some form of transaction analysis to appreciate and understand the role of accounting in recording, summarizing and reporting economic data. This may be appropriate for general business education but it is less relevant for entrepreneurs. At the concept/seed stage of the commercialization process, transaction-based accounting is overshadowed by cash flow considerations. Where will the cash come from, how much is needed for early stage working capital requirements, what role is played by family, friends, and angel investors to move the idea forward? Students also learn the differences between

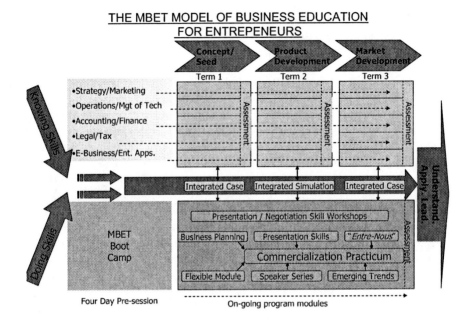

Figure 8.3. The MBET curriculum.

income and cash flow concepts and, in combination with their entrepreneurial finance and strategy courses, must complete a major analysis of a local publicly listed technology company. At the end of the term, the CEO or CFO of approximately eight local firms come to the classroom to listen as teams of four students provide an analysis of their firm and hear the group's conclusion as to whether their analysis leads them to conclude that they would, or would not, invest in their company. This is a riveting experience for both students and executives. Because they must defend their choices in front of executives, students know this is no idle exercise and the quality of research is excellent. For their part, executives learn how technology-savvy future investors perceive their firms' strategy and results.

This high involvement approach continues during Term 2 (the product/service development phase of the commercialization process) and Term 3 (the market execution phase). For example in the second term, students get exposure to the type of introductory accounting package they will need for early stage business and training in the fundamental managerial accounting concepts of budgeting, basic cost systems, break-even and cost analysis. The final term deals with the accounting requirements of going-concern organizations with a diverse product and customer base.

Course materials include activity accounting elements and reporting systems consistent with a balanced scorecard approach. In short, the accounting requirements for technological entrepreneurs differ from those of students enrolled in traditional graduate programs, and a unique course was designed to meet their needs.

*The marketing course.*   Marketing courses in MBA programs are often designed from the perspective of large companies (often in fast-moving consumer goods sectors) with established marketing departments. The curricula is loosely organized around the marketing management tradition of the "4-Ps" (product, price, physical distribution, and placement), with some exposure to concepts from consumer behavior, and perhaps the unique contexts of marketing in services, international and business-to-business situations. In some ways, the traditional marketing curriculum is disingenuous when teaching technology entrepreneurs, as it reinforces the misperception that "marketing" is something that comes after technology and product development, and is solely focused on advertising, sales, distribution, and other processes associated with getting products in the hands of consumers. Further, technology entrepreneurs deal with a specific context of launching a new product/service, often into a business market that is dispersed globally.

Marketing is crucial to the formation of a successful technology-based new venture. The first term focuses on understanding how market-based assets add value to an organization, communications between R&D and marketing, sources of opportunities, identifying vertical market applications, conducting market feasibility studies, and demand forecasting. In addition to specific market research skills, a goal of the first term is to shift attitudes and build appreciation for the role of marketing in the commercialisation process. It is sometimes difficult to get students with a technology background to understand that few buyers appreciate new technology for its own sake. Rather, the technology must be applied to a significant problem and offer a compelling value proposition. During the second term, the course addresses product development issues including standards, platform design, and flexible product/service offerings and alternative business models. Market planning issues of pricing, sales, distribution and communications leading up to the launch are also examined. In the final term, topics include developing a brand, public and investor relations, sales management (salesmanship is practiced in another part of the program), and marketing performance metrics.

Assessment is closely linked to the commercialization practicum—students prepare a market assessment for their practicum during the first term, complete a marketing plan during the second term, and establish in detail how to execute one of the tactics from the plan during the third term. An element of the overall grade is also based on performance in an integrated case and other activities that emphasize the integration between marketing and other business disciplines.

### *"Doing" Component*

In addition to the "knowing" courses, the program emphasizes the "doing" element. The primary purpose of class work is to support outside study and further the development of ideas. Metaphorically, MBET students not only become skilled with "a saw and hammer but also emerge from the program with the ability to become cabinet makers." Examples of innovative features in the "doing" part of the curriculum include:

- A commercialization practicum in which students start to develop their business, or help an existing business commercialize a new technology-based product or service.
- Integration between disciplinary areas in the curriculum, including an online integrated case each term that is specially written about a new technology under development.
- Student attendance at seminars and networking events offered by Communitech (the local technology industry association).
- Weekly guest speakers from the entrepreneurial or service communities.
- Encouragement to enter local and international business competitions.

The following sections describe two of these innovations—the commercialization practicum and a course that is designed to coordinate many of the "doing" themes that are listed above.

*The commercialization practicum.*   In their final two terms, students participate in a commercialization practicum where they work with real technologies and produce assessments and plans for bringing these new technologies to market. The practicum accommodates two broad categories of students. The first are students who enter the program with an already well-defined idea for a new business. The second are students who believe that building their own business is what they want to do in the future, but realize that their ideas are not yet adequately formed. Students in the first category are encouraged to build on their course knowledge and use the expertise of the faculty, advisory council and service providers to continue the development of their own businesses as their practicum. Students in the second category are paired with local companies and industry advisors to develop a commercialization plan for a specific company or promising intellectual property.

Irrespective of the type of practicum (self or company sponsored), each team's final project—which may include market research, a design for a product, profiles of desired management teams, licensing plans, technical and marketing feasibility studies, and/or a start-up business plan—is jointly evaluated by a faculty advisor and the institution that originated the technology. The practicum gives students insights and experience in the early stages of entrepreneurial technology commercialization, various aspects of company formation and finance, and technology licensing and intellectual property issues.

*Business planning, skills, and applied leadership.*   The doing elements in the MBET program (listed earlier and also shown in the middle and bottom sections of Figure 8.3) are managed through an additional academic credit course—Business Planning, Skills and Applied Leadership. This course provides a formal link from the "knowing" to the "doing" part of the curriculum and was inspired by discussions with the advisory council. As the council reviewed early drafts of the curriculum, they were asked, "If you had had the opportunity of being in program like MBET, what additional features would you like your program to cover that may not be captured in the proposed curriculum?" Responses included the themes of networking, negotiations, sales skills, business process integration, presentation skills, and the opportunity to pitch ideas to experienced entrepreneurs, business angels and venture capitalists.

To respond to these needs, a course was created to manage the ongoing development of key business planning and business execution skills. The course is a major differentiator for the program and adds richness to the student experience. Not only do the modules reinforce academic concepts with critical entrepreneurial analytical and soft skills, they also create a sense of fun, excitement, and connectedness. Examples of these "rubber-to-the-road" activities, include Ignition Week (a boot camp), entrepreneurship week, preparing business plans, enhancing presentation skills, developing a personal vision statement, integrative business games, cases and simulations, negotiation strategies, sales modules, movie nights, speaker series, *entre-nous* (an opportunity to discuss business challenges with volunteers from the professional services community), and business competitions. Students are encouraged to enter business and licensing plan competitions to further refine their ideas, improve their presentation skills and get access to critical individuals and groups that can assist them to commercialize their innovations. Success at these competitions builds self-confidence for the participants, reinforces UW's reputation for innovation and entrepreneurship, and advances the goal of establishing new market-leading businesses.

## Measuring Progress

Over the next decade, the success of the MBET program will, in part, be measured by its ability to generate relatively more new ventures and commercialized intellectual property than less focused graduate business programs. During the first 3 years, the program nurtured five new student led businesses, worked with several local start-ups, and several graduates are self-employed as consultants or trainers. There are also less demonstrable measures of success for a program like MBET. Paradoxically, for example, one of the successes may be in helping individuals to realize that despite their passion for creating a new venture, their ideas or technologies may not be sufficiently robust to be commercially viable. Additionally, a number of students end up as corporate entrepreneurs, or intrapreneurs, who will add significantly to the success of their employer, but whose outputs are difficult to measure. Nevertheless, our primary objective is to encourage innovation. A balanced scorecard helps the MBET management team to track progress toward this objective, and the others identified in the MBET strategy map. Figure 8.4 illustrates this scorecard—one perspective for each of the stakeholder, financial, internal processes, and renewal perspectives on the strategy map. For each of the four perspectives, there are performance indicators for four to seven goals that measure actual performance against a target and stretch objective. As an example, Figure 8.5 shows the scorecard for the stakeholder perspective.

From the stakeholder perspective, the first goal is to increase the number of applications to the program. This is an important indicator because there is evidence that the number of applications to MBA programs, in general, have been declining (Kedrosky, 2005; Lavelle, Di Meglio, & Sparks, 2005). For competitive reasons, some of the metrics on the scorecard are not shown. An example is the number of applications received, which has grown substantially each year.) The second goal is an important indicator of success in differentiating the program from other graduate business programs. Indications are that students often "shop" around for an MBA program, resulting in many offers but a much smaller number of acceptances. The objective for MBET is to differentiate itself so that the goals and purposes of the program are clear, and a high proportion of those offered admission actually enrol. Indeed, many applicants indicate that MBET is the only program they are considering. Based on these comments, and the importance of maintaining this "unique" style of program, we set a high target and stretch ratio of acceptances to offers—75% and 80% respectively.

**MBET Program**
**Balanced Scorecard**
**Sept. 2004 - Aug. 2005**

| Financial Perspective | | Stakeholder Perspective | |
|---|---|---|---|
| Goals | Measures | Goals | Measures |
| Achieve financial self-sufficiency | Actual surplus/deficit ($K) | Increase number of 2005/6 applications | Actual number of 2005/6 applications |
| Increase scholarship funding | Actual scholarship funding ($K) | Maximize ratio of 2005/6 acceptances to offers | Actual ratio of 2005/6 acceptances to offers |
| Increase non-scholarship funding from community | Actual non-scholarship funding from community ($K) | Maximize student satisfaction | Actual student satisfaction survey overall score (max. 7) |
| Increase cash flow from Outreach program | Actual contribution margin from Outreach program ($K) | Maximize student loyalty score | Maximize student loyalty score (max. 7) |
| Increase university financial support | Actual university financial support | Maximize Advisory Council survey score | Actual Advisory Council survey score (max. 7) |
| Succeed in obtaining government "innovation" support | Actual government funds obtained | Maximize Commercialization Practicum survey score | Actual Comm. Practicum survey score (max. 7) |
| | | Increase faculty involvement in CBET activities | Number of faculty members actively participating in 3 or more CBET defined activities |

| Internal Perspective | | Renewal Perspective | |
|---|---|---|---|
| Goals | Measures | Goals | Measures |
| Build quality of MBET faculty | Results of relevant student satisfaction question (max. 7) | Link faculty research interests to CBET interests | Actual number of research activities by CBET faculty related to innovation or entrepreneurialism |
| Continue to build an effective advisory council program | Number of AC members actively participating in 3 or more CBET defined projects. | Optimize number of new sources for donations | Actual number of new sources for donations |
| Maximize effectiveness of commercialization practicum | Student survey question results (max. 7) | Continue to introduce new concepts to keep current | Actual number of new concepts introduced into BET 611 |
| Build an effective Outreach certificate program | Number of Outreach certificate streams presented to Senate | Improve design of curriculum to remain differentiated | Student survey question results (max. 7) |
| Create and deliver effective and unique courses and modules | Results of relevant student satisfaction question (max. 7) | Optimize number of visitors with relevant expertise | Actual number of visitors |
| | | Develop plan for scaling up of MBET program | Actual plan development |

Figure 8.4.   MBET's balanced scorecard for fiscal year ending August 2005.

The third goal is to maximize student satisfaction and is measured through an exit survey consisting of questions such as the degree to which MBET served as a preparation for developing and running a business, was relevant to career goals, matched students' expectations, and provided the culture (networks, competitions, etc.) consistent with entrepreneurial expectations. Responses to the questions, coupled with direct student feedback, provide the basis for understanding where required adjustments must be made.

A *Harvard Business Review* article titled, "The One Number You Need to Grow" (Reichheld, 2003), inspired the fourth goal. Reichheld argues that a single loyalty question can be substituted for the "complex black box" of the typical customer satisfaction survey. This advice is followed by asking our students to rate the following statement on a 7-point scale, "I would recommend the MBET program to a friend or colleague." This is perhaps the most revealing insight into the future success of MBET—the

| Goals | Weight | Measures | Target | Stretch | Actual | Score | Weighted Score |
|---|---|---|---|---|---|---|---|
| **MBET Program** <br> **Stakeholder Perspective** <br> **Sept. 2004 - Aug. 2005** | | | | | | | |
| Increase number of 2005/6 applications | 10% | Actual number of 2005/6 applications | | | | | |
| Maximize ratio of 2005/6 acceptances to offers | 10% | Actual ratio of 2005/6 acceptances to offers | 75% | 80% | 82% | 107% | 11% |
| Maximize student satisfaction | 30% | Actual student satisfaction survey overall score (max. 7) | 6 | 6.5 | 5.5 | 95% | 28% |
| Maximize student loyalty score | 20% | Maximize student loyalty score (max. 7) | 6 | 6.5 | 6.0 | 100% | 20% |
| Maximize Advisory Council survey score | 10% | Actual Advisory Council survey score (max. 7) | 6 | 6.5 | 5.3 | 93% | 9% |
| Maximize Commercialization Practicum survey score | 10% | Actual Comm. Practicum survey score (max. 7) | 6 | 6.5 | 5.7 | 97% | 10% |
| Increase faculty involvement in CBET activities | 10% | Number of faculty members actively participating in 3 or more CBET defined activities | | | | | |
| **Total Weight (must = 100%)** | **100%** | | | | | | |
| | | | | **Stakeholder Perspective Score:** | | | **98%** |

*Note:*   There are various approaches to scoring results in the Balanced Scorecard. These have to do with motivational factors that are beyond the scope of this chapter. In our case, we achieve 100% if actual targets are achieved and higher than 100% if stretch targets are met. Scores below target indicate areas where we must improve.

Figure 8.5.   MBET's balanced scorecard-stakeholder perspective.

degree to which current graduates are willing to be advocates for the program.

The final goals and measures relate to different elements of the stakeholder domain—the advisory council, practicum sponsors, and faculty. In each of these cases, the program is approaching targets, but still has a way to go. There are areas that need to be addressed. In summary, the scorecard has proven to be a very helpful tool to assist us in monitoring the degree to which our vision and strategies are being accomplished.

## The Future

In many respects, the development of MBET is similar to the start up organizations it is designed to foster. MBET began at the concept/seed stage with the vision of a small handful of individuals who believe that UW is well positioned to develop a graduate business program in entrepreneurship that can assist in reducing Canada's innovation gap. This vision had to be conveyed to others and needed to be convincing enough to attract stakeholders who were willing to invest time and money into its development. Most importantly, the MBET program needed to offer an experience that was genuinely viewed to be distinctive and of high quality to attract students.

MBET was successful at the seed stage of development. An external reviewer of the program wrote:

> The University of Waterloo's MBET program is the right program in the right place at the right time—the very definition of innovation. MBET's emphasis on problem solving ability, intellectual fluency and the other skills of "entrepreneurship" constitute a dynamic response to Canada's innovation agenda and addresses the nation's stated need to develop and cultivate its best entrepreneurial talent. (Robert Richards, PhD, Hubert W. Kelly Chair in Youth-focused Technological Entrepreneurship, PJ Gardiner Institute for Enterprise and Entrepreneurship, Memorial University, 2002)

Now in the third year of operation, MBET has moved through the product development phase, and with enrollments climbing,[1] we are experiencing similar opportunities, pressures and tensions that most early venture organizations encounter as they grow their market base. For example, CBET is currently housed in what a recent business publication (Bogomolny, 2005) called the "basement" in one of UW's buildings. More space is required and a vision for an Entrepreneurship Centre is part of the University's ongoing capital campaign. Growth opportunities include partnering with select Canadian and international universities, and offering the MBET program on a part-time basis over the Internet. Beyond the MBET program, a series of outreach programs to provide business skill knowledge to area entrepreneurs and intrapreneurs was launched in 2004.

As with all growing young organizations, future success will depend not only on the quality and uniqueness of the product, but also on the ability to develop the appropriate organizational structure to support the vision and strategies. The university showed considerable foresight in establishing CBET as a cross campus multidisciplinary unit—signaling that entrepreneurship development is not the prerogative of any one specific faculty. Paradoxically, however, not being aligned with a faculty has created its own tensions. For example, CBET must compete for internal and external resources in much the same way as do individual, more established, faculties. Bigger, more visible, campus projects often take the spotlight, so CBET needs to work hard to keep its message and promise in front of both internal and external stakeholders.

CBET is not also yet a stage where it has the university authorization to hire its own tenure track faculty. Thus, it must convince Deans to share their faculty resources or attract internal faculty and outside professionals who are inspired enough by the promise of MBET that they are willing to teach on an overload basis. And, similar to many early stage ventures, MBET receives no university subsidy, so it must also set its pricing (tuition) at levels sufficient to cover its operating costs while still keeping the program at levels that entrepreneurial students can afford. These are all areas of active negotiation that will eventually be resolved.

Despite these impediments, good progress is being made on our objective that MBET become a catalyst for the development of successful innovation and entrepreneurship. Several new businesses have been formed and capital has been provided. Entering business competitions throughout North America and overseas is becoming the norm. In this year's class, for example, close to 80% of the students will have entered at least one business competition either with their own business idea or a company sponsored practicum idea.

## Summary

Innovation has become the defining theme for global competitiveness. Any nation's ability to create wealth for its citizens depends on creative people who are constantly looking for new and better ways to improve things. However, considerable doubt is expressed in Canada and the United States about the role that traditional graduate business programs play in encouraging innovation.

MBET was created as a response to these well-documented problems. One solution for improving competitiveness lies in improving the quality of future business leaders through focused programs that begin by attracting innovative students, and then providing experiences that help them to develop the managerial skills that assist in converting opportunities into viable commercial businesses. The objective of the MBET program is to help graduates achieve these accomplishments by leveraging their existing entrepreneurial talents and backgrounds with a knowledge of contemporary business skills and practices. This is accomplished through a "knowing-doing" curriculum that simulates the commercialization process and provides students with a nurturing environment in which they can test out new ideas, develop networks, gain self-confidence, and start their entrepreneurial journeys equipped to avoid many of the common causes of small and medium enterprise failure.

The distinct value proposition and the differentiated educational adventure that MBET provides is resonating well with the entrepreneurial audience that CBET seeks to attract. Enrolments are increasing and the scorecard indicates the MBET program is making good progress in achieving the objectives that lead to reaching our vision. Future success will depend on realizing new opportunities and developing an organizational structure consistent with these growth opportunities.

## NOTE

1.  We started MBET with 22 students and are now at our physical space capacity level of approximately 35 students.

## REFERENCES

Bogomolny, L. (2005) The real deal. *Canadian Business*, *78*(6), 51-52.

Bossidy, L., & Charan, R. (2002). *Execution: The discipline of getting things done.* New York: Crown Business.

Merritt, J. (2005, April 18). MBA applicants are missing in action. *Business Week*, 3929, 28-31.

Canadian Manufacturers and Exporters. (2001). *The business case for innovation.*

Conference Board of Canada. (2001). *Investing in innovation: 3rd annual innovation report.*

Conference Board of Canada. (2002). *Innovation Challenge Paper Series* 1-4.

Conference Board of Canada. (2004). *The Canadian skills imperative: Building and sustaining a culture of innovation.*

DeAngelo, H., DeAngelo, L., & Zimmerman, J. (2005). What's really wrong with U.S. business schools? Retrieved May 21, 2006, from http://ssrn.com/abstract=766404

Financial Post and COMPAS Inc. (2001, December 21). M.B.A.s, business schools. Retrieved June 28, 2006, from http://www.compass.ca/html/archives/mba_surv.html

Gartner, J. (2005, June 19). Are business schools failing the world?: Interview with Jeffrey Gartner, Dean, Yale School of Management. *New York Times*, sec. 3, 13.

Government of Canada. (2002). *Achieving excellence: Investing in people, knowledge and opportunity.* Retrieved June 28, 2006, from www.innovationstrategy.gc.ca/cmb/innovation.nsf/pageE/Contents

Government of Canada. (2002). *Knowledge matters: Skills and learning for canadians.* Retrieved May 23, 2005, from www.hrdc-drhc.gc.ca/sp-ps/sl-ca/home.shtml

Kaplan, R. S., & Norton, D. P. (2004). *Strategy maps: Converting intangible assets in to tangible outcomes.* Boston: Harvard Business School.

Kedrosky, P. (2005). The problem with B-schools. *Canadian Business*, *78*(14/15), 19.

Lavelle, L., Di Meglio, F., & Sparks, W. (2005). MBA applications: Still skidding. *Business Week.* Retrieved June 28, 2006, from http://www.businessweek.com/bschools/content/aug2005/bs2005089_9256_bs001.htm

Little, B. (2005, May 9). RBC's Nixon takes aim at corporate Canada's competitive failures. *Globe & Mail* (Toronto), B19.

Martin, R. L., & Porter, M. E. (2000). *Canadian competitiveness: Nine years after the crossroads.* Toronto, Canada: Rotman School of Business.

Mintzberg, H. (2004a). *Managers not MBA's: A hard look at the soft practice of managing and management development.* San Francisco: Berrett and Koehler.

Mintzberg, H. (2004b). MBA programs turning out "unqualified elite." *Canadian HR Reporter, 17*(4), 1-2.

Pitts, G. (2003, May 29). Departing Ivey Dean urges emphasis on elite schools. *Globe and Mail,* B1, B6.

Pfeffer, J., & Fong, C. (2002). The end of business schools? Less success than meets the eye. *Academy of Management Learning & Education, 1*(1), 78-96.

Pfeffer, J., & Fong, C. (2004). The business school "business": Some lessons from the U.S. experience. *Journal of Management Studies, 41*(8), 1501-1520.

Pfeffer, J., & Sutton, R. (2000). *The knowing-doing gap: How smart companies turn knowledge into action.* Boston: Harvard Business School Press.

Reichheld, F. (2003, December). The one number you need to grow. *Harvard Business Review,* 46-54.

CHAPTER 9

# REVERSE INNOVATION IN MBA EDUCATION

## Local Actors as Catalysts for Change in Global MBA Provisions

**Anne Herbert and Kari Lilja**

There are pressures to change the MBA template from both the core, and the periphery. The core is where the template originates and is maintained, and from where many of the MBA doctrines are exported. The periphery is comprised of managers and businesses embedded in institutional settings where the MBA template requires adaptation to suit local needs and variations of liberal market models. This chapter argues that local peripheral actors are creating a "reverse innovation" that will ultimately affect the MBA template at the core. The development of the Helsinki School of Economics MBA programs is used as an example to illustrate the pressures from the periphery, and how they could influence the core.

### INTRODUCTION

In spite of the persistent popularity of the MBA degree, there are pressures for changing it. The pressures to change the MBA come both from

*New Visions for Graduate Management Education,* 247–266
Copyright © 2006 by Information Age Publishing
All rights of reproduction in any form reserved.

the core, and the periphery. The core is the place where the MBA originated and from whence, still, many of the doctrines taught in MBAs orig-
inate and are maintained and exported. The core is constituted by the
complex web of U.S. ways of developing and delivering the MBA curriculum, based on the doctrines of functional and general management in a
liberal market economy. The assertion that this U.S. model is the archetypal core model of the MBA curriculum is summed up by Starkey and
Tempest:

(a) the vigorous expansion of U.S. programs overseas;
(b) the fact that schools that directly compete with leading US business
schools do so mostly according to the rules established by the U.S.
schools; and
(c) the increasing recruitment of U.S. trained faculty by places such as
London Business School and INSEAD (2001, p. 10).

Other authors such as Costea (1999) and Pfeffer and Fong (2004) have
elaborated on the way in which most models of MBA curricula are socio-
culturally embedded in conceptualizations of U.S.-based capitalism. The
influence and prevalence of the core is sustained furthermore by mechanisms such as rankings and accreditations that maintain the status quo in
MBA education, and is reflected and reinforced in the dominance of U.S.
based programs in active lobby groups such as the Executive MBA Council.

In relation to this core, there is also a periphery where actors can be
found who are not involved at the core of operations and, who both
overtly and covertly, are trying to do the "MBA thing" somewhat differently. Those actors are, for example, faculty and program directors who
try new initiatives, or participants who pressure MBA providers to tailor
the standard offering to meet better their particular situation and needs.
These actors who initiate and implement innovations to address local
demand typically wish to keep the "MBA" name and identity.

When new ways of doing things begin to influence activity at the core,
then we have a phenomenon of "reverse innovation." The concept of
"reverse innovation" comes from studies of multinational companies
(MNC) that have given leeway for their subsidiaries to act differently from
the operations of the country of origin (Hedlund, 1986). According to a
wide range of empirical studies, reverse innovation arises when demands
from contexts and experiences that differ from those of the original centre of operations, force local actors in such conditions to respond earlier
than those operating closer to the antecedent conditions of the first wave
of the innovation. (cf. Ferner & Quintanilla, 2002). Developing and
implementing a reverse innovation requires synchronization of various

local actors and situational conditions. Specific local competences are needed alongside incremental mobilizations of local ecosystems and national institutions. Such mobilizations include managerial actions, generative dialogues and institutional mechanisms at multiple levels which effectively aggregate actions to implement and sustain the innovative effect, until the effect is so significant that it influences the operations at the core (Sabel, 2005). In reverse innovation the multilevel dialogues and experimental learning aggregate to reaffirm and reinforce the change. Ultimately, in reverse innovation, new collective practices and actor identities affect the original centre of operations. In multinational companies (MNCs), the institutionalization of centers of excellence at different host countries of operations is based on the assumption that reverse innovation is possible (Holm & Pedersen, 2000).

In this chapter we focus on the pressures from the periphery[1] to reform U.S. prototypes of MBA education, and consider the case of Helsinki School of Economics (HSE) MBA programs as a contributor to reverse innovation. Two main drivers for reforming the U.S.A model of MBA education are recognized. The first is related to various national contexts, which differ from the U.S. style capitalism, and thus the assumed best practice in management characteristically taught in a generic MBA. The second is the need to differentiate from competitors and draw intellectual resources from new academic traditions that take into account the varieties in capitalisms in the current phase of globalization.

Our proposition is that the MBA will remain a desirable educational qualification world-wide if it can be transformed so that the doctrine of U.S.-style capitalism is taught as an option to be modified as appropriate, rather than a prescription for economic success, and that the participants are taught skills so that they can identify and implement appropriate modifications to address local circumstances.

The structure of the chapter is in five parts. First, we elaborate the core and especially the periphery of MBA operations, using the MBA portfolio and business model of HSE as an example. As a provider in the MBA market, HSE has taken initiatives at a local level that have contributed to coevolutionary mechanisms producing reverse innovations in MBA education. Second, these initiatives and mechanisms shall be described. Third, we offer a description of the reverse innovation pipeline in MBA operations, and fourth, the next desirable innovation from the periphery is suggested. Finally we describe how HSE can implement the desired innovation and what would signal and support the institutionalization at the core of such an innovation.

## At the Core: The Archetypal MBA

Today the MBA is the recognized flagship of generalist management education around the world (Costea, 1999). MBA programs are designed to develop practical managers who can contribute to organizational success, predominantly, but not only, the success of privately owned organizations with success measured by financial returns in a free market system. The label "MBA" indicates a set of disciplinary knowledge that has been stabilized and reinforced around the world by accreditation authorities. As academic awards, MBAs emerged in the twentieth century in industrialized America and spread around the world alongside American models of capitalism and industrial management. The MBA model of management education has been sold as a generic model of education and business that can be applied usefully in every context. Thus, most MBA curricula are designed on the basis that there are unitary principles and relatively definable best ways to do business effectively and efficiently, and that people could learn these via an academic award.

Throughout the twentieth century, as especially the American perceptions of the business environment changed, themes and emphases in the MBA changed accordingly. Growing emphasis on uncertainty and risk can be observed in the 1980s (Costea, 1999), and in the last part of the century there was a clear rush to "internationalize" MBA curricula as more and more western business organizations saw themselves operating across national boundaries. "International business" became a popular topic and "globalization" a favorite theme and lens for looking at the world of business operations. Likewise, since the publicity about crises in Enron, Anderson, and WorldCom, the trend to teach more ethics and corporate responsibility in MBA programs has been reinforced by corresponding changes in accreditation standards. These are examples of innovations at the core, changes in the generic model in response to the external environment and perceived needs of businesses located very close to the core.

## At the Periphery: The HSE Experience

The Helsinki School of Economics (HSE), the leading business school in Finland, was the first university in the Nordic region to offer an MBA program. From the outset fees were charged for participation in the program. That was a radical step because academic education was (and still is) counted as a public good in Finland, and by law no tuition fees may be charged for any nationally-recognized degrees. Yet, in the 1980s, alongside the publicly funded programs a leading university introduced MBAs as fee-charging, postexperience, generalist but advanced practical education for managers.

The initiative was the brainchild of a very energetic, entrepreneurial Finn, Professor Veikko Jääskeläinen, who maintained strong academic and business connections both in Finland and in the United States. His vision was that an American style MBA education would provide Finnish business and individuals with more internationally competitive business competence and confidence at a time *when* the Finnish economy was in transition and opening up to global forces (Tainio, Lilja, & Santalainen, 1997; Tainio, Pohjola, & Lilja, 2000). While an MBA was not and is not an officially recognized "degree" under Finnish law, Jääskeläinen knew that such an award should be associated for its prestige with HSE. Extraordinary negotiations were required to create the space to enact a market-based education initiative in a publicly funded university. Through his networks and by his reputation, the professor was able to gain agreement for a special unit in the university, and win capital grants from a number of nontraditional sources. The MBA was launched successfully.

The initiative was not only radical in the context of the Finnish education system. From the outset, the HSE MBA also innovated on the archetypal U.S. model of MBAs in at least three ways: first, it was initiated as a post experience qualification (an entry level MBA was offered later); second, it was delivered mainly by visiting faculty, and third, it was a delivered in a modular format. These characteristics would not be so remarkable for a new entrant in the MBA today (due to reverse innovation), but they were in the 1980s.

The first intakes targeted local persons who already had academic degrees and managerial experience without formal management education, and who sought a better understanding of general management issues and to be more effective on the job. The first MBA in Nordic countries was therefore not positioned as qualification to enter the labor market as a manager (cf. traditional MBA). On the contrary, due to the education system in Finland[2] most of the participants not only had more than a few years managerial work experience, they also held specialized Masters degree qualifications. The experience of participants was considered important, and was expected to be shared as an important part of the education, with the participants' employing companies being used as live business examples.

The teaching faculty for the MBA were recruited from North America where Jääskeläinen had good contacts. He was convinced of the value of international faculty with highly engaging teaching skills, and with close linkages to contemporary business experience in international contexts that could effectively be shared with a class of business people. The local HSE faculty was fully employed with the existing master's and doctoral programs, and unable for various reasons to take on teaching roles in the MBA program. Thus, instructors with high academic standing (mostly professors), complemented with having experience in teaching practicing managers, and with very high student ratings for their academic content and pedagogic practice were identified. The intention was that those instructors could teach their courses, highly rated by students at their home institutions, to the students enrolled in the MBA program in Helsinki.

HSE was not in a position, as a government funded university where faculty members are employed as Finnish civil servants, to recruit the MBA faculty to ongoing appointments. The dominantly U.S.-based faculty were hired on a sessional basis to teach the courses as modules that comprised the HSE MBA. This was in the 1980s when modular formats had not yet become popular for MBA programs. The chosen faculty were happy to oblige: they had the satisfaction of teaching eager learners, a course for which they needed to do little additional preparation, the program manager in Helsinki took care of all practical logistics; Helsinki is a comfortable place to spend 3 weeks, and the reimbursement was good. Thus, from the first annual intake, in 1984, the programs were full-time modular programs, designed for cohorts to commence, progress, and graduate together.

After four intakes, a strong demand for a part-time version of this MBA had arisen in Helsinki. A part-time offering, primarily a weekend version of the full-time program, was launched as an executive MBA, and like its full-time parent program, the executive program has had an annual intake until now. Initially the instructors for the part-time program were the same people as in the full-time program. From the point of view of participants and their learning outcomes the weekend delivery worked well, participants especially valuing the opportunities to share experiences and perspectives with other practicing managers in other companies, while continuing to work full-time. From the instructor point of view, the weekend work was challenging on top of teaching during the week. The weekend days were long, and the participants demanded a lot of interaction with the instructor and each other. Under these pressures, the network of instructors who came to teach in the Helsinki School of Economics full time and executive MBA was expanded. In 1990 another part-time option was made available by also delivering the program on weeknights in Helsinki, and the faculty network expanded further, including not only Americans or faculty from American universities. From the beginning, until now, there has developed a core of faculty who come regularly to teach in the programs, and who over the years have contributed a great deal of constructive suggestions for improvements that have been implemented.

Faculty and business contacts encouraged HSE to offer the MBA program abroad because the practical and flexible model seemed transportable as well as desirable. HSE has used various forms of partnerships to expand delivery of its MBA from Finland to Korea, Singapore, Poland, China, and Taiwan. In particular, in Korea, Poland, and Taiwan, HSE has taken an early mover advantage offering a foreign-branded program on the MBA market. The faculty network has had to expand further to teach in all these programs. Cohort sizes are usually around 40. In 2004, 500 people were enrolled in HSE MBAs. Just fewer than half the participants were non-Finnish by citizenship. This constitutes a significant international business activity for the university.

These MBA programs are successful by measures of faculty satisfaction, participant satisfaction, graduation rates, and profitability. With each MBA cohort, a program director ensures a flow of topics that complement and build upon one another as far as possible. All HSE MBA programs demand face to face attendance. The program director helps manage participants' expectations and positive working relationships between all the participants. Other tools used to help integrate the curriculum are learning logs with guiding questions in the log to help the participants make links between modules and issues in their own workplaces; and cross-disciplinary project work tied to the participants' workplaces.

After more than 20 years, it is evident that many of the initiatives that HSE has taken, which were new or radical at the time and in the context of MBA operations, are now widely accepted and used, affecting operations at the core. The current acceptability at the core of all these initiatives is affirmed by the accreditation of HSE and its portfolio of MBA programs.

## The Reverse Innovation Pipeline

The previous section has described how HSE made various innovative moves to deliver MBA programs in contexts where the product was new or immature. Many of the moves are now adapted and widely used in one form or another even at the core, which illustrates the effect of reverse innovation. The archetypal MBA concept and "best-practice" models for its delivery are increasingly being debated, and pressures persist for further innovation which could well emerge from the periphery.

When HSE first implemented an MBA operation, the curricula content was largely copied from North America by the faculty who specifically were employed for their expected ability to import that curriculum to Finland. The practical solution to the barriers which existed for recruiting these faculty on a long term basis was a modular curriculum, with practical supplementary mechanisms to support integration. In the 1980s modular delivery by visiting faculty for all courses in an MBA program was not yet a common thing. Nevertheless, the flexibility of the model was appreciated and adopted in other locations. It is now widely accepted even at the core of operations.

Faculty have been able to take advantage of the modular system to market themselves and their MBA courses around the world, so that many providers effectively can buy-in the faculty expertise. This mode of operations has become so popular that the competition for "good faculty" has become a key issue for provider networks. Every provider wants to reduce faculty costs and prefers paying only for what they use, not necessarily having to fund a full time position. Many providers still source "good faculty" from the U.S.-based institutions and those institutions have to struggle to retain their "good faculty."

HSE experience is that the "good faculty" are learning also at the periphery and feeding their experience and interpretations, not only back to HSE, but also to their ongoing employer, and networks at the core. Most of the faculty in the HSE MBA portfolio are employed elsewhere and the faculty become cross-fertilizers of experiences and ideas about MBA programs and possibilities. As already explained, many of the faculty are senior professors who can have considerable influence at the core of operations, as well as at the periphery. However, without the initiating actions of organizations like HSE, there would not be a mechanism for these senior professors so easily to access the periphery and the variety of managerial experiences and institutional contexts.

In the process of expanding and internationalizing the MBA operations, HSE has recruited excellent local faculty to teach at each location. Nowadays, HSE aims to have Asia and Poland-based professors teach in the other HSE MBAs around the world, so that each MBA cohort can benefit from a wide diversity of perspectives.

The individual faculty and the partner relations provide significant conduits of information to HSE about local needs in delivery locations remote from Helsinki. HSE's experience is that working with partners in foreign locales means that efforts must be spent to ensure the partners' maintenance of HSE standards for the MBA award. The local partners engage with all the systemic and institutionalized dimensions of product and service delivery in their location, and in turn create reverse pressure on HSE for changes in the HSE MBA product and service. The most tangible consistent pressure is to ensure that via the MBA curriculum the participants can address their local needs and issues.

Curricula issues are a major concern that may be addressed from the periphery. Opponents of the current core model suggest that MBA graduates would be better equipped if they were more aware of the diversity and debates surrounding the management knowledge and its formation, better able to contextualize and interpret the interface of business activity with wider society, and in turn better appreciate plurality and diversity. Twenty-first century managers, in practice, need to be able to strategically manage the ever-changing internal and external relations that affect business success (CEMP, 2001). This signals the need for sophisticated critical and synthesis skills, more than provided by the typical MBA focus on analytical skills (e.g., Grey, 2004; Mintzberg, 2004). "Contemporary companies want creative collaborative thinkers and leaders" according to Booz Allen Hamilton consultants, Doria, Rozanski, and Cohen (2003, p. 2)— who also complain that current MBA programs are producing "look alike" graduates who can assert their ideas but are not highly effective communicators. In this ambiguous and uncertain world, the biggest challenge for managers is not "decision-making" but "sensemaking" (Weick, 2001). The key skill of sensemaking is typically underdeveloped in MBA graduates (Doria, Rozanski, & Cohen, 2003; also Mintzberg & Gosling, 2002). Further, the way that the contents of many MBA programs promote rapid growth of turnover and profits especially by restructuring, outsourcing and cost cutting, without considering local, moral, social, and cultural implications is criticized (e.g., Locke, 1996; Pfeffer & Fong, 2002; Starkey & Tempest, 2005).

A new vision of MBA curriculum needs to teach managers to be intelligent consumers of existing theory and disciplinary knowledge, and, among other things, to be collaborative authors of local hypotheses about their context, current choices, and likely effects of action. This could be the next innovation, and it could well be another reverse innovation, that is arising from the periphery, as described in the following section.

## The Next Innovation

The model and operations of HSE's MBA delivery have gone through two major phases of development, and are ripe for the next. The initial model was to imitate the standard U.S. model for an MBA and transfer it to Finland by using North American professors extensively. The next phase developed based on internationalizing the operation, creating a network of local MBA providers under the HSE brand and bringing in other international and Finnish professors along with local professors from each of the new countries in the network. However, currently the network of HSE's MBA programs around the world is subject to intensified competition due to the proliferation of providers and many similar and substitute management education products in every location. In the face of such competition, all MBA providers are seeking innovations and differentiations that provide a unique and desirable value proposition associated with their program (see Friga, Bettis, & Sullivan, 2003 for one analysis of strategic options).

Notwithstanding the increasing crowd of MBA providers in the market, there are widely recognized shortcomings in the standard MBA template. There are indications of a variety of design and delivery challenges regarding intellectual and practical content, academic standards, pedagogy, and relevance of MBAs for tomorrow's managers (see e.g., Andrews & Tyson, 2004; Currie & Knights, 2003; Mintzberg, 2004; Pfeffer & Fong, 2002). Thus the critical issue to be tackled is how could the current MBA operation be modified or at least incrementally reformed to meet the local challenges of globalizing business.

At each delivery location, unique local conditions create pressure for HSE to innovate and ensure local flavor in the program, while at the same time maintaining a "HSE identity" and recognizable "HSE MBA" brand for the individual programs. The economies in the national settings where HSE currently delivers its MBA are clearly divergent from liberal market economies (Hall & Soskice, 2001). They can be characterized as variants of coordinated market economies, transition economies with strong traditions of central planning processes or economies driven by developmental states. In these contexts, a company is not usefully managed or studied as an isolated hierarchy, as a unified, individual actor (cf. Whitley, 1999); although that is the way many companies are represented in typical MBA case studies (see Liang & Wang, 2004). Each of the HSE MBA programs is delivered in a nation-state that has earlier or is currently opening up markets for international companies to operate; with a variety of business cultures operating within the same system. The participants, and their sponsors, are keen to understand better the principles and practices of liberal market economies, of archetypal U.S. ways of acting, and that of multinational businesses. The participants are also acutely aware that they are "different" from people brought up and educated in Anglo American liberal market economies, and they demand faculty members who appreciate their local business environment and its conditions.

The innovation that seems possible but that has not been widely discussed or tried is to incorporate content on studies of varieties of capitalism and comparative studies of national business systems (Hall & Soskice, 2001; Whitley, 1992) into the curricula. The varieties of capitalism and national business systems perspective does not assume that one type of economic entity, like the Chandlerian multidivisional corporation, is inherently superior in all contexts (Whitley, 1999). Instead, local actors can make use of specific location-based advantages, institutional legacies, traditions of the civil society and build alliances with the national elites.

By so doing they invent and mobilize resources that are unique and invisible to external observers. Ideally the practising manager in a MNC learns ways to enact and use different nationally specific business systems and assess their operational viability for specific objectives (Djelic & Quack, 2003; Morgan, Kristensen, & Whitley, 2001; Morgan, Whitley, & Moen, 2005). At national and even regional level in some places, managers of organizations aiming to compete effectively in business need to understand local and national institutional factors and how they affect the translation of business models in that locale. By understanding systematic differences in ways of acting and being able to recognize distinctive local ways of acting and ways to improve them, managers access the possibility to use more intelligently local resources not well understood by competitors (Kristensen, 1994; Kristensen & Zeitlin, 2005).

The main advantage of these interrelated actor-system approaches is that they provide conceptual tools to understand dynamic complementarities of national institutions and intercompany relations. Such dimensions are missing in more specialized disciplinary studies and especially in MBA curricula that tend to be organized around functional practices, doctrines and disciplines. The historical and institutional contents of these approaches bring in legacies and contingences that are far more relevant for management and practical strategy making than abstract dimensions of cross-national behavioral orientations (Hofstede, 1991).

There are several reasons why country-specific "naturalistic" experience and tacit knowledge or systemic models of varieties of capitalism do not easily translate to learning experiences in MBA modules. The systemic frameworks of national business and innovations systems are based on the duality of deep historical studies of individual cases and a large number of comparative dimensions that are context and period specific. Such heuristic and epistemologically complicated knowledge is not easily turned into practical tools for strategy making in concrete situations or embraced in MBA modules. However, this kind of knowledge is what MBA participants frequently acknowledge they need and seek. Moreover, some of the systemic frameworks of varieties of capitalisms and national business systems are static, that is, the dynamic aspects based on actors' agency in micro-macro interrelations cannot be analyzed with them (Sorge, 2005). This lowers their apparent immediate relevance in practitioner-oriented education such as the MBA. Despite the intellectual and relevance gap between static frameworks and actors' agency, both the country-specific diversity and the frameworks that conceptualize these midrange national comparisons need to be taken into account by managers working across borders and cultures. Understanding the action implications of these frameworks may direct those that design MBA curricula to consider ways to develop the participants' opportunities for agency, their political capacity to negotiate across sectors, and their abilities to generate unique social capital.

Finally, for realizing the potential for a reverse innovation in MBA education the pedagogy must be partially experiential. The experiences of participants recorded in the MBA portfolio of the HSE demonstrate that interesting learning approaches can be built by using the career-based competence of the participants to highlight all the elements discovered so far by academic research, and to go further to the tacit dimensions and articulation of their individual and collective cross-cultural and cross-national understandings. That is to say that experience, awareness and consciousness among participants in a MBA program are important elements of design alongside issues of the new economy and new relational patterns in business. Project-based learning processes can provide MBA participants with the tools and space to practice making sense in complex situations and practise being agents. This situational- and experience-based content in the curriculum is a useful complement and testing ground for generic and normative best practice models.

The next innovation then may be a MBA curriculum that can help participants develop personal theories and agency related to the specificity of their contexts.

## Visions for HSE's Innovative Offer

The vision of a renewed MBA offering from HSE builds on lessons learned from the peculiarities of the national business system at home and from delivery of MBA programs in nonliberal market economies. Finland, being a variant of a coordinated market economy has been able to implement institutional changes at a pace that has met the requirements of the global competition (see e.g., Castells & Himanen, 2002; Moen & Lilja, 2005; Tainio & Lilja, 2003; for the Finnish success story), contrary to doctrinal predictions that coordinated economies are less flexible and slower to adapt (Hall & Soskice, 2001). Finnish business organizations such as pulp and paper companies and companies developing information and communication technologies have succeeded by their demonstrated capacity to identify core businesses and build a critical mass for their knowledge base and capacity to build confidence in and for distributed leadership. The latter has generated distinctive social capital and other opportunities for agency in Finland, which enhances actors' political capacity to negotiate across sectors in the economy and society. The evidence shows that the capacity for cross-sectoral collaboration has also been transferred to transnational epistemic communities and standard setting bodies (Braithwaite & Drahos, 2000; Lilja & Moen 2003; Moen &

Lilja, 2001; Morgan, 2001; Steinbock, 2001, 2003). In such a context copying best practices is not any more enough to survive. Instead, successful managers have identified unique development paths and ways of acting in the global business and competition regime, and must do so repeatedly, almost continuously.

Building on these Finland-based lessons, and responding to the calls from participants, alumni and companies in other and various parts of the world, means offering an MBA program that assists managers to think and act differently, not instinctively, but consciously knowing well the text book and consulting templates, and yet able to invent new paths. When it is so clear that generic best practice models of business do not fit the experience and perceived opportunities of many participants in MBA programs, sense making skills are going to be of premium import. This requires that MBA graduates are competent to deduct from existing doctrines and analyze available data, but much more importantly, (1) to initiate experiments that fit their local context and international reach; (2) to reflect on the emerging outcome by making comparisons with relevant benchmarks; (3) to alter their own identities as actors based on collaborative learning; and (4) to improve pilot experiments and to extend them to other contexts (cf. Beck, 1994; Holman & Thorpe, 2003; Sabel, 1994; Weick, 2001; and for more detailed descriptions of these competencies).

This vision does not demand a complete overhaul of the current curriculum offered, but we will describe the sort of changes required to some elements. Not only does the vision suggest teaching inductive ways of theorizing and applying conceptual tools from varieties of capitalism and national business systems research in a novel way, but elements of pedagogy should be addressed. There are many ways to implement it and the more widespread the idea becomes the better it is for the first movers.

The action plan is based on the view that only incremental changes can be made to existing MBA offerings. The current existing template is so strong that radical changes would cause a shock for the participants and their potential sponsors. In addition, the human resources and capabilities for implementing the action plan take time to mature. Thus the action plan consists of the following elements:

1. Introducing a new module that teaches participants the ideas, basic frameworks and research results typical for studies in the varieties of capitalisms.

2. Integrating the basic conceptual ideas and research results into the project assignments that are made as part of the program requirements and organizing faculty support for that as a complementary form of supervision.

3.  Educating the program directors about the basic theoretical ideas and breakthrough research results in the area of varieties of capitalism and business systems, and paying special attention to the institutional contexts from which the participants come or in which they are employed (e.g., Finland, South Korea, Taiwan, Singapore, Poland, etc).

4.  Dedicating time during face-to-face educational situations for explicit dialogical forums where participants have space to narrate incidents, based on their own experience. In such stories unique institutional and cultural legacies are intertwined with business operations.

For internationally experienced managers it is not a surprise that strategic action and business operations are institutionally conditioned. In international companies, such competence is taken for granted in senior positions. One potential gap in the competence of such managers is that they are not able to explicate their tacit understanding to other managers within the company. This concerns the managers with less experience in international exposure and even more so with expatriates from other countries having different experience and educational background. Such a gap means top managers are not able to communicate the strategic vision of the company and its institutionally set strengths and weaknesses to others, even though these are taken for granted by them. Neither are they capable of acting as effective mentors for the next generation of top managers if they cannot make this knowledge explicit and communicable. A module on the varieties of capitalism and business systems research frameworks and findings would offer tools to close this competence gap.

A major bottleneck for making use of the varieties of capitalism and business systems research is that it is done in a paradigm that relies primarily on case studies and inductive reasoning, even though there are plenty of abstract conceptual tools that are used to specify the historical and institutional contexts. The primary message is that there are no universal best ways to craft company strategies and conduct business even though period specificity is taken into account, as made evident by the emerging new phase of globalization. Thus, on the one hand, the capacity to be sensitive to specific situational contexts in an analytical and comparative way is needed. On the other hand, the constantly changing context is an obstacle for using the research findings and conceptual tools as such, without adaptation to fit local specificities and new situational contingencies.

From the practitioner point of view, the benefits of the varieties of capitalism and national business systems research can only be harvested if the basic paradigm is put to use in practice in an inductive way. To get such an initial touch, the strategy project work will be tutored in a new way. We are practising with a dual supervisor approach. The first supervisor takes the overall responsibility for securing the integration of generic management doctrines and tools in the project implementation while the second supervisor is chosen to help embed varieties of capitalism and business systems type of research into the project analysis and final report. This could happen in various ways, for instance, in the forms of inductive sense making and justification of arguments based on situational knowledge, as well as applying and inventing conceptual tools that help to express complex interrelations of different aggregate levels of analysis and dynamic cross-sectoral complementarities.

In line with the varieties of capitalism and national business systems research and thinking, the importance of some unique institutional, geo-political, and industry specific issues cannot be predicted and taken into account by teachers alone. Thus, considerable rethinking of the pedagogical approach is needed. A skilled facilitator in knowledge exchange (Locke, 1996) and conflict management is required, who can develop and sustain a relational and dialogical approach to pedagogy and the development of a mutually supporting and challenging learning culture within each MBA cohort. What is essential is for the participants to be able to draw on one's own and other's experience and knowledge for a reflexive praxis. This learning culture is already clearly within the scope of HSE goals and often achieved to some extent; yet there is always need for maintenance and conflict management in this culture, and different demands on the learning culture are made in each delivery location. Here, local program directors at each delivery site have an important role to play, understanding the varieties of capitalism and national business systems paradigm and to act as facilitators of learning. The essential intent is that when a teacher, participating manager or a working-group presents an example or theoretical point that is linked with the varieties of capitalism and national business systems research tradition, the program director makes an appropriate intervention and stimulates other participants to explicate their own experiences by similar or contrasting phenomena. In this way teaching situations become multivoiced and participants recognize tacit understandings based on their own experience and expertise. While some program directors already may capably act as facilitators, there is no doubt about the need to educate them to understand the epistemology and major contents of the varieties of capitalism and national business systems research tradition.

To secure the implementation of the aim that this kind of thinking becomes an essential integrated element of the curriculum, the final item in the action plan is to organize group work and dialogues as part of the tasks assigned to the participants. Such events can be linked with teaching cases or other pedagogic tools used. The procedure suggested is not new as such. Similar attempts have been made to integrate themes and learning objectives from organizational behavior and ethics courses into other modules and learning situations in a program.

The expected outcome of such an action plan is that MBA graduates are capable of diagnosing changing institutional contexts and making use of the resources and competences those contexts provide when doing strategy work, making strategic decisions and conducting more operational work. Such a capacity is essential in international companies and cannot be substituted by other intellectual and practical tools taught in MBA programs and widely used by managers.

As for the sentiments of managers from transition economies and coordinated market economies, we have considerable evidence that the usefulness of course modules, materials, and lectures in MBA programs do not adequately reflect the concrete contexts of the participants. This message is not always sent further because participants have an instrumental orientation to the completion of the program. But if such managers start to get conceptual tools from the varieties of capitalism and business systems research they could also better challenge managerial frameworks and tools that are too generic.

## Conclusions: Institutionalizing the Reverse Innovation

To maintain the usefulness of the MBA qualification and to deliver the promise of being a leading management education provider, HSE must continue to innovate. In addition to learning ways of measuring economic performance and constructing balanced scorecards, pressures are to provide an MBA curriculum that helps practitioners make sense of the situational complexity and evaluate options for translating generic models or stories of best practices. By drawing on varieties of capitalism and national business systems research we can help MBA participants to better appreciate local idiosyncratic dynamics and, as providers, find a way to translate MBA programs to effectively meet idiosyncratic local needs. Based on historically and institutionally embedded case studies, varieties of capitalism and national business systems research also provides a rationale for promoting reflexive praxis that can appeal to those wanting a scientific logic based on empirical research for management education. It offers conceptualizations and guide posts for focusing the reflective thinking and to inform future action by practising managers. To make this change in MBA curriculum builds on unique, deep and world class experience based at HSE. Together these moves provide a desirable offering in very competitive market conditions.

To use varieties of capitalism and national business systems research in this way can be considered a reverse innovation in the MBA business because the driver for this innovation comes from the periphery of MBA education provision in Finland, Asia and Eastern Europe, not the mainstay of the market in United States and United Kingdom. The innovation pipeline is at an early stage, but some small experiments have been initiated in Helsinki. The MBA applicants and participants recognize that they need to understand, not just tacitly, the persistent systemic differences in their local business conditions, not to mention in the "foreign" places where they may be required to manage. They need to learn and practice using inductive reasoning, to synthesize and create plausible meanings and reasonable predictions. Of course, reasonableness can only be judged in retrospect, but that is business—taking manageable risks.

The systemic context that supports such a reverse innovation as we are describing is multilayered. The most diffuse layer consists of the practicing managers who participate in programs. They have heterogeneous educational backgrounds and employment experiences and a diversity of expectations related to MBA education. The next layer is the heated debate, centered on the shortcomings of the MBA template that was briefly reviewed above. Parallel to this is the advancement in the study of national business systems and other streams of the variety of capitalisms, as presented in this chapter. These academic interventions in typical business school topics have created a fruitful intellectual milieu for mobilizations of academics.

The debate catalyzed by the academics for renewing the MBA template resonates with the core message of the varieties of capitalism and national business systems type of research. This means that these intellectual streams are supporting each other. In Europe, national business system type of research has become part of the mainstream in organizational research and many of the major scholars are already teaching in MBA programs. Linked with available books, course materials, and pedagogic innovations, a wider reform movement could be mobilized. HSE academics have been among the first movers in academic research on varieties of capitalism and national business systems (see Lilja, 2005). Thus, HSE is positioned well to catalyze again new pan-European initiatives.

The final and most concrete contingency is related to the accreditation authorities. One signal that this innovation is being supported, and to make such an intellectual and practical change more visible, is to get the accreditation bodies such as AMBA, EQUIS and AACSB[3] to promote it. An existing example of how an innovation has been endorsed and encouraged by accreditation authorities is the incorporation of new requirements to integrate the teaching of ethics into MBA curriculum. In the next round of accreditation, a target with respect to varieties of capitalisms and national business systems could be set from different national contexts. Once those accreditation bodies include this innovation into their standards, the institutionalization of the reverse innovation at the core is virtually complete.

## NOTES

1. There are also pressures emanating at the core, in the United States, for the reform of MBA education. Pressures from the core and the periphery intersect, but the focus of this chapter is restricted to the pressures from the periphery.

2. Since the 1970s until very recently, Finnish universities followed the European model of management education (Engwall, 2004) offering students, directly after their high school baccalaureate, a specialized academically-focused "Master of Science" degree in business studies and economics. The model where students first take a more general bachelor's degree and then take an optional master's degree, is just being reintroduced.

3. AMBA, Association of MBAs (UK), EQUIS, European Quality Improvement System (Belgium), AACSB, Association to Advance Collegiate Schools of Business (USA).

## REFERENCES

Andrews, N., & Tyson, L. D. (2004). The upwardly global MBA. *Strategy + Business, 36*, 1, 9.

Beck, U. (1994). The reinvention of politics: Towards a theory of reflexive modernization. In U. Beck, A. Giddens, & S. Lash (Eds.), *Reflexive modernization. Politics, tradition and aesthetics in the modern social order* (pp. 1-55). Cambridge, England: Polity Press.

Braithwaite, J., & Drahos, P. (2000). *Global business regulation.* Cambridge, MA: Cambridge University Press.

Castells, M., & Himanen, P. (2002). *The information society and the welfare state. The Finnish model.* Oxford, England: Oxford University Press.

CEMP. (2001). *Final report of "The Creation of European Management Practice" research program.* Retrieved June 28, 2006, from http://www.fek.uu.se/cemp/publications/cempreports.html

Costea, B. (1999). International MBAs and globalization: Celebration or end of diversity? *Human Resource Development International, 4*(4), 309-311.

Currie, G., & Knights, D. (2003). Reflecting on a critical pedagogy in MBA Education. *Management learning, 34*(1), 27-50.

Djelic, M., & Quack, S. (Eds.). (2003). *Globalization and institutions: Redefining the Rules of the Economic Game.* Cheltenham, England: Edward Elgar.

Doria, J., Rozanski, H., & Cohen, E. (2003). What business needs from business schools. *Strategy + Business, 32*, 1-8.

Engwall, L. (2004). The Americanization of Nordic management education. *Journal of Management Inquiry, 13*(2), 109-117.

Ferner, A., & Quintanilla, J. (2002). Between globalization and capitalist variety: multinational and the international diffusion of employment relations. *European Journal of Industrial Relations, 8*(3), 243-250.

Friga, P., Bettis, R., & Sullivan, R. (2003). Changes in graduate management education and new business school strategies for the 21st century. *Academy of Management Learning and Education, 2*(3), 233-249.

Grey, C. (2004). Reinventing business schools: the contribution of critical management education. *Academy of Management Learning and Education, 3*(2), 178-186.

Hall, P., & Soskice, D. (2001). *Varieties of capitalism. The institutional foundations of comparative advantage.* Oxford, England: Oxford University Press.

Hedlund, G. (1986). *The hypermodern MNC—A heterachy? Human Resource Management, 20*(1), 9-25.

Hofstede, G. (1991). *Cultures and organizations: Software of Mind.* New York: McGraw-Hill.

Holm, U., & Pedersen, T. (2000). *The emergence and impact of MNC centres of excellence: A subsidiary perspective.* London: Macmillan.

Holman, D., & Thorpe, R. (2003). *Management and language.* London: Sage.

Kristensen, P. H. (1994). Strategies in a volatile world. *Economy and Society, 23*(3), 305-334.

Kristensen, P. H., & Zeitlin, J. (2005). *Local players in global games. The strategic constitution of a multinational corporation.* Oxford, England: Oxford University Press.

Liang, N., & Wang, J. (2004). Implicit mental models in teaching cases: An empirical study of popular MBA cases in the United States and China. *Academy of Management Learning and Education, 3*(4), 397-413.

Lilja, K. (Ed.). (2005). *The national business system in Finland.* Helsinki: Helsinki School of Economics.

Lilja, K., & Moen, E. (2003). Coordinating transnational competition: changing patterns in the European pulp and pager industry. In M. Djelic & S. Quack (Eds.), *Globalization and institutions. Redefining the rules of the economic game* (pp. 137-160 Cheltenham, England: Edward Elgar.

Locke, R. (1996). *The collapse of the American management mystique.* New York: Oxford University Press.

Mintzberg, H. (2004). *Managers not MBAs.* London: Prentice Hall.

Mintzberg, H., & Gosling, J. (2002). Educating managers beyond borders. *Academy of Management Learning and Education, 1*(1), 64–76.

Moen, E., & Lilja, K. (2001). Constructing global corporations: contrasting national legacies in the Nordic forest industry. In G. Morgan, P. H. Kristensen, & R. Whitley (Eds.), *The multinational firm. Organizing across institutional and national divides* (pp. 97-121). Oxford: Oxford University Press.

Moen, E., & Lilja, K. (2005). Change in coordinated market economies: The case of Nokia and Finland. In G. Morgan, R. Whitley, & E. Moen (Eds.), *Changing capitalisms?* (pp. 352-379). Oxford, England: Oxford University Press.

Morgan, G. (2001). The development of transnational standards and regulations and their impacts on firms. In G. Morgan, P. H. Kristensen, & R. Whitley

(Eds.), *The multinational firm. Organizing across institutional and national divides* (pp. 225-252). Oxford, England: Oxford University Press.

Morgan, G., Kristensen, P. H., & Whitley, R. (Eds.) (2001). *The multinational firm. Organizing across institutional and national divides*. Oxford, England: Oxford University Press.

Morgan, G., Whitley R., & Moen E. (Eds.). (2005). *Changing capitalisms?: Internationalisation, institutional change and systems of economic organization*. Oxford, England: Oxford University Press.

Pfeffer, J., & Fong, C. T. (2002). *The end of business schools? Less success than meets the eye. Academy of Management Learning and Education, 1*(1), 78-95.

Pfeffer, J., & Fong, C. T. (2004). The business school "business": Some lessons from the U.S. experience. *Journal of Management Studies, 41*(8), 1501-1520.

Sabel, C. F. (1994). Learning by monitoring: The institutions of economic development. In N. J. Smelser & R. Swedberg (Ed.), *The handbook of economic sociology* (pp. 137-165). New York: Princeton University Press.

Sabel, C. F. (2005). *Globalisation, new public services, local deomcracy: What's the connection?* In *Local governance and drivers of growth* (pp. 111-131). Paris: OECD

Sorge, A. (2005). *The global and the local. Understanding the dialectics of business systems*. Oxford, England: Oxford University Press.

Starkey, K., & Tempest, S. (2001). *The world-class business school: A UK perspective*. London: Council for Excellence in Management and Leadership.

Starkey, K., & Tempest, S. (2005). The future of the business school: Knowledge challenges and opportunities. *Human Relations, 58*(1), 61-82.

Steinbock, D. (2001). *The Nokia Revolution. The story of an extraordinary company that transformed an industry.* New York: AMACOM.

Steinbock, D. (2003). *Wireless Horizon. Strategy and competition in the worldwide mobile marketplace*. New York: AMACOM.

Tainio, R., & Lilja K. (2003). The Finnish business system in transition: Outcomes, actors and their influence. In B. Czarniawska & G. Sevón (Eds.), *Northern light—Organization theory in Scandinavia* (pp. 69-87). Trelleborg: Liber/Abstrakt/Copenhagen Business School Press.

Tainio, R., Lilja, K., & Santalainen, T. (1997). Changing managerial competitive practices in the context of growth and decline in the Finnish banking sector. In G. Morgan & D. Knights (Eds.), *Regulation and deregulation in European financial services* (pp. 201-215). London: Macmillan.

Tainio, R., Pohjola, M., & Lilja, K. (2000). Economic performance of Finland after the Second World War. In S., Quack, G. Morgan, & R. Whitley (Eds.), *National capitalism, global competition, and economic performance* (pp. 275-287). Amsterdam: John Benjamins.

Weick, K. E. (2001). *Making sense of the organization*. Boston: Blackwell.

Whitley, R. (Ed.). (1992). *European business systems: Firms and markets in their international context*. London: Sage.

Whitley, R. (1999). *Divergent capitalisms: The social structuring and change of business systems*. Oxford, England: Oxford University Press.

# Part IV

**PARTNERSHIPS IN MBA INNOVATION**

CHAPTER 10

# USING A NONPROFIT BUSINESS PARTNER TO DEVELOP BUSINESS MANAGEMENT SKILLS FOR MBA EDUCATION

**Hugh D. Sherman, Deborah Crown Core, and Gary Coombs**

Recent critics have advocated that business schools should move away from the current scientific model of graduate business education to a professional model. These critics have identified two key problems with the majority of existing programs. The first problem is that most graduate students do not learn how and when to apply appropriate academic tools and models. The second problem is that many business schools do not have faculty with extensive professional business experience, or are unable to access professional business executives who can assist faculty in integrating practical business experiences with disciplinary knowledge. This paper discusses how in an effort to address these issues, we redesigned our graduate MBA program utilizing a critical partnership with the Voinovich Center for Leadership and Public Affairs. We found that the most important task to make this partnership and professional degree program effective for our students is the coordination and integration of the academic faculty and professional staff. The different roles and functions of the participating faculty and staff are discussed.

*New Visions for Graduate Management Education*, 269–282
Copyright © 2006 by Information Age Publishing

## INTRODUCTION

Henry Mintzberg in the opening sentence of his latest book (2004), *Managers not MBAs: A Hard Look at the Soft Practice of Managing and Management Development*, has written; "It is time to recognize conventional MBA programs for what they are—or else to close them down" (p. 5). He contends that MBA programs recruit the wrong people, teach them the wrong things, and do it in the wrong way. He calls for graduate programs to integrate the content of the various business disciplines and to build on students' actual managerial experience.

Graduate business education has been criticized for more than 25 years as missing the mark in educating future managers and leaders (Mintzberg, 2004). Pfeffer and Fong (2002) found no evidence of long term return on investment, in terms of advancement and salary, for those who completed an elite MBA program. Hill (1992) cites a survey which found that 65% of the graduates of MBA programs reported not using, or only marginally using skills they learned in their programs. She concluded that business schools "provide little to prepare managers for their day to day responsibilities" (p. 274). As a result some scholars have called for radical restructuring of existing MBA programs, combining management education with action based learning (Reynolds & Vince, 2004).

At Ohio University's College of Business, we have a history of attempting to address such criticisms. For more than 2 decades we have used a problem or action learning based curriculum. Over the years we have made countless changes as new faculty joined the College, and the target audience for the program changed. The change process has not always been smooth. Faculty has had very different ideas as to what is the correct balance between the time spent using problems that require students to integrate the various disciplines versus teaching students specialized discipline knowledge.

In recent years, our current faculty have become increasingly concerned about the relevance of the problems that are used (stories out of the current business press), the need for additional expertise to assist in problem design and management, and the continuing concern about students not learning enough specialized content knowledge.

In this paper we discuss how we tried to address these challenges. Most importantly, we have developed a partnership with a nonprofit organization that is the University's largest service provider to the 29 county Appalachian Ohio region. Through this organization we have established relationships with regional economic development officials, bankers, and a for-profit venture capital firm. We believe that this partnership has allowed us to accomplish a fundamental improvement in the development and learning for our students.

## Recent Criticisms of MBA Programs

In reviewing the literature that is critical of the approach of the majority of graduate business programs, we identified two common broad themes. The first theme is that the primary focus of faculty should be to educate professionals to be effective practicing managers. Bennis and O'Toole (2005) argue that business schools have become ineffective in recent decades because they have moved from a professional model of education to a scientific model. The scientific model assumes that business is an academic discipline like chemistry or biology. Bennis and O'Toole (2005) argue that business is a professional school more similar to medicine and law, where practice is integral to learning the skills required to be effective in the real world. Business managers must work with people, make deals and process often vague and contradictory information (Mintzberg, 2004).

As schools have adopted the scientific model, they have increasingly been hiring professors with little real-world business experience. Faculties often have not developed the skills and competencies necessary to be a manager; hence, it is challenging for them to pass along these skills to their MBA students. Bennis and O'Toole (2005) further contend that, "today it is possible to find tenured faculty who have never set foot inside a real business, except as customers." And to make the problem worse, untenured faculty members are urged by senior faculty not to work with practitioners doing fieldwork, but to instead focus on narrow scientific subjects. Many leading business schools have measured themselves by the rigor of their scientific research rather than in terms of the competence of their graduates.

A second theme concerns the need for graduate programs to be designed to teach students how to integrate materials across disciplines to be better able to solve the interrelated, complex business problems faced by today's managers (Mintzberg, 2004; Pfeffer & Fong, 2002). This integrated thinking approach requires practice and experience (Mintzberg, 2004). Perhaps as a result of these criticisms, many schools have added integrative practical, action learning components to their programs. However, few programs integrate this experience across their curriculum (Feldman, 2005).

Students need to be provided with the theories, concepts, and techniques in a classroom environment. After receiving a base of content knowledge, the students need to be able to practice experiences that a manager encounters. The next step is critical—reflection. Faculty need to engage students individually, and as a group, to connect, synthesize, probe, and analyze what happened and what they learned during and after their experience (Feldman, 2005; Mintzberg, 2004). Faculty assist in the reflection, questioning and guiding around theoretically-driven, yet self-reflectant principles and models concerning effective management practices. Additionally, Mintzberg (2004) and Feldman (2005) claim that **throughout their course of study, students need to explore their own beliefs in relation to theories and empiricism about the way things need** to be done. This helps students think about their experiences in a broader context so they can make connections with the issue and the solution. This "experienced reflection" is reciprocal and can be applied to new business situations (Mintzberg, 2004).

The importance of reflection raises the question about whether many faculty members have the ability to be effective "teachers" in this type of professional program. Few have been trained to recognize and draw the connections between organizational realities and the theories which they test and refine. If the purpose of graduate business education is to develop managers and leaders, then the faculty must have expertise in more than fact collection (Bennis & O'Toole, 2005). Faculty must be able to examine an organizational situation with the ability to delve into the hidden strategic, human, and political complexities which must be identified for managers to make effective decisions (Armstrong, 2005; Bennis & O'Toole, 2005; Feldman, 2005; Mintzberg, 2004). Bennis and O'Toole (2005) contend that some faculty members may be uncomfortable analyzing multifaceted questions concerning strategy and policy which often require judgment based on experience and wisdom. If this is true, then business schools need to find other approaches to augment the skills of faculty so that business schools can still accomplish the mission of educating the next generation of effective organizational managers and leaders.

## The Ohio University MBA: Historical Experience

For almost 2 decades, our graduate program has used an action learning pedagogy which is consistent with the professional model of business education. Action learning was first proposed by Reginald Revans in the 1940s (Revans, 1971, 1981). Action learning is a process through which a group of learners engages in solving a real or authentic problem while concurrently reflecting on their learning and its application and benefits to them individually and to their organization (Marquardt, 1999). The key elements of action learning are the authenticity and salience of the problems, the interactions among the members of the action learning group, a focus on the process of inquiry, and the opportunity for reflection.

It is the problem that sets the environmental context for learning and serves as the stimulus for learning. Problems must be significant and sufficient in scale to provide a challenge that an individual would be unlikely to surmount in the time available. For team learning to occur, the problem must require the collaborative efforts of the team members.

Action learning occurs in a group or team, typically comprising four to eight members. The objective is to bring multiple perspectives to bear on the problem and to encourage members to challenge teammates' views constructively in order to generate better solutions. It is within the action learning group, and through the interactions of the learning group with the faculty serving as guides and tutors, that social negotiation occurs and individual understandings are tested.

The action learning model emphasizes inquiry. One objective is to develop better questions about the problem in order to refine the research and problem-solving processes. As Marquardt (1999) points out, action learning attends to both what is known and what is not known about the problem, with the objectives of discovery and shifting the balance from the latter to the former. The learner is constantly challenged to consider sources of information, to assess their credibility, and to make judgments about conflicting information.

Reflection should center on the learning accomplished in solving the problem abstracted from the specifics of the problem itself. Thus, it is not the particular solutions to the problem that matter, as much as the process of solving the problem and learning the skills that can be applied to future problem situations.

Although we have had some success with the action learning elements we have incorporated into our program, we still faced several problematic issues. Hence, we sought to identify major ways in which we could improve what our graduate students learn and how the learning is accomplished. As a result, we talked to alumni and our executive advisory board, read the management education literature, and benchmarked our program against other graduate programs. The following issues were identified.

The first major issue, which has always been identified as critical, concerns the development of authentic business problems that met the desired learning outcomes. An ongoing challenge in administering a program of this type is coming up with new and relevant business problems that address critical learning issues at an appropriate level of ambiguity and complexity.

In the past we have used simulated situations created by faculty members to replicate typical business scenarios. One example is projects developed in conjunction with managers of actual organizations seeking input and fresh perspectives on problems they are facing. Another is the use of case studies drawn from current business issues that are being discussed in the press. In contrast, real problems, worked in partnership with actual organizations, provide the most engaging and memorable experiences with real-world managerial problem solving. However, they are also the most difficult to "acquire" as they are dependent on a steady supply of businesses willing to open their doors to student consultants.

A related issue was that to use "real" business clients necessitated faculty who understood actual, comprehensive business problems. As has been identified by Mintzberg (2004) and Feldman (2005), a critical task of faculty is to integrate the experiences with disciplinary knowledge. This can only be done by faculty who are able to facilitate the necessary reflection/discussion in an integrated manner that captures the comprehensiveness of actual business problems and solutions.

The third issue was that faculty and some of our graduates believed we had not provided enough specialized course content. This had been an on going debate from the inception of implementing an action learning approach. By utilizing this approach throughout the program we previously had to reduce some of the specialized discipline related course content.

## Improving Ohio University's Graduate Program: Partnership With Voinovich Center for Leadership and Public Affairs

After collecting information from benchmark programs and our alumni, we decided we could only accomplish our desired learning outcomes by developing partnerships to leverage the classroom educational experience with actual business experience. We wanted to continue to capitalize on our historical knowledge of using a problem-based, action-learning platform, but we needed to deal with three of the inherent weaknesses that we have continued to experience over the history of our program. As discussed previously, these were the quality of the "business experiences" we were providing the student, the limited professional experience and skills of our faculty, and the need to maximize student learning of critical content knowledge necessary to guide the business experiences. Consequently, we made the decision to only use authentic business problems, and to utilize professional practitioners to augment the skills of our faculty. In addition, we decided to increase the rigor and the coverage of specialized discipline content throughout our program. We could not make this change by ourselves. We were only able to accomplish this change by developing a partnership with the Voinovich Center for Leadership and Public Affairs.

## Description of Voinovich Center and Development of Relationship

The Voinovich Center is Ohio University's largest public service organization, engaged in providing technical assistance and research services to local government, nonprofit, and business organizations throughout the 29 counties of Appalachia Ohio. The Center has four major different initiatives that include public service, energy, and environment, an executive leadership institute and a business development group. It employs approximately 60 full-time professionals.

The Business Development Group (BDG) offers an integrated set of business technical assistance services to new, existing, and fast growing businesses throughout Appalachian Ohio. The BDG operates an international trade assistance program, a Procurement Technical Assistance Center (PTAC) which assists businesses in selling goods and services to local, state, and federal governments, and several small business development centers. In addition, they are partners with Adena Ventures, the nations' first New Markets Venture Capital Company (a program administered by U.S. Small Business Administration). Adena Ventures is a for-profit $32 million equity fund, created to provide equity financing to high-growth potential firms located in southern Ohio and West Virginia. The BDG provides high-end business consulting services to potential firms that may apply to Adena Ventures for financing or to firms in which Adena has already invested. The BDG employs 11 professional staff people and has four regional offices.

We believe that by using a nonprofit organization this has helped us to gain the support of local businesses and government officials. This program has received quite a bit of positive publicity in the regional press. We have been able to gain the endorsement of many of the local legislative leaders for our work helping businesses to become sustainable and to increase employment in the region.

## Description of Ohio University's New MBA Program

The alliant relationship with the Voinovich Center provided an immediate solution to our problem of needing relevant application and experience for our students. However, to secure the optimal learning environment we needed to structure our program in such a way as to facilitate specialized knowledge while also ensuring that students would both apply what they learned, and learn from their experience. Consistent with Mintzberg (2004) and Bennis and O'Toole's (2005) mandate, we needed an integrated delivery system where the integration crossed disciplines, skills of instructors/faculty, modes of learning (i.e., declarative and procedural knowledge acquisition), and levels of analysis. And although we are still in the early stages of implementation, we are confident the structure of our redesigned program meets these objectives.

As previously mentioned, the facilitation of a truly integrated program required us to partner with an organization dedicated to delivering business solutions to regional businesses (i.e., the Voinovich Center). This relationship provides a number of opportunities and challenges. The first benefit of this relationship is the Center's ability to provide us with an authentic and diverse range of problems we can use as application opportunities for our students. These experiences range from high growth potential businesses seeking venture capital, existing midsized manufacturing businesses aiming for growth, and new venture start ups seeking initial debt or angel investment. Further augmenting this benefit, partnering with the Center allowed us to restructure our program in such a way as to enhance the amount of specialized course content we could offer, while simultaneously providing more appropriate applications. We achieved this efficiency by removing more contrived applications from the classroom—which allowed us to include more specialized course content, and synergistically develop students toward applying their knowledge in an integrated manner.

In addition to providing relevant, year-round applications, The Center also provided us with a professional staff, all of whom have significant business experience. However, the majority of the professional staff is also hired for their ability to teach, coach, and mentor students. Their experience, coupled with their managerial skills form the basis for their ability to analyze multifaceted organizational problems in a variety of industries. Conversely, many of the academic faculty's skills are more suited to delivering specialized content knowledge, although several faculty members have a range of experience as business professionals. Hence, it was imperative to create an internal structure that blended and built the full range of skills necessary for delivering the program.

As we were redesigning the program, we identified two dimensions of the program's content that required coordination. The first dimension, which has troubled academics for years, is the integration of content knowledge across disciplines. The second dimension was even more challenging to coordinate, the integration of declarative and procedural knowledge (i.e., content knowledge and the ability to apply that knowledge). We employed two strategies to achieve this coordination. The first strategy was the coordination of curriculum and knowledge delivery systems, while the second was to create an integrated internal structure with the development of specific roles for academic and professional faculty members.

Coordinating curriculum and knowledge delivery systems required a considerable amount of information sharing prior to the launch of the program. A series of meetings were held between academic faculty members, as well as between academic and professional faculty. Both types of content were considered equally critical and so the coordination for both was handled simultaneously. Professional faculty are employees of the Voinovich Center who have extensive business experience.

During this process, the development of the integrated curriculum was led by academically-trained course instructors, with professional faculty, and faculty application leaders assisting with evaluating content for synthesis, organizational relevance, and its contribution toward improving managerial skills. Additionally, professional faculty identified specific content areas needed by students before the students engaged in professional experiences. Developing the program's content in this manner allowed us to integrate across disciplines, and equally important, it allowed us to prepare for the integration of education and experience.

The second coordination mechanism was employed to assist with the integration of curriculum by providing a vehicle by which faculty could coordinate, build, and blend managerial knowledge and skills. Four primary roles were developed, faculty application leaders, faculty application guides, faculty content instructors, and professional faculty. Because integrating education and experience requires both planning and adapting to be successful, our program used the coordinating mechanisms of identified roles and weekly faculty and student/faculty meetings to facilitate the mutual adjustment necessary for optimal learning (Mintzberg, 1980). Three roles were specifically designed to facilitate integration and mutual adjustment throughout the program, with the fourth serving only a quasi-integrative role.

The first role created to facilitate integration was that of the faculty application leader. Faculty application leaders are all academically trained, but also have professional experience at the managerial and executive levels. These individuals teach specialized content in the MBA program, and they also work directly with professional faculty and the faculty application guides to supervise, evaluate, and guide students throughout their academic and business experiences. These individuals have the requisite knowledge, skills, and abilities to deliver specialized content, while also understanding and embracing complex, comprehensive business issues. In addition to mentoring students, Faculty application leaders are asked to contribute to the "seasoning" of inexperienced faculty members. Faculty application leaders also work directly with professional faculty to ensure the infusion of cutting edge information into students' work experiences. Finally, faculty application leaders are also part of the faculty team which participates in weekly reflective sessions with students, and the faculty team that evaluates the students' progress on skill development and knowledge acquisition.

The second integrative role is that of faculty application guides. These individuals also come from the academic environment and teach specialized course content, but are involved in more of the day to day operational issues with students during their application experiences than faculty application leaders. Additionally, faculty application guides do not have the planning, directing, or mentoring responsibilities of faculty application leaders. Finally, the faculty application guides are part of the faculty team which meets weekly to engage students in reflection, and to discuss students' progress.

The third integrative role is that of professional faculty members. As previously stated, these individuals have significant business experience and are proficient in solving complex business problems. In addition to participating in classroom sessions, Professional faculty members deliver content designed to facilitate the application of knowledge. Professional faculty members work directly with students as they engage in a wide range of business activities. Professional faculty members also structure the students' experiences consistent with a learning acquisition model, as students are heavily mentored during the initial stages of application, with more responsibility entrusted to individuals and teams of students as they gain experience, knowledge, and confidence.

The final role of faculty content instructor is less integrative, and more traditional. These individuals are academically trained, and deliver specialized content, yet still in an integrated format.

The pedagogical structure for the program is based on initially presenting a *comprehensive model* that serves as the framework for integrating application and knowledge. The other elements of the pedagogical structure include *intense content delivery, mentored application*, and *model-based, mentored, self-regulated reflection*. The time dedicated to each element, and the reciprocity elements are a function of the stage of learning both individually and collectively.

Initially presenting a comprehensive model is essential for ensuring that specialized and general knowledge can be built around a central theme that is organizationally relevant. Additionally, this model serves as the frame by which experiences, skills, and reflection can be interwoven with knowledge.

In our program we have used a model describing the concept of adding value to organizations. In the opening classes a team of faculty with cross-disciplinary and across-the-board professional and academic backgrounds, present the model to students. In addition to allowing an integrated forum for defining terms and articulating relationships in concert with other disciplines, this format also allows us to present the interdependencies necessary between knowledge and application.

The comprehensive model was developed by a cross-disciplinary team of faculty, including both seasoned professionals and traditional academics. To help students understand this comprehensive model, we developed an initial project that requires students to develop a strategy for adding value to two regional businesses in disparate industries. During the time students are working on this project, faculty offer intense classroom instruction directed at understanding how various disciplines add value to businesses in general, and to the targeted organizations and industries specifically.

Earlier we discussed the importance of reflection that is guided by faculty, but which fosters reflective skills in individual students (Feldman, 2005; Mintzberg, 2004). This step is even more influential in developing effective management practices if it is done within a schema that allows individuals to reflect upon their experiences and newly acquired knowledge against some integrated standard (i.e., the model). Hence, in our program we provide students with almost immediate summary feedback that helps them evaluate their experience and deliverable within the framework of the comprehensive model. Additionally, within days, students meet with a team of cross-disciplinary, professional and academic faculty members to reflect upon their first experience. In fact, the first iteration of this project is only presented as constructive development, rather than a graded requirement. This facilitates the likelihood that students will focus on learning, a necessary element in the early stages of knowledge and skill development. This process of reciprocal content delivery, application, and mentored reflection is repeated with the second portion of the project the following two weeks.

In the next 8 weeks students engage in acquiring intense declarative knowledge, still within the rubric of integrating this knowledge back to the comprehensive model. Additionally, each piece of knowledge it required to pass the test of organizational relevance. However, instead of relying solely on academically-trained faculty to generate the content of this knowledge, it was constructed using the reciprocal processing mechanism previously described.

During this period students also begin a formal orientation geared toward helping them gain procedural knowledge, or the application of content knowledge. This orientation is also done in concert with professional and academic faculty, taking specialized content and putting it in a format that highlights ways to apply this information. The applied orientation culminates with a project that is again facilitated by cross-disciplinary academics and professionals. Once again, the process of reciprocal content delivery, application, and mentored reflection is utilized. Additionally, the project is broken into portions where the initial deliverable is followed by heavily mentored reflection without an academically-oriented evaluation (i.e., a letter grade) to foster learning, and a learning-orientation. At the end of the applied orientation, students enter a 4 week window where no new content knowledge is delivered, and the focus is exclusively on applying knowledge. This concentration on application is due to the heavy attentional demands required for skill development during initial training phases (Kanfer & Ackerman, 2000).

Following the period of stand alone application, students are immersed into simultaneous content delivery and application of that knowledge. Consistent with earlier curriculum development, this stage was developed by the cross-disciplinary, professional and academic faculty members. Again, weekly reflective sessions with students, faculty application leaders, the faculty application guides, and professional faculty are held to foster the development of skills within a self-reflectant framework. Weekly evaluation sessions are also held with all faculty members to ensure coordination of delivery, the mutual adjustment necessary to adapt to emerging needs from the professional experiences, and to assess students' development. During this time frame MBA students take on increasing responsibility to manage the client relationship, their consulting team, and themselves.

Throughout the program, students' development is monitored, with the goal of building effective managers and leaders. As such, the final 4½ months of the program attempt to transition students toward independence, both in national and international environments. The culmination of the program is an international consulting project for the MBA students.

The students select from among two or more destination countries where we have established relationships with partner educational institutions. Following a period of predeparture preparation, including familiarization with the host country business culture and environment, students travel to the host country to engage in an intense 2-week consulting project in teams that integrate students from the two institutions (Coombs & Yost, 2004). In essence, the projects mirror the types of client-based consulting projects that they have been doing in the domestic arena, under tight time pressures and with the added complexity of operating in an unfamiliar business and cultural context, teamed with and somewhat dependent on peers from a different educational, cultural, and linguistic background. As with prior projects, the outcome is a consulting report and presentation to the client. Following the experience, the students are asked to submit a paper to the faculty reflecting on their international project experience.

## CONCLUSION

To make graduate business programs relevant to the success of their graduates, Bennis and O'Toole (2005), as well as Mintzberg (2004) have contended that business schools must put the practice of management into graduate programs. Bennis and O'Toole (2005) recommend that business schools need to adopt a professional school approach to educating their graduates. This requires an emphasis on the needs of the client and most importantly the integration of knowledge and practice.

However, this is not an easy transition. As we have discussed there are two critical issues that must be overcome. These are identifying the range and complexity of business problems to meet program learning outcomes and faculty with business experience. Faculty need to be able to guide students in interpreting messy, available data; understand the indirect and long term implications of business decisions; and be able to make decisions in the absence of desired information.

To address these issues we recommend that business schools look for innovative solutions. Very few schools will have continual access to firms, or the comprehensive expertise among their faculty to undertake developing a professional education curriculum. In our case we looked externally for a partner that could help us overcome these problems. The Voinovich Center for Leadership and Public Affairs possesses the contacts in the region so that they are able to provide the necessary variety of businesses in terms of size, stage of development and industry sector. In addition, they have an extensive experienced professional staff of business consultants. Finally, they have the willingness and desire to work with graduate students and faculty. To enhance this partnership the Center has altered the job descriptions and annual performance forms to incorporate coaching and mentoring of students as a key job requirement.

Even though we were successful in finding an excellent partner, the redesign of our MBA program required an extremely high level of coordination and integration of the College's academic faculty and the Center's professional staff. We had numerous meetings with faculty and professional staff to get everyone comfortable with their new roles. But we were all in agreement that the purpose of the program and the measure of our success will continue to be the competence of our graduates.

We believe that we have developed a program that integrates knowledge with experience. The result is that our graduates possess strong business specialized knowledge, management skills and experiences that are proving highly attractive to potential employers. These are skills that are necessary for successful business careers.

## REFERENCES

Armstrong, S. (2005). Postgraduate management education in the UK: Lessons from or lessons for the U.S. model? *Academy of Management Journal of Learning & Education, 4*(2), 229-234.

Bennis, W. G., & O'Toole, J. (2005). How business schools lost their way. *Harvard Business Review* [Online version]. Retrieved May 29, 2005, from harvardbusinessonline.hbsp.Harvard.edu

Coombs, G. & Yost E. (2004) Teaching international business through international student consulting projects: The GCP/JSCP at Ohio University. In C. Wankel & R. DeFillippi (Eds.), *The cutting edge of international management education*. Greenwich, CT: Information Age.

Feldman, D. (2005). The food is no good and they don't give us enough: Reflections on Mintzberg's critque of MBA education. *Academy of Management Journal of Learning & Education, 4*(2), 217-220.

Kanfer, R., & Ackerman, P. L. (2000). Individual differences in work motivation: Further explorations of a trait framework. *Applied Psychology, An International Review, 49*, 47-482.

Hill, L. (1992). *Becoming a manager: Mastery of a new identity.* Boston: Harvard Business School Press.

Marquardt, M. J. (1999). *Action learning in action: Transforming problems and people for world-class organizational learning.* Palo Alto, CA: Davies-Black.

Mintzberg, H. (2004). *Managers not MBA's: A hard look at the soft practice of managing and management development.* San Francisco: Berret-Koehler.

Pfeffer, J., & Fong, C. (2002). The end of business schools? Less success than meets the eye. *Academy of Management Learning & Education, 1*(1), 78-96.

Revans, R. W. (1971). *Developing effective managers: A new approach to business education.* London: Longman.

Revans, R. W. (1981). The nature of action learning. *Omega, 9*, 9-24.

Reynolds, M., & Vince, R. (2004). Critical management education and action-based learning: Synergies and contradictions. *Academy of Management Learning & Education, 3*(4), 442-456.

CHAPTER 11

# AMCHAM-BASED INTERNATIONAL INTERNSHIPS

## A Cost-Effective Distance Field Learning Model For Improving MBA International Business Education

**Charles M. Vance and Yongsun Paik**

Students who wish to succeed in international business can enhance their international competencies and increase the likelihood of career success by obtaining international work experience. A model prescribing a cost-effective approach for expanding the utilization of international internships for obtaining this vital work experience is long overdue for U.S. MBA programs. In this chapter we examine major obstacles of traditional international internship efforts that combine to limit MBA student utilization of these powerful learning experiences. We then propose an improved model, integrated with distance coursework and direct field learning assignments, and based in American Chambers of Commerce (AmChams) located throughout the world.

*New Visions for Graduate Management Education*, 283–305
Copyright © 2006 by Information Age Publishing

## INTRODUCTION

Many U.S. organizations are now placing a premium on job candidates'competencies as these organizations strive to compete in an increasingly globally integrated marketplace (Ball & McCulloch, 1993; Shetty & Rudell, 2002; *Wall Street Journal*, 1994). This emphasis on global competencies should come as no surprise with the widely held realization that the best growth opportunities for U.S. multinationals over the next several decades will be abroad (Garten, 1997). For individuals planning and developing their future career, it is becoming increasingly apparent that the development of international business and global competencies—such as the ability to effectively adjust and relate to different cultures, adjust and respond to differing competitive and political environments, deal with rapid change and uncertainty, and deal with the challenge of duality involving thinking global yet acting local—should be a top priority (Parker, 2005; Mendenhall, Kuhlmann, & Stahl, 2001).

As organizations and individuals planning their future careers consider how to most effectively begin to develop essential global competencies (whether ultimately practiced domestically or in a foreign assignment), they may do well to consider the old maxim, "Experience is the best teacher." In one survey on developing global leadership competencies, 80% of the executives interviewed described their foreign work assignment as the single most influential developmental experience in their lives (Black, Morrision, & Gregersen, 1999). Another study examining multinational corporation (MNC) executives' perceptions about obtaining needed global competencies to contribute to future company success concluded that overseas experience generally was valued more than traditional classroom-delivered university education or executive development programs (Reynolds & Rice, 1988). Osland (1995) outlines important forms of beneficial personal transformation in cognition, attitudes, and social relationships as a result of working abroad for an extended period of time. Therefore, there is strong evidence that at some point in their planned professional career development individuals should seriously consider an extended work experience in a foreign business environment as a very productive "experiential field learning classroom" for building important competencies in international business and global leadership.

In recent field research among current American expatriates in Asia, Vance (2005) identified international internships as a frequently used and highly recommended strategy for individuals in developing their international careers. Several other studies also point to an international internship as extremely valuable in preparing future international managers for the challenges of the global marketplace, and place squarely upon academia the expectation and responsibility of providing this powerful form of experiential learning (Fugate & Jefferson, 2001; Marlowe & Santibanez, 2000; Toncar & Cudmore, 2000). Consistent with Black, Morrison, and Gregersen's (1999) evidence of the preeminence of significant international field experience for developing global leadership competencies, some studies even assert that international internships as a form of intense experiential learning, built upon a solid international business interdisciplinary foundation, represent the most effective approach for helping students develop critical international business competencies (Toncar & Cudmore, 2000; White & Griffith, 1998).

In this chapter we will briefly examine the nature and quality of international business education in the United States and for MBA programs in particular. Specific limitations and difficulties involved with existing efforts to provide international internships for enhanced student learning and development also will be discussed. We finally will present a cost-effective model, combining current technological innovations and experiential field learning, for delivering international internship opportunities in a manner that will enhance the effectiveness of U.S. MBA education. We believe that the adoption of this model can lead to a greatly increased utilization of quality international internship curriculum options, and ultimately enhance the international competitiveness of talent graduating from US MBA programs.

## A Current Assessment Of U.S. International Business Education and International Internships

Several researchers in business education have claimed that the responsibility of educating tomorrow's managers lies with business schools (Aggarwal, 1989; Frear & Metcalf, 1988; Kaynak, Yucelt, & Barker, 1990; Porter & McKibbin, 1988; Schoell, 1991). However, many believe that U.S. business school curricula fall far short in effecting student acquisition of vital international business competencies. Additionally, U.S. business schools and the overall educational system have been blamed for the decline in the competitiveness of U.S. MNCs (Beamish & Calof, 1989; Kwok & Arpan, 1994; Kwok, Arpan, & Folks, 1994; Tung & Miller, 1990). They assert that for US corporations to remain a competitive force in the global economic arena, the educational focus of our business schools must change.

In comparing U.S. business school effectiveness in preparing future managers for the global marketplace with the performance of European business schools, Kwok and Arpan (1994) surveyed nearly 400 business schools in the United States and Europe. They found that European schools, in comparison with those in the United States, sought higher levels of internationalization, were more likely to require international business courses, were more likely to offer specialized degrees in international business, had more faculty with greater international expertise and involvement, *and placed more emphasis on foreign experience in the educational process.* They concluded that European universities seem to have responded to the demands of internationalization in a much more proactive and comprehensive fashion than their American counterparts. Their more recent global survey of business schools (Kwok & Arpan, 2002) found that non-U.S. business schools were more likely than their U.S. counterparts to offer international internships. Although this study also concluded that in the United States and abroad significant progress continued to be made in the internationalization of business schools, including an increase in the use of international internships, it surfaced dissatisfaction with the continuing lag of business schools behind the accelerating pace of businesses responding to the growing opportunities and challenges of globalization.

Nevertheless, in their extensive study of U.S. business schools, Kwok, Arpan, and Folks (1994) reported extraordinary commitment and achievement on the part of individual programs and a general sense that progress toward internationalization was being made. And many of these schools with a clear focus and commitment to international business education, such as the federally-funded CIBER (Centers for International Business Education and Research) schools, often require a significant international internship component for graduation (Sowinski, 2002). In fact, in competing for talented business students within our increasingly global economy, these schools are strengthening their programs with international internship options and requirements. However, these changes are likely more due to the resulting increased attractiveness and relevance of their programs than to their sense of duty to enhance the international competence of future U.S. managers and their corporations (Kwok & Arpan, 2002).

Despite the notable curricular advances of relatively few leading U.S. international business programs, a great majority of accredited U.S. business schools—even those that claim to have an emphasis or specialization in international business—fail to require, adequately encourage, or even offer their students opportunities to gain the valuable experiential learning provided by international internships. To gain a sense of the nature and degree of utilization of international internships in U.S. graduate business programs, we contacted by telephone interview 34 AACSB-accredited (Association to Advance Collegiate Schools of Business) U.S. full-time MBA programs with an international focus, selected at random and evenly spread across five U.S. regions from a list of 120 provided by

*Business Week* online. We expected that due to the recognized value of international internships in building international competencies, programs that offer an international concentration or focus would commonly feature this curriculum component. We were surprised that of the 34 programs we contacted (speaking by phone with a program director or coordinator), only 10 or 29% provided some kind of required or even optional international internship component in their curriculum. Of the 24 (71%) of the schools with an international focus that *did not* offer an international internship component, 83% did offer one or more forms of international exposure, including a managed international tour (71%), an exchange program or study abroad experience (42%), a relatively brief (e.g., two or three weeks) international trip involving a consultancy project (21%), and coursework in business plan development followed by foreign travel (17%).

Some of the most common barriers (in order of magnitude) reported by our sample for *not* having an international internship component were lack of resources (especially funding, faculty, and administrative staff), lack of student foreign language proficiency, lack of internship availability, communication difficulties between departments (e.g., between MBA program and study abroad program), and internships simply not being a priority for the particular school interviewed. Of the 10 schools that offered an international internship arrangement, 60% handled the program internally, 30% had an external provider to administer the program, and 10% had both internal and external people working on the program. In most of these schools students were limited to one or only a few foreign city locations for international internships, often administered by foreign partner schools with which student exchange or study abroad arrangements had been made. Yet even in these cases, students often were expected to secure their own international internships. Some of the challenges of administering an international internship program internally were reported to include difficulties in obtaining work visas for the students at the foreign location, the double cost of going overseas and loss of domestic earning opportunity, the expense of an administrator's travel to foreign sites to monitor internship arrangements, inadequate foreign language proficiency for student international internship placement, lack of quality internship opportunities abroad, and insurance and liability issues.

We believe that the extreme lack of utilization and availability of international internships as a curricular option, even among those AACSB-accredited MBA programs that claim to have an international specialization, speaks very poorly about the general quality and effectiveness of U.S. graduate business education in preparing future managers for the global marketplace. Also, these programs fall short of supplying U.S. corporations with experienced globally-thinking talent needed to success-fully compete in the future. This evident lack adds weight to the increasing voices that seriously question the curricular relevance of today's American business schools (Mintzberg & Gosling, 2002; Pfeffer & Fong, 2002). We believe that a great deal more can be done, utilizing readily available communications technologies and curricular innova-tions, to make international internships more effective and available on a much more economical basis to more U.S. MBA students—even to those enrolled in regular MBA programs without a clear international special-ization.

## Limitations: Surrounding Current International Internships

Based on our review of the literature, an analysis on the Internet of existing study abroad programs providing international internships, and telephone interviews with coordinators of U.S. MBA programs that include international internships, we have identified several limitations of existing graduate business programs for delivering international intern-ship opportunities for their students. We now will briefly describe these limitations.

## Prerequisite of Foreign Language Fluency

Although the universal language of business tends to be English, living and working in a country where the predominant language is not English poses a significant obstacle that could easily impede the international internship learning process or rule out the possibility of the experience completely (Elmore, 2004). For example, most study abroad programs providing international internships require a basic level (e.g., intermedi-ate) of predominant language proficiency in the country of internship placement. There is always the solution of participating in an internship in a country whose primary language is English, like England or Austra-lia. However, this option may not provide the extent of a developmental opportunity provided by working and living in a non-English speaking country, and does not always fit with the student's foreign experience interest.

## Student Learning Experience Quality Control

Current graduate programs that either outsource the coordination of the internships or handle the internships internally may have difficulty controlling or validating the quality of the student's learning experience because of lack of direct control. If an external provider is coordinating the internship experience, the home university loses direct control over the student's learning experience. An external internship provider or an international university overseeing the internship may not have the same expectations that the home university possesses, and therefore the internship experience may not be as rich. In the interest of preserving a partnering relationship with a foreign school and not offending the international partner, administrators may be hesitant to closely scrutinize and especially find fault with the quality of the foreign partner's instructional program. One of our MBA students recently participating in an established study abroad exchange program with a partnering university in another country, and which included the option of an international internship experience, was very disappointed in the low quality of her foreign business instruction, especially when compared with her previous domestic studies. She also was greatly disappointed that although a foreign internship option was available, there was very little assistance in securing the internship.

## Vague Learning Objectives and Assignments

Of the nine universities surveyed that currently have international internships that are *internally* administered, three of them only require the student to keep a journal and/or write a final paper detailing their experience. There is no close control over or reliable attention to specific learning objectives or assignments. Much learning depends on chance. In these types of highly variable international internship programs, the educational rigor and quality of the experience provided by the internships are inevitably inconsistent and questionable at best.

## Challenge of Managing a Great Variety of International Internship Organizational Sites

As every internship will be different and pose different challenges, the sponsoring organizations also typically vary dramatically, and thus provide different experiential learning contexts and challenges. If the international internship effort is handled internally, there is a huge management challenge with the typically wide variety of internship sites available and in need of periodic monitoring to ensure quality field learning experiences. Each internship represents a different and unique organization for the internship administrator to understand for preparing valuable international learning experiences. Of the internally administered international internship programs that we surveyed, all are handled by only one or two staff members. It is extremely difficult for these few people with limited time and resources to keep quality relationships with and awareness of the unique aspects of all internship sites. Some form of internship standardization would be extremely helpful in these situations.

## Predominant Focus on Large MNCs

When discussing internship sites, multinational corporations (MNCs) typically are considered as the most obvious and preferred choice for strong internship experiences. Clearly, an internship with a large MNC in a foreign country can present advantages. One of the most distinct advantages, especially if the intern is given a picture of the overall global operation of the MNC, is the opportunity to begin to build an experience-based awareness of "duality" (Black, Morrison, & Gregersen, 1999) in managing the organization for global efficiencies yet maintaining responsiveness to local conditions. In addition, with a student making a favorable impression, an internship may eventually lead to a regular job offer, whether in the present foreign location or elsewhere in the MNC operations around the world.

However, working at an MNC may provide only a quite specialized or narrow exposure to international business and its players, rather than a broader exposure to multiple functions, business skill disciplines, and different companies in work related to entrepreneurship and new business development. In a large MNC setting there may be minimal opportunities for cross-functional contacts and exposure to broad perspectives faced by the organization in the larger competitive global environment. An international internship assignment in a large MNC also will likely preclude exposure to ongoing local new business development and creation of new job activities, essential to the long-range economic development of the foreign business location, and especially critical for less-developed economies. Another key potential benefit of the internship experience is international networking opportunities. The international internship experience within the MNC may limit the intern's exposure to other companies and business professionals in the international region, thus limiting the extent of potentially valuable interorganizational networking opportunities for future career developments.

## High Overhead Costs for Internally Managed Programs

Business schools with international internship programs involving large numbers of students often have high associated overhead costs. These costs typically range from having some type of regular local support staff in the host countries to the added costs of regular professional and support staff at the parent institution. Other costs also include traveling to the foreign sites to set up the internship and other local arrangements, as well as ongoing site visits for internship monitoring purposes. High overhead costs are a substantial obstacle to current programs that wish to expand their international internship opportunities for students, or that struggle to maintain quality relationships and student learning experiences with their existing company sites and partnering educational institutions.

## Lack of Home Country Faculty Active Involvement

As mentioned previously, of the existing programs surveyed that are internally managed, one-third require that the student submit only a journal and/or final paper at the end of the internship experience. In these types of relationships, the home country business faculty assigned to the interning student typically has only remote and passive involvement. There usually is no opportunity for the faculty to provide ongoing advice, coaching, or other instructional resources for the intern as needs arise in the field—very much an "out of sight, out of mind" curricular arrangement. Sometimes there is a local supervisor to assist the intern, but in many cases this person has minimal interaction with the home university's business faculty.

Yet the home country faculty can play a pivotal role in the success of internships—particularly in international settings which require a comprehensive understanding of the cultural dimensions of work and of internships (Chapel, 1998). Feldman, Folks, and Turnely (1999), in examining demographic diversity between local mentors and students on international internships, found evidence that difference in nationality contributed to decreased task-related, social-related, and career-related support. And these deficits are associated with poorer socialization to the internship assignments, lower levels of learning about international business, and lower likelihood of receiving and accepting job offers from internship employers. Back home active involvement of faculty of like nationality can help to overcome this local mentoring deficit due to nationality differences.

## Limited Availability of Established International Business Internship Programs

Although many students choose to have their internships in established business environments and countries, there are significant challenges for an intern who wants to go to a country with underdeveloped or non-existent internship programs. Even where students desire an internship in a developed country, especially where academic credit is involved, those opportunities are often limited to those countries with which the home institution has established an international education partnership. Thus, many MBA students, even in programs with an international emphasis, may face a very limited geographic choice for their international internships.

### Requirement of Full or Near Full-time Internship Work

Many internship sites are looking for full time or near full time work from their interns. To many organizations, this extended time commitment is the only way to get the full value from an intern. However, from the intern's perspective, they cannot balance their extensive internship work commitment with time required for completing concurrent coursework, as well as fulfill their strong desire to explore the host country. Thus participation in some international internship programs can possibly present a somewhat discouraging obstacle by putting students behind in their coursework, requiring them to take an additional semester or year to finish their degree.

### Proposed New Delivery Model for MBA International Internships

Based on initial work presented by Vance (1997) on international internship delivery, and our review of existing trends and limitations in international internships for MBA students, we developed and field-tested a new delivery model for MBA international internships. The field test involved an e-mailed survey regarding international internship arrangements and procedures with 18 American Chambers of Commerce (AmChams) in Europe, South America, and Asia. The e-mailed survey was followed by our conducting 17 field interviews with university international student offices, AmChams, non-U.S. chamber trade/commerce development organizations, independent business professionals, American firms, and U.S. Consulate Commercial Service offices located in five cities in New Zealand and Australia: Auckland, Christchurch, Melbourne, Perth, and Sydney. This field research was part of a 3-week MBA international business studies tour conducted in May and June of 2003.

The design of the resulting model consists of three major components: (1) American Chamber of Commerce or equivalent new venture development internship site; (2) curriculum; and (3) local support services. We now will examine each of these components in more detail.

### American Chamber of Commerce

AmChams are influential organizations that represent the interests of American businesses in the various countries in which they are hosted. These organizations typically promote commerce between the U.S. and the host country, support measures to benefit and protect the interests of U.S. companies with operations in those countries, and present a variety of programs that keep chamber members abreast of current local business practices and trends. AmChams are extremely gregarious entities that actively promote receptions and other networking activities that bring together local business players with American businesses. Members of AmChams include representatives from both American companies, large and small, and local host country firms.

We noted from our field interviews and e-mail survey that the AmChams generally have had positive experiences and are active in utilizing student interns, both from local universities and from schools in foreign countries. Typically, however, these internship arrangements are sought out by the AmChams or the students themselves, with little initiative taken by educational institutions. The internships also are typically unpaid (often due to local restrictions against hiring foreign employees), or the intern receives a nominal stipend to help cover local housing and travel. The following are several reasons why AmChams may serve as ideal sites for business students' international internships:

(a) AmChams serve as a generally standard internship organizational site wherever they are found in the world, thus greatly reducing internship context variation and administrative challenge to internship program quality control.

(b) There are 96 accredited (by the U.S. Chamber of Commerce) AmCham offices located outside of the U.S. in 84 countries (Moore, 2004). Since each AmCham represents a potentially viable international internship site, MBA students are presented with a great variety of geographic choices for obtaining international internship experiences.

(c) The activities associated with the work of an AmCham provide a very rich context for a broad range of experiential learning relevant to developing international business competencies, including cross-cultural differences, new venture development, local and regional international economic studies, international government relations, and functional applications of business (e.g., marketing, finance, accounting) within the international business environment of the AmCham and international internship.

(d) For English-fluent only students, an AmCham represents a site where there is likely to be relevant English-language projects for the students while they are concurrently studying the local foreign language. This situation removes a significant barrier of prerequisite foreign language fluency that places an international internship experience in the near future out of reach for many U.S. students.

(e) AmChams are very frequently involved in networking events with local businesses, and allow students to attend various social and business events with local business leaders, often in a support staff capacity. This regular networking activity will potentially lead to useful contacts as sources of information and learning about the international business environment, as well as valuable connections for promoting future international career opportunities.

(f) Partnerships with AmChams represent a stable and relatively low-cost and high quality alternative to traditional international internships arranged by current international internship providers. In exchange for the qualified service provided by the interns, AmChams require no placement fee.

Table 11.1 represents several possible kinds of tasks that students could perform in working for an AmCham for approximately 20-30 hours per week (Vance, 1997, 1999). Many of these and other tasks useful to an AmCham and its members would not have to be performed at an AmCham office, but could easily be performed elsewhere, such as in using the student facilities of a nearby local university. We acknowledge that some of the tasks in Table 11.1 may seem too clerical and basic for MBA students, and even undergraduate students. However, the primary purpose of these tasks is to provide service to the often insufficiently staffed AmCham and a justification for allowing the student's service work involvement with the AmCham internship. As will be discussed more specifically in the following section on curriculum, a local presence and active involvement at the AmCham affords the student with the opportunity to follow-up on other important course learning objectives. For example, by simply providing logistical support and even ensuring an adequate sup-

### Table 11.1.  Potential Tasks for
### AmCham-Based International Internships

1. Assist with the detailed preparation for and carrying out of sponsored AmCham events (e.g., receptions, conferences, seminars, luncheons);
2. Survey AmCham members by phone or in writing and provide an analysis of their needs, level of satisfaction with the AmCham, suggestions, etc.
3. Research relevant data bases and information resources to fulfill AmCham member information/research requests.
4. Serve as active research and administrative assistant in support of the chairperson of various AmCham member volunteer committees.
5. Assist with the preparation of various communications to AmCham members.
6. Assist with tasks related to government agency affairs (both domestic government and foreign government agencies located locally).
7. Assist with research and information gathering for AmCham publications.
8. Provide administrative support for meetings of ongoing groups sponsored by the AmCham (e.g., Young Professionals Committee).
9. Assist with activities related to new member prospecting and promotion.
10. Assist with the interactions, communications, coordination, partnering, etc., with other local chambers and economic development centers.
11. Provide placement and ongoing support services for interns in AmCham member companies, based on identified member company needs.
12. Assist with the development of press releases to the general public.
13. Assist with specific tasks or projects requested by member companies of local AmChams.

ply of napkins at an AmCham reception will place the student in an ideal context for afterwards mixing with local business professionals, thus supporting the student's active professional networking requirement. Therefore, an AmCham represents a rich and stimulating context providing a variety of opportunities for tasks that are associated with various specific field learning assignments of graduate coursework taken concurrently.

### Curriculum

The proposed curriculum includes up to a maximum of three primary MBA courses over a 3-month summer period or during a regular semester: International Professional Development, International Entrepreneurship, and Regional Studies. These courses would be conducted through "distance field learning," involving a form of asynchronous distance learning and direct field learning assignments managed by home university faculty on a tutorial (one-on-one) and small group basis via online communications (i.e., using e-mail and a course management platform, such as Blackboard or a similar online instruction provider). Thus students at their various AmCham sites would have direct and frequent interaction with their home university faculty, as well as very rich experiential and empirical field learning opportunities through direct application assignments within their foreign environment. The faculty member teaching one of these courses could have up to 15-20 students (often the maximum class size recommended for online asynchronous courses) at different AmCham sites located around the world. Where possible, an attempt would be made to design AmCham work tasks to correspond to specific course assignments. However, many of the course learning objectives are unrelated to actual AmCham internship tasks. As mentioned before, the primary purpose of those AmCham tasks (such as in Table 11.1) are to provide the justification for the student to be in this rich foreign context within which the student course learning objectives can be addressed through specific, powerful field learning assignments.

The International Professional Development course would focus on the development of important international professional career competencies inherently associated with the overall international experience (Black, Morrison, & Gregersen, 1999; Osland, 1995). This course would involve the international internship experience, regular internship insight journal entries, and reflective written assignments based on assigned readings, faculty lecture notes, and direct field learning experience. The primary learning objectives for this course are:

- Enhanced self-understanding that is useful for future international career planning;
- Increased ability to adapt and adjust to new international working environments;
- Enhanced skills in diagnosing and understanding cultural differences;
- International business professional preparation through relevant work experience and valuable networking connections in an international setting.

The International Entrepreneurship course is very fitting for the AmCham context that emphasizes new venture development. This course also is very appropriate for tapping into the growing new venture opportunities attendant to globalization. This course would focus on international business venture start-ups, and seeks to develop student knowledge and skills in three key components of international entrepreneurship: initiating an entrepreneurial venture, managing basic international business transactions for new ventures and small businesses, and dealing with multicultural business environments. Through the use of lecture notes, assigned readings, and specific field projects with companies associated with the AmCham (e.g., active local AmCham member companies), students would develop knowledge and skills in the following areas:

- Key issues, concepts, and steps in the international entrepreneurship process;
- Major sources of information resources and assistance in international entrepreneurship, with a focus on electronic databases;
- Conducting a feasibility study resulting in a viable business plan for an international small business venture.

Last, the Regional Studies course would provide a broad exposure to several important technical, political, social, and economic environments affecting international business markets and practices within the geographic region of the student's foreign study experience. The primary learning objectives for this course include:

- Increased awareness and direct observation of basic issues and practices involved in the management of business within a geographic region;
- Increased understanding of the key environments affecting business in this region;
- Increased understanding of how local companies can successfully compete within the larger global marketplace;
- Increased awareness of differences in business practices between businesses of the selected region and those in the United States.

These three courses could provide a valuable contribution to the student's overall learning experience, with conceptual learning integrated with actual internship experience and local field learning assignments (e.g., interviews with local business executives contacted through AmCham connections regarding business environment challenges). The courses also provide academic credit toward student degree completion. Internship placements within AmChams will not require American students to be fluent at the start of the internship assignment, although concurrent local foreign language instruction would be very highly recommended as part of these international learning experiences, and could be provided by a local language institute.

### Local Support Services
The local support services act as a liaison between the AmCham, the intern and the intern's professor and/or home university. These local ser-

vices, paid for on a per student basis, provide direct and individual support to the intern to fulfill personal and academic needs surrounding the international experience, thus removing basic logistical and student support responsibility and added burden from the AmCham. Within the category of local support services there are two subcategories: (a) local coordinator, and (b) local logistics support.

(a) **Local Coordinator:**   This individual would be a local professional who is hired and compensated on a contingency basis by the home university. Feasible responsibilities for the local coordinator would include meeting with the local AmCham to identify and organize appropriate internship tasks associated with course assignments, providing the intern with some orientation assistance within the city, periodically meeting with the intern to assess student needs and monitor progress, and reporting to the home faculty member. An individual who may fit this role could be a local businessperson who is associated with the location of where the intern is working. For example, an owner of a business who has connections within the business community and is a member of the AmCham where the intern is placed would be very qualified to serve as a local coordinator. Important criteria for the local coordinator would include strong familiarity with the location and business environment where the intern is located, a strong network of local business contacts, and the time and flexibility to participate in this type of project.

(b) **Local Logistics Support:**   An international student office of a local college or university can fulfill this function very well. The primary responsibilities of this role would be providing for basic support needs for the student outside of the academic experience of the internship, and would include helping with various necessary tasks such as getting the intern acclimated to the foreign environment, assisting with obtaining a visa for the intern (whether a work visa or student visa, depending upon the local government's requirements), and providing housing arrangements. As a common service provided for other international students, this office or department could provide attractive cultural awareness experiences and local tours of interest, as well as activities offering a source of social support for the MBA intern. In addition, the local school could make available campus resources where student interns can work on tasks that can be performed away from the AmCham office.

*Discussion*

The results of our field interviews in Australia and New Zealand, combined with the results of our e-mail survey with AmChams in Europe, South America, and Asia, yielded considerable agreement. They confirmed overall that our proposed model is innovative, very feasible, and overdue. All those interviewed were emphatic that an international internship that is geared to instill cultural immersion, work experience, and allow for educational benefits—all on a very cost-effective basis—was vitally important.

## Advantages of Proposed Model in Addressing Limitations of Traditional Efforts

The following discussion briefly examines how the present AmCham-based international internship model addresses the limitations of existing efforts that were identified earlier.

### Prerequisite of Foreign Language Fluency

Although students would be strongly encouraged to concurrently take instruction in the practical use of the local language, much of the student's valuable work at the AmCham could be on projects where English is required, such as working with local AmCham members and business people who are interested in developing and marketing products and services for American and other English-speaking customers.

### Student Learning Experience Quality Control

Student experiential learning at different AmChams in the world can vary significantly, greatly due to the various kinds of experiences available at different AmChams within different socioeconomic contexts. However, in all cases students would have significant immersion experiences with their extended foreign learning assignment. In addition, faculty at the home school who are in frequent online contact (as well as possible telephone contact in some cases) would maintain quality control over the student learning through monitoring progress in achieving the consistent course objectives, which would not vary depending upon the internship placement. Although in some cases, as mentioned previously, course assignments could be integrated with particular internship work activities, many of the course assignments would be incidental to the AmCham internship but would be facilitated by the local business context associated with the internship.

### Vague Learning Objectives and Assignments

Related to the above quality control strength of our proposed model, general course learning objectives and more specific assignments are set from the beginning and are not dependent upon the actual international internship placement, and on what actually happens in the course of the international working experience. Certainly the desirable serendipitous learning of such an international experience is important and will be included and explicitly addressed as part of the International Professional Development course, as briefly described above. However, the consistent application of multiple course objectives will also provide clarity and consistency in quality in the achievement of learning objectives.

### Challenge of Managing a Great Variety of International Internship Organizational Sites

Although the activities, structure, and practices of AmChams are greatly influenced by their local social, political, and economic context and are not identical throughout the world, they do have significant similarities and standardized objectives and practices that simplify their supervision as an international internship site. In addition, the important course learning objectives discussed above can be addressed within the internal and external context of AmChams throughout the world, and do not depend upon the nature of the international internship assignment.

### Predominant Focus on Large MNCs

The present model of AmCham-based international internships is very consistent with the growing trend of small and medium-sized enterprises (SMEs) going abroad. A large number of AmCham members with which students would interact are from local and American SMEs. Nevertheless, several large MNCs also are active AmCham members, and their organizations may also provide valuable exposure for students. An important point here is that the AmCham-based international internship potentially provides the students with exposure to and experience with a much larger number and range of businesses in the foreign environment than would a traditional international internship within one large MNC.

### High Overhead Costs for Internally Managed Programs

There would be variable costs associated with online faculty and the outsourced on-site support services provided by a local coordinator (the on-site logistics support would be provided by a local university international student office, any costs of which each MBA student would handle directly). Thus, local supervision costs would be contingent upon the internship placement, and there would not be the need of a separate regular professional staff at the home university, beyond existing university study abroad staff, to manage the international internship program. Of course, there may be increased cost implications to the university for increased online faculty load, as well as for the overseeing of this largely outsourced localization service that our model describes.

### Lack of Home Country Faculty Active Involvement

Unlike traditional international internships, home country business faculty would be closely involved with the students in the course of their international experience to provide suggestions, guidance, coaching, and online resources. This active, direct involvement, albeit virtual, by home country faculty can be helpful in overcoming the nationality differences between the intern and local supervisor that may tend to diminish the value of the internship in terms of student learning and future career impact (Feldman et al., 1999). Active involvement of faculty with their students working in foreign environments can also serve as a valuable source of vicarious learning for the faculty themselves.

### Limited Availability of Established International Business Internship Programs

Although there is a large number of international business internship programs, universities typically present a very limited geographic range of choices for their students. With an establishment of an international internship partnership with AmChams located throughout the world, universities could provide a much broader choice for academic credit of valuable international internship experiences.

### Requirement of Full or Near Full-Time Internship Work

According to the present model, students would work at an AmCham approximately 20-30 hours per week, which would allow students to have time to further their progress toward graduation by pursuing their online coursework, including course assignments associated with field learning objectives within and outside the AmCham. This part-time arrangement would also allow students extra time to tour and explore their physical and cultural surroundings, a very important source of learning from such an extended international experience.

## Summary and Conclusion

The potential value that this international internship opportunity can provide for students is considerable. Students who have direct international work experience strengthen their preparation for leadership responsibilities within the global marketplace. In addition, due to their contacts made through interaction with local business leaders, students who participate in this international learning experience may develop a much broader international professional network to tap into for possible future career opportunities. Students also would be educated in the business culture practices of a particular country, and demonstrate their ability to adjust to international work challenges. Their subsequent desire to return and work in a particular international region where they had an international internship would likely meet with company confidence that there will not be serious international adjustment problems, which are often encountered by expatriates with little previous experience in a particular international region.

In our model we have begun to attempt to address current limitations in MBA program efforts to provide international internships. Our model represents a cost-effective approach that can make available international work experience for academic credit for many more students than are currently taking advantage of these critical international competency development opportunities, including students from MBA programs that do not have a special focus in international business. We have an opportunity to enhance the quality of our international education efforts, extending them beyond traditional abstract classroom learning intermingled with brief tourist-oriented international travel experiences to include far richer forms of experiential learning in the international workplace.

Although we received considerable convergence and support from our field interviews and survey involving AmChams throughout the world, our model presented here is as yet untested in actual operation. Questions remain about precisely how to make arrangements with AmChams, as well as arrangements (including clear tasks and expectations in exchange for a fair fee per student) with the local support services of a professional coordinator and a local educational institution. It is also unclear about how many interns, working on various projects and assignments on a part-time basis and not requiring AmCham work space, can be accommodated by a single AmCham. In a recent interview by one of the authors with the AmCham director and her assistant in Vienna, Austria, it was concluded that, with the organization of student work and regular support of a local coordinator and educational institution described in our model, as many as 15-20 student interns could be readily used to the benefit of the AmCham and the students in fulfilling their international internship experience.

Besides the current obstacles to the broad utilization of international internships identified in this chapter, others should be further analyzed, especially when they inescapably become more apparent upon initial program implementation. For example, it may be found that MBA students prefer to utilize summer months as a time for full-time jobs or paid internships in the United States to earn money for further educational support, which might therefore serve as a significant obstacle for utilizing the proposed "unpaid" international internship model during the summer. In addition, it might be more viable to encourage students to schedule the international internship experience for a semester early on, such as near the middle of their program rather than at the end when immediate job placement may be more of a concern for the student. Although the AmCham-based international internship experience could lead to an immediate job offer, this purpose is much less central to the experience than is the case with a more traditional domestic internship near or at the end of the MBA program. Efforts should now be made on a pilot basis, limiting initial international internship placements to one or two countries, to implement and test our model, and make revisions as needed. Eventually, relevant outcomes related to international competencies also should be examined and compared between students completing our proposed international internship program and students completing traditional domestic MBA and even international MBA programs, where opportunities for obtaining quality international work experience remain rather limited.

## ACKNOWLEDGMENTS

The authors are indebted to their following former MBA students who, as part of their Comparative Management Systems capstone requirement, provided invaluable assistance through field research and analysis in the development of the present work: Marybeth Collins, Wendi Glodery, Kara Jaffe, Tyler Lamb, Victor Nguyen, and Allison Weinreich.

## REFERENCES

Aggarwal, R. (1989, Fall). Strategies for internationalizing the business school: Educating for the global economy. *Journal of Marketing Education*, 59-64.

Ball, D. A., & McCulloch, W. H., Jr. (1993). The views of American multinational CEOs on internationalized business education for prospective employees. *Journal of International Business Studies, 24*(2), 383-391.

Beamish, P. W., & Calof, J. L. (1989). International business education: A corporate view. *Journal of International Business Studies, 20*(3), 553-564.

Black, S., Morrison, A., & Gregersen, H. (1999). *Global explorers: The next generation of leaders*. New York: Routledge.

Chapel, W. (1998). Advising graduate students for successful international internships. *Business Communication Quarterly, 61*(4), 92-103.

Elmore, B. (2004). Internships a go go. *Baylor Business Review, 21*(2), 40-43.

Feldman, D., Folks, W., & Turnley, W. (1999). Mentor-protégé diversity and its impact on international internship experiences. *Journal of Organizational Behavior, 20*(5), 597-611.

Frear, C. R., & Metcalf, L. E. (1988, Spring). International project workshops: Merging education with enterprise. *Journal of Marketing Education*, 21-28.

Fugate, D. L., & Jefferson, R. W. (2001). Preparing for globalization—do we need structural change for our academic programs? *Journal of Education for Business, 76*(3), 160-166.

Garten, J. E. (1997). *The big ten: The big emerging markets and how they will change our lives.* New York: Basic Books,

Kaynak, E., Yucelt, U., & Barker, A. T. (1990, Fall). Internationally oriented marketing curriculum development: A comparative study of Canada, the USA, and New Zealand. *Journal of Marketing Education*, 53-63.

Kwok, C. C. Y., & Arpan, J. S. (1994). A comparison of international business education at US and European business schools in the 1990s. *Management International Review, 34*(4), 357-379.

Kwok, C. C. Y., & Arpan, J. S. (2002). Internationalizing the business school: A global survey in 2000. *Journal of International Business Studies, 33*(3), 571-581.

Kwok, C. C. Y., Arpan, J. S., & Folks, W. R., Jr. (1994). A global survey of international business education in the 1990's. *Journal of International Business Studies, 25*(3), 605-623.

Marlowe, J., & Santibanez, R. R. (2000). Consumer education for a global marketplace: The need for an issue and policy focus. *Advancing the Consumer Interest, 12*(2), 11-15.

Mendenhall, M. E., Kuhlmann, T. M., & Stahl, G. K. (Eds.). (2001). *Developing global business leaders: Policies, processes, and innovations.* Westport, CT: Quorum Books.

Mintzberg, H., & Gosling, J. (2002). Educating managers beyond borders. *Academy of Management Learning and Education, 1*(1), 64-76.

Moore, D. (2004). Personal telephone conversation on January 29 with Moore, staff representative of the International Division, US Chamber of Commerce.

Osland, J. S. (1995). *Adventures of working abroad: Hero tales from the global frontier.* Hoboken, NJ: Wiley.

Parker, B. (2005). *Introduction to globalization and business* (2nd ed.). Thousand Oaks, CA: Sage

Pfeffer, J., & Fong, C. (2002). The end of business schools? Less success than meets the eye. *Academy of Management Learning and Education, 1*(1), 78-96.

Porter, L. W., & McKibbin, L. E. (1988). *Management education and development: Drift or thrust into the 21st century.* New York: McGraw-Hill.

Reynolds, J., & Rice, G., Jr. (1988). American education for international business. *Management International Review, 3*, 48-57.

Schoell, W. F. (1991, Summer). International students: An underutilized resource in internationalizing marketing education. *Journal of Marketing Education*, 31-35.

Shetty, A., & Rudell, F. (2002). Internationalizing the business program: A perspective of a small school. *Journal of Education for Business, 78*(2), 103-110.

Sowinski, L. L. (2002, May). It's not just about books anymore. *World Trade, 15*(5), 50-52.

Toncar, M. F., & Cudmore, B. V. (2000). The overseas internship experience. *Journal of Marketing Education, 22*(1), 54-63.

Tung, R. L., & Miller, E. L. (1990). Managing in the twenty-first century: The need for global orientation. *Management International Review, 30*(1), 5-18.

Vance, C. M. (2005). The personal quest for building global competence: A taxonomy of self-initiating career path strategies for gaining business experience abroad. *Journal of World Business, 40*(4), 374-385.

Vance, C. M. (1999, July). *Kung Fu master in cyberspace: Using e-mail tutorials to enhance learning in study abroad and international internship experiences.* International Organizational Behavior Teaching Conference, Bocconi University, Milan, Italy.

Vance, C. M. (1997, September). *Practicum in international entrepreneurship.* Fourth Conference of Educational Innovation in Economics and Business, Edinburgh, Scotland.

*Wall Street Journal.* (1994, March 22). Labor Letter Section, A1.

White, D. S., & Griffith, D. A. (1998). Graduate international business education in the United States: Comparisons and suggestions. *Journal of Education for Business, 74*(2), 103-115.

# Part V

**POTPOURRI OF INNOVATIVE CONTRIBUTIONS TO
GRADUATE MANAGEMENT EDUCATION**

CHAPTER 12

# HYBRID LEARNING NETS

## APPLICATIONS TO EXECUTIVE
## MANAGEMENT EDUCATION

**Owen P. Hall, Jr.**

Distance learning has come a long way since Sir Isaac Pitman initiated the first correspondence course in the early 1840s. Today the number of working managers returning to the classroom is growing rapidly as a result of globalization and technological developments. These dynamics call for new and innovative learning systems for providing management education. This is particularly the case for working managers enrolled in executive MBA type programs. To meet these challenges the traditional classroom model for delivering executive business education is giving way to a more holistic learning paradigm in which both the pedagogical and andragogical focus is on knowledge acquisition and management. The one-size-fits-all educational approach of the past is being augmented by Web-based customized learning systems. The purpose of this chapter is to introduce a hybrid net learning system that combines the best of both Web-based learning and time-honed classroom practices for delivering cost-effective executive management education.

## INTRODUCTION

The number of working managers returning to the classroom is growing (Edgington, 2004). Executive business education calls for a combined pedagogical and andragogical learning approach for this cohort group. This mixed strategy is based on the proposition that working managers possess both a rich experiential base and a process focus for learning (Monks, 2001). Managers returning to the classroom are interested in a practical curriculum that focuses on results and convenience. To meet these demands, the traditional method of knowledge transfer that features the constraints of fixed location, time, and learning pace is being replaced with more user friendly and customized learning systems (Smith, 2001). The Internet is the key ingredient in this new delivery paradigm. Many students who have been exposed to Web-based learning tend to favor this education on-demand delivery format (Lundgren, 2003). Program cost and convenience are two major factors that significantly contribute to the decision to enter an MBA program. Executive MBA (EMBA) programs are pricey. Today, the average price for U.S. based programs is on the order of $60,000 and at some of the premier schools is approaching $125,000. This cost is two to three times that of a standard MBA, but usually includes books, meals, and related expenses (Tyler, 2004). In Europe the costs for an EMBA program can exceed E100,000. Interestingly, recent survey data shows that corporate sponsorship of EMBA students is almost recession proof (Karaian, 2003).Typically, EMBA programs are more flexible than the standard MBA program and are presented in a substantially different format. Flexibility, learning format, and corporate sponsorship are keys to their continued popularity and growth potential.

The complexities and interrelated nature of modern business practice call for an integrated learning approach to executive management education (Sparrow, 2004). One learning strategy that recognizes the need for an integrated yet flexible learning experience is the Instructional Management System (IMS) cooperative initiative (Graves, 1999). This initiative is designed to promote systematic thinking regarding the delivery of higher education, to improve learning outcomes, and to increase return on instructional investments. Specific principles of the IMS initiative are: (1) Education involves more than a single course; (2) A course is more than content; (3) Content is more important than lecture notes; (4) Convenience is important and (5) Quality assurance requires an integrated learning approach. The IMS initiative calls for the increased use of Internet resources to promote integrated learning and to improve outcomes. One Internet based approach that embodies the IMS initiative is hybrid learning nets (HLN). These systems offer the student engaged in a graduate management education degree program both a customized and an integrated learning experience through the use of both traditional classroom learning combined with the power of the Internet. In this regard, HLN are well suited to meet the challenges associated with executive management education since they can provide instructional content at a time, location and pace convenient to the student (Jorgensen, 2002).

## EXECUTIVE MBA PROGRAMS

EMBA programs are usually conducted in a style and format different than standard MBA programs (Fessler, 2001). Some specific characteristics unique to most EMBA programs include the following:

- Reduces emphasis on traditional lecture format
- Uses lock-step cohort student groups
- Focuses on collaboration and hands-on exercises
- Caters to student work demands and travel schedules
- Permits students to use actual work projects in courses
- Features more learning from other students (andragogical) as compared with traditional MBA programs

Table 12.1 illustrates the distribution of teaching methods for selected domestic and international EMBA programs currently ranked in the top 25. The other category includes simulations, team projects, experiential, and distance learning.

The data in Table 12.1 illustrates the "significant" role nontraditional teaching methods, as characterized by the "other" category, are now play-

**Table 12.1.   Distribution of Teaching Methods for Selected EMBA Programs[1]**

| Method/School | Northwestern | IMD[2] | Duke | Cornell | Queens[3] | LBC[4] |
|---|---|---|---|---|---|---|
| Lecture | 30 | 5 | 20 | 30 | 10 | 30 |
| Case Study | 30 | 25 | 30 | 30 | 40 | 30 |
| Other | 40 | 70 | 50 | 40 | 50 | 40 |
| Rank | 1 | 7 | 9 | 18 | 21 | 25 |

Source:   1. BusinessWeek Online — EMBA Comparator, 2. International Institute for Management Development, 3. Queens University, Ontario, 4. London Business School.

ing in top tier EMBA programs. The average of the "other" category for the top 25 ranked EMBA programs is nearly 50% and has been steadily growing over the past decade. This trend toward more nontraditional learning can be further enhanced through the use of Web-based applications

Many EMBA programs also recognize the need for content integration (Schmotter, 2004). The focus of an integrated business learning environment is on how management functions such as operations, finance, and marketing are linked. Accordingly, the educational direction is away from "course silos" and toward "content and theme integration" (Cotner, 2003; Steiner, 2000). To meet these challenges the EMBA curriculum needs to serve as a gateway connecting the various business disciplines to the specific learning theme constructs. Presented below are some of the more common themes associated with EMBA programs:

- *Leadership:*   To inspire and work with others to achieve common goals.
- *Change management:*   To improve critical thinking and decision-making skills and to formulate cost-effective plans having specific performance metrics.
- *Innovation*:   To foster an appreciation of the growing reliance on technology and how it can be used to enhance competitive advantage.
- *Globalization*:   To develop an international mindset including an awareness of different belief structures and cultural sensitivities.
- *Strategic perspectives:*   To integrate economic, social, technological and political trends into a holistic approach to business management.

These themes transcend any given discipline. Table 12.2 illustrates one possible arrangement for linking these EMBA learning themes with two specific first level disciplines, and also, examples of second level topics and corresponding virtual applications. There are many other possible combinations which would be driven based on the specifics of the curriculum.

In the past, the introduction of multidisciplinary topics such as leadership was often accomplished using a teaching team strategy. This approach is still viable today. However, there are many issues associated with using an exclusive team teaching approach including "burn out" (Wenger, 1999). Another approach for helping implement a theme driven curriculum is Internet based learning nets.

**Table 12.2.   Themes to Discipline Content Map**

| Theme | 1st Level | 2nd Level | Virtual Application |
|---|---|---|---|
| Leadership | Behavior | Sense of community | Personal blog |
| | Information systems | ERP | Facility tour |
| Change Management | Finance | Capital markets | Seminar |
| | Operations | Supply chains | Simulation |
| Innovation | Technology | Robotics | Streaming video |
| | Decision systems | Forecasting | Data analysis |
| Globalization | Marketing | E-business | Professional blog |
| | Economics | Currency valuation | Threaded chatroom case |
| Strategic Perspectives | Planning | Project management | Simulation |
| | Law and ethics | Intellectual property | Linear chatroom case |

**Table 12.3.   Examples of Internet Type EMBA Programs**

| Institution | Accreditation | Delivery Mode | Assessments |
|---|---|---|---|
| Arizona State (U.S.) | AACSB | Hybrid | Online |
| University of Wyoming (U.S.) | AACSB | Online | Online |
| Henley College (U.K.) | AACSB | Online | On Campus |
| Curtin University (AU) | EQUIS | Hybrid | On/off Campus |

## HYBRID LEARNING NETS

Learning nets (LN) are Internet-based platforms that provide educational content and conductivity on a 24/7 worldwide basis. Basically, there are two learning net formats: (1) Hybrid, a combination of in-class and online learning, and (2) all online learning (Harvey, 2003). A recent survey of distance learning based MBA programs indicates that approximately 60% of the programs are hybrid and 40% are exclusively online (Ubon, 2002). Table 12.3 presents some examples of Internet oriented EMBA programs both domestic and overseas.

Figure 12.1 illustrates the structural concept of a hybrid learning net (HLN) for EMBA programs. In this setting, the learning net serves as a conduit that connects students with the course content, peers, instructors and the external business environment.

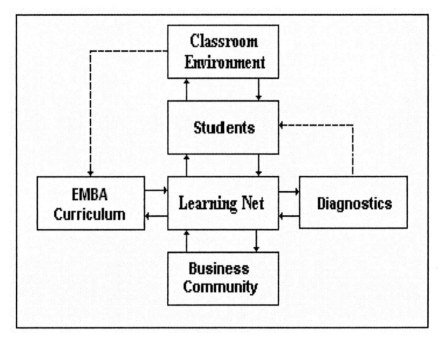

Figure 12.1.    EMBA hybrid learning net concept.

This learning support system is geared to support the student throughout the EMBA program. Specific characteristics of the hybrid learning environment include the following:

- A balanced approach between traditional and Internet learning formats.
- Archival student performance data gathered throughout the entire program.
- Possibility for students to engage in extensive virtual collaboration.
- Proactive learning diagnostics
- Remedial instructional support for students.

This last characteristic is of particular importance since many students enrolled in an EMBA program do not have an undergraduate degree in business. Therefore, specific topics such as statistical reasoning and accounting basics can be presented via a Web-based "bootcamp" on a customized basis. By providing self-paced "customized" instructional content, HLN can enhance the learning experience for working managers with a variety of backgrounds (Kasworm, 2003).

## System Design

One of the main attributes of HLN is providing course content in an integration format at one convenient portal. Figure 12.2 highlights the learning supportive elements of this design approach. This integrative system combines e-books, lecture notes, simulators, databases, computing applications, virtual tours, and other supportive resources all in a digital learning environment.

A central component of learning nets (hybrid and asynchronous) is the e-book. An e-book is a digitized learning resource that is both readable

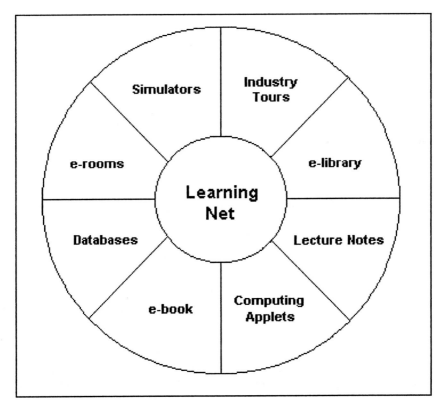

Figure 12.2.   HLN support systems.

and downloadable from the Internet. One primary advantage of an e-book is that it can be customized to meet specific course requirements thus avoiding the one size fits-all approach of the past (Chen, 2003). Unlike print books (p-books), e-books are designed to support the feedback process through interactive student participation. For example, after reading a section on benefit-cost analysis, the student is connected to an on-line benefit-cost simulation. Such navigational enhancements are a key ingredient to increased e-book acceptance throughout academe (Shiratuddin, 2005).

Business simulations have long been found particularly effective in developing both individual and team management skills (Aguino, 2005). Furthermore, evidence has shown that students engaged in simulations retain about 75% of the instructional material compared to 5% for lectures, 20% for audiovisual presentations, and 50% for discussion groups (Johne, 2003). A large number and variety of business simulations are available on the Internet. One specific simulation that has found widespread use in EMBA-type programs is the Internet-based MIT Beer Game (Hong-Minh, 2000). This simulation is used to teach supply chain management principles in an interactive environment. Another important feature of learning nets is the availability of virtual facility tours (Pettijohn, 2000). The Internet offers a wide range of virtual sites that can be easily integrated into the lesson plan. These tours provide students with direct insight into the integrative nature of business management. In the future, learners will be able to experience real time guided facility tours that feature the ability to interact directly with on-site management and staff. The hybrid format also provides direct access to the digital library, Harvard business cases and large databases such as the Bureau of Labor Statistics. Virtual computing provides the student with direct access to a wide range of analytical Internet-based models (e.g., regression) and is receiving increased usage throughout industry (Vizard, 2002).

Figure 12.3 shows the three dimensional structure associated with the HLN design. This learning paradigm represents a natural extension to the two dimensional model (flexible time and flexible location) introduced by Cukie, Grant, and Susla (2002). The third dimension is learning pace flexibility. Clearly, this is the most challenging aspect both from a technical and content delivery perspective.

The basic faces of the HLN Cube are defined as follows:

- **Customized asynchronous distance learning** (different time, location, pace)—The primary vehicle for providing personalized content based on basic background and performance. Examples include statistical and accounting boot camps.

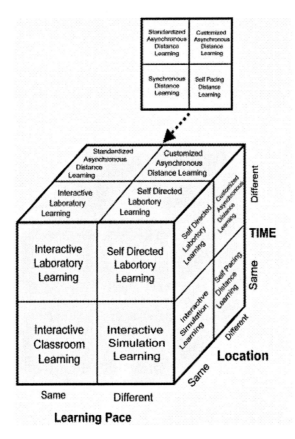

Figure 12.3.   HLN cube structure.

- **Standardized asynchronous distance learning** (different time and location, same pace)—The delivery mode for distributing basic study plan content. Specific content includes e-text and lecture notes.
- **Interactive laboratory learning** (different time, same location and pace)—The primary focus is on providing virtual facility tours and computing applications such as forecasting.
- **Self-directed laboratory learning** (different time and pace, same location)—Presents business principles videos and specific computer skill tutorials such as Excel usage.
- **Interactive classroom learning** (same time, location, pace)—The standard venue for team case presentations, personal interactions and instructor based lectures.

- **Interactive simulation learning** (same time and location, different pace)—Team based simulations in which the level of learning complexity is based on team skill levels.
- **Interactive synchronous distance learning** (different location, same time and pace)—Instructor-led lectures and discussions via broadcast conferencing.
- **Self-pacing synchronous distance learning** (different location and pace, same time)—Individual and team-based assignments with instructor coaching via broadcast conferencing.

A major learning objective in executive management education is to enhance decision-making skills. These include the ability to develop cognitive competencies such as problem solving, critical thinking, formulating questions, searching for relevant information, making informed judgments, using information efficiently, conducting observations, and creating new ideas. Business decisions invariably are outcomes of multi-discipline discussions featuring extensive interactions. Standardized asynchronous distance learning provides an ideal vehicle for enhancing students' experiences in understanding how to capture inputs from a distributed group. This process tends to mirror the work environment that many working managers experience. Another learning focus for managers is to develop a comprehensive understanding of sources of business information. The continuing enhancement of search engines and digital libraries provides an opportunity for students to "drill down" on topics, such as industry analysis, technology and globalization.

## Learning Support Systems

Figure 12.4 illustrates the variety of learning support systems associated with the hybrid model. This graphic underscores ways in which traditional and Web-based learning methods can be used in combination to optimize knowledge and content delivery.

The HLN environment also supports group analysis via linear and threaded chatrooms. The learning net provides a vehicle for stimulating "common interest groups" by allowing individuals to link across classes to other students working on similar projects. For example, the traditional classroom setting (Synchronous, Personal) tends to be effective for team presentations that require a great deal of face-to-face interaction. On the other hand, the threaded chatroom environment (Asynchronous, Internet) supports the working manager's requirement for flexibility. Develop-

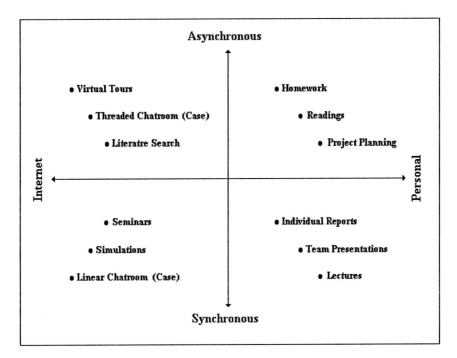

Figure 12.4.   Learning dimensions.

ing a sense of community (SOC) is an essential ingredient for a lock step degree program such as an EMBA. Specific SOC characteristics include feelings of belonging, influence and membership (Blanchard, 2004). Blogs provide an approach for maintaining SOC in a virtual environment and for facilitating team assignments (Flatley, 2005). A blog, short for Web log, is a Web page that provides individual or group views on a particular subject or topic, current events or a personal journal (Clyde, 2005). In this regard, blogging is receiving increased attention throughout academe (Oravec, 2003).

## Customized Learning

A fundamental tenet of the HLN design is that one size does *not* fit all. That is, students do not learn at the same pace, and they are impacted differently by the learning environment. One key to effective learning via HLN is a customized lesson plan wherein the specific strengths and weaknesses of each student are identified and measured and appropriate feedback is provided. This is where artificial intelligence (AI) systems can play a helpful role. AI can be used to design lesson plans and learning experiences based on student performance and background. The use of AI to assist in the learning process is receiving increased attention (Lin, 2005). More specifically, synthetic agents, a major branch of AI, can generate customized learning plans derived from student accomplishments and expectations using a set of conditional rules. For example, if a student is having difficulty mastering business forecasting as detected by simulation or self-assessment, then the synthetic agent would prescribe specific additional learning content to be provided to the student via the HLN. This content can take the form of videos, computing tutorials or simulations. Figure 12.5 illustrates the overall design concept.

Typically, synthetic learning agents should possess the following four basic characteristics: autonomy, proactivity, adaptability, and sociability. A well-designed synthetic tutorial agent should be able to assess the student's current knowledge state and to modify both the lesson plan and content level. One approach, albeit not the only one, for evaluating a learner's knowledge state is via real time simulation. Additionally, the "social" interface between the agent and the learner should be highly visual. It is within this type of design context that the specific learning objectives can be achieved and maintained (Matsatsinis, Moraitis, Psomatakis, & Spanoudakism, 2003).

The identification of customized content via AI can be based on both simulation outcomes and student characteristics such as industry group, management level and functional work area, for example, finance. Typically, testing is not use extensively in most EMBA programs. Where testing is employed it can also be used to support the customization process. Customized materials can be selected for a specific student who is having difficulty in mastering a particular concept or is interested in more details, for example, how benchmarking is used to evaluate an organization's forecasting system. This capability of providing customized content based on specific factors is particularly useful for working adults whose job assignments often mirror the specifics found in the identified content. Used in this way a student can directly apply the lesson plan material to the workplace.

Table 12.4 shows more specifically how AI could be used to support a lesson plan involving business forecasting. The first column lists some basic learning plan objectives. The second column identifies the primary resources used by a student in connection with each session objective. The third column shows additional material identified by the instructor that is designed to support each lesson objective. For example, after developing a forecast using a virtual applet a student may wish to better understand the mechanics behind how a forecast is developed. At this point an inter-

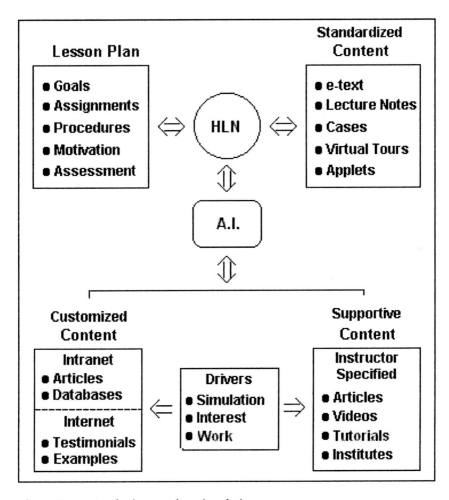

Figure 12.5.   Synthetic agent learning design.

active simulation can provide the student with an in-depth view of the forecasting process. This type of capability is sufficiently general to evoke a wide range of interest among students. The fourth column highlights some examples of customized content discovered by AI based on both student performance and characteristics. For example, after reviewing and discussing a case on improving the forecasting process via benchmarking a student can choose to view specific applications. This level of detail and specificity helps reinforce the basic ideas introduced in the forecasting process case. Again the specific applications are "captured" by the AI agent in real time.

**Table 12.4.    Example Application of AI Support**

| Session Learning Objectives | Primary Resource | Support Resources | Customized Resources |
| --- | --- | --- | --- |
| Appreciate the role of forecasting in business operations | Introductory lecture notes | Slide show on how forecasting is being used | Industry specific forecasting applications |
| Understand the different types of forecasting systems | Forecasting e-chapter | Articles that illustrate the various types of forecasting methods | Role planning simulation based on management background |
| Accessing large-scale databases | Streaming video | Bureau of labor statistics | Data marts associated with a student's industry. |
| How to develop a forecast using computer models | Forecasting applet | Interactive simulation | Slide show based on industry and management level |
| How to improve the forecasting process | Case on benchmarking and best practices | Articles on implementation issues | Industry specific performance testimonials |

## Effectiveness and Perceptions

A variety of studies have been conducted regarding the use of Web-based learning systems to support management education (Condone, 2004; Sauers & Walkers, 2004; Shih, 2003; Wang, 2003; Webb, 2005). The general consensus of these investigations, particularly for working adults, is summarized below:

- Offer a high degree of interaction and collaboration that, in some instances, can be more effective than are traditional methods.
- Represent a long sought solution to the ongoing challenges associated with adult education by providing a dynamic, flexible, personal and scaleable experience for continuous learning.
- Provide the learner with a purposeful entry to the Internet and thus to a new era of learning technologies.
- Connect learners, instructors and content on a 24/7 basis.
- Underpin the development of new relationships between education and business through a variety of virtual arrangements.

Students report that in using Web-based support systems, they were able to remain current with assignments and in contact with their study team even while on extended travel status. Students appreciate the fact that course material is available at one convenient location on a 24/7 basis. On the other hand, students show an increased dependency on the Internet and a low tolerance for out-of-date information.

## IMPLEMENTATION

The use of Web-based systems throughout the b-school community is growing rapidly albeit unevenly (Blass, 2003). Developing a comprehensive implementation plan is a necessary condition for insuring a successful system deployment. Implementing an HLN-type design for an executive EMBA program is not a simple task. A number of specific steps must be taken to insure a successful system deployment. These steps include:

- **Think Long Term**:   Link the HLN design to the mission statement of the institution. Look ahead 5 years in terms of development direction and tempo.
- **Develop Content**:   The development and acquisition of Web-based content can account for upwards of 50% of the overall budget.
- **Comparison Shop**:   Carefully evaluate the portal providers. There are over 100 potential vendors. Any disruption in providing 24/7 learning will court disaster.
- **Implement a Phased Approach**:   Consider prototyping the HLN in a specific EMBA section for gaining experience and confidence.

To reap the full potential of the hybrid model the design must be more than simply "attaching" a series of Web sites to the standard classroom format (Skill & Young, 2002). Generally, the course structure must be redesigned to provide a seamless transition between face-to-face learning and asynchronous learning (Conway, 2005).

Student "buy-in" represents a key factor to the successful implementation of the HLN paradigm. Students must be convinced that the convenience and richness of Internet resources offsets the perceived notion that they can only learn in a classroom. One way to accomplish this is to have EMBA students, with their extensive managerial experience, serve as co-producers thus giving the class additional ownership (Brown & Murti, 2003). Other keys to success are to insure that the system is operational on a 24/7 basis and is easy to use. Another "buy-in" modality is to organize the students into self-sustaining support teams. This helps insure that no one is left behind. In this regard, students tend to participate to a greater extent in learning systems that are content rich and that feature extensive variety (Kathawala, Abdou, & Elmuti, 2002).

Arguably, the single most important element of the hybrid model is faculty "buy-in" and orientation. Some faculty has been reluctance to embrace a hybrid course structure let alone an asynchronous course format. This is due to technology phobia, a lack of motivation and no additional compensation (Crooks, Yang, & Duemer, 2003). While some institutions do provide some incremental resources for course development the general perspective is that faculty need to make the transition as part of the modernization of academia. One approach to help ameliorate some faculty concerns is through the use of Web-based training modules. These systems not only introduce the faculty to the "power" of the Internet but also show how to design and implement a hybrid based course.

Some specific administrative challenges in implementing the HLN paradigm include the following:

- Training faculty for successful system deployment and usage
- Providing high quality and consistent system access
- Setting specific performance goals and metrics
- Preparing students for entry and ongoing use
- Sustaining system operation and flexibility
- Establishing the overall culture

Developing the internal capability to deploy the HLN is complex and expensive. Furthermore, an internalized approach may not take advantage of the ongoing developments in delivery technology, for example, search engine technology. One possible implementation strategy that helps overcome these issues consists of developing institutional partners with both content and application service providers (Sorel, Dear, & Edge, 2001). This approach draws on the basic ideas behind supply chain management and is consistent with the increased use of suppliers in large volume operations such as those found in most business programs. Measuring ongoing effectiveness and performance is key to the successful sustainability of a hybrid system such as the one outlined in this chapter (Bersin, 2002; Creaser, 2002).

## CONCLUSIONS

Interest in executive management education is growing, due in part, to the impact of globalization, technology and demographics on the job market and corporate operations. Additionally, the use of Web-based learning systems in business education is also on the rise (Coppola, Hiltz, & Rotter, 2002). These learning systems hold out considerable promise for enhancing executive management education in a changing global environment. As a result of these developments, many EMBA programs are moving toward an increased focus on customization, experiential learning and results assessment (Fry & Carter, 2002). The purpose of this chapter has been to introduce hybrid learning nets (HLN) that are designed to support these trends and opportunities. HLN optimize the use of the Internet to deliver learning content for business courses and programs while simultaneously enhancing faculty and peer group inter-actions. HLN provide an opportunity for collaborative learning that has a positive impact on the educational experience (Graham & Scarborough, 2001). Another feature of the HLN is real time feedback. This capability can be provided in a variety of ways including business simulations and related experiential learning assignments. Real time feedback presents both the instructor and student with insights into subject areas that require more in-depth attention. Providing the broadest range of tutorial instruction optimizes students' opportunities for effective learning. Asynchronous real time feedback is particularly attractive for working managers engaged in extensive travel and other work related assignments. The HLN strategy outlined herein is designed to significantly alter the three pillars of traditional EMBA instruction—fixed time, fixed location, and fixed learning pace—with a more flexible and customized learning process. The hybrid learning net also can be used to improve the delivery and effectiveness of traditional MBA programs (Latham, Latham, & Whyte, 2004).

Specific benefits of the HLN paradigm for EMBA type programs include the following:

- Affords an integrated perspective on the course/program
- Presents instructional rich content including real time feedback
- Offers courses designed for specific learning applications with real time feedback
- Increases student team participation and interaction
- Improves quality control through content integration
- Supports quality assurance through rubric measurements
- Provides direct linkage with Internet and library resources

A number of additional developmental tasks need to be addressed to further improve the effectiveness of HLN for EMBA education. These efforts include enhanced interactive simulations, real time videos, virtual experiential exercises, and improving the sense of community through, for example, the use of blogs. Furthermore, the introduction of artificial intelligence models for student assessment and mentoring will greatly improve the capability of the HLN to deliver effective customized content. In terms of an implementation strategy, consideration should be given to developing a strategic partnership with both content and application service providers. Specifically, using an "outsourcing" implementation strategy should insure both a reliable learning resource as well as timely technological updates.

Higher education, in general, and management education, in particular, is undergoing a fundamental shift from a teacher centric process to a learning centric environment that focuses on customized learning (Hitz & Turnoff, 2005). In graduate management education, this transformation is being fueled by the need to produce educated managers that can compete on a global basis. The vehicle for facilitating this reformation is the Internet. Hybrid learning nets, which combine the best in classical learning with Web-based support systems, provide both the rigor and flexibility to meet the challenges and requirements of today's managers.

## REFERENCES

Aquino, K., & Serva, M. (2005). Using a dual role assessment to improve group dynamics and performance. *Journal of Management Education, 29*(1), 17.

Blass, E., & Davis, A. (2003). Building on solid foundations: Establishing criteria for e-learning developments. *Journal of Further & Higher Learning, 27*(3), 227.

Bersin, J. (2002). Measuring e-learning effectiveness: A five-step program. *e-Learning, 3*(3), 36.

Blanchard, A. (2004). *Blogs as virtual communities: Identifying a sense of community.* University of Minnesota. Retrieved June 28, 2006, from http://blog.lib.umn.edu/blogosphere/blogs_as_virtual.html

Brown, R., & Murti, G. (2003). Student partners in instruction: third level student participation in advanced business courses. *Journal of Education for Business, 79*(2), 85.

Chen, Y. (2003). Application and development of electronic books in an e-Gutenberg age. *Online Information Review, 27*(1), 6.

Clyde, L. (2005). Educational blogging. *Teacher Librarian, 32*(3), 43.

Condone, S. (2004). Reducing the distance: A study of course Web sites as a means to create a total learning space in traditional courses. *IEEE Transactions on Professional Communication, 47*(3), 190.

Conway, R., & Easton, S. (2005). Strategies for enhancing student interaction and immediacy in online courses. *Business Communication Quarterly, 68*(1), 23.

Coppola, N., Hiltz, S., & Rotter, N. (2002). Becoming a virtual professor: Pedagogical roles and asynchronous learning networks. *Journal of Management Information Systems, 18*(4), 169.

Cotner, J., Jones, R., & Kashlak, R. (2003). Effectively Integrating an International Field Study into the EMBA Curriculum. *Journal of Teaching in International Business, 15*(1), 5.

Creaser, K. (2002). Online education tools. *Australian CPA, 72*(10), 49.

Crooks, S., Yang, Y., & Duemer, L. (2003). Faculty perceptions of Web-based resources in higher education. *Journal of Educational Technology Systems, 31*(2), 103.

Cukier, W., Grant, K. A., & Susla, J. (2002, November). *The costs and benefits of learning technologies.* San Antonio, TX: ISECON2003.

Edgington, R. (2004). Application Trends, Survey Executive Report 2004, Graduate Management Admission Council, McLean, Virginia, 22102.

Fessler, N. (2001). Surviving an executive MBA riot. *Accounting Education, 10*(3), 325.

Flatley, M. (2005). Blogging for enhanced teaching and learning. *Business Community Quarterly, 68*(1), 77.

Fry, B., & Carter, L. (2002). Executive education for state and local government: A survey. *International Journal of Public Administration, 25*(8), 953.

Graham, M., & Scarborough, H. (2001). Enhancing the learning environment for distance education students. *Distance Education, 22*(2), 232.

Graves, W. H. (1999). The instructional management system cooperative: converting random acts of progress into global progress. *Educom Review, 34*(6), 32.

Harvey, K. (2003). It's all in the mix. *The Banker, 153*(927), 135.

Hitz, S., & Turnoff, M. (2005). Education goes digital; the evolution of online learning and the revolution in higher education. *Association for Computing Machinery, Communication of the ACM, 48*(10), 59.

Hong-Mihn, S., Disney, S., & Naim, M. (2000). The dynamics of emergency transshipment supply chains. *International Journal of Physical Distribution & logistical Management, 30*(9), 788.

Johne, M. (2003). Virtual environments. *CMA Management, 76*(10), 28.

Jorgensen, D. (2002). The challenges and benefits of asynchronous learning networks. *Reference Librarian, 77*, 3.

Karaian, J. (2003, February). Master plan: Executive MBA programmes are proliferating but are they worth their high price tags? *CFOEurope.com.* Retrieved June 28, 2006, from http://www.cfoeurope.com/

Kasworm, C. (2003). Adult meaning making in the undergraduate classroom. *Adult Education Quarterly, 53*(2), 81.

Kathawala, Y., Abdou, K., & Elmuti, D. (2002). The global MBA: a comparative assessment for its future. *Journal of European Industrial Training, 26*(1), 14.

Latham, G., Latham, S., & Whyte, G. (2004). Fostering integrative thinking: adapting the executive education model to the MBA program. *Journal of Management Education, 28*(1), 3.

Lin, F. (2005). *Designing distributed learning environments with intelligent software agents.* Greenwich, CT: Information Age.

Lundgren, T., & Nantz, K. (2003). Student attitudes towards Internet courses: A longitudinal study. *Journal of Computer Information Systems, 43*(3), 61.

Matsatsinis, N., Moraitis, P., Psomatakis, V., & Spanoudakism, N. (2003). An agent-based system for products penetration strategy selection. *Applied Artificial Intelligence, 17*(10), 901.

Monks, K., & Walsh, J. S. (2001). The role of postgraduate education in management development. *Journal of European Industrial Training, 23*(2), 148.

Oravec, J. (2003). Blending by blogging: Weblogs in blended learning initiatives. *Journal of Educational Media, 28*(2), 225.

Pettijohn, J. (2002). Virtual tours—A tool for enhancing and enlivening the international business class. *Journal of Business education, 75*(5), 291.

Sauers, D., & Walker, R. (2004). A comparison of traditional and technology-assisted instructional methods in the business communication classroom. *Business Communication Quarterly, 67*(4), 430.

Schmotter, J. (2004). On two-plus decades: A world of difference. *Selections, 4*(1), 3.

Skill, T., & Young, B. (2002). Embracing the hybrid model; Working at the intersection of virtual and physical learning spaces. *New Directions for Teaching and Learning. Wiley Periodicals, 92*, 23.

Shih, Y. (2003). A survey of distance education challenges and technologies. *International Journal of Distance Learning Technologies, 1*(1), 1.

Shiratuddin, N. (2005). E-books in higher education: Technology, e-marketing prospects, and pricing strategy. *Journal of Electronic Commerce in Organizations, 3*(2), 1.

Smith, L. (2001). Content and delivery: A comparison and contrast of electronic and traditional MBA marketing planning courses. *Journal of Marketing Education, 23*(1), 35.

Sorel, R., Dear, R., & Edge, D. (2001), Evolution of Web-based distance learning strategies. *International Journal of Educational Management*, 15(4/5), 245.

Sparrow, S. (2004, January). The trend to blends. *Personnel Today*, p. 22.

Steiner, T. L., & Wells, R. (2000). Integration of the business curriculum: The case of finance and marketing in a MBA program. *Financial Practice & Education, 10*(2), 148.

Tyler, K. (2004). Getting value from executive MBA programs. *HR Magazine, 49*(7), 105.

Ubon, A. (2002). *A report on distance learning programs.* York University, UK: Management and Information Systems Research Group

Vizard, M. (2002). Virtual computing. *CRN, 1020*, 38.

Wang, Y. (2002). Assessment of learner satisfaction with asynchronous electronic learning systems. *Information and Management, 41*(1), 75.

Webb, H. (2005). Teaching with the case method online: Pure versus hybrid approaches. *Decision Sciences Journal of Innovation Education, 3*(2), 223.

Wenger, M., & Homyak, M. (1999). Team teaching for higher level learning: A framework of professional collaboration. *Journal of Management Education, 23*(3), 311.

CHAPTER 13

# TAKING BUSINESS ETHICS SERIOUSLY

## Best Practices in Teaching and Integrating Business Ethics Within a Business Program

**Denis Collins**

Business ethics professors stand at the epicenter of many higher education reforms directed at business schools. For many decades, business schools have been criticized for being too isolated from the liberal arts, emphasizing functional knowledge to the detriment of integrative knowledge, and relying too heavily on traditional lecturing and memorization classroom techniques. This chapter describes how to integrate the teaching of ethics into the business curriculum by applying innovative teaching methods that engage students in higher level learning and through a host of other activities. The Business Ethics course described in this chapter is designed according to Kohlberg's stages of moral development (Kohlberg, 1981). Students begin the semester exploring egoism, advance through social group relativism and cultural relativism, and conclude in the realms of utilitarianism and deontology. In addition to being based on relevant theories and empirical research, the chapter reflects the author's 15 years of experience teaching business ethics to undergraduate and MBA students and dialoguing with both business ethics professors and functional business school professors about what works and does not work.

*New Visions for Graduate Management Education,* 329–359
Copyright © 2006 by Information Age Publishing
All rights of reproduction in any form reserved.

## INTRODUCTION

Socrates maintained that the unexamined life is not worth living. Although the famous statement is overly dramatic—even unexamined lives are worth living—Socrates' analysis highlights the central importance of ethics in management education. Business ethics professors should provide a safe environment for students to critically examine their own ethics within the context of business activities.

In addition, business ethics professors are at the vortex of two other educational reforms in business education—experiential education and curriculum integration. More than 30 years ago, Pablo Friere (1971) critiqued the banking style of education characterized by a sage on stage who deposits information into the minds of passive students and then withdraws the knowledge from the student's memory system at exam time to determine if any interest has been earned on the retained knowledge. A practical outgrowth of Friere's alternative style of education can be found in the management education literature about higher levels of learning activities, wherein students participate in experiential exercises and dialogue with each other under a professor's supervision, which purportedly provides deeper levels of understanding. This chapter summarizes some of the experiential and dialogical pedagogies professors can employ in the teaching of business ethics.

Second, external pressures from businesses and alumni are forcing business programs to develop a more cross-functional curriculum, where professors challenge students to make connections between functional streams of knowledge (Hamilton, McFarland, & Mirchandani, 2000; Schlesinger, 1996). In the business world, accounting, marketing, and finance are interrelated, not separate, entities. Business ethics professors can provide cross-functional knowledge by addressing ethical problems that arise within the course content of each business school discipline.

The American Assembly of Collegiate Schools of Business (AACSB) has been highlighting the cross-functional potential of business ethics since the 1970s by requiring that ethics be integrated throughout the curriculum or explored in a separate course. Many business ethics scholars, as well as undergraduate and MBA students (Power & Lundsten, 2001; Stewart, Felicetti, & Kuehn, 1996; Swanson & Frederick, 2003), maintain that the optimal strategy is to employ both a separate course *and* ethics integration across the curriculum. There is abundant material unique to the topic "business ethics" and central to the functioning of business to require a separate course taught by an expert in the field.

Despite the occasional teasing title on books and articles—that is, the Harvard Business School faculty titled their contribution to the subject *Can Ethics Be Taught?* (Piper, Gentile, & Parks, 1993)—ethics has been taught since the beginning of time to people of all ages and will continue to be taught until the end of time. The ethical knowledge taught in high schools and other mediating institutions is not adequate for handling the complex ethical problems with which managers wrestle on a daily basis. Newspaper and magazine headlines scream out the latest business misdeeds, informing the public that something is wrong with the way some businesses operate and something should, and can, be done about it.

This chapter addresses a pragmatic question: How should business ethics be taught as a separate course and integrated throughout the curriculum? Part I provides a brief history of business ethics education. Part II explores some best practices in teaching a separate business ethics course by addressing topics such as course goals, social desirability, logical flow of the semester along Kohlberg's theory of moral development, an ethical decision making framework, establishing relevancy, developing a moral solution, creating a personal moral code, sharing ethical dilemmas, journaling, ethical persuasion, role playing, service-learning, and a purposes in life essay. Part III examines a wide range of methods for integrating business ethics throughout a student's higher education experience, including student orientation, first-year forums, other courses, student organizations, and community outreach.

Much of the analysis that follows reflects my own experiences teaching business ethics to undergraduate and MBA students for nearly 20 years.

## PART I: A BRIEF HISTORY

Business ethics topics appear in the earliest known legal writings of western civilization. In the opening paragraph of Hammurabi's *Code of Laws*, written in 1780 B. C., the Babylonian King notes that the purpose of his laws are "to bring about the rule of righteousness in the land, to destroy the wicked and the evil-doers; so that the strong should not harm the weak" (http://eawc.evansville.edu/anthology/hammurabi.htm). Inspired to create a society worthy of divine approbation, Hammurabi codified rules for governing economic transactions, such as the ownership and theft of agricultural products, animals, and slaves. Governments have been developing laws to restrict unethical business practices ever since.

According to the Council for a Parliament on the World's Religions (1993), there is significant agreement among the major world religions on five principles that should govern human behavior in all realms of life, including business: (1) "Do unto others as you would have them do to you," (2) "Thou shall not commit sexual impropriety," (3) "Thou shall not steal," (4) "Thou shall not lie," and (5) "Thou shall not kill" (Koys, 2001). Systematic violations of these principles have given rise to major changes in the rules governing economic systems. Adam Smith's conception of capitalism followed from his critique of mercantilist policies that kept many Scottish people immersed in poverty (Collins, 1988). Karl Marx's conception of communism followed from his critique of capitalist activities that exploited laborers.

The AACSB has long ensured that accredited business programs in higher education institutions were not devoid of ethical considerations. The AACSB—recently renamed the Association to Advance Collegiate Schools of Business—was created in 1916 when business school deans met to establish common standards for their programs (Dirksen, 1966). Early curriculum standards included the teaching of business law to educate students about broader societal concerns. But in the late 1950s, reports by the Ford and Carnegie Foundations concluded that the business law course had become too narrow in content and they recommended a more broad-based course that dealt with the social, political, and legal environments of business (Swanson & Frederick, 2003). As a result, business ethics was granted a prominent place in the common body of business knowledge (Collins & Wartick, 1995).

The AACSB granted business schools flexibility to determine how they should meet the business ethics standard. Accredited schools could either offer a separate business ethics course or infuse ethics into other business courses, a position reinforced in the latest AACSB standards drafted in 2003. Based on an informal survey, the AACSB reports that only one-third of accredited programs currently offer a required business ethics course (Stewart, 2004), similar to the number of required offerings more than a decade ago (Collins & Wartick, 1995). Barriers precluding the offering of a separate business ethics course include scarce space in an already overcrowded business curriculum and the employment of business ethics scholars, who are few in number.

Most business schools have chosen to implement the infusion model by encouraging discipline-based professors to address the now mandatory ethical dilemmas found in functional textbooks. Unfortunately, students report that their discipline-based professors avoid raising ethical issues in their courses, thus inadequately preparing graduates for the types of ethical dilemmas they are likely to encounter during their careers (Adams, Taschian, & Shore, 1999).

The AACSB business ethics flexibility rule came under attack following the most recent wave of corporate scandals. Swanson and Frederick (2003), in *A Call for Business School Responsibility*, urged the AACSB to adopt more rigorous standards because most business schools do not take teaching business ethics seriously. They conclude their call to arms with the obvious solution: "require a course in ethics while striving for across-the-board infusion of ethics" (p. 161).

What such a solution could look like is explored in the next two sections.

## PART II: THE SEPARATE BUSINESS ETHICS COURSE

Separate business ethics courses are often treated as peripheral to the business school curriculum—a moral band-aid to the more substantive functional business school courses. As a result, many business ethics professors feel isolated and not respected by their business school colleagues, and there is a perceived intellectual bias against the field, particularly at large research institutions (Hosmer, 1999). Although the primary objections against providing curriculum space to business ethics courses are fallacious (Acevedo, 2001), they tend to be deeply held by many functional business school faculty.

Framing the business ethics course as one that questions the moral assumptions of other business school disciplines alienates the business ethics professor from business school colleagues. Instead, the business ethics course should be framed as a unifying one at either the beginning or conclusion of a business education. The business ethics course can serve as an introductory course that provides a common body of knowledge usable in functional courses, as a capstone course that integrates all previous functional courses, or in the middle of a student's business education where connections are explicitly made with previous and future functional courses.

Business education reformists have called for improving the quality of a business education through the development of a student's higher level skills (National Commission on Excellence in Education, 1983; Porter & McKibbin, 1988; U.S. Department of Education, 1990). Students can enhance their analytical, problem solving, communication, and team building skills by grappling with the rich complexity of ethical issues (Smith, 2003). The remainder of this section will address course goals, establishing relevancy and a host of learning activities.

### Course Goals

The business ethics course is where the liberal arts intersects the business curriculum by raising ethical awareness and applying ethical analysis to business issues. According to Brinkman and Simms (2001), this gives rise to values and teaching styles that opponents of a separate course consider discordant to the rest of the curriculum. Functional business school professors can feel as though some of their core beliefs are under attack, which can be epitomized in the battle between the long maintained shareholder theory of the firm and the newly formulated stakeholder theory of the firm. This unhealthy tension can be minimized by initially obtaining buy-in on course goals from other business school professors.

Some business ethics professors might object to the need to obtain consensus from other faculty on the grounds that such a technique creates a double standard applicable only to business ethics courses, or that it infringes on their academic freedom. But accounting professors typically obtain consensus for course goals from their departmental peers, particularly in this age of course and program assessment, and then determine how best to achieve the goals within their own individual courses.

If the business ethics course is to be truly integrative and unifying, then every stakeholder should have the opportunity to provide input in course design, particularly given the nature of academic politics and faculty assumptions about the business ethics course being antibusiness. A consensus among business faculty could be achieved around four goals that many business ethics professors usually adopt for their courses (Brinkmann & Sims, 2001):

1. Awareness of one's moral values and thresholds
2. Ability to identify and manage moral issues, conflicts and responsibilities
3. Ability to share moral understanding
4. Ability to exhibit moral courage

These four goals can be obtained while simultaneously honing a student's higher order skills—analytical thinking, problem solving, communication, negotiation, and team development (Carlson & Burke, 1998; Smith, 2003). In terms of assessment, the first, third, and fourth goals may be difficult to measure. The second goal is probably the easiest to assess because the information is contained in most business ethics textbooks.

## The Social Desirability Issue: What the Course is not About

Many functional business school professors and students express concern as to whether students enrolled in business ethics courses are being taught that there is one correct moral answer to the complex issues surrounding management decision making. It is essential to clarify that the business ethics course is about stimulating debate about right and wrong, not ending the debate. The business ethics course fails if at the end of the semester students merely repeat the professor's own ethical viewpoints. The course should not be about generating politically correct opinions.

I continually remind students of the Shakespearean line inspired by Socrates: "To thine own self be true." Student class contributions should be fueled by their own observations and previous behaviors. The more honest students are about themselves and their life experiences, the more they will learn.

Nor should the course be about generating ethical anarchy. Whereas accounting professors teach generally accepted accounting principles to help students generate appropriate answers, business ethics professors teach generally accepted ethical principles to help students generate appropriate answers. As will be discussed below, business ethics professors should develop a student's ability to apply universal ethical principles—namely deontology (respect for everyone) complemented by utilitarianism (greatest good for the greatest number)—to the myriad of ethical dilemmas faced by managers on a daily basis. On contentious social issues, utilitarians disagree with utilitarians, deontologists disagree with deontologists, and utilitarians and deontologists disagree with each other, which makes for very interesting class discussions. The emphasis should be about helping students to use good reasons based on facts, and not about students agreeing with the professor's political conclusions.

## Overall Course Logic

Students arrive at a business ethics course with a set of preconceived ideas about right and wrong. These ideas are based on their life experiences and what they have absorbed from the surrounding culture, including parents, friends, teachers, and the media. Similar to other business courses, the business ethics course should begin with the exploration of the most basic ethical principle (egoism) and evolve toward the highest standard (deontology). See Table 13.1 for definitions of the five most prevalent ethical theories. A more in-depth discussion of egoism, social group relativism, cultural relativism, utilitarianism, and deontology appears in Collins and O'Rourke (1994) and Collins and Page (1997).

Lawrence Kohlberg (1981) found that people sequentially progress through the six stages of moral development listed in Table 13.2, beginning with punishment avoidance and culminating at the level of universal

## Table 13.1.  Five Prevalent Ethical Theories

*Five Ethical Theories—From Most Basic to Most Desirable*

**EGOISM:**  How does the action relate to me? If the action furthers my interests, then it is right. If it conflicts with my interests, then it is wrong.

**SOCIAL GROUP RELATIVISM:**  How does the action relate to my social group (peers, friends, etc.)? If the action conforms with the social group's norms, then it is right. If it is contrary to the social group's norms, then it is wrong.

**CULTURAL RELATIVISM:**  How does the action relate to the national culture, particularly its laws? If the action conforms with the law, then it is right. If it is contrary to the law, then it is wrong.

**UTILITARIANISM:**  How does the action relate to everyone who is affected by it? If the action is beneficial to the greatest number of people affected by it, then it is right. If it is detrimental to the greatest number, then it is wrong.

**DEONTOLOGY:**  How does the action relate to my duty to become an ideal human being who treats others in the way that I would want to be treated? Does it treat *every stakeholder* truthfully and with respect and integrity? If it does, then it is right. If it does not, then it is wrong.

## Table 13.2.  Kohlberg's Stages of Moral Development and Ethical Theories

| Age Group | Stage Of Moral Development | Ethical Theory |
|---|---|---|
| Mature Adulthood | Stage 6:  Universal ethical principles—justice, equality, fairness for everyone, universal human rights | Deontology (Does the action treat every stakeholder with respect?) |
| Mature Adulthood | Stage 5:  Prior rights, social contract, utilities—human rights | Deontology, utilitarianism (Is the action the greatest good for the greatest number?) |
| Adulthood | Stage 4:  Social system—duty to society's customs, traditions, laws | Cultural relativism (Does the action maintain laws and customs?) |
| Early Adulthood, Adolescence | Stage 3:  Mutual interpersonal expectations—well-being of friends and coworkers | Social group relativism (Is the action supported by my peers?) |
| Adolescence, Youth | Stage 2:  Reward seeking—self-interest, fairness to me, reciprocity | Egoism (Does the action benefit me?) |
| Childhood | Stage 1:  Punishment avoidance—obedience to rules due to fear of authority | Egoism (Does the action hurt me?) |

ethical principles. People admire those at the next highest stage, but consider those who reason at a level two stages higher to be naïve. Moral development can stop at any stage. Most managers and college-age students reason at stages 2 and 3 (Weber & Gillespie, 1998). At stage 2, a person's determination of right and wrong is based on seeking rewards from others and at stage 3 a person is significantly influenced by his or her peers' moral sentiments. In other words, most managers determine right and wrong based on reward mechanisms (what behaviors earn bonuses or promotions) and peer approval.

Table 13.2 suggests linkages between the six stages of moral development and the five dominant ethical theories. Moral reasoning in stages 1 and 2 reflects egoism, stage 3 moral reasoning reflects social group relativism, stage 4 moral reasoning reflects cultural relativism, and stages 5 and 6 reflect utilitarianism and deontology.

The evolution of a semester should parallel advancement through Kohlberg's six stages of moral development, beginning with egoism and ending with deontology. Defending deontology at the beginning of a semester to a group of egoists or social group relativists is like speaking English in rural Japan—a few loose connections can be made but much will be lost in translation. Egoists feeling threatened by the professor's deontological logic will unite, making for a very long and unrewarding semester.

According to Kohlberg, students cannot leap from egoism to deontology; they must gradually and sequentially pass through each stage of moral reasoning. Individuals advance to the next higher level of moral reasoning only when they become dissatisfied with the beliefs and outcomes associated with their current level of moral reasoning. The dissatisfaction has to be personally experienced and recognized by the student, it cannot be intellectually imposed or injected by the professor.

Rather than imposing utilitarianism and deontology on a group of egoists comfortable with their level of moral reasoning, business ethics professors should begin the course with a defense of egoism. In *Theory of Moral* Sentiments and *Wealth of Nations*, Adam Smith emphasizes that people very naturally make economic decisions based on self-interest (Collins, 1988). The pursuit of self-interest, restrained by concerns raised by utilitarianism and deontology, justifies the extensive granting of liberty found in democratic capitalist societies.

As such, students and business people are more likely to adopt the highest ethical standards if they can be shown that doing so is in their self-interests and good for business. Researchers have noted that ethical behavior is positively associated with employee trust and commitment, customer trust and satisfaction, and organizational reputation, all of which have a positive impact on financial performance (Ferrell, Fraedrich, & Ferrell, 2005). It is in a company's financial self-interest to behave ethically; unethical behavior can result in fines and jail.

I have found that students are much more receptive to learning about the higher ethical theories after the professor has reinforced the dominant mode of ethical analysis, namely egoism. Students are now more willing to begin the trek up the ethics ladder.

Through the use of textbook material, cases, dilemmas, and experiential exercises, students should learn that applying social group relativism tends to generate better ethical outcomes than egoism, cultural relativism tends to generate better ethical outcomes than social group relativism, utilitarianism tends to generate better ethical outcomes than cultural group relativism, and deontology tends to generate better ethical outcomes than utilitarianism. By the end of the semester, students should be comfortable applying utilitarianism and deontology—Kohlberg's highest stages of moral reasoning—to business situations.

As demonstrated in the "Developing a Moral Solution Framework" (see Table 13.3), all five ethical theories provide useful information, with utilitarianism and deontology pointing in the most ethically defensible direction. Students are often so focused on their own self-interests that simply listing all the stakeholders affected by a decision can be very illuminating. We examine how the act of cheating on an assignment can have a negative impact not only on the student getting caught, but also other students taking the exam, the reputation of the college, and family integ-

### Table 13.3.   Developing a Moral Solution Framework

*Instructions:*   Answer Questions 1 through 6 to gather the information necessary for performing an ethical analysis. Based on this information, develop a policy option that has the strongest ethical basis.

1. Who are all the people affected by the action (stakeholder analysis)?
2. Is the action beneficial to me (egoism)?
3. Is the action supported by my social group (social group relativism)?
4. Is the action supported by national laws (cultural relativism)?
5. Is the action for the greatest good of the greatest number of people affected by it (utilitarianism)?
6. Are the motives behind the action based on truthfulness and respect/integrity toward each stakeholder (deontology)?

- *If answers to Questions 2 through 6 are all "yes,"* then do it.
- *If answers to Questions 2 through 6 are all "no,"* then do not do it.
- *If answers to Questions 2 through 6 are mixed,* then modify your decision.
  - *If answers to Questions 5 and 6 are "yes,"* this action is the *most* ethical. You may need to modify this decision in consideration of any "no" answer to Questions 2 through 4.
  - *If answers to Questions 5 and 6 are "no,"* this action is the *least* ethical. Modify this decision in consideration of these objections.
  - *If answers to Questions 5 and 6 are mixed,* this action is *moderately* ethical. Modify this decision in considerations of objections raised by Questions 5 or 6. You may need to further modify this decision in consideration of any "no" answer to Questions 2 through 4.

rity. A more in-depth discussion of using the "Developing a Moral Solution Framework" appears in Collins and O'Rourke (1994) and Collins and Page (1997).

## Establishing Relevancy During the First Class Meeting

Business ethics professors should establish subject relevancy during the very first class meeting. Students are predominantly egoists and social group relativists and need to be shown that the course is relevant to their personal development, careers, and organizational performance.

I begin the *first class* distinguishing between being selfish and self-interested by describing situations I experienced during the past week. Students must categorize the described behaviors as being either selfish (was the person concerned solely about herself or himself) or self-interested (did the person take into consideration the interests of others as well as himself or herself). The examples include my decision to show up to teach today's class, otherwise I might get reprimanded.

We then discuss how the pursuit of self-interest constructively fuels a capitalist economy. As noted earlier, we brainstorm why it is in an organization's self-interest to be ethical, including how high levels of integrity and earned trust within a company can reduce supervisory costs and enhance profitability.

After establishing self-interest as an appropriate guiding value, we review several articles in that day's *Wall Street Journal,* a newspaper with high legitimacy among business students (Schaupp & Lane, 1992). Every issue of the newspaper provides information on ethical and legal mishaps, as well as business decisions that have negative social effects. Using that day's edition minimizes student objections regarding bias against choosing a day of unusually high unethical activities.

In small groups students discuss why the executives or companies got into trouble. The overwhelming answer is that they were either selfish or pursued their self-interests in a way that generated a harm. I then survey the students as to whether the executives whose unethical activities are exposed in the newspaper represent a "few bad apples" or good people who made a bad decision due to the competitive marketplace or some other job pressure.

We conclude the first class with an exercise developed by the Josephson Institute (Lampe, 1997). Students, concerned with protecting their own self-interests, derive a list of core ethical values for guiding society, first independently, then in small groups, and lastly as an entire class. The list typically includes deontological concepts such as trustworthiness, respect, responsibility, justice, fairness, caring, and good citizenship.

Although some students consider these values unobtainable in a business setting due to egoistic concerns about profit and promotion, the student-generated conceptions about the values associated with a "good society" can be referred to throughout the semester.

## Developing a Moral Solution

In the *second class* we discuss two ethical dilemmas experienced by people similar to them, students who took the course the previous semester. These real-life dilemmas typically include observing coworkers stealing money or a boss verbally abusing a subordinate or misusing his/her authority (MacFarlane, 2003).

I read the first dilemma, require students to write down what they would do, and then facilitate a free flowing discussion where they question one another about what response would be appropriate. I conclude the discussion after about 10 minutes and ask students to critique what just happened. Most students express dissatisfaction with the superficiality of the discussion, complain that viewpoints were ignored and very little progress occurred.

I then read the second dilemma and require the students to use the "Developing a Moral Solution Framework" shown in Table 13.3 to develop a moral solution. This trains the student to consider the perspectives of all affected stakeholders (Collins & Page, 1997) and to consider the impact of one's actions based on egoism, social group relativism, cultural relativism, utilitarianism, and deontology. Hosmer (2000) offers a more complex set of questions for deriving a moral solution. We then discuss the dilemma one ethical theory at a time, reaching a consensus on each question before moving forward. Sometimes the students will reach a consensus at the end of the discussion, sometimes they do not. In either case, all perspectives are explored and treated respectfully.

Given the personal dimension of the ethical issues discussed during this class session, I instruct the students to construct their own personal moral anchor, or set of rules, to adequately guide them when ethical issues arise, one that clearly states principles and aspirations (Ferris, 1996). Most students use an inspiring quote from literature or someone they admire that moves them to do the right thing, whatever the right thing happens to be. This personal code is representative of their worldview or meaning of life. Students share their personal codes with each other, highlighting similarities and differences.

## Comfortably Sharing Personally Experienced Ethical Dilemmas

Discussing unethical issues involving strangers written about in a newspaper and students who previously took the class opens students up to discussing ethical dilemmas they have personally experienced at work. By now the students have a general understanding as to what it means to face an ethical dilemma.

For the *third class,* students compose a brief paragraph describing an incident at work that represented an ethical dilemma, either something that bothered their conscience or was contrary to the firm's interests, industry standards, national laws, not to the greatest good of the greatest number affected by it, or disrespectful toward other human beings. They also comment on their personal feelings about the actions taken. I briefly share stories about ethical dilemmas I experienced as a 12 year old with a newspaper delivery route, an 18 year old working part-time at a summer job, a 25 year old manager, and a professor.

As an ice-breaking activity, Sims (2004) recommends that students share their ethical stories with a partner, who then conveys the story to the rest of the class. In the process of public self-disclosure, students practice listening and communication skills and form special bonds with other classmates. When facilitated appropriately, a safe conversational learning environment begins to take shape. Later in the semester, students are put in teams to further develop one of the dilemmas and facilitate an in-depth class discussion about it.

In many of the ethical dilemmas shared by the students, they either did nothing or what everyone else did when the ethical problem arose. I ask the students if their behavior upheld the values of a "good society" that we developed during our first class session or the personal moral codes they developed during our second class session. If not, why not? This helps the students to better understand the distinction between knowing what is right and doing what is right. We also explore the obstacles that prevented them from taking right action and discuss how difficult it can be at times to behave ethically in the workplace.

In addition, I introduce the concept of journaling during the second class. Throughout the semester students write about their experiences inside and outside the classroom, reflecting on the types of ethical dilemmas they experience or observe in terms of the personal code of ethics they constructed and the core values of a "good society" developed by their classmates. Students write about how people, including themselves, responded to the dilemmas and how a more socially desired outcome could have been achieved (Dennehy, Sims, & Collins, 1998; McNeely, 2000). Journaling provides an important outlet for students who are not comfortable with public disclosure, particularly international or shy students (Sims, 2002), and can be particularly effective in response to public policy (Lenn, 1997) or service-learning experiences.

## Persuading Others by Speaking the Same Ethical Language

By the *fourth class,* many students are curious to know where they stand on the ethics continuum and how this knowledge can help them become better managers. Students complete a Machiavellian survey instrument to enhance self-understanding (Christie & Geis, 1970). In addition, I have modified a managerial dilemma developed by Mallinger (1997) to provide some insight on their preferred ethical style.

In the ethical dilemma, a seismologist receives data predicting an 80% probability of a 7.3 magnitude earthquake hitting one of four fault lines in Southern California within the next 2 days, including the populated San Andreas fault. Should the seismologist disclose this information to the public? Each prompt response to the dilemma represents the application of one of the five ethical theories, ranging from egoism to deontology.

I group together the students who applied the same ethical theory to the dilemma (i.e., all those who chose the social group relativist response are put in the same group). The groups then develop persuasive arguments to convince students one step lower on Kohlberg's stages of moral development to join their group. For instance, the social group relativists must develop egoistic reasons why egoists should adopt the social group relativist action response, cultural relativists must develop social group relativistic reasons why the social group relativists should adopt the cultural relativist action response, and so on. Egoists are assigned the task of convincing deontologists to choose the egoist option.

This activity demonstrates how to successfully persuade others. Egoists are unlikely to change behavior unless provided with an egoistic reason for doing so. Similarly, giving a deontologist egoistic reasons for changing behavior will most likely be unsuccessful. However, an egoist could influence a deontologist by reasoning like a deontologist, framing the desired behavior in terms of duties and respect for all stakeholders.

We end this class session the way we end all class sessions, with the question "What did you learn today in class?" Debriefing is essential to connect the student's experience with the conceptual knowledge being taught and reinforce the learning that has taken place (Dennehy, Sims, & Collins, 1998; Sims, 2002)

## Role Playing to Understand Social Group and Cultural Relativism

As noted earlier, the class is structured to move students through Kohlberg's stages of moral development, from egoists to deontologists. I do not expect all the students to reason like deontologists and utilitarians by the end of the semester, but I do expect them to have a more sympathetic understanding of how these higher stages of moral development reason through ethical dilemmas. Role playing is a very useful technique for achieving this goal.

Typically, professors use role playing to provide students with an opportunity to consider alternatives from different stakeholder perspectives (Brown, 1994; Raisner, 1997). Role playing also provides a unique opportunity to demonstrate (1) the superiority of social group relativism over egoism and (2) the inadequacy of social group relativism.

Landrum (2001) constructs an ethical dilemma wherein the decision maker must decide whether to recommend Morgan, an ethically-challenged friend, for a job. I have modified the dilemma slightly to enhance its relevancy for students. The central decision maker is now a student working as an assistant weekend store manager. Morgan, who had falsified records at a previous employer, requests a favorable recommendation for a job opening as the second assistant weekend store manager. Most students would recommend Morgan for the position without informing anyone about Morgan's past misbehaviors. They justify the decision using egoism (Morgan would praise or blame the decision maker) and social group relativism (Morgan, as a friend, deserves special consideration). Students generally agree that social group relativism—an obligation developed out of friendship—provides a stronger ethical reason than egoism.

Then we change roles. The student is now the current store manager rather than Morgan's friend. If the store manager, most students would want to be informed about Morgan's previous misbehaviors. Most students are uncomfortable with right or wrong being dependent on whether the student is either the one making the recommendation to the manager or the manager receiving the recommendation. They desire greater moral consistency.

Eventually, a student has an "aha" experience and asks about the status of the law on this matter. I explain that it is illegal to knowingly provide false information. The law provides moral guidance that addresses ethical problems associated with the application of social group relativism. The law encourages honesty independent of one's social group preferences.

I further reinforce this lesson with an ethical dilemma developed by Sanyal (2000). I have modified the dilemma by putting the decision maker into five different roles—an uninformed consumer, an informed consumer, the purchasing manager, the CEO, and a societal perspective.

A person shopping in a national hardware store must choose between two identical hammers of similar quality, one costs $5.99 and the other $8.29. Which hammer should the shopper purchase? Most students would purchase the lower-priced hammer. Next the person notices that the lower-priced hammer has a "Made in China" sticker on it and the higher-priced hammer does not have any sticker. Which hammer should the person purchase? Most students would still purchase the lower-priced hammer.

The decision maker is now the purchasing manager of a national hardware company that employs many people. Managers at every unit were directed to cut costs and increase revenues to prevent bankruptcy. The purchasing manager locates a Chinese supplier of hammers, screwdrivers and other hardware with prices way below that of other suppliers, enabling the company to simultaneously lower prices and increase profits on each item sold. Unfortunately, the Chinese supplier, which sells to other American hardware companies, employs prisoners required to work long hours under very harsh conditions and no wages. Money paid the supplier goes to pay the prison officials rather than the prisoners. Most American consumers are unaware of the Chinese prison labor conditions, while others have heard about it but do not care. Should the purchasing manager recommend to corporate headquarters that the company switch to the Chinese supplier? If, instead of purchasing manager, the student was the CEO, would the student sign the contract with the Chinese supplier?

Last, students evaluate the same dilemma from a societal perspective. In the United States, the use of prison labor to manufacture products for commercial sale is generally banned, otherwise American companies paying regular labor costs could not compete on price. Should the United States government ban importing Chinese hardware made by unpaid prison laborers? Most students—even those who would have purchased the product in their roles as consumers, CEO and purchasing agent— vote to ban such products. Typically, they justify their decision change based on utilitarianism or deontology. This leads to a discussion as to why we prefer laws to be based on utilitarianism or deontology, rather than egoism or social group relativism.

A similar role play dilemma could be developed based on the Maquiladora vignette on sweatshop labor provided by Raisner (1997). Students can determine the ethics of where to locate a new production facility by comparing the perspectives of a United States labor union member, a Guatemalan laborer, the CEO, and a human rights activist. The use of a "mock trial" also generates lively discussions by forcing students to struggle with the incongruity of applying the logic of social group relativism to people in different roles facing the same information. In the mock trial, students must defend, prosecute or serve on a jury in a case involving an executive who committed a questionable behavior (Orlitzky, 1997). Such discussions push students into using utilitarian and deontological analysis to smooth out the moral ambiguity of social group and cultural relativism.

One other classroom activity that confronts students with the ethical shortcomings of social group relativism is an ethical analysis of papers or homework assignments they submitted to professors teaching functional business courses. I have offered this assignment to students wanting extra credit points. Students typically compartmentalize their learning, which is why curriculum integration is so important. In accounting courses, students seek to please their accounting professors by thinking like accountants. The same is true for marketing, finance, and even business ethics. After applying the "Developing a Moral Solution Framework" in Table 13.1 to the papers they wrote for other classes, students are quite surprised at the unethical nature of some of their recommendations.

## Service-Learning

Service-learning projects are increasingly seen as a viable pedagogical tool for learning college course material. According to the 2002 National Survey of Student Engagement, 42% of graduating college seniors have participated in a community-based project as part of a regular course, and nearly two-thirds performed community service or volunteer work during the college years (National Survey of Student Engagement, 2002). The addition of a service-learning component to courses has been found to positively effect a student's moral development (Bass, 1994) and enhances critical thinking (Eyler & Giles, 1999), even beyond graduation (Astin, Sax, & Avalos, 1999).

Many schools have service-learning centers that can help professors develop projects associated with business ethics course learning objectives, such as enhancing a student's sensitivity to social issues, developing a deeper understanding of how businesses can address social problems, and learning how to manage a community service project (Collins, 1996; Lamb, Swinth, Vinton, & Lee, 1998; Shaffer & Collins, 1997). Businesses engage in community service activities to enhance their reputation in the community, as a form of team and management development, and to attract and retain employees. Participation in service-learning projects prepares students for this work expectation.

I have been conducting service-learning projects out of my business ethics courses since the early 1990s, ranging from a one-time serving of food at a homeless shelter to several weeks addressing a nonprofit agency's management needs. Students continually report that the service-learning project is one of their most enjoyable college learning experiences, even those students who begin the assignment with negative preconceptions about the subject matter. Business ethics professors can help students learn course content by tapping into their desire to become more involved in the local community and positively impact their values and opinions (Kracher, 1999; McCarthy & Tucker, 2002; 1999; Weber & Glyptis, 2000).

I allocate approximately 25% of my class time during a semester to service-learning activities. My course meets for 75 minutes, twice a week, for 15 weeks. Teams of three or four students apply the skills and knowledge they are learning in their business programs to a service-learning project during eight class sessions. I have formed a partnership with a nearby Boys & Girls Club and meet with its managers prior to the semester to design projects beneficial to the Boys & Girls Club that coincide with my curriculum goals. Many of the projects are on management's "to-do" list, but have not been accomplished due to a lack of time and resources. During the 2003-2004 academic year, student teams designed a program brochure, created manuals for hiring employees and managing volunteers, developed program guidelines for new member and new employee orientations, and reorganized the library. During class time I oversee the evolution of their work and provide feedback as needed.

The importance of team development as part of course goals and the business program should not be underestimated. Team activities at work will dominate the future lives of many students. Business ethics professors should assist students in interacting with team members, performing multiple team roles, and developing their social and group processing skills (Siciliano, 2001; St. Clair & Tschirhart, 2002).

The service activity could be directed at the college campus rather than the local community. I recently taught students how to use The Natural Step framework for improving environmental performance (James & Lahti, 2004; Nattrass & Altomare, 1999). Students applied the first three principles to the college campus and developed recommendations for improving our environmental performance, such as more recycling in the library, reducing energy usage in the dormitories, and providing locally grown organic food in the cafeteria. The students met with the appropriate administrator and collaboratively developed an action plan that the students then implemented.

## Table 13.4.   Purposes In Life Essay Assignment

*"The unexamined life is not worth living." —Socrates*

*"This is the true joy in life—the 'being' used for a purpose recognized by yourself as a mighty one; the 'being' a force of nature instead of a feverish, selfish little clod of ailments and grievances, complaining that the world will not devote itself to making you happy." —George Bernard Shaw*

Every day we recreate ourselves, though we tend to be a lot like the person we were the previous day. As Socrates suggests, personal reflection on our own lives is very important to our evolution as individuals, community members, and a species. As George Bernard Shaw suggests, a life of meaning generates tremendous joy as we travel through life's adventures.

Edgewood College's Dominican educational tradition consists of study, reflection and action. Throughout the semester we have studied, reflected and acted. Now it is time to study yourself and reflect on the data you gather about yourself.

*Part I:   Compose a 4-6 page, double-spaced typed response to the following questions:*

(1) What three characteristics best describe who you are? Assume a judge responds: "That's not true!" Defend each characteristic you listed with a real experience that exemplifies it is true.

(2) The five values at the heart of Edgewood College are: Truth, Justice, Compassion, Partnership and Community. Write five short paragraphs about whether people in your work organization (a) are truthful, (b) pursue justice, (c) are compassionate, (d) develop partnerships, and (e) engage others in the spirit of community, one short paragraph per value. Support your conclusions with examples.

(3) At some point in your life an injustice to someone else cried out to your heart and mind that led you to demand justice. Whether it was a news story, an article, a talk you attended, a call from a friend, or something you observed, it moved you to seek justice. What was it? What did you do?

(4) In class we examined ethical dilemmas, critical incidents and business scandals. Reflect on your journal entries regarding the positions you took in these discussions and summarize how they represent your belief system about human beings, business, and society.

*Part II: Compose a 4-6 paged, double-spaced type response to the following questions*

(1) What is the purpose of life?
(2) How will you fulfill this purpose through your work, career, and family?

## Purposes in Life Essay

My business ethics course culminates with the composition of a "Purposes in Life" essay that effectively provides a reflective debriefing of the entire semester. As shown in Table 13.4, students articulate their own purposes in life based on their journal entries, course activities and other life experiences. By the end of the assignment students have developed their own worldview, one that will influence the types of decisions they make during their professional careers.

## Other Classroom Activities

The business ethics and management education literature abounds with many other innovative teaching methodologies, including in-depth case study analysis (Bezold, Wokutch, & Gerde, 1997; Dean & Fornaciari, 2002; Desiraju & Gopinath, 2001; Nelson & Wittmer, 2001; Schaupp & Lane, 1992; Siciliano & McAleer, 1997), crisis management simulations (Fryxell & Dooley, 1997; Muir, 2001; Weber, 1997; Zych, 1999), field trips to discuss ethics training with corporate ethics officers (Jones & Ottaway, 2001) or to observe how white collar criminals are processed and incarcerated (McPhail, 2002), theatrical movies that dramatize complex ethical dilemmas (Giacalone & Jurkiewicz, 2001; Hosmer & Steneck, 1989), novels (Garaventa, 1998), current events presentations (Ferris, 1996), and exploration of diversity issues (Clair, Crary, McDaniels, Spelman, Buote, & MacLean, 1997; Eylon & Langton, 1998; McQuarrie, 1998; Muller & Parham, 1998; Thompson, 2002). All of these activities can generate lively and meaningful discussions and understandings.

## PART III: AN INTEGRATED BUSINESS ETHICS PROGRAM

In addition to a separate business ethics course, business ethics topics should be infused into other business courses. Business ethics professors can serve as change agents by developing partnerships with key subunits within the business school and local community. Business ethics integration programs have been created at private institutions, such as Wharton (http://ethics.wharton.upenn.edu), and public institutions, such as the University of Nebraska-Lincoln (http://www.cba.unl.edu/outreach/busethsoc/information.html). This section is written from the perspective of a one-professor operation with limited resources. I have tried, with various degrees of success and failure, to infuse business ethics into student orientations, first-year forums, other courses, student organizations, and community outreach.

## Orientation Activities

Business ethics education should begin with a student's orientation to the university and business program. It is essential to build moral expectations at the front end of the higher education process. The National

Resource Center for the First-Year Experience & Students in Transition surveyed 1,013 higher education institutions in 2000 and found that 62% offered an extended orientation or college survival seminar, and half of them required this of all first-year students (www.sc.edu/fye/research/surveyfindings/surveys/survey00.html). Approximately 80% of these programs involved faculty in orientation activities.

Communication between faculty and students outside the classroom is an important predictor of student engagement and retention. At the University of Wisconsin-Madison, I conducted half-day orientation workshops in which new MBA students debated an ethical dilemma and learned an ethical vocabulary they could bring to their functional courses (Collins & Page, 1997). Incoming students can also participate in a service-learning project with a business ethics dimension, such as an environmental clean-up activity, that helps them develop communication, teamwork and leadership skills.

## First-Year Forum Activities

For undergraduate students, first-year forum activities are an important layer in their socialization process. The Policy Center on the First Year of College reports that 94% of the schools they surveyed offered first-year seminars, and more than 40% required student participation (Barefoot, 2002). The first-year forum could be an ethics course that covers business issues, or a management course that covers ethics issues (Lamb, Lee, & Vinton, 1997). These courses should include student collaboration, active learning, a high degree of faculty interaction, and high expectations (Chickering & Gamson, 1987).

Many incoming freshman have participated in high school service-learning projects (Duckenfield, 2002; Fusco, 2002) and, as a result, are very receptive to deeper service-learning projects linked to the curriculum (DeVitis, Johns, & Simpson, 1998; Zlotkowski, 2002). Edgewood College offers a nonmandatory, one-credit, first-year forum course. During the Spring 2004 semester, three professors from different academic disciplines designed an environmental immersion course that begins during orientation and extends into the student's first semester. The students and professors canoed around an adjacent lake, stopping at various points to hear guest lectures along the shoreline. My group of students studied the storm drain system within the local watershed and glued decals noting "this drain dumps to lake" on the storm drains nearest the lake. The objective of our first-year forum is to habituate students into the cycle of study, reflection, and action, followed by more study, reflection, and action.

## Brown Bag Workshops on Teaching Ethics

As discussed earlier, many functional business professors are reluctant to raise ethical issues in their courses. Business ethics professors can organize brown bag workshops on how to integrate ethics into other business disciplines. I achieved mixed results conducting these workshops at the University of Wisconsin-Madison Business School.

Importantly, I had the support of the then dean of the business school, who sent a memo to each department requesting that they sponsor an ethics teaching workshop. My goal was to train each professor to facilitate one ethics discussion during the semester. The dean's more modest goal was for me to train one professor per department to facilitate one ethics discussion per semester. Attendance was voluntary and very few professors attended. Integrating ethics into their courses was not a high priority among the professors at this research institution.

I achieved slightly more success sponsoring my own brown bag workshops available to all business school faculty. Most of the attendees were nontenured professors sincerely interested in the subject, though they expressed concern that tenured colleagues preferred they spend more time conducting research rather than improving teaching pedagogy.

Prior to conducting the first workshop, I met with MBA students from each discipline and developed ethical dilemmas based on their previous work experiences. At the faculty workshops, I modeled how to facilitate an ethics discussion for the student developed dilemmas (Collins & Page, 1997). I read the real-life ethical dilemma, the participants wrote down what they would do and why, and I empowered those with the minority point of view to question those who held the majority point of view. We then developed a consensus around what would be the most ethical thing to do, and examined how to do it without alienating a powerful stakeholder (such as a boss or colleague). Most attendees found this format very helpful and simple to adopt in their own courses.

The business ethics and management education literatures contain many examples of ethical topics that can be addressed in functional courses, including courses in Accounting, Computer Science, Communication, Marketing, Operations Management, Organizational Behavior/ Management, Personnel Administration, and Public Relations (Agarwal & Mallow, 2002; Buerck, 2002; Eylon & Langton, 1998; Piper, Gentile, &

Parks, 1993; Sims, 2000; Sims & Brinkmann, 2003). Most functional course textbooks contain ethical dilemmas that professors can assign to students for classroom discussion.

## Integrating Ethics and Social Responsibility Into Management Courses

At Edgewood College I teach management courses as well as the business ethics course. According to a poll of business student recruiters conducted in 2003, the top five student attributes recruiters consider most important are: (1) communication and interpersonal skills, (2) ability to work well within a team, (3) analytical and problem-solving skills, (4) personal ethics and integrity, and (5) leadership potential (*Wall Street Journal*, 2003). As part of our assessment efforts, the full-time management faculty agreed on the following five learning outcome goals for the introductory management course required of all business majors: problem-solving, communication, teams, leadership/motivation, and ethics/social responsibility.

I have designed an extensive service-learning project that addresses all five learning outcome objectives around the teaching of "project management," a concept assigned to the course. Students learn project management by conducting an educational outreach project at a public or private grade school, middle school or high school. In conjunction with the mission of Students-In-Free-Enterprise (SIFE), which is discussed later in this section, student teams present workshops on how free markets work in the global economy, how entrepreneurs identify and serve market needs, skills needed to successfully compete in a free market economy, and practicing business ethics.

Similar service-learning projects can be built into other management courses. Students in my capstone management course on improving organizational effectiveness act as small business consultants by addressing a current organizational inefficiency, such as how to better market the company's products or services. My strategy students at the University of Bridgeport conducted a customer satisfaction survey for a nearby tutoring center and marketed the services of a free medical clinic to low-income families.

Integrating ethics and social responsibility in management courses can also be done on a much smaller scale. For an upper-level undergraduate management course that addresses diversity, my students interview someone of a different race, ethnic group, or religion about their life experiences. Shortly after the 9/11 tragedy, many students attended a local

Islamic service and interviewed attendees about their religious beliefs. This increased student awareness and empathy.

## Student Organizations and Activities

Many student organizations have a statement in their constitutions about serving the campus or broader community. While at the University of Wisconsin-Madison, I held brainstorming sessions with student organization leaders to determine ways they could serve the local community. Some organizations decided to apply the skills they were learning, such as accounting club members providing free bookkeeping services to non-profit agencies. Other student organizations preferred undertaking a community service project unrelated to their area of study, such as finance club members participating in an environmental clean-up project.

Student organizations are notoriously understaffed and compete against each other to recruit new members. As the faculty advisor to the Edgewood Business Association (EBA), I encourage student organization members to cooperate with, rather than compete against, other student organizations. EBA members offer their services to other student organizations for joint projects, such as helping the Psychology Club advertise their events. In addition to reinforcing the habit of service among students, these joint activities help reduce the stereotypes different college majors have toward each other.

During the 2003-2004 academic year we created a Students-in-Free-Enterprise (SIFE) chapter at Edgewood College. SIFE's mission is "to provide college and university students with an opportunity to make a difference and to develop leadership, teamwork and communication skills through learning, practicing and teaching the principles of free enterprise" (www.sife.org). SIFE teams are active on more than 1,500 college/ and university campuses in 37 nations. Edgewood College SIFE team members conducted community workshops on business topics, and participated in a regional competition against SIFE teams from other colleges and universities.

Another possibility is student participation in an annual Ethics Bowl. Initiated by Robert Ladenson of the Illinois Institute of Technology in 1993, the national contest takes place in conjunction with the Association for Practical and Professional Ethics' annual February meeting (Borrego, 2004; Ladenson, 2001). Forty teams participated in the 2004 Ethics Bowl. A panel evaluates the teams according to intelligibility, depth, focus, and judgment.

Last, business ethics professors can assist student services in creating a cohesive life experience at college based on ethics. At Maharishi University of Management a student's daily schedule includes time for exercise, sports, and meditation (Schmidt-Wilk, Heaton, & Steingard, 2000). The school focuses on the emotional, social, and moral growth of students, in addition to cognitive growth.

## Business Ethics Center

An increasing number of higher education institutions are sponsoring business ethics and leadership centers. Extensive lists of domestic and international centers and other very useful business ethics Internet links are available at http://ecampus.bentley.edu/dept/cbe/resources/ ethicsorgs.html and www.web-miner.com/busethics.htm#orgs.

A primary activity of most centers is distributing information through conferences, workshops, and newsletters to local companies, the media, other professors, and alumni. Founded in 1976, the Center for Business Ethics at Bentley College is one of the earliest business ethics centers housed at an institution of higher education (http://ecampus.bentley.edu/ dept/cbe). In addition to conferences, the center provides a variety of publications, research and teaching materials, and consulting services. In 1991, the center helped establish the Ethics Officer Association (www.eoa.org) for professional ethicists.

At Edgewood College, we are exploring the creation of a business executive support network wherein ethical issues can be confidentially addressed among colleagues and informed stakeholders. This format can be extended to practitioners in other fields and academic disciplines, such as political science, law, and medicine. Another possibility is the creation of a survey research center that researches public sentiments on business ethics issues.

## Community Outreach

The business ethics professor's audience extends beyond the classroom and campus. Opportunities to educate the local, national, and international community includes op-ed essays for newspapers, media interviews, and presentations to professional groups and community organizations. One of my most recent rewarding activities is serving as a judge for the Wisconsin Business Ethics Award sponsored by the Society of Financial Services Professionals. The regional award feeds into a national competition. We have designed the judging process to include business students from several Wisconsin colleges and universities. Student teams evaluate the nominees according to the judging criteria and then present their conclusions to the business practitioners, community leaders, and academics judging the contest.

## CONCLUDING COMMENTS

Business ethics professors can influence the lives of students, the business curriculum, and the culture of their institutions in a way unlike that of professors teaching more functional disciplines. The course content—the integration of ethics with professional skills—is central to the mission of higher education institutions. Although at times the mission can be burdensome and isolating, this article's emphasis on partnering with key units throughout the institution suggests that it need not be. We are uniquely positioned to assist in the implementation of higher education reforms that have long been called for and central to keeping colleges and universities active players in shaping our future leaders.

## REFERENCES

Acevedo, A. (2001). Of fallacies and curricula: A case of business ethics. *Teaching Business Ethics, 5*, 157-170.

Adams, J. S., Taschian, A., & Shore, T. H. (1999). Frequency, recall and usefulness of undergraduate ethics education. *Teaching Business Ethics, 3*, 241-253.

Agarwal, J., & Malloy, D. C. (2002). An integrated model of ethical decision-making: A proposed pedagogical framework for a marketing ethics curriculum. *Teaching Business Ethics, 6*, 245-268.

Astin, A. W., Sax, L. J., & Avalos, J. (1999) The long-term effects of volunteerism during the undergraduate years. *The Review of Higher Education, 21*(2), 187-202.

Barefoot, B. O. (2002). *Second national survey of first-year academic practices.* Brevard College, NC: Policy Center on the First Year of College.

Bezold, M. P., Wokutch, R. E., & Gerde, V. W. (1997). If it's Monday, this must be a crisis! In S. Waddock (Ed.), *Research in corporate social performance and policy: Teaching business and society courses with reflective and active learning strategies* (Supplement 2, Special issue, pp. 63-78). Greenwich, CT: JAI Press.

Borrego, A. M. (2004, March 5). Ethics bowls exercise students' moral muscles. *Chronicle of Higher Education, 50*(26), 31-32.

Bass, J. A. (1994). The effect of community service work on the moral development of college ethics students. *Journal of Moral Education, 23*(2), 183-198.

Brinkmann, J., & Sims, R. (2001). Stakeholder-sensitive business ethics teaching. *Teaching Business Ethics, 5*, 171-193.

Brown, K. M. (1994). Using role play to integrate ethics into the business curriculum: A financial management example. *Journal of Business Ethics, 13*(2), 105-110.

Buerck, J. P. (2002). Ethics—A curriculum enhancement initiative in applied computer science technology degree programs. *Teaching Business Ethics, 6*, 167-177.

Carlson, P. J., & Burke, F. (1998). Lessons learned from ethics in the classroom: Exploring student growth in flexibility, complexity and comprehension. *Journal of Business Ethics, 17*(11), 1179-1187.

Chickering, A. W., & Gamson, Z. F. (1987). *Seven principles for good practice in undergraduate education,* Racine, WI: The Johnson Foundation.

Christie, R., & Geis, F. I. (1970). *Studies in Machiavellianism,* New York: Academic Press.

Clair, J. A., Crary, M., McDaniels, M., Spelman, D., Buote, J. D., & MacLean, T. (1997). A cooperative inquiry into teaching and taking a course on managing diversity. In S. Waddock (Ed.), *Research in corporate social performance and policy: Teaching business and society courses with reflective and active learning strategies,* (Supplement 2, Special issue, pp. 25-62). Greenwich, CT: JAI Press.

Collins, D. (1988) Adam Smith's social contract. *Business and Professional Ethics, 7*(3/4), 119-146.

Collins, D. (1996). *Community involvement and service learning student projects,* a special issue. *Journal of Business Ethics, 15*(1).

Collins, D., & O'Rourke, T. (1994) *Ethical dilemmas in business.* Cincinnati, OH: South-Western.

Collins, D., & Page, L. V. (1997). A Socrates/Ted Koppel paradigm for integrating the teaching of business ethics in the curriculum. In S. Waddock (Ed.), *Research in corporate social performance and policy: Teaching business and society courses with reflective and active learning strategies* (Supplement 2, Special issue, pp. 221-242). Greenwich, CT: JAI Press.

Collins, D., & Wartick, S. L. (1995). Business and society/business ethics courses: Twenty years at the crossroads. *Business & Society, 34*(1), 51-89.

Council for a Parliament of the World's Religions. (1993). *Towards a global ethic: An initial declaration.* Chicago: Council for a Parliament of the World's Religions.

Dean, K. L., & Fornaciari, C. J. (2002). How to create and use experiential case-based exercises in a management classroom. *Journal of Management Education, 26*(5), 586-603.

Dennehy, R. F., Sims, R. R., & Collins, H. E. (1998). Debriefing experiential learning exercises: A theoretical and practical guide for success. *Journal of Management Education, 22*(1), 9-25.

Desiraju, R., & Gopinath, C. (2001). Encouraging participation in case discussions: A comparison of the MICA and the Harvard case methods. *Journal of Management Education, 25*(4), 394-408.

DeVitis, J. L., Johns, R. W., & Simpson, D. J. (1998). *To serve and learn: The spirit of community in liberal education.* New York: Peter Lang.

Dirksen, C. J. (1966). *The American Assembly of Collegiate Schools of Business: 1916-1966.* Homewood, IL: Irwin.

Duckenfield, M. (2002). Look who's coming to college: The impact of high school service-learning on new college students. In Ed Zlotkowski (Ed.), *Service-learning and the first-year experience: Preparing students for personal success and civic responsibility* (pp. 39-50). University of South Carolina: National Resource Center for the First-Year Experience & Students in Transition.

Eyler, J., & Giles, D.W. (1999). *Where's the learning in service-learning?* San Francisco: Jossey-Bass.

Eylon, D., & Langton, N. (1998). Discrimination in the forest industry: A teaching module. *Journal of Management Education, 22*(2), 173-192.

Ferrell, O. C., Fraedrich, J., & Ferrell, F. (2005). *Business ethics: Ethical decision making and cases* (6th ed.). New York: Houghton Mifflin.

Ferris, W. P. (1996). The effectiveness of teaching business ethics using moral philosophy and personal ethical codes. *Journal of Management Education, 20*(3), 341-357.

Friere, P. (1971). *Pedagogy of the oppressed,* New York: Herder and Herder.

Fryxell, G. E., & Dooley, R. S. (1997). Saving the commons: A behavioral simulation for experiencing the role of collaboration and trust in devising workable solutions to environmental and other social issues. In S. Waddock (Ed.), *Research in corporate social performance and policy: Teaching business and society courses with reflective and active learning strategies* (Supplement 2, Special issue, pp. 149-184). Greenwich, CT: JAI Press.

Fusco, A. (2002). High school service-learning and the preparation of students for college: An overview of research. In E. Zlotkowski (Ed.), *Service-learning and the first-year experience: Preparing students for personal success and civic responsibility* (pp. 3-14). University of South Carolina: National Resource Center for the First-Year Experience & Students in Transition.

Garaventa, E. (1998). Drama: A tool for teaching business ethics. *Business Ethics Quarterly, 8,* 547-555.

Giacalone, R. A., & Jurkiewicz, C. L. (2001). Lights, camera, action: Teaching ethical decision making through the cinematic experience. *Teaching Business Ethics, 5,* 79-87.

Hamilton, D., McFarland, D., & Mirchandani, D. (2000). A decision model for integration across the business curriculum in the 21st century. *Journal of Management Education, 24*(1), 102-126.

Hosmer, L. T. (1999). Somebody out there doesn't like us: A study of the position and respect of business ethics at schools of business administration. *Journal of Business Ethics, 22*(2), 91-106.Hosmer, L. T. (2000). Standard format for the case analysis of moral problems. *Teaching Business Ethics, 4,* 169-180.

Hosmer, L. T., & Steneck, N. H. (1989). Teaching business ethics: The use of films and videotape. *Journal of Business Ethics, 8,* 929-936.

James, S., & Lahti, T. (2004). *The natural step for communities: how cities and towns can change to sustainable practices.* British Columbia, Canada: New Society.

Jones, G. E., & Ottaway, R. N. (2001). The effectiveness of corporate ethics on-site visits for teaching business ethics. *Teaching Business Ethics, 5,* 141-156.

Kohlberg, L. (1981). *The philosophy of moral development.* New York: Harper Collins.

Koys, D. J. (2001). Integrating religious principles and human resource management activities. *Teaching Business Ethics, 5*, 121-139.

Kracher, B. (1999). What does it mean when Mitchell gets an "A" in business ethics? Or the importance of service learning. *Teaching Business Ethics, 2*, 291-303.

Ladenson, R. F. (2001). The educational significance of the ethics bowl. *Teaching Ethics, 1*(1), 63-78.

Lamb, C. H., Lee, J. B., & Vinton, K. L. (1997). Developing a freshman seminar: Challenges and opportunities. *Journal of Management Education, 21*(1), 27-43.

Lamb, C. H., Swinth, R. L., Vinton, K. L., & Lee, J. B. (1998). Integrating service learning into a business school curriculum. *Journal of Management Education, 22*(5), 637-654.

Lampe, M. (1997). Increasing effectiveness in teaching ethics to undergraduate business students. *Teaching Business Ethics, 1*(1), 3-19.

Landrum, N. E. (2001). My friend Morgan: An exercise in ethics. *Journal of Management Education, 25*(5), 606-616.

Lenn, J. (1997). The personal journal in business and public policy courses. In S. Waddock (Ed.), *Research in corporate social performance and policy: Teaching business and society courses with reflective and active learning strategies* (Supplement 2, Special issue, pp. 185-200). Greenwich, CT: JAI Press.

MacFarlane, B. (2003). Tales from the front-line: Examining the potential of critical incident vignettes. *Teaching Business Ethics, 7*, 55-67.

Mallinger, M. (1997). Decisive decision making: An exercise using ethical frameworks. *Journal of Management Education, 21*(3), 411-417.

McCarthy, A. M., & Tucker, M. L. (2002). Encouraging community service through service learning. *Journal of Management Education, 26*(6), 629-647.

McNeely, B. L. (2000). One-point wonders: Using student experiences as a way to make OB theory come alive. *Journal of Management Education, 24*(4), 520-523.

McPhail, K. (2002). Using porridge to teach business ethics: Reflections on a visit to Scotland's most notorious prison and some thoughts on the importance of location in teaching business ethics. *Teaching Business Ethics, 6*, 355-369.

McQuarrie, F. A. E. (1998). Expanding the concept of diversity: Discussing sexual orientation in the management classroom. *Journal of Management Education, 22*(2), 162-172.

Muir, C. (2001). Responding to public issues: An exercise in managerial communication. *Journal of Management Education, 25*(5), 572-578.

Muller, H. J., & Parham, P. A. (1998). Integrating workforce diversity into the business school curriculum: An experiment. *Journal of Management Education, 22*(2), 122-148.

National Commission on Excellence in Education. (1983). *A nation at risk: The imperative for educational reform*. Washington, DC: U.S. Dept. of Education.

National Survey of Student Engagement. (2002). *The college student report: 2002 Overview*. Bloomington: Indiana University Center for Postsecondary Research.

Nattrass, B., & Altomare, M. (1999). *The natural step for business: Wealth, ecology and the evolutionary corporation*. British Columbia, Canada: New Society.

Nelson, D. R., & Wittmer, D. P. (2001). Developing a learning community approach to business ethics education. *Teaching Business Ethics, 5,* 267-281.

Orlitzky, M. (1997). Developing intellectual ability, moral insight, active involvement, and objectivity through the ethics mock trial simulation technique. In S. Waddock (Ed.), *Research in corporate social performance and policy: Teaching business and society courses with reflective and active learning strategies* (Supplement 2, Special issue, pp. 201-220). Greenwich, CT: JAI Press.

Piper, T. R., Gentile, M. C., & Parks, S. D. (1993). *Can ethics be taught? Perspectives, challenges and approaches at Harvard Business School.* Boston: Harvard Business School.

Porter, L. W., & McKibbin, L. E. (1988). *Management education and development: Drift or thrust into the 21st century?* New York: McGraw-Hill.

Power, S. J., & Lundsten, L. L. (2001). MBA student opinion about the teaching of business ethics: Preference for inclusion and perceived benefit. *Teaching Business Ethics, 5,* 59-70.

Raisner, J. A. (1997). Using the "ethical environment" paradigm to teach business ethics: The case of the maquiladoras. *Journal of Business Ethics, 16*(12/13), 1331-1346.

Sanyal, R. N. (2000). An experiential approach to teaching ethics in international business. *Teaching Business Ethics, 4,* 137-149.

Schaupp, D. L., & Lane, M. S. (1992). Teaching business ethics: Bringing reality to the classroom. *Journal of Business Ethics, 11,* 225-229.

Schlesinger, P. F. (1996). Teaching and evaluation in an integrated curriculum. *Journal of Management Education, 20*(4), 479-499.

Schmidt-Wilk, J., Heaton, D. P., & Steingard, D. (2000). Higher education for higher consciousness: Maharishi University of management as a model for spirituality in management education. *Journal of Management Education, 24*(5), 580-611.

Shaffer, B., & Collins, D. (1997). Active learning for business and society students: Community service models. In S. Waddock (Ed.), *Research in corporate social performance and policy: Teaching business and society courses with reflective and active learning strategies* (Supplement 2, Special issue, pp. 291-310). Greenwich, CT: JAI Press.

Siciliano, J. I. (2001). How to incorporate cooperative learning principles in the classroom: It's more than just putting students in teams. *Journal of Management Education, 25*(1), 8-20.

Siciliano, J., & McAleer, G. M. (1997). Increasing student participation in case discussions: Using the MICA method in strategic management courses. *Journal of Management Education, 21*(2), 209-220.

Sims, R. L. (2000). Teaching business ethics: A case study of an ethics across the curriculum policy. *Teaching Business Ethics, 4,* 437-443.

Sims, R. R. (2002). Debriefing experiential learning exercises in ethics education. *Teaching Business Ethics, 6,* 179-197.

Sims, R. R. (2004). Business ethics teaching: Using conversational learning to build an effective classroom learning environment. *Journal of Business Ethics, 49*(2), 201-211.

Sims, R. R., & Brinkmann, J. (2003). Business ethics curriculum design: Suggestions and illustrations. *Teaching Business Ethics, 7,* 69-86.

St. Clair, L., & Tschirhart, M. (2002). When and where? Facilitating group work beyond the borders of the classroom. *Journal of Management Education, 26*(4), 449-461.

Smith, G. F. (2003). Beyond critical thinking and decision making: Teaching business students how to think. *Journal of Management Education, 27*(1), 24-51.

Stewart, C. S. (2004, March 21). A question of ethics: How to teach them? *New York Times,* Section 3, p. 11.

Stewart, K., Felicetti, L., & Kuehn, S. (1996). The attitudes of business majors toward the teaching of business ethics. *Journal of Business Ethics, 15*(8), 901-911.

Swanson, D. L., & Frederick, W. C. (2005). Denial and leadership in business ethics education. In O. C. Ferrell & R. A. Peterson, (Eds.), *Business ethics: The new challenge for business schools and corporate leaders.* Armonk, NY: M.E. Sharpe.

Swanson, D. L., & Frederick, W. C. (2003). Campaign AACSB: Are business schools complicit in corporate corruption? *Journal of Individual Employment Rights,"* 10(2), 151-165.

Thompson, C. A. (2002). Managing the work-life balancing act: An introductory exercise. *Journal of Management Education, 26*(2), 205-220.

U.S. Department of Education. (1990). *National goals for education.* Washington, DC: Government Printing Office.

*Wall Street Journal.* (2003, September 17). Business School Forum Section, p. 4.

Weber, J. (1997). Corporate policy simulation: An interactive, group learning exercise for business and society courses. In S. Waddock (Ed.), *Research in corporate social performance and policy: Teaching business and society courses with reflective and active learning strategies* (Supplement 2, Special issue, pp. 79-116). Greenwich, CT: JAI Press.

Weber, J., & Gillespie, J. (1998). Differences in ethical beliefs, intentions and behaviors: The role of beliefs and intentions in ethics research revisited. *Business & Society, 37*(4), 447-467.

Weber, J., & Glyptis, S. M. (2000). Measuring the impact of a business ethics course and community service experience on students' values and opinions. *Teaching Business Ethics, 4,* 341-358.

Zlotkowski, E. (2002), *Service-learning and the first-year experience: Preparing students for personal success and civic responsibility.* University of South Carolina: National Resource Center for the First-Year Experience & Students in Transition.

Zych, J. M. (1999). Integrating ethical issues with managerial decision making in the classroom: Product support program decisions. *Journal of Business Ethics, 18*(3), 255-266.

CHAPTER 14

# INTEGRATING CULTURAL DIVERSITY IN GRADUATE MANAGEMENT EDUCATION

**Loykie Lomine**

This chapter examines how graduate management education may further engage with cultural diversity. The underpinning argument is that graduate management students would benefit from more structured opportunities to develop their knowledge and understanding of cultural diversity and its implications for business management. The chapter starts with a framework to typify cultural diversity, applying Milton Bennett's Developmental Model of Intercultural Sensitivity (DMIS) to evaluate current provision. The chapter then critically analyses the reasons why management education often tends to remain monocultural. It eventually provides and exemplifies concrete suggestions in order to integrate cultural diversity in management education, with regard to staff development, curriculum audit and curriculum development.

## INTRODUCTION

Graduate management education can more deeply involve cultural diversity, with graduate management students utilizing more structured

*New Visions for Graduate Management Education*, 361–379

opportunities for the learning and understanding of cultural diversity's importance in business practice.

> How many of your management graduates are aware that, in French business culture, meetings are less organized to reach a collective decision than to exchange information, with the Chairperson ultimately deciding? Managers from different national backgrounds will have different approaches to collective decision making, and awareness of such intercultural differences is paramount to avoid faux-pas.

> How many of your management graduates remember that during the holy month of Ramadan, Muslims will normally fast during daylight hours? This may be important when scheduling meetings and allocating tasks with Muslim workers or partners. Within a company, irrespective of its size, cultural misunderstandings may offend both parties, as they show a lack of sensitivity and knowledge.

> How many of your management graduates appreciate the fact that questionnaires which ask for "marital status" discriminate against same-sex couples in most countries (with the exception of Spain or Canada where gay marriage is now legal)? In several Western countries, changes in the legislation are currently taking place on issues pertaining to sexuality (e.g., adoption by same-sex couples) and managers need to understand the complexity of the issues involved (e.g., parental leave and pensions rights).

For reasons identified in this chapter, graduate management education tends to remain monocultural. Program and courses often ignore certain issues pertaining to cultural diversity, which is paradoxical, given the importance of cultural issues in society as a whole, and for business management in particular, be it locally, regionally, nationally, or internationally. Irrespective of students' industry destinations, educational background, and personal preferences, graduate management education needs to address cultural diversity and to integrate it in the curriculum. Some students may already be quite aware and knowledgeable, but for others it might be a challenging experience with a mental shift in the way they perceive the world and, ultimately, the way they define and construct their own cultural identity. The aim is to give students opportunities to develop their awareness, knowledge and understanding, these three concepts (awareness, knowledge, and understanding) providing a simple cognitive model that underpins the whole chapter:

- **Awareness:**   refers to the fact that many students, even graduate management students, may not spontaneously think of cultural diversity and related issues. This could be due to their own monocultural background or to the fact that their previous studies may not have taught them or trained them to "think across cultures" and to problematize aspects of cultural diversity in relationship to business management.

- **Knowledge:**   refers to the fact that some students may simply lack knowledge (even basic knowledge) of cultures other than their own. Knowledge follows awareness: recognizing the existence of other cultures, with their own values and beliefs, is the first step in learning about them and in broadening one's cultural horizon.
- **Understanding:**   refers to the importance for business management students, particularly at graduate level, of appreciating and evaluating the business implications of cultural diversity. Understanding follows knowledge: learning about other cultures is not an end in itself, as that newly-acquired knowledge must then be critically applied to concrete business situations in order to understand cultural diversity in context.

The structure of the chapter follows that model of awareness-knowledge-understanding:

- Section 1 develops an *awareness* of key concepts, proposing both a framework to typify cultural diversity and a model to evaluate intercultural awareness.
- Section 2 provides *knowledge* of two types of reasons why management education often fails to include cultural diversity in its curriculum.
- Section 3 develops an *understanding* of what can be done concretely in order to integrate cultural diversity in management education, with regard to staff development, curriculum audit and curriculum development.

## SECTION 1. AWARENESS: CONCEPTUAL CONSIDERATIONS

### Subsection 1.1:   A Framework to Typify Cultural Diversity

Although the term "cultural diversity" is an invitation to consider a plurality of cultures, at a practical level one needs to work within a systematic frame around specific identity characteristics. As the operational objective is to identify and map cultural groups within a larger population, the criteria and overall methodology will be reminiscent of market segmentation. Numerous factors, criteria, and variables could be used for that purpose; the framework proposed here relates to the six areas where employment discrimination is now illegal in Great Britain (either as a result of established British antidiscrimination law or as a consequence of the European Equal Treatment Directive): race/ethnicity, religion, sex/gender, sexual orientation, age, and dis/ability. The politics of discrimination explain the choice of these six factors, which are commonly referred to as "the six equality strands" in British higher education parlance. Cultural diversity and discrimination go together—within an educational program, many groups are being discriminated against as they are not properly presented or represented in a curriculum that rather reflects a dominant culture. That dominant culture, in Western industrialized English-speaking societies, is White, Anglo-Saxon, male-dominated, able-bodied, middle-aged, Christian, and heterosexual. Graduate management education tends to take that hegemonic culture as the norm, which explains why many groups tend to be misrepresented or underrepresented in universities in general, in learning resources (such as textbooks and case studies) and in learning activities (such as debates and assignment topics). The six factors of race/ethnicity, religion, sex/gender, sexual orientation, age and dis/ability may not all have been spontaneously chosen by many academics and curriculum developers to map and examine issues of cultural diversity; other factors could be taken into account, for example with regards to household disposable income or family life cycle, as they all may have cultural implications. The six equality factors offer a conceptually precise and legitimate framework though, which is why British universities and higher education colleges are now increasingly using them for equality audits and similar activities such as risk assessments. This section outlines and illustrates why management education too ought to take them into account.

## Race/Ethnicity

Race and ethnicity are two related concepts. Strictly speaking, ethnicity is linked to ideas of societal groups marked by cultural and traditional origins and backgrounds, including a shared language, as well as shared values and group acceptance, while race is related to notions of biological classification and morphological features (such as skin color or facial characteristics). If nowadays the term "race" is usually avoided because of its discriminatory connotations (racism), some legislators do employ it, as illustrated by the 2000 Race Relations (Amendment) Act in Great-Britain, which is why the two terms are jointly used here. As illustration, in Canada, where the Official Multiculturalism Act was passed in 1988, the nexus race/ethnicity will mainly (though not exclusively) refer to the coexistence of a Francophone culture, principally in Québec, and an Anglophone one in the other Provinces. In the United States, it will mainly (but not exclusively) refer to the amalgamation of immigrant cultures with limited state intervention: the famous metaphor of the melting pot, a model of assimilation which many multiculturalism scholars dispute, arguing that assimilation weakens and ultimately eradicates minority cultures). In terms of management education, students can examine notions of race and ethnicity as well as their implications for business, for example concerning inclusive representations of ethnic groups in advertising, or understanding that White people too constitute an ethnic group. Besides, some students may not be aware of the way attitudes and behavior are shaped by one's experience of racial discrimination; their graduate education can further enhance their understanding of the process of identity development.

## Religion

Religion is both about belief systems (theological questions, eschatology, spirituality, ethical frameworks) and about the organisations which support the exercise and practice of the faith (for instance, churches and religious groups). With an increase in secularization and the rejection of religion by the younger generations, some students may lack awareness of the importance of religion in society as a whole. Besides, lacking knowledge of major religions' beliefs and principles may occasionally be detrimental to managers, as illustrated by the following two examples. First example: *riba* (the idea of financial interest), is prohibited in Islam, which is why many Muslims following that ruling from the *Sharia* (law) will rather bank with financial institutions that offer "Islamic banking" (Lewis & Algaoud, 2001). Business managers need some basic awareness, knowledge and understanding of *riba* and Islam in order to appreciate the double significations of Islamic banking, both its financial signification and its religious signification. Second example: the first lay precept of Buddhism prohibits killing, and in certain Mahayana *sutras*, the Buddha strongly denounces the eating of meat (Walters & Portmess, 2001). Most Buddhists will consequently be vegetarians, which is important to know when organising catering for business meetings or when developing international projects potentially involving Buddhists. Not all Buddhists will be vegetarian though, so one must be wary of generalizations.

## Sex/Gender

As a sociocultural concept, gender is more complex than most people think: not solely limited to biological sex, the concept of gender encompasses other characteristics such as appearance, speech and movement, which is why it is often presented, at least in scholarly works, as a social construct and as a performance (Kimmel, 2000). Feminism, gay studies, and queer theory have all contributed to problematizing gender and related issues of gender identity, gender roles, and gender associations (illustrated by the fact that the color pink was considered masculine in the early 1900s but has since long been viewed as feminine). In terms of management education, students may benefit from some sociological input that can help them conceive of gender differently, in a more sophisticated way, and which can concretely relate to issues of equal opportunities, sexual harassment and sexism.

## Sexual Orientation

Sexual orientation might be a difficult topic to address for some students who may consider it private and inappropriate in a management course at graduate level, yet it is an important aspect of social identity, of cultural diversity, of equality politics and also of discrimination, which is why graduate management education should not coyly discard it. Because of their own experience, LGBT (lesbian, gay, bisexual, and transsexual) students are more likely to have considered the cultural dimension of their sexual identity (Harris, 1997)—heterosexual students will here gain awareness, knowledge, and understanding into other ways of being, behaving, and thinking. Courses are generally heterosexualized, with few references, if any, to gay and lesbian communities, and graduate management education may really need to modify some of its heteronormative premises in order to acknowledge the existence of a part of the population whose economic and political contribution cannot be overestimated (Chasin, 2000).

## Age

Age may well be considered in marketing (for example about market segmentation) and human resources management (for example about retirement procedures) but the cultural diversity coming from age and experience is rarely mentioned in business books and in books about business pedagogy. Although age groups and generations have different cultures, there is a tendency to underplay the importance of age in management education, possibly to sound inclusive and to prevent criticisms of ageism (prejudice and preconceived ideas on the basis of age) and age discrimination (the unfair treatment and unequal opportunities because of age). Age differences between students (typically a 25 year old sitting next to a 50 year old who could be their parent) represent major advantages in graduate management education as these students have often extremely varied life and work experiences. These differences ought to be celebrated and used pedagogically, resisting the temptation to treat all students as if they were identical.

## Dis/ability

The concept of dis/ability is difficult to circumscribe because individuals, organizations and governments use different definitions; one can nonetheless distinguish between physical impairments (such as muscular dystrophy and cerebral palsy), sensory impairments (such as visual or hearing impairments), cognitive impairments (such as autism or Down's syndrome) and psychiatric conditions (such as depression and schizophrenia). Some able-bodied healthy students may not have thought about the various types of disabilities, their impacts on people's lives, on business and on society as a whole—and they may not have had any training about interacting with, say, visually impaired people. Here again, graduate management education may need to revisit its curriculum so as to integrate references to disabled cultures (from sign language to wheelchair-access through mental health problems), not only to reflect society as a whole, but also to prepare students for a real world that is not as sanitized and monocultural as many management textbooks imply.

## Subsection 1.2: A Model to Evaluate Intercultural Awareness

In 1986 the American scholar Milton Bennett proposed a developmental model of intercultural sensitivity (now commonly abbreviated as DMIS) to compare, map, and explain the varied reactions of people to cultural differences. A director of the Intercultural Communication Institute (ICI), Bennett has written extensively on intercultural issues (1993, 1998), further refining the DMIS whose use is now widespread in training programmes for intercultural education. The DMIS may also help curriculum developers and management course leaders, even at MBA level, appreciate how their students may lack awareness, knowledge and understanding of other cultures. Briefly summarized, Bennett's model is composed of six stages:

1. Denial:   one does not recognize cultural differences.
2. Defence:   one recognizes some differences, but sees them as negative.
3. Minimization:   one is unaware of the projection of one's own cultural values, which are seen as superior.
4. Acceptance:   one shifts perspectives to understand that the same "ordinary" behavior can have different meanings in different cultures.
5. Adaptation:   one can evaluate others' behavior from their frame of reference and can adapt behavior to fit the norms of a different culture.
6. Integration:   one can shift frames of reference and deal with subsequent identity issues.

With regards to the six cultural factors previously identified (race/ethnicity, religion, sex/gender, sexual orientation, age, and dis/ability), it is a helpful to apply Bennett's DMIS and to consider whether students are aware of the way these six factors have cultural consequences—or are they in denial? Do they accept and celebrate the differences, or do they tend to minimize them? Do they have opportunities to examine a variety of cultural differences from a management perspective or does their course dismiss and deny cultural issues? A culturally-aware graduate education ought to make students move higher on Bennett's scale, helping them develop their intercultural sensitivity—what other authors call "multicultural competency" (Pope-Davis, Coleman, Liu, & Toporek, 2003) or "multicultural competence" (Constantine, 2005).

## SECTION 2. KNOWLEDGE: THE CAUSES OF THE CURRENT SHORTCOMINGS

This section examines why graduate management education tends to neglect issues of cultural diversity. Two sets of reasons are identified and analyzed: first, in terms of pedagogical reproduction, and second, in terms of pedagogical assumptions.

## Subsection 2.1: Pedagogical Reproduction

Curriculum developers tend to reproduce what they are familiar with, that is, the expected constitutive components of graduate management education, following a blueprint that may limit innovation. In business management, curriculum developers themselves tend to have a particular sociocultural profile; without generalizing, one may anecdotally note that the majority tend to be able-bodied, Anglo-Saxon, White, heterosexual, middle-aged Christian males (precise research, in the spirit of Anderson's study of faculty demographics (2002) would be useful to evaluate that hunch). Because of their background, training and sociocultural identity, they unconsciously design courses in a hegemonic way, making their own profile "the norm," embedding it in the curriculum, failing to problematize it and expecting students to understand and accept that silent hegemony.

The benchmarks and criteria from organizations such as the AMBA (Association of MBAs) or the AACSB (Association to Advance Collegiate Schools of Business) reinforce the unchallenged reign of a pedagogical status quo that does not pay much attention to cultural diversity. In 2005, the AMBA published a revised list of criteria for MBA accreditation; one may appreciate evidence of a broad movement toward the recognition of the importance of social values within the curriculum, as recognized by the AMBA Web site:

> Some aspects of the curriculum have gained special attention. Firstly, that it should reflect the increasingly international aspect of business, secondly, that it should pay attention to ethical and social issues, and thirdly, that it should include the so-called "soft" largely interpersonal skills of management in practice.

Yet terms such as "culture" and "multicultural" are not mentioned even once; put another way, even AMBA-accredited MBAs are not explicitly expected to engage with cultural diversity. Similarly, in the United States, the AACSB does not refer once to cultural diversity in its standards accreditation for business courses (the official documentation is currently being revised though, and the new version might). Likewise, in the United Kingdom, the Quality Assurance Agency has benchmarks statements for academic standards for postgraduate courses in business and management, yet none of them refers to culture, let alone cultural diversity. The EFMD (European Foundation for Management Development) is more culturally aware: as part of its EQUIS (European Quality Improvement System), it now has guidance notes and quality criteria which support and promote multiculturalism, with references to the "*development of multicultural skills*' for students, '*a concern for intercultural exchange in the classroom*" and the benefits from having "*intercultural teams*" of teaching staff. Internationalization is clearly on their agenda, which explains why the EFMD has started to recognize and support the explicit integration of multiculturalism in the curriculum.

Curriculum development is a very difficult task, particularly for postgraduate courses in business management where so many issues are at stake (such as the institution's reputation, its financial health, and its research expertise), which is why curriculum developers often remain within the confines of well-established pedagogical comfort zones. Likewise, lecturers and tutors may not always be confident enough to address issues pertaining to race/ethnicity, religion, sex/gender, sexual orientation, age, and dis/ability: it may seem politically sensitive, and one falls back onto generic views that tend to overlook cultural diversity.

## Subsection 2.2: Pedagogical Assumptions

Three pedagogical assumptions may also explain why graduate management curricula are not always engaging with cultural diversity:

- The assumption that the presence of students from several cultures or nationalities will, by itself, make a course multicultural.

- The assumption that all students, because they have enrolled on the same programme in the same institution, will be culturally identical.
- The assumption that cultural diversity is not relevant for a specific institution, for its faculty and its students.

### Assumption 1

Assuming that the presence of students from several cultures or nationalities will, by itself, make a course multicultural. In fact, that diversity will only be an asset if it is used pedagogically and valorized in the course. Recruiting international students can be a "cross-cultural blessing" as students may then be able to learn from one another and to become "cultural learning resources" for one another—but this process must be facilitated and channelled, for example through group activities that encourage students to explore and discuss their cultural differences. A good method, which may also help graduate management students become more reflective and self-critical, is to have students discuss how their cultural differences may account for differences in their management styles. The danger, with a mixed cohort, is to try to make students melt into the same academic mould (like a "pedagogical melting pot") on the basis of cohesion and standards. To help students become more culturally aware, cultural diversity must be celebrated and not minimized. In the case of a classroom with both home students and foreign students, foreign students will learn from a different pedagogical culture (thereby really becoming "international students" that is, literally students between nations) but home students may learn from the foreign students too. They can benefit from their presence and input—everyone will benefit, as long as the course team does not try to treat and consider all students as if they were home students.

### Assumption 2

Assuming that all students, because they have enrolled on the same programme in the same institution, will be culturally identical. Even when student cohorts seem homogeneous, when students have similar ages and cultural backgrounds, it will be possible to identify subcultures based on other criteria such as interests and professional preferences. Making students identify their differences and complementarities is a first step that may help bonding, especially at the start of a course, by encouraging students to communicate together and to discover how they differ and how they can learn from one another. The absence of manifest expressions of cultural diversity in a classroom is not an excuse for ignoring the issue. One does not need to have visually impaired students to discuss issues pertaining to visual impairment in a business management perspective (for example about legislation, rights, and service provision); likewise, one does not need to have openly gay students to discuss the economic importance of the so-called "pink dollar" or the fact that gay male couples tend to have more disposable income that their heterosexual counterparts, thereby creating a niche for leisure and tourism service providers. The apparent homogeneity of students' demographics should not prevent cross-cultural education.

### Assumption 3

Assuming that cultural diversity is not a relevant theme for a specific institution, for its faculty and its students. Such an attitude of denial may actually prove detrimental for graduates at a later stage of their career. Even in homogeneous communities where cultural diversity does not seem locally topical and pertinent, management students should be given the chance to learn to think multiculturally and to develop multicultural skills—their professional career may lead them to meet and work with people from other cultures, even in a neighboring town. Management education is a holistic project that goes beyond the major areas that underpin general management (such as production, marketing, organization theory, and accounting): it is also about preparing students to work, at management level, with people they may not have previously met.

## SECTION 3: UNDERSTANDING WHAT CAN BE DONE

This section outlines concrete ways to integrate cultural diversity in graduate management education. It covers issues of staff development, curriculum audit and curriculum enhancement.

### Subsection 3.1: Staff Development

Any attempt to change the way cultural diversity is tackled pedagogically will prove fruitless unless academic staff themselves are motivated and interested. The cognitive model of awareness-knowledge-understanding can readily be used for professional development purposes: firstly, to raise staff awareness of the fact that their students may benefit from a more culturally-aware management education; second, to develop their own knowledge of the reasons why their program so far may not have optimally engaged with notions of cultural diversity; third, to enhance their understanding of what, concretely, they can do in the foreseeable future to further integrate cultural diversity in the curriculum. A workshop lasting half-a-day can prove an effective start to address these issues amongst faculty who, in turn, will later have to address them with their own students. While Bennett's model of intercultural sensitivity may help staff map their own competences, caution, and patience may be required. For reasons linked to pedagogical reproduction and misconceptions, some staff may have problems to accept cultural differences and their significations (Bennett's stages 1 to 3: Denial, Defence, Minimization).

In terms of pedagogical resources, there is a plethora of books and articles about issues pertaining to cultural diversity in education, especially with a focus on working across cultures; they can be used as teaching material with students, but also for faculty, as part of their own professional development. Publishers, catalogues, Web sites, libraries, and bibliographies may use different headings and subcategories to present these resources, with keywords such as "cross-cultural communication," "transcultural training," "intercultural education" sometimes used interchangeably; likewise, books will often have similar-sounding titles juggling with the same terms, from *Intercultural Interactions* (Brislin & Cushner, 1995) to *Coaching Across Cultures* (Rosinski, 2003) via *Foundations of Intercultural Communication* (Chen & Starosta, 1998). All major publishers tend to have books about cultural diversity, yet it is worth mentioning the small specialist publisher Intercultural Press (based in Boston, Massachusetts as well as London under the name Nicholas Brealey Publishing) which has over 100 titles, all potentially useful depending upon the reader's perspectives, from a book such as Kras (1995) *Management in Two Cultures: Bridging the Gap between U.S. and Mexican Managers* to a video on the experience of being an international student learning to adapt in a North American College environment (Czarnawska, 2001). Like in all other subjects, academic textbooks will sometimes have a single author (e.g., *Cultural Diversity*, Diller, 1999) or be in the form of edited collections (e.g., *Handbook of Intercultural Training*, Landis, Bennett, & Bennett, 2001); some will be more theoretical (such as *Culture's Consequences: International Differences in Work-Related Values*, Hofstede, 1980, now a classic), others more empirical and impressionistic (such as *Transculturalism*, Grunitzky, 2004). No scholar has ever tentatively drafted a canon, possibly because of the ever expanding size of the field, reflected in the multiplication of academic journals such as the *International Journal of Intercultural Communications* the *International Journal of Intercultural Relations* and the *Journal of Multiculturalism in Education*, to name a few.

Regarding the six cultural factors of race/ethnicity, religion, sex/gender, sexual orientation, age, and dis/ability, one can also find specific academic resources, for example books on gender and management such as *Capital Culture: Gender at Work in the City* (McDowell, 1997), *Managing Like a Man: Women and Men in Corporate Management* (Wajcman, 1998) and *Challenging Women: Gender, Culture and Organization* (Maddock, 1999) or articles from the *Women in Management Review*, yet nonacademic material can also provide a very good starting point. Current affairs, debates about bills, even tabloid-type scandals and Hollywood films may be a good basis for sophisticated discussions. They help raise awareness of some issues, which is the first cognitive step, to be followed by knowledge and understanding: learning more about the context and issues, then analyzing the implications for business management.

## Subsection 3.2: Curriculum Audit

In most cases, one may not objectively appreciate the extent to which a graduate management course already engages with cultural diversity. A curriculum audit is the most efficient method to assess how cultural diversity is currently addressed (the present) and how certain areas could be further developed (the future). The audit does not have to be time-consuming or threatening: it is a tool to critically identify existing strengths as well as opportunities for improvement. Although methodologically a

**Table 14.1.  Methodological Framework for a
Simple Curriculum Audit of Cultural Diversity**

| | |
|---|---|
| Overall methodology | A qualitative research strategy rather than a quantitative one (as the aim is not so much to score and quantify, but rather to identify and map). |
| Method | Semistructured interviews with as many staff as possible (either one by one, or together in a focus-group) as the course leader alone may not be aware of some aspects of cultural diversity covered in teaching and assessment. |
| Auditor | An internal auditor already familiar with institutional terminology, though not directly involved in the course delivery (as this could hinder their critical distance). A colleague from another department could be a good auditor, as long as they are thoroughly briefed on the purpose and modalities of the audit. |
| Areas of audit | Three areas:<br>    First, at a generic level, about strategic approaches to cultural diversity: Is cultural diversity already mentioned in the programme philosophy, as one of the learning outcomes of the programme? Are there some specific, local issues that need to be taken into account, for example, about students' demographics? How does it fit with the department or the institution's mission and vision?<br>    Second, a focus on cultural factors (for example race/ethnicity, religion, sex/gender, sexual orientation, age and dis/ability), one by one, to identify the extent to which they are (or are not) covered in the course in terms of awareness, knowledge, and understanding.<br>    Third, an assessment of the possible "resistance to cultural diversity" that is, the challenges that may come from staff or students alike, because of their own backgrounds and cultural assumptions. |
| Results | The results, as analyzed by the auditor, are best presented under two headings:<br>    Strengths (factors that are already well covered and problematized, good practice worth celebrating and disseminating).<br>    Opportunities for development (possibly with suggestions in terms of prioritizing). |

range of approaches are possible, for a first exploratory audit one will recommend a simple approach as outlined in Table 14.1.

## Subsection 3.3: Curriculum Enhancement

Three methods may help integrate cultural diversity in graduate management programmes:

- Adapting current practice.
- Adding a course component about cultural diversity.

**Table 14.2.   Comparison of the Three Methods of Curriculum Enhancement**

| | *Implementation* | | |
| --- | --- | --- | --- |
| | *Difficulty Level* | *Planning Requirements* | *Mode of Intervention* |
| Method 1: Adapting current practice. | Easy | Short term | Minimal |
| Method 2: Adding a course component about cultural diversity. | Moderate | Medium term | Operational |
| Method 3: Embedding cultural diversity in the course's overall pedagogy. | Difficult | Long term | Strategic |

- Embedding cultural diversity in the course's overall pedagogy.

The three methods are suitable for all types of course (full-time, part-time, distance learning) but they present differences in terms of implementation of change (difficulty level, planning requirements and mode of intervention), as showed in Table 14.2.

## Method 1: Adapting Current Practice

Teaching teams may decide to improve current practice without making any substantial alterations to the course structure. Pedagogical activities, within existing modules and sessions, may help reach the cultural learning outcomes whilst helping students progress up Bennett's developmental model of intercultural sensitivity, as illustrated in Table 14.3.

## Method 2: Adding a Course Component About Cultural Diversity

Instead of instilling elements of cultural diversity throughout existing modules and course components, program developers may decide to offer an extra taught element dedicated to cross-cultural issues. For example, the MA in Organizational Management at Antioch University Santa Barbara, California, has a unit titled "Multicultural Management"; the MBA from Wits Business School (University of the Witwatersrand, Johannesburg, South Africa) has an elective in "International Management and Culture," and the MBA from The Richard Ivey School of Business (Uni-

**Table 14.3.   Examples of Activities to Gradually Implement a Culturally-Aware Pedagogy**

|  | Learning Outcomes | Examples of Pedagogical Activities | Bennett's DMIS |
|---|---|---|---|
| Awareness | To make students aware of the importance of cultural factors and variables. To make students think of cultural diversity in relationship to business management. | Awareness quiz Awareness activities Case studies (primary material from the media, for example, current affairs, bills, or local debates) | Level 1-2 |
| Knowledge | To give students opportunities to learn about cultural diversity. To help students learn how and why cultural factors affect business management. | Learning resources including guest speakers Access to books or articles about cultural diversity | Level 3-4 |
| Understanding | To develop students' empathy through a mental shift that leads them to think across cultures. To help students learn how to manage cultural diversity. | Discussions, debates Role-plays assignments (assessed or not) | Level 5-6 |

versity of Western Ontario, Canada) has a module ("Competing Successfully in a Global Environment") which contains a cross-cultural project assignment. This enables students to focus on issues of cultural diversity, to rapidly develop their awareness, knowledge and understanding, which is otherwise difficult as graduate courses already have intense syllabuses.

Instead of a taught module or unit, a learning experience (typically in another country) can also fulfil that cross-cultural function, even as part of a graduate course in business management. This is an increasing trend in many European MBAs, for example MBA students from Lancaster University Management School, England, can spend 3 months in one of the partner institutions (such as Vienna Wirtschaftsuniversität in Austria or Bilbao Universidad Comercial de Deusto in Spain); students enrolled on the Euro-Australian MBA (EAMBA) from the ESG (Paris Graduate School of Management) complete half of their studies in Paris and half in Perth, and the MBA in International Business from the European Business School London combines two semesters of academic work in London with an integral study period in either New York or Hong Kong. Such "study abroad" schemes are most valuable in terms of multicultural awareness although one needs to be careful not simply to equate "cultural diversity" and "multiculturalism": the notion of cultural diversity is broader than multiculturalism, as it includes other demographic and sociocultural factors also contributing to the dynamic development of cultures.

## Method 3: Embedding Cultural Diversity in the Course's Overall Pedagogy

Some universities have started to design graduate management courses that purposefully do not follow the traditional functional breakdown of management disciplines (such as finance and economics) but, instead, start with intended learning outcomes articulated in terms of cultural diversity. The MA in Managing Contemporary Global Issues from the University of Winchester (England) is a good example, with students completing modules such as "Socio-cultural analysis of contemporary global issues" and "Management responses to contemporary global issues." Other institutions start with a vision and mission statement espousing globalization and diversity, and then design courses that reflect that international ambition: this is the case of the INSEAD Business School, with its mission statement proudly claiming how "*a unique global perspective and multicultural diversity are reflected in all aspects of its research and teaching.*" This ethos of multicultural diversity underpins program design as well recruitment of both students and staff: students are from over 70 countries, with no one nationality accounting for more than 12% twelve of the class, and academic staff are from nearly 30 different countries; this makes the institution itself a place of cultural diversity (though again the focus might be on international multiculturalism to the detriment of other cultural aspects such as age and dis/ability).

## CONCLUSION: THE VISION OF A CULTURALLY-RICHER GRADUATE MANAGEMENT EDUCATION

This chapter has examined how graduate management education may further engage with cultural diversity. Business success cannot short-circuit culture and cultural values; monocultural managers are more limited cognitively and may fail to appreciate subtle cultural differences with colleagues, staff, stakeholders, and customers. The financial argument for a culturally-enriched curriculum would deserve a chapter of its own; the focus here is on pedagogical aspects, from awareness raising among staff to intervention in curriculum design.

Integrating cultural diversity in management education is difficult because of the many curricular demands which are given priority, especially with regards to "hardcore" business disciplines and functions. An explicit commitment to cultural diversity gives a positive image of a given institution though: it shows to the outside world that graduate education recognizes also has a humanistic agenda, as it aims to ensure that students will later make culturally-informed and culturally-sensitive business decisions in their professional careers. The end goal is to make tomorrow's leaders and managers more aware of the nexus of culture and management—and eventually these culturally-aware people will be better managers and better citizens, better global managers, and better global citizens.

## REFERENCES

Anderson, E. L. (2002). *The new professoriate: Characteristics, contributions and compensation*. Washington, DC: American Council on Education.

Bennett, M. J. (1986). A developmental approach to training for intercultural sensitivity. *International Journal of Intercultural Relations, 10*(2), 179-195.

Bennett, M. J. (1993). Towards ethno-relativism: A developmental model of intercultural sensitivity. In R. M. Paige (Ed.), *Education for the intercultural experience* (pp. 109-135). Yarmouth, ME: Intercultural Press.

Bennett, M. J. (Ed.). (1998). *Basic concepts of intercultural communication: Selected readings*. Yarmouth, ME: Intercultural Press.

Brislin, R. W., & Cushner, K. (1995). *Intercultural interactions: A practical guide*. Thousand Oaks, CA: Sage.

Chasin, A. (2000). Interpenetrations: A cultural study of the relationship between the gay/lesbian niche market and the gay/lesbian political movement, *Cultural Critique, 44*, 145-168.

Chen, G. M., & Starosta, W. J. (1998). *Foundations of intercultural communication*. Boston, MA: Allyn & Bacon.

Constantine, M. G. (Ed.). (2005). *Strategies for building multicultural competence in mental health and educational settings*. Somerset, NJ: Jossey-Bass.

Czarnawska, I. (2001). *The aliens: Being a foreign student* [video]. Boston: Intercultural Press.

Diller, J. V. (1999). *Cultural diversity, a primer for the human services*. New York: Brooks/Cole.

Grunitzky, C. (2004). *Transculturalism: How the world is coming together*. New York: Powerhouse.

Harris, M. B. (Ed.). (1997). *School experiences of gay and lesbian youth: The invisible minority*. Binghampton, NY: Haworth Press.

Hofstede, G. (1980). *Culture's consequences: International differences in work-related values*. Newbury Park, CA: Sage.

Kimmel, M. S. (2000). *The gendered society*. New York: Oxford University Press.

Kras, E. (1995). *Management in two cultures: Bridging the gap between U.S. and Mexican managers*. Boston: Intercultural Press.

Landis, D., Bennett, J., & Bennett, M. (2001). *Handbook of intercultural training*. Thousand Oaks, CA: Sage.

Lewis, M., & Algaoud, L. M. (2001). *Islamic banking*. Cheltenham, England: Edward Elgar.

McDowell, L. (1997). *Capital culture: Gender at work in the city*. Oxford, England: Blackwell.

Maddock, S. (1999). *Challenging women: Gender, culture and organization*. London: Sage.

Pope-Davis, D. B., Coleman, H. L. K., Liu, W. M., & Toporek, R. L. (Eds.). (2003). *Handbook of multicultural competencies in counselling and psychology*. Thousand Oaks, CA: Sage.

Rosinski, P. (2003). *Coaching across cultures: New tools for leveraging national, corporate, and professional differences*. London: Nicholas Brealey.

Wajcman, J. (1998). *Managing like a man: Women and men in corporate management*. Philadelphia: The Pennsylvania State University Press.

Walters, K. S., & Portmess, L. (Eds.) (2001). *Religious vegetarianism: From Hesiod to the Dalai Lama*. Albany, NY: State University of New York Press.

## WEB SITES

AACSB (Association to Advance Collegiate Schools of Business) www.aacsb.edu

AMBA (Association of MBAs) www.mbaworld.com

ECU (Equality Challenge Unit) www.ecu.ac.uk

EFMD (European Foundation for Management Development) www.efmd.org

ICI (Intercultural Communication Institute) www.intercultural.org

Intercultural Press www.interculturalpress.com

QAA (Quality Assurance Agency) www.qaa.ac.uk

# ABOUT THE AUTHORS

**Howard M. Armitage,** PhD, FCMA, is the Gordon H. Cowperthwaite professor of accounting and the director of the Centre for Business, Entrepreneurship, and Technology at the University of Waterloo in Ontario.

**Jos A. R. Arts,** currently he is active in quality assurance and the design of active learning environments at the Technical University of Eindhoven, the Netherlands. The theme of his 2006 doctoral dissertation is stimulating managerial knowledge use and managerial reasoning in a student-directed learning environment.

**Stephen R. Ball,** Stephen R. Ball, associate professor and chair of the Leadership Studies department at Lourdes College, received his doctorate in organizational behavior and management from the Center for the Study of Higher and postsecondary education at the University of Michigan. Dr. Ball helped develop the ETS MBA-Major Field Test and has designed and taught in MBA programs. He was a banking executive in "a previous life."

**Robert J. Bies,** professor of management and academic director of the Executive Master's in Leadership program at the McDonough School of Business at Georgetown University. He received his PhD from Stanford University. His current research focuses on leadership and the delivery of bad news, revenge and forgiveness in the workplace, and organizational justice.

**Henny P. A. Boshuizen,** Dean, School of Education, Open University, Netherlands, researches the development of professional expertise. She has published both in cognitive psychosocial, scientific, general, and professional educational journals. She is on the editorial board of *Learning in Health and Social Care.*

**John C. Byrne,** PhD is an assistant professor of management in the Lubin School of Business at Pace University. He received his PhD in technology management from Stevens Institute of Technology. John has a BS in marketing management from Dominican College and an MBA from Pace University. Prior to entering academia, John spent more than 30 years in several technology fields: biotechnology, electronic instrument manufacturing, and precision optics. He has managed capital biotechnology projects for many of the world's leading biotechnology companies, and acted as a corporate and technical liaison with facilities in France, Switzerland, and England. John maintains a consulting practice addressing the pharmaceutical/biotechnology industries, and publishes with Akgün, Dominick, Reilly, Smither, and Lynn on leadership, organizational learning and peer feedback.

**Arnaldo Camuffo** is professor of management at the University of Padova, Italy. He holds a PhD from the Ca'Foscari University of Venice. His work on HRM&D has appeared in the *MIT Sloan Management Review, Industrial Relations, International Journal of Training and Development, International Journal of Human Resource Management, Journal of Management and Governance, International Journal of Innovation and Learning* and *Human Resource Development International.*

**Francesca Chiara** is contract professor of Organizational Behavior and Human Resource Management at the Ca'Foscari University of Venice, Italy.

**Denis Collins,** professor of business at Edgewood College, received a PhD in business administration from the University of Pittsburgh. At the University of Wisconsin-Madison he won Most Outstanding MBA Faculty Member in three consecutive alumni surveys conducted by *Business Week.* His books include *Gainsharing and Power* (Cornell University Press, 1998), *Sustaining the Natural Environment* (JAI, 1996), *Ethical Dilemmas in Business* (South-Western, 1994), and *Behaving Badly: Ethical Lessons from Enron* (Dog Ear). He is on the editorial boards of *Journal of Business Ethics* and *Journal of Academic Ethics.*

**Gary Coombs,** Associate Professor of management and former MBA director at Ohio University, received his PhD from the University of Colorado at Boulder in 1994 in organizational behavior and organization theory and a minor in social psychology. His research interests are management pedagogy and creativity and innovation management. Recent publications have appeared in *The Cutting Edge of International Management Education, Journal of Management Education, Journal of Computer Information Systems,* and *Public Performance & Management Review.*

**Deborah Crown Core,** MBA director at Ohio University, received her PhD from the University of Colorado in 1992 in Organizational Behavior and Human Resource Management. Her primary research interests include organizational work teams, motivation, ethics, and issues relating to professional and collegiate sports. Her research has been published in the *Journal of Applied Psychology, Organizational Behavior and Human Decision Processes,* and *Group and Organizational Management,* and featured in the *Wall Street Journal, Entrepreneur,* CNN, ABC National News, and the *New York Times.*

**Robert DeFillippi** is professor of management and director of the Center for Innovation and Change Leadership www.ciclsuffolk.org at Suffolk University Business School, where he is also academic coordinator for the innovation and design management program in executive education. Dr. DeFillippi is also an international visiting fellow to the Tanaka Business School, Imperial College of London. He publishes in leading United States and European journals on issues related to how knowledge creation and learning can be fostered through the effective organization and management of innovative and creative work-based projects. He is associate editor for the *International Journal of Management Reviews* and serves on the editorial boards of *Management Learning, Journal of Organizational Behavior* and *Organization Management Journal.* Dr. DeFillippi was 2001-2002 Chairperson for Management Education and Development (MED) Division of the Academy of Management and currently serves on the MED division executive board. He is a frequent international conference speaker and workshop leader to executive and scholarly audiences on a wide range of innovation and management education issues. E-mail: rdefilli@suffolk.edu.

**Peter G. Dominick,** assistant professor of management, is coordinator of leadership development education for the Stevens Institute of Technology, W. J. Howe School's Executive MBA, Project Management and Undergraduate Business and Technology programs. Leadership and behavioral skills development are major themes for his writing and research. Other research interests include project leadership, and virtual team effectiveness.

**Mark Fenton-O'Creevy,** director of curriculum and programs (associate dean) and professor of organizational behavior at the Open University Business School, has played a lead role in the redesign and development of it's MBA curriculum. He holds a PhD and MBA from London Business School and is a member of the U.K. Higher Education Academy. He is also director of the center for Practice Based Professional Learning. He led the development of the Open University's Professional Diploma in Management.

**Fabrizio Gerli,** assistant professor of organizational behavior at the Ca'Foscari University of Venice, holds a PhD in management from the Ca'Foscari University and has published essays on competency-based HRM and on organizational design and articles in *Industrial Relations* and *International Journal of Training and Development.*

**Wim H. Gijselaers**, professor of education at the Faculty of Economics and Business Administration, Maastricht University, the Netherlands. His current research focuses on the instructional design of powerful learning environments, expertise development in management education, and shared cognition in teams. He received several grants from the Dutch government and the Dutch Science Foundation for educational development projects and fundamental research. Currently he serves as associate dean, and Chair of the Department of Educational Development and Educational Research at the Faculty of Economics and Business, Maastricht University.

**Owen P. Hall, Jr.**, professor of decision and information systems, Pepperdine University, received his PhD from the University of Southern California and undertook postdoctoral studies at the Center for Futures Research. He is the recipient of a Charles Luckman teaching fellowship. He has authored four textbooks on computer based decision support systems and over 50 technical papers on the subjects of decision support systems, forecasting software design, distance learning systems and neural networks. His current research includes the application of artificial agents for search engine technology and the development of Internet based hybrid learning nets.

**Anne Herbert,** senior researcher in organization and management and academic director at the Helsinki School of Economics Executive Education, completed doctoral studies in Education in Australia. She is interested in management education practices and promoting the use of action research by managers. Recently she has used action research to explore issues and changes in public and private education management, especially in the higher education sector.

**Brooks Holtom,** assistant professor of management, McDonough School of Business, Georgetown University. His research focuses on how organizations can attract, develop, and retain top talent. He is particularly interested in better understanding the dynamics surrounding the MBA talent pool. In 2005, he received the Western Academy of Management's Ascendant Scholar Award.

**Edward J. Inderrieden,** associate professor of management, College of Business Administration, Marquette University, received his PhD in organizational behavior from the University of Colorado-Boulder. His research interests include organizational justice and fairness, performance appraisal, organizational attachment, and gender issues.

**Peter Knight** is director of the Open University's Institute of Educational Technology. He wrote a defining report on the role of higher education in relation to the creation of research-informed knowledge economies in Europe, *Measures to improve HE/R in order to strengthen the strategic basis of the ERA. The report of an independent high level expert group set up by the European Commission.* He was also founding director of the center for Practice Based Professional Learning.

**Kari Lilja,** professor in organization and management, Helsinki School of Economics, currently is the coordinator of the EU-funded "Transnational learning through local experimenting" (Translearn) project. His publications cover topics in such areas as workplace industrial relations, resource based strategies and globalization of forest industry corporations and the dynamics of change of national business systems.

**Loykie L. Lominé,** program director for an international MA in cultural and arts management and instructor at the University of Winchester. He has published on e-learning and assessment strategies.

**Judith Margolis,** senior lecturer in marketing at the Open University Business School, until recently Chaired the professional diploma in management at the Open University Business School. She spent a number of years in the publishing field, as co-owner of a small publishing house and as an advertising sales executive.

**Rod B. McNaughton,** Eyton Chair in entrepreneurship at the University of Waterloo, holds PhD's from the University of Western Ontario and from the University of Lancaster. His background is a multidisciplinary mix of marketing management, international business, and entrepreneurship. His research focuses on the growth of knowledge-based ventures, especially development of a market orientation, early internationalization, financing, and their role within industrial clusters.

**Tunç D. Medeni** is a doctoral student at JAIST, School of Knowledge Science. He earned his master's degree in management and organizational learning from Lancaster University, U.K, and bachelors degree in management from Bilkent University, Turkey. Besides his academic background in management learning and knowledge management, he has experience as an internal auditor, consultant, and educator.

**Yongsun Paik** is a professor of international business and management at Loyola Marymount University, Los Angeles. His primary research interests focus on global strategic alliances, Asian Pacific business studies, and international human resource management. He has published widely, and is the immediate past president of Association of Korean Management Scholars (AKMS).

**Mien Segers** is professor of educational sciences at the Department of Educational Sciences of the University Leiden, the Netherlands, and at the Department of Educational Development and Research of the University Maastricht, the Netherlands. Her major research interests are the evaluation and optimization of learning in learner-centered learning environments and the characteristics of new modes of assessment within these environments.

**Hugh D. Sherman,** professor of strategy and associate dean at Ohio University, received his PhD from Temple University in 1995 in strategy and international business. His research interests are corporate governance, international management, entrepreneurship, and economic development. His most recent publications have appeared in *Journal of International Management, Journal of Teaching International Business, Economic Development Quarterly, Long Range Planning,* and *Corporate Governance: An International Review.*

**Charles M. Vance,** PhD, teaches human resource management at Loyola Marymount University, Los Angeles. Based on his graduate studies in organizational behavior and instructional technology, Vance has focused much of his consulting in training and management development, and has been active in business and management curriculum innovation in the United States and abroad.

**Charles Wankel** is associate professor of management at St. John's University, New York. Dr. Wankel publishes and presents research on the use of information technologies in support of management education and development. He is the premier director of scholarly virtual communities for management professors, currently directing 10 with thousands of participants in more than 70 nations. He has taught in Lithuania at the Kaunas University of Technology (Fulbright Fellowship), University of Vilnius, (United Nations Development Program and Open Society Foundation funding). Recent invited lectures include 2005 distinguished speaker at the E-ducation Without Border Conference, Abu Dhabi, and 2004 keynote speaker at the Nippon Academy of Management, Tokyo. Corporate management development program development clients include McDonald's Corporation's Hamburger University and IBM Learning Services. Pro bono consulting assignments include reengineering and total quality management programs for the Lithuanian National Postal Service. He is editor of *The Handbook of 21st Management* (Sage, 2008) and is on the editorial boards of the *Academy of Management Learning and Education* journal and *Social Science*. Information on other books in the Research in Management Education and Development series is available at http://management-education.net. E-mail: wankelc@stjohns.edu.

Printed in the United States
68552LVS00001B/13-16

9 781593 115531